The Best
in American Cooking

The Best
in American Cooking

Recipes collected by Clementine Paddleford

DECORATIONS BY ANNA KOPCZYNSKI

CHARLES SCRIBNER'S SONS / NEW YORK

Foreword

"To my Little Girl, Remember and remember." That is what Clementine inscribed in my copy of "How America Eats." On school vacations I was her tag-along, sharing so many of these eating events, listening to her interviews, eagerly helping out on the tasting. Clementine was a cracker-jack reporter and a skilled writer, working from early dawn until late night to achieve the reputation that seemed to grow up so easily around the end of her pencil.

She is gone now, and I do remember. I see her yellow pencil racing across the soft-back steno books as she took down recipes that had come mother to daughter, friend to friend. Recipes that had begun on the farm, moved to the city, and then out to the suburbs. Recipes carried in heads and in worn suitcases from lands around the world; recipes that fell into our national melting pot and emerged with a special flavor—American regional cooking. Her home files grew and grew until they overflowed our apartment, marching down the hall and into a second apartment, the walls soon lined with cabinets packed with recipes, unpublished and painstakingly gathered.

These regional recipes, now arranged under food categories, are the harvest of Clementine's interviews, the windfalls of her food reporting for over thirty years.

Arrowsic, Maine, 1969

CLAIRE JORGENSEN

Publisher's Note

All the recipes in this book appeared in an earlier volume, *How America Eats* by Clementine Paddleford (Scribners, 1960), now out of print. The material, based on her articles in the *New York Herald Tribune* and *This Week*, was arranged regionally and the recipes were part of a narrative telling how and where they were acquired. For the present volume, only the recipes are given, with a notation of their origin, and they are arranged by food categories instead of state by state.

Contents

Appetizers, Dips and Spreads

CHEESE-WALNUT BALLS · MAXINE THORPE, HOLLYWOOD, CALIF.

A holiday hors d'œuvre uses 1 package of cream cheese mashed with 1 teaspoon grated onion with Tabasco sauce to taste, this mixed with enough ground walnut meats to make a thick paste. Roll into small balls. Take walnut halves, twice as many as there are cheese balls, and run into the oven until toasted and brown. Sandwich each cheese ball between walnut halves and serve hot.

CHEESE BALLS · MRS. GREYTON TAYLOR, HAMMONDSPORT, N.Y.

Blend 4 ounces cream cheese and ¼ pound butter together. Mix in 1½ cups sifted flour. Form into 24 balls. Place on baking sheet. Bake at 350°F. about 25 minutes or until lightly browned. While still warm, cut with a sharp knife and fill with a dot of wine jelly. Yield: 24 balls.

CHEESE STRAWS · MARY CALL COLLINS, TALLAHASSEE, FLA.

1 pound sharp Cheddar
   cheese
½ pound butter or margarine
3 cups sifted flour
1 teaspoon paprika
½ teaspoon salt

Grate cheese very fine. Cream cheese with butter. Add flour, paprika and salt and mix thoroughly. Roll dough on floured surface to ¼-inch thickness. Cut in strips about ½-inch wide and 4 inches long. Place on ungreased cooky sheet. Bake at 400°F. for 8 to 10 minutes.

Yield: about 7 dozen sticks.

1

CHEESE BALLS · MRS. GUY ROCKWELL, EAST CLEVELAND, OHIO

One-eighth pound of butter or margarine brought to room temperature, blended with a six-ounce crock of a neutral sharp Cheddar spread, or you could use the bacon-Cheddar spread which is around in the markets. Into the cheese add butter, work in ¾ cup of all-purpose flour, form the mixture into balls to refrigerate several hours. Just before serving, into a hot oven for 10 minutes' baking. Serve piping hot. Crusty on the outside, soft within. Don't burn your tongue!

NETTIE ROSE'S CHEESE RIBBONS · MELANIE DE BEN, PASS CHRISTIAN, MISS.

¼ pound butter or margarine,
   melted
2 cups sifted flour
1½ teaspoons salt
½ to 1 teaspoon cayenne
   pepper
1 pound sharp Cheddar
   cheese, finely grated

Mix buttter, flour, salt and pepper. Stir in cheese, blending thoroughly. Place bowl in warm water until dough is pliable. Using a 1½-inch ribbon disc, put dough through a cooky press into long ribbons, onto an ungreased baking sheet. Cut strands into 3½-inch lengths. Bake at 350°F. for about 10 minutes or until lightly browned and crisp.

Yield: about 100 cheese ribbons.

BEEF BURGUNDY BALLS · MRS. GREYTON TAYLOR, HAMMONDSPORT, N.Y.

Combine ½ pound round steak (ground), 1 egg, 2 tablespoons flour, 2 teaspoons finely chopped onion, ¼ teaspoon Worcestershire sauce, 1 tablespoon Burgundy wine, salt and pepper. Mix ingredients well. Form into small balls. Roll in fine cracker crumbs. Fry in deep fat at 375°F until brown. Drain. Serve hot on picks.

G'FILLTI GAPICKELTI OYER (STUFFED PICKLED EGGS)

LANCASTER COUNTY, PENNA.

6 hard-cooked eggs
1 cup beet juice
2 small cooked beets
1 cup vinegar
¾ teaspoon salt
¼ teaspoon pepper
½ teaspoon cloves
¼ teaspoon allspice
¼ teaspoon mace
2 teaspoons lemon juice
Mayonnaise
Parsley

Cut eggs in half lengthwise. Remove yolks. Combine beet juice, beets, vinegar, salt, pepper, cloves, allspice and mace. Place egg whites in the juice and soak until whites are dyed red (about an hour). Remove and drain dry. Mash yolks. Combine with lemon juice and enough mayonnaise to moisten. Fill centers with the mashed yolks. Top with small sprig of parsley.

Yield: 12 egg halves.

SAVORY MEAT BALLS (RAW BEEF) · MARY TURNER, WASHINGTON, D.C.

1½ teaspoons salt
½ teaspoon pepper
½ teaspoon Worcestershire
    sauce
1 pound top round steak,
    ground twice
1 can French fried onions
½ cup minced parsley

Add seasonings to raw ground round steak; mix thoroughly. Shape into small balls. Chop French fried onions very fine; add parsley. Roll balls in onion mixture. Chill.

Yield: 60 small meat balls.

CHICKEN LIVER BALLS · MRS. FLOYD L. RHEAM, TULSA, OKLA.

1 pound chicken livers
3 tablespoons butter or
    margarine
2 tablespoons minced onion
4 cooked chicken gizzards,
    cut up
2 hard-cooked eggs, cut into
    quarters
Salt
Pepper
Finely chopped parsley

Sauté livers in 2 tablespoons of the butter until lightly browned. Remove. In same pan sauté onion until tender. Put chicken livers, onion, gizzards, and eggs through meat grinder twice. Melt remaining tablespoon of butter; blend with liver mixture. Season to taste. Shape into 1-inch balls. Roll in parsley. Serve at room temperature.

Yield: approximately 40 balls.

SAUERKRAUT BALLS · GRUBER'S RESTAURANT, CLEVELAND, OHIO

½ pound lean, boneless ham
½ pound lean, boneless pork
½ pound corned beef
1 medium-sized onion
1 teaspoon minced parsley
3 tablespoons shortening
2 cups all-purpose flour
1 teaspoon dry mustard
1 teaspoon salt
2 cups milk
2 pounds sauerkraut, cooked
    and drained
Flour
2 eggs, slightly beaten
Dry bread crumbs

Put meats and onion through food grinder; add parsley. Blend well and sauté in shortening until browned. Add flour, mustard, salt, and milk; blend. Cook, stirring constantly, until thick. Add sauerkraut and put entire mixture through food chopper. Mix thoroughly. Return to skillet and cook, stirring constantly until very thick. Cool. Form into balls about the size of a walnut. Roll in flour; dip in eggs; roll in bread crumbs and fry in hot, deep fat (370°F.) until browned. Serve hot as an appetizer.

Approximate yield: 90 to 100 sauerkraut balls.

HAM-STUFFED MUSHROOM CAPS · MRS. GREYTON TAYLOR, HAMMONDSPORT, N.Y.

Scoop out centers of 1 medium-sized can of mushroom caps. Fill with mixture of ½ cup pork sausage meat, 2 tablespoons Burgundy wine and a dash of red pepper. Broil until tender. Serve hot on picks.

MUSHROOMS HORS D'ŒUVRES · ARECE ANDERSON, COATESVILLE, PENNA.

1 clove garlic
¾ cup vegetable oil
¼ cup olive oil
½ cup lemon juice
1 medium onion, chopped
1 teaspoon salt
¼ teaspoon pepper
½ teaspoon dry mustard
3 bay leaves
1 can (4 ounces) button
    mushrooms

Rub mixing bowl with cut clove of garlic. Pour in oils and lemon juice. Add onion, salt, pepper, mustard and bay leaves. Drain mushrooms and add to sauce. Be sure the sauce is sufficient to cover mushrooms. Let stand in refrigerator for 24 hours. Before serving, drain mushrooms, lay on paper towel, insert picks. Spike the picks into a grapefruit and lace in English ivy. Place grapefruit on tray or plate and circle with greens.

Yield: about 30 mushroom caps.

SYE NOOF-GAWICKELT (PIGS IN BLANKETS) · LANCASTER COUNTY, PENNA.

Oysters
Bacon
Pepper
Lemon juice

Wrap oysters in ½ strip of bacon. Fasten with toothpicks. Broil until bacon is crisp. Sprinkle with pepper and lemon juice. Serve hot.

SHRIMP HORS D'ŒUVRES · MRS. JAMES D. COMPTON, SEA ISLAND, GA.

1 pound fresh shrimp,
    cleaned and cooked
1 tablespoon minced onion
1 teaspoon minced celery
1 teaspoon minced green
    pepper
2 teaspoons lemon juice
½ teaspoon grated lemon rind
¼ teaspoon salt
4 to 5 drops Tabasco
Dash of pepper
¾ cup mayonnaise
Bread for canapés

Cut shrimp into very fine pieces. Mix together all ingredients and add more seasoning if desired. Cut 36 rounds about the size of a half dollar, from bread sliced ¼ inch thick. Pile a heaping teaspoon of shrimp mixture on each round. Garnish with parsley or pretty green leaves.

Yield: 3 dozen hors d'œuvres.

SHRIMP CANAPÉS · MARIE GRAFTON, NEW ORLEANS, LA.

2 pounds raw shrimp
2 quarts boiling salted water
⅛ teaspoon thyme
Dash of cayenne
1 bay leaf
1 bunch celery leaves
1 envelope unflavored gelatin
1 can (12 ounces) vegetable
   juice cocktail
50 bread pieces, 1 × 2-inches
1 bunch watercress

Drop shrimp into rapidly boiling water; add thyme, cayenne, bay leaf and celery leaves. Cook 5 to 8 minutes, or until shrimp turns pink. Drain and cool. Remove shells and vein; mince finely. Soften gelatin in 2 tablespoons of the vegetable cocktail for 10 minutes. Heat remaining cocktail juice and stir in gelatin until dissolved. Add minced shrimp. Chill overnight. Sauté bread pieces in butter. Stir shrimp mixture and mound on bread. Serve garnished with leaves of watercress.

Yield: about 50 canapes.

TOMATOES FLORENTINE · MRS. FLOYD L. RIIDAM, TULSA, OKLA.

20 to 24 cocktail-size
   tomatoes, 1¼ inch
   diameter
5 tablespoons butter or
   margarine
1 bay leaf
Juice of 1 small clove garlic
1 package frozen chopped
   spinach, cooked and
   drained
1½ teaspoon lemon juice
¼ teaspoon nutmeg
2 drops Tabasco
Salt
2 tablespoons grated
   Parmesan cheese

Cut slice off bottoms of tomatoes so they will sit upright. Scoop out pulp and juice. Turn tomatoes upside down to drain. Melt 3 tablespoons of the butter in medium skillet. Add bay leaf and garlic juice; simmer a few minutes. Discard bay leaf. Stir in spinach, lemon juice, nutmeg, Tabasco, and salt to taste. Place tomatoes in shallow baking pan; sprinkle cavities lightly with salt. Stuff with spinach mixture. Sprinkle tops with cheese. Melt remaining 2 tablespoons butter; spoon over cheese. Bake at 350°F. for 20 minutes.

Yield: 20-24 hors d'œuvre portions.

MARINATED CHAYOTE · DR. GEORGE SELLECK, SAN FRANCISCO, CALIF.

4 chayote (sub-tropical
   squash)
1 quart water
2 teaspoons salt
3 tablespoons tarragon wine
   vinegar
3 tablespoons olive oil

Peel squash; cut in lengthwise pieces about ½ inch thick. Cover with water and add salt. Boil 15 to 20 minutes or until tender. Drain. Spread on platter and while still warm sprinkle with vinegar. Allow to cool. Dress with olive oil. Serve as appetizer with thin slices of prosciutto ham.

Yield: 12 portions, 2 strips each.

DUNK FOR PRETZELS *OR* CELERY SPIKES · MRS. STAFFORD WENTWORTH, PALERMO, CALIF.

Take six ounces of cream cheese, add milk to soften, stir in one-eighth teaspoon curry powder, one-fourth teaspoon grated lemon rind, one-half cup chopped ripe olives with a dash of pepper.

LEMON BUTTER DIP · MRS. JOHN T. RUSSEL, JR., CHATHAM, MASS.

Juice of two lemons
1 cup soft butter or
  margarine
2 teaspoons crumbled dried
  parsley

Add lemon juice to butter drop by drop and keep stirring for 15 to 20 minutes. Add parsley. Serve cold as a dip.

Yield: about 1½ cups.

To oven-dry the parsley: the leaves are picked from the stems, and placed in a 350°F. oven, the door left open until the dampness is out. Close the oven door, turn the heat up to 400°F. for 5 minutes. Off again, and leave the parsley until it dries to a crumble.

CHILI CON QUESA DIP · MRS. ROBERT E. BOGUE, WICHITA, KAN.

1 pound process American
  cheese
1 pound process Cheddar
  cheese
2 tablespoons minced green
  chili peppers
1 clove garlic, mashed
¼ cup milk

Melt cheese in double boiler. Stir in chili peppers, garlic, and milk. Keep warm over hot water or in chafing dish. Serve as a dip for corn chips.

Yield: about 4 cups dip.

AVOCADO DIP SAUCE · TICO TACO CAFÉ, SCOTTSDALE, ARIZ.

3 ripe avocados
½ cup grated longhorn cheese
  (or use a sharp
  Cheddar)
½ cup grated white Mexican
  cheese (or use a mild
  Cheddar)
Salt to taste
1½ tablespoons mayonnaise
½ cup water
1 tablespoon chopped onion

Peel avocados; split and remove seeds. Finely chop two of the avocados. Break the third into pieces and place in blender with remaining ingredients except salt. Blend for 10 minutes or until the consistency of thick cream. Remove from the bowl and mix with the chopped avocado. Salt to taste. Store in container of a size for sauce to fill to the top, so removing all air spaces which prevents browning. Tightly cover and chill until ready to serve. Serve in individual small cups adding a drop of Tabasco, firing to taste.

Yield: about 5 cups sauce.

TEXAS BEAN DIP · ARTHUR AND BOBBIE COLEMAN, SAN ANTONIO, TEX.

4 cups pinto beans
2 cups chopped onion
3 cloves garlic, mashed or
*   chopped*
2 teaspoons ground cumin
*   seed or 4 teaspoons of*
*   the seed, crushed*
6 tablespoons bacon
*   drippings or lard, or a*
*   fist-size chunk of salt*
*   pork*
6 tablespoons chili paste or
*   chili powder*
Salt to taste
1 cup butter or margarine
½ pound sharp Cheddar
*   cheese, grated*
Dash of salsa picante
*   (Mexican hot sauce)*

Wash beans thoroughly and remove any foreign particles. Soak beans overnight (or boil for 2 minutes in 10 cups of boiling water, remove from cover and let stand for 1 hour). Put in a pottery, enamel or glass pot with soaking water. Add onion, garlic, cumin seed and fat. Simmer until beans are very soft, 3 to 4 hours, stirring occasionally with a wooden spoon to prevent sticking. If additional water is needed, use boiling water as cold water will darken the beans. When beans are soft add chili paste and continue cooking a few minutes. Add salt to taste, about 3 teaspoons. (Salting too soon hardens the beans.) While beans are still warm, mash in butter, cheese and Mexican sauce. Blend until smooth. Serve warm.

Yield: about 2 quarts bean dip.

FRONTIER BEAN DIP · DALLAS, TEX.

4 cups pinto beans
1 cup hot bacon fat
2 tablespoons Tabasco
1 tablespoon Worcestershire
*   sauce*
1 teaspoon garlic salt
Juice of lemon

Cook beans; drain. Heat bacon fat in a large skillet. Add beans and fry, stirring constantly, until lightly browned. Drain off surplus bacon fat. Mash the beans to a smooth consistency. Blend in remaining ingredients. Add salt and pepper, if desired. Serve hot with corn chips or cheese crackers.

Yield: about 6 cups dip.

CRAB DIP · WINN BRINDLE, WARD'S COVE, ALASKA

1 cup sour cream
¼ cup mayonnaise
1 can (6½ ounces) Dungeness
*   crab meat, drained and*
*   flaked*
1 tablespoon capers
1 tablespoon grated onion
1 tablespoon lemon juice
Salt and pepper

Combine all ingredients. Chill thoroughly. Use dip for crackers, toast, pretzels, cauliflowerettes, celery sticks.

Yield: 2 cups dip.

CHILI BOWL · MRS. ORVILLE BURTIS, ASHLAND BOTTOM, KAN.

4 pounds red kidney beans
3 No. 10 cans tomato juice or
    6½ No. 5 cans
¼ cup salt
¾ cup chili powder
10 pounds chuck beef,
    ground
1 medium-size onion, grated

Wash beans; cover with cold water and soak overnight in large heavy kettle. Cover and cook beans in water in which they have soaked. Simmer 2½ to 3 hours or until beans are tender, adding tomato juice from time to time to keep beans covered as liquid boils away. Add salt. Remove ½ cup of liquid from bean pot and blend with chili powder to make a paste; add to beans, blending well. Cook beef in large skillet, stirring continuously until all the particles are browned. Add beef and grated onion to beans. Cook mixture over low heat, stirring continuously, about 5 minutes longer. Serve with rolls or crackers. Approximate yield: 20 portions.

PISSALDIÈRE · DR. GEORGE SELLECK, SAN FRANCISCO, CALIF.

3 tablespoons olive oil
¾ cup chopped onion
¼ clove garlic, minced
1 green pepper
2 cans (1 pound, 4 ounces)
    solid pack tomatoes
2 cans (8 ounces each)
    tomato sauce
1 teaspoon salt
⅛ teaspoon pepper
1 can (4 ounces) pimiento,
    chopped
4 tablespoons grated Parmesan cheese
3 tablespoons chopped olives
1 8-inch baked pie shell
7 fillets flat anchovies
Black olive slices
Whole olive

Heat olive oil in heavy iron skillet. Add onion and garlic and sauté until golden. Cut pepper in half, remove core and seeds and cut into strips ¼ inch wide. Add to onion and cook until soft. Add tomatoes, tomato sauce, salt and pepper. Reduce heat to very low and cook sauce until thickened, about 2 hours, stirring occasionally with wooden spoon. (Do not cook in double boiler or the mixture turns brown. The wide bottom of the skillet is important to the success of this sauce.) Remove from heat. Add pimiento, 3 tablespoons of the cheese, and chopped olives. Turn into pastry shell. Arrange over mixture flat fillets of anchovies in spoke-of-wheel fashion, allowing one to a portion. Stud between "spokes" with cuts of black olives and center with whole olive. Sprinkle with remaining tablespoon of Parmesan cheese. Bake at 300°F. until the mixture is heated. Serve while warm as an hors d'œuvre.

Yield: 7 portions.

Pastry: Use recipe for rich pie pastry. Roll dough ⅛ inch thick and line cake tin, 8 inches wide, 4 inches high. Place greased paper over dough and spread on bottom ¼ cup beans to keep pastry from bubbling. Bake at 425°F. for 15 minutes. Cool slightly before adding the filling.

GUACAMOLE · MRS. HUGH B. MCDUFFEE, LONG BEACH, CALIF.

3 very ripe avocados
1 clove garlic, minced
1 tablespoon lemon juice
½ teaspoon salt (optional)

Cut avocados in half, remove seed, spoon out flesh. Mash and whip, using fork. Add garlic, lemon juice and salt. Yield: 4 to 6 portions.

ADMIRAL'S GOLDEN BUCK · MRS. HAMILTON POLK JONES, NEW ORLEANS, LA.

1 pound sharp processed
   cheese, grated
1 tablespoon butter or margarine, softened
1 egg, beaten
½ teaspoon salt
1 tablespoon Worcestershire
   sauce
¼ teaspoon cayenne
2 dozen rounds (3 inches in
   diameter) thinly sliced
   bread, toasted

Mix together cheese, butter and egg. Add seasonings. If not smooth enough, force through medium-fine sieve. Cover and chill. Spread mixture on rounds and broil until cheese melts. Serve hot. Yield: 2 dozen canapés.

NOTE: Cheese mixture may be spread on toasted rounds several hours in advance and broiled just before serving.

MRS. DECKER'S CHEESE POT · MRS. CLARENCE DECKER, KANSAS CITY, MO.

8 pounds bleu cheese
2 pounds cream cheese
6 tablespoons dry mustard
4½ tablespoons curry
6 tablespoons monosodium
   glutamate
4 tablespoons garlic salt or
   garlic juice
1 quart olive oil
1 pint sherry wine
Port or sherry wine
Rum, port, brandy

Combine cheeses in large earthenware bowl and beat with an electric mixer until blended. Let stand overnight to soften. In another bowl, mix dry ingredients and stir in oil and sherry. Pour this mixture over the cheese and mix well with wooden fork, then beat until creamy. Place a half gallon of the mix in an earthen crock; lace generously with port or sherry (about 1 cup). Store in refrigerator. (This constitutes the "mother" to be added to the next batch.)

Divide the remainder of the mixture as desired into large gallon or one-half gallon crocks. Part of it may be dipped into attractive quart ceramic jars with wide tops to bring to the table at serving time. Gash the cheese with a fork and trickle your favorite liquid seasoning into the jars. Into one may go rum; into another port, or Cognac for a change. Two to four jiggers of this "seasoning" is allowed to each quart, according to taste. Let stand at least a week in the refrigerator before serving. Yield: 2 gallons cheese.

FLAISH UN KAIS (CURRIED TURNOVERS) · LANCASTER COUNTY, PENNA.

PASTRY:
1 cup sifted flour
¼ pound butter or margarine
1 package (3 ounces) cream
  cheese
Salt
Curry powder

Sift flour. Work butter and cream cheese into flour with fingers until well blended. Form into roll. Wrap in waxed paper. Chill several hours or overnight. Roll very thin. Cut into 2-inch circles. Place a teaspoon of the filling on each round. Fold over and seal. Bake at 400°F. for 5 to 8 minutes or until brown. Sprinkle lightly with salt and curry powder. Serve hot. Yield: 2½ dozen.

FILLING:
½ cup boiled chicken livers
2 hard-cooked eggs
1 teaspoon grated onion
¼ teaspoon salt
⅛ teaspoon black pepper
1 teaspoon curry powder
3 to 4 tablespoons heavy
  cream

Combine livers and eggs. Chop very fine or press through fine sieve. Add remaining ingredients using just enough cream to moisten.

SHRIMP MOLD OR PASTE · MRS. STUART DAWSON, CHARLESTON, S.C.

2 pounds shrimp, cooked and
  cleaned
½ cup butter or margarine
3 tablespoons mayonnaise
  (optional)
1 teaspoon Worcestershire
  sauce
¼ teaspoon lemon juice
Few drops Tabasco
Ground mace or celery seed
Salt and pepper to taste

Put shrimp through meat grinder twice. Combine with butter until well blended. If desired, add mayonnaise to soften slightly. Blend in seasonings. Chill mixture thoroughly, serve with crackers or thin, crisp toast. A delicious dish served with hominy for breakfast. Yield: 3 cups paste.

PICKLED FILLETS OF HERRING · MRS. ORREN SAFFORD, MINNEAPOLIS, MINN.

Drain and place a layer of herring in shallow glass dish. Cover with a layer of peeled, thinly sliced Bermuda onion, over this finely cut chives, and a scattering of capers. Cover with thick sour cream seasoned to taste with salt and a touch of mustard. Chill the dish almost to freezing. Serve on crisp all-wheat crackers. Pass with fork and spoon.

CHEESE MASTERPIECE · DR. GEORGE SELLECK, SAN FRANCISCO, CALIF.

1 pound ripe Camembert
    cheese
½ cup Amontillado sherry
1 pound sweet butter
3 tablespoons dry bread
    crumbs

Remove rind from Camembert. Soften cheese in bowl. Cover with sherry; let stand in a cool place overnight. Cream butter in a warm bowl. Drain sherry from cheese and reserve. Mash cheese with fork. Add butter and cream thoroughly. Blend in drained sherry and chill until cheese sets. Immerse bowl to rim 1 minute in warm water to unmold neatly to serving plate. Garnish with dry bread crumbs.
Yield: 2 cups.

MUSHROOM SANDWICH SPREAD · ARECE ANDERSON, COATSVILLE, PENNA.

1½ pounds mushrooms
½ cup butter or margarine
1 tablespoon cornstarch
1 teaspoon salt
¼ teaspoon pepper
1 tablespoon chopped parsley

Chop mushrooms very fine. Sauté in butter, covered, using stainless-steel saucepan, just long enough to draw out the juices. Remove 2 tablespoons of butter from pan, cool slightly, blend with cornstarch to make a smooth paste. Add to mushrooms, stirring in well. Add salt and pepper and cook, stirring, until thick and smooth. Mix in parsley. Chill. Spread between thin slices of white bread, with crusts removed and each slice cut into 3 thin fingers. Yield: 2¼ cups spread.

LEMON BOODER No. 1 (LEMON BUTTER) · MRS. PALMA CLIFFORD BAKER, COCHRANVILLE, PENNA.

2 lemons
4 eggs
1½ cups sugar
¾ teaspoon ground mace

Grate lemons. Beat eggs. Combine with sugar, mace and the grated rind. Place in double boiler and cook over hot water until thick, about 20 minutes, stirring constantly. Store, covered, in refrigerator. Yield: 1 pint.

LEMON BUTTER No. 2 · MRS. PALMA CLIFFORD BAKER, COCHRANVILLE, PENNA.

3 eggs, beaten
2 cups sugar
3 lemons, juice and grated
    rind
¼ pound butter or margarine

Combine eggs, sugar, lemon juice and rind and butter in a saucepan. Cook over low heat, stirring constantly, only until thickened. Serve hot or cold. Yield: about 3 cups.

Soups

PEPPERPOT · PHILADELPHIA, PA.

¾ pound fresh honeycomb
    tripe
2 pounds knuckle of veal
3 quarts cold water
1 small bunch parsley
10 whole cloves
16 peppercorns, crushed
¼ teaspoon marjoram
¼ teaspoon savory
¼ teaspoon basil
¼ teaspoon thyme
3 green peppers, chopped
3 medium onions, chopped
3 medium beets, chopped
3 tablespoons butter or
    margarine

1 tablespoon salt
⅓ cup uncooked rice
1½ cups canned tomatoes

Wash tripe thoroughly; cut into ¼-inch cubes. Place in pot with veal knuckle; add water. Heat slowly to boiling point and boil 10 minutes; skim. Cover and simmer gently 2 hours. Add parsley and herbs tied in a cheesecloth bag. Cover pot; continue slow cooking 1 hour; remove bag. Sauté fresh vegetables in butter until lightly browned. Add salt. Add to soup mixture with rice. Cover and simmer 30 minutes. Add tomatoes and cook ten minutes. Remove veal knuckle and cool soup. Skim. Reheat before serving. Yield: about 8 portions.

12

PAINLESS BORSCHT · LUCY CORBETT, GROSSE ILE, MICH.

1 can (12½ ounces) consommé
    or bouillon
2 jars (7½ ounces each)
    chopped beets
1½ cups water
3 tablespoons grated onion
2 tablespoons tarragon
    vinegar
1 teaspoon coarse salt
½ teaspoon garlic salt

¼ teaspoon black pepper, freshly ground
⅛ teaspoon cayenne
2 tablespoons commercial sour cream

Combine all ingredients, except sour cream. Heat thoroughly. Serve topped with sour cream, a teaspoonful added to each bowl. Yield: 6 portions.

BEEF BOUILLON WITH DUMPLINGS · MRS. JOSEPH A. GAMMA, MILWAUKEE, WIS.

1 marrow bone
Cold water
2 teaspoons salt
¼ teaspoon pepper
2 carrots, sliced
1 onion or leek, chopped
3 stalks celery, diced
5 sprigs parsley

Crack marrow bone; cover with cold water. Bring to boil. Skim. Add salt, pepper, and vegetables: continue cooking 1 hour. Strain. Add dumplings. Yield: 1 quart soup.

NUTMEG DUMPLINGS:
2 eggs
½ cup milk
½ teaspoon salt
1 cup flour
Nutmeg
1 tablespoon chopped parsley

Beat eggs slightly; stir in milk and salt. Place flour in bowl making a well in center, add liquid in hollow and stir until mixed; beat until smooth. Drop by teaspoonfuls into boiling water. When the dumplings float dip out with slotted spoon, drain a minute and drop into hot soup. Allow three to a portion. Dust well with freshly grated nutmeg, sprinkle with chopped parsley.
Yield: 18 small dumplings.

RICE SOUP WITH CELERY AND PARSLEY · TOSCANINI'S COOK, ANNA

1 tablespoon butter or
    margarine
3 tablespoons chopped celery
2 tablespoons rice
2 cups beef stock
1 tablespoon minced parsley

Heat butter or margarine in saucepan, add celery and cook until slightly softened, add rice and stir a minute or two, add one cup stock. Cover and cook until rice is done. Add remaining stock, reheat, add parsley. Serve with toast. Yield: 1 portion, a big bowl full.

BARLEY LAMB BROTH · MRS. CORNELIUS STOB, LISLE, ILL.

⅓ cup coarse barley
2 lamb shanks
2 quarts cold water
2 teaspoons salt
⅓ cup brown rice, washed
½ cup minced carrots
½ cup minced onion
1 cup minced celery
1 can (10½ ounces) condensed
    tomato soup

Soak barley in water to cover overnight. Wash lamb shanks. Combine with barley, cold water, salt, and rice. Cover and simmer 1½ hours. Add boiling water as needed to keep liquid at 2 quarts. Add vegetables and soup. Simmer 30 minutes. Cool and skim fat. Remove meat from shank bones; cut in small pieces; return to soup. Refrigerate overnight to reheat the following day.

Yield: 6 portions.

MINESTRONE · TOSCANINI'S COOK, ANNA

1 tablespoon olive oil
1 tablespoon butter or
    margarine
¼ cup finely chopped onion
½ cup finely chopped celery
½ cup finely diced carrot
2 tomatoes chopped
1 small whole turnip
    chopped
⅓ cup chopped cabbage
1 small potato, chopped
2 quarts seasoned beef stock
¼ cup lentils
½ cup cooked fresh peas

½ cup cooked kidney beans
½ cup rice

Heat oil and butter or margarine, add onions and cook until transparent. Add celery, carrots and tomatoes; cook a few minutes to soften. Add all other vegetables except peas, along with one quart beef stock and lentils which have been soaked in cold water one hour. Cook until the lentils are almost tender. Add peas and beans. Add remaining stock and the rice. Cook 15 minutes. Remove from heat, let stand 10 minutes and serve with bread sticks or crusty rolls.

Yield: 6 portions.

CHARLESTON OKRA SOUP · MARY HUGUENIN, CHARLESTON, S.C.

1 large beef bone, with
    plenty of meat on it
3 quarts water
3 pounds fresh okra, finely
    chopped
1 slice bacon diced
8 large tomatoes, peeled, or 2
    cans (1 pound, 13 ounces
    each) tomatoes
2 bay leaves

2 medium onions
Salt and pepper to taste

Gently simmer beef bone in water, partially covered, for 2 hours. Add okra, bacon, tomatoes, bay leaves, onions and salt and pepper to taste. Cook another 2 hours, adding more water if necessary. When serving, add steamed rice if desired. Hot buttered cornsticks are a tasty accompaniment.

Yield: 5 quarts soup.

ESCAROLE SOUP · TOSCANINI'S COOK, ANNA

Outside leaves of escarole
2 eggs
2 tablespoons grated Parmesan cheese
6 cups beef stock

Remove outside leaves from head of escarole, retain heart for salad, cook leaves in boiling salted water until tender. Drain, chop very fine to measure three tablespoonfuls. Beat eggs, add escarole and cheese. Gradually add boiling stock and serve immediately. Yield: 4 portions. A quite different soup, one you'll enjoy.

KIDDLEY BROTH · CAROLINE BANCROFT, DENVER, COLO.

12 leeks
1½ quarts water
6 tablespoons butter or margarine
Salt and pepper
3 slices bread, cut in squares
Finely chopped shallot tops
Marigold heads

Wash and trim leeks. Simmer in water for 30 to 40 minutes. Strain. Add butter. Season to taste with salt and pepper. Serve hot with bread squares in soup bowl. Garnish with shallot tops and marigolds. Yield: about 6 portions.

Variation: Dissolve 3 to 4 beef bouillon cubes in broth and serve with leeks, cut in slices.

SCOTCH BROTH · NANCY FINCH, SALT LAKE CITY, UTAH

1½-pound piece chuck beef
1½-pound piece rump beef
1½ pound beef-leg bone, cracked
2 quarts water
2 quarts beef stock
2 bay leaves
2 tablespoons salt
Pepper, freshly ground
1 tablespoon chopped onion
1 cup finely diced carrot
1 cup finely diced turnip
1 small parsnip, diced
1 tablespoon barley
1 cup cooked dried beans (lima, pea, etc.)
1 cup cooked garbanzos (chick-peas)

1 can (16 to 17) green peas
Salt and pepper
Dash of Tabasco sauce

Place meat and bones in large kettle. Add water, stock, bay leaves, salt, pepper, and onion. Simmer, covered, 3 to 4 hours or until meat is very tender. Strain, cool meat and cut into bite-sized pieces. Add carrot, turnip, parsnip and barley to strained broth and cook until tender. Add beans, peas, and cut-up meat; heat. Season to taste with salt, pepper and Tabasco. Yield: 8 portions.

CHICKEN-CORN SOUP · EDNA EBY HELLER, HERSHEY, PENNA.

1 4-pound chicken, disjointed
2 teaspoons salt
¼ teaspoon saffron
2 cups noodles
2 cups fresh corn kernels
1 teaspoon chopped parsley
⅛ teaspoon pepper
2 hard-cooked eggs, chopped

Put chicken in pot with water to cover, about 3 quarts. Add salt and saffron. Stew until tender. Remove chicken from stock and set aside the legs and breast for a future potpie, along with 1 cup of the stock. Cut up the remaining meat and return to stock in kettle. Bring to a boil. Add noodles and corn. Boil for 15 minutes. Add parsley, pepper and eggs. Yield: about 2½ quarts.

WILLIAMSBURG INN OLD-FASHIONED TURKEY SOUP · WILLIAMSBURG, VA.

3 large onions
3 stalks celery
2 medium carrots
½ pound butter or margarine
1½ cups flour
3 quarts turkey (or chicken)
     stock
1 pint light cream
Salt and white pepper to
     taste
¼ cup finely diced cooked
     turkey (or chicken)
¼ cup cooked rice

Chop onions, celery and carrots very fine. Cook with a little water for 20 minutes or until tender. Melt butter and blend in flour thoroughly. Heat stock and cream and add very gradually to butter and flour mixture, stirring until lumps disappear. Add vegetables, water and all; stir and cook over low heat for 10 minutes. Season to taste. Add turkey and rice.
     Yield: about 4½ quarts soup.

MAIN DISH VEGETABLE SOUP · MRS. RUTH PHILLIPS, ARIZONA

Beef-shank bone
2 tablespoons salt
6 outside stalks celery
1 large potato, pared
1 large Bermuda onion
6 medium carrots
1 small head cabbage
2 white turnips
2 tablespoons chopped
     parsley
2 cups canned tomatoes
Salt to taste

Place shank bone in deep pot and cover with cold water. Add salt. Bring water to a boil, and reduce heat. Cover and simmer for 2 hours. Put celery through meat grinder using coarse blade; grind potato next to catch the celery juice. Run other vegetables through grinder. Add parsley and tomatoes. Combine vegetable mixture with meat stock (about 2 quarts); add salt to taste. Simmer gently for 1 hour.
     Yield: 8 portions.

HAMBURGER BALL SOUP · MRS. CORNELIUS STOB, LISLE, ILL.

2 pounds marrow bones with
    meat
2 quarts cold water
2 teaspoons salt
4 stalks celery, coarsely
    chopped
1 small onion, coarsely
    chopped
½ cup minced parsley

Combine marrow bones, water, and salt. Cover and simmer 1½ hours. Remove bones and meat and put aside to use for stew later. Add vegetables and Meat Balls to stock. Cover and continue cooking about 30 minutes. Yield: 6 portions.

MEAT BALLS FOR SOUP:
1 pound ground very lean
    round
1 cup flour
½ teaspoon pepper, freshly
    ground
2 teaspoons nutmeg, freshly
    grated
Salt to taste

Mix ingredients with hands until well blended. Shape into marble-sized balls.

ALBONDIGAS DE CARNE · MRS. DOROTHEA DALTON, CALIF.

½ pound each, lean beef and
    very lean pork or fresh
    ham, ground together
    twice
¼ cup masa (to make, put one
    can hominy through food
    grinder to form a paste)
1 onion, finely chopped
1 canned hot chili, finely
    chopped
2 small tomatoes, finely cut
1 tablespoon finely cut mint
    leaves
1 teaspoon coriander seed,
    crushed
1 egg
2 tablespoons butter or
    margarine

Salt and pepper to taste
1½ quarts boiling water
1 can chicken or beef broth

Mix meat and *masa*. Combine chopped vegetables, mint leaves, coriander and salt and pepper. Drain, saving liquid for soup. Add half of vegetables to meat. Add egg, mix well; let stand while soup is being prepared. Melt butter in large kettle. Sauté other half of vegetables for 5 minutes. Add boiling water, broth and vegetable liquid; keep boiling rapidly. Pinch off small balls of meat mixture and drop into boiling soup. Do as quickly as possible. Cover. Simmer for 25 to 30 minutes. Yield: 6 portions.
NOTE: Some cooks add 1 finely chopped garlic clove.

ALBONDIGAS SOUP · MRS. ELMA VAN ZANDT, PHOENIX, ARIZ.

MEAT BALLS:

2 pounds ground round steak
1 pound ground fresh pork
3 eggs
1 green chili pepper, finely
 chopped
3 bunches scallions, finely
 chopped
3 sprigs mint, finely chopped
½ clove garlic, finely shaved
1½ cups corn meal
¼ cup chopped parsley
1 cup canned tomatoes,
 drained

½ teaspoon cloves
Dash of savory thyme
¾ teaspoon sage

Grind the ground steak and pork together twice. Add remaining ingredients, mixing well. Form into small balls about size of marbles and drop into hot soup. Cover. Simmer 1 hour or until tender. Keep adding water if necessary.

SOUP:

6 quarts water
3 cans beef bouillon
1 cup tomato juice
Salt and pepper to taste
Dash of savory thyme
¼ cup chopped parsley
½ clove garlic, shaved
1 green chili pepper, finely
 chopped

Combine water with beef bouillon, tomato juice, and salt and pepper to taste. Add remaining ingredients. Bring to a boil. Yield: 20 portions (9 meat balls each; 2 gallons soup).

CRAB MEAT AND MUSHROOM SOUP · WARREN POSEY, NEW ORLEANS, LA.

½ cup butter or margarine
½ cup minced onion
1 scallion including top,
 minced
3 tablespoons minced parsley
2 cups fresh mushrooms,
 sliced
3 cups medium white sauce
2 cups light cream
3 cups flaked cooked crab
 meat
1 egg yolk
2 tablespoons milk

Melt butter in frying pan; add onion, scallion, parsley and mushrooms. Sauté until soft but not brown. Add to white sauce; stir in cream. Bring to a slow boil over low heat; add crab meat. Simmer 5 minutes. Add to egg yolk which has been beaten with milk. Yield: 8 portions.

NOTE: The soup can be made with watercress instead of mushrooms. Use 1 bunch of cress; parboil, drain, mince and add just before stirring into egg yolk.

SUNDAY SUPPER CRAB SOUP · MRS. EDWIN FENDIG, ST. SIMON, GA.

3 tablespoons butter or
    margarine
½ cup finely diced celery
3 tablespoons flour
1 quart milk
1 pint light cream
1 pound white crab meat
2 teaspoons salt
¼ teaspoon pepper
Sherry to taste
2 lemons, thinly sliced

2 hard-cooked eggs

Melt butter in saucepan. Add celery and cook until just tender. Blend in flour to a smooth paste. Heat milk almost to boiling point and slowly add to paste. Add cream, stirring constantly. Heat crab meat in double boiler and add to soup mixture with seasonings and sherry. Place 2 thin slices of lemon and 2 slices of hard-cooked egg in each service plate and pour in soup.
Yield: 6 large portions.

BRETZEL SUPP MIT CLAMS (PRETZEL CLAM SOUP) · READING, PA.

1 can (7 ounces) minced
    clams and liquor
2 cups canned clam broth
2 cups milk
½ teaspoon ground thyme
    leaves
½ teaspoon salt
1 teaspoon garlic salt
¼ teaspoon pepper
2 tablespoons grated onion
2 tablespoons dried parsley
    flakes
4 tablespoons butter or
    margarine
2 tablespoons flour

½ cup light or heavy cream
Paprika
12 large pretzels

Drain clams. Place liquor in saucepan. Add broth, milk, thyme, salt, garlic salt, pepper, onion and parsley Simmer very gently for 5 minutes. Do not allow to come to a full boil. Melt 2 tablespoons of the butter in saucepan. Stir in flour. Remove from heat and gradually stir in 1 cup of the milk mixture. Add remaining milk mixture; heat and stir until slightly thickened. Add minced clams, cream and remaining butter. Heat thoroughly. Serve sprinkled with paprika. Crumble pretzels over soup when serving.
Yield: 6 portions.

CREAM OF CLAM SOUP · MADELEINE AND MILDRED BURRAGE, WISCASSET, ME.

1 pint shelled clams
1 quart milk
3 tablespoons butter or
    margarine
1½ tablespoons flour
Salt
Paprika
Freshly ground pepper

Put clams through meat grinder. Place in saucepan, adding just enough water to cover. Simmer 3 minutes. Heat milk. Blend butter with flour. Add a little of the milk to make a smooth paste. Pour paste into hot milk and stir until it thickens. Add clams, salt, paprika and pepper, quite a lot of pepper.
Yield: 6 portions. Wonderfully good when it's left to stand and mellow for a day and reheated.

GRANDMOTHER BARTON'S CORN SOUP · EDITH B. CRUMB, DEARNBORN, MICH.

2 cups water
1 can (1 pound, 4 ounces)
    cream-style corn
1 onion slice
2 cups milk
3 tablespoons butter
2 teaspoons flour
1 teaspoon salt
¼ teaspoon pepper
2 tablespoons whipped cream
½ teaspoon paprika

Combine water and corn, and simmer 20 minutes. Strain and press through a sieve. Scald onion slice in milk over hot water. Melt a tablespoon of butter; blend in flour and seasonings and add to corn. Bring just to a boil and remove from heat. Add milk, removing onion. Heat thoroughly but keep under boiling point after milk is added. Serve immediately, adding ½ teaspoon butter to each cup and 1 teaspoon whipped cream. Fleck with paprika. Yield: 6 portions.

ENDIVE SOUP · MRS. ABRAHAM ELKTON, PURCHASE, N.Y.

1 pound endive
5 cups chicken stock
⅛ teaspoon cayenne pepper
1 cup thick cream sauce
1 beef bouillon cube
3 egg yolks
2 tablespoons heavy cream

Wash endive and trim root ends. Cook until very tender, about 20 minutes, in chicken stock to which pepper has been added. Remove endive from broth and press through a food mill. Return to broth. Add cream sauce and bouillon cube and bring to a boil, stirring until bouillon cube is dissolved. Add egg yolks which have been beaten with cream, stirring until soup comes to a boil. Remove from heat immediately.
Yield: 6 portions.

LOBSTER STEW · MILDRED RICHARDSON, ROCKLAND, ME.

3 fresh lobsters, 1½ to 1¾
    pounds each (1½ pounds
    lobster meat)
1 cup butter or margarine
2 quarts milk
½ teaspoon salt
⅛ teaspoon pepper

Cook lobsters in about 5 quarts of rapidly boiling water in a large kettle, using 1 tablespoon salt for each quart water. Cover and boil rapidly 5 minutes per pound (7 to 10 minutes) counting cooking time after water returns to boiling. Plunge into cold water; remove immediately and cool. Crack shell and discard craw or crop near head, as well as the black vein. Remove meat from body and claws and cut into large-size pieces. Melt butter in heavy frying pan: sauté lobster meat in butter about 4 minutes. Turn heat to lowest point; add milk and cook, stirring constantly, until milk bubbles around the edges, 10 to 15 minutes. Add salt and pepper. Yield: 4 portions. Two days' aging isn't a bit too much—every hour the stew waits, the flavor multiplies. So set it aside in a cool, dark place for the flavors and savors to merge and blend and meld together.

DR. COFFIN'S LOBSTER STEW · ROBERT P. TRISTRAM COFFIN, PENNELLVILLE, ME.

12 medium lobsters (about 1¼
  pounds each)
2 cups Maine sea water or 2
  cups fresh water with 1
  tablespoon salt
½ pound butter
3 quarts milk
1 quart light cream

Bring water to a boil and lay in lobsters shell side down, to steam in their own juices. Cover tightly, steam at high heat 10 to 15 minutes. Pick meat from shell while hot. Remove intestinal vein and lungs. Let picked meat cool overnight. Melt butter in a large pot and add lobster meat; cook until meat and butter seethe. Turn heat low and add 1 quart of the milk, stirring clockwise constantly to keep the mixture from coagulating; bring almost to a froth. Add the second quart of milk a little at a time. Bring to a froth and immediately stir in third quart of milk and continue stirring clockwise. Let come to a boil and add 1 pint of cream. When this starts to bubble add second pint of cream. Simmer for a few minutes, do not boil, then remove from heat. Cool 12 to 24 hours while flavor develops. Reheat before serving. Season to taste. Yield: 10 to 12 portions.

OYSTER-MILK SOUP · MRS. DELAWARE VOLLRATH, FRANKLIN, LA.

4 tablespoons butter or
  margarine
8 scallions, finely chopped
2 tablespoons chopped
  parsley
2 stalks celery, minced
36 oysters, drained
1 pint oyster liquor
1 pint milk
1 pint light cream
Salt and pepper
Paprika
Mace and oregano (optional)

Melt butter in a soup pot. Add vegetables: cook until scallions just begin to soften. Add oysters and when the edges curl, add oyster liquor, milk and cream. Season to taste. Serve hot with a sprinkle of paprika and mace and oregano.

OYSTER BAR STEW, FAMILY STYLE · GRAND CENTRAL STATION, NEW YORK CITY

28 oysters
6 tablespoons butter or
*   margarine*
2 teaspoons Worcestershire
*   sauce*
½ teaspoon celery salt
1 teaspoon paprika
1 cup oyster liquor
1 cup milk
1 cup light cream
Salt to taste

Pick over oysters, removing bits of shell. Melt 4 tablespoons of the butter in saucepan. Add Worcestershire, celery salt and paprika. Add oysters, bring to a simmer; add oyster liquor, bring to a boil. Add milk and cream. Stir once or twice. Bring almost to a boil; salt to taste and turn into bowls. Add to each portion ½ tablespoon butter. Yield: 4 portions.

OYSTER SOUP · MARY DUNN, AVERY ISLAND, LA.

1 quart milk
3 tablespoons butter or
*   margarine*
2 tablespoons flour
36 oysters and juice
1 tablespoon chopped parsley
½ cup chopped celery
Salt to taste
Tabasco to taste
2 tablespoons whipped cream

Heat milk. Blend butter and flour and add to hot milk, mixing in to make a smooth sauce. Cook oysters in oyster juice with parsley and celery until edges curl. When ready to serve, pour in cream sauce. Add salt and Tabasco. Pour into bowls; top each with 1 teaspoon whipped cream.
    Yield: 6 to 8 portions.

SEAFOOD STEW · COLUMBIA RESTAURANT, YBOR CITY, FLA.

2 quarts boiling water
1 tablespoon salt
1 pound dried split peas
4 celery stalks, cut in pieces
1 onion, chopped
3 soft-shell crabs
½ pound small raw shrimp
¼ cup oil
18 bay scallops
12 cherrystone clams
12 oysters
2 small lobster tails
1 package (12 ounces) frozen
*   okra, thawed*

1 can (12 ounces) whole-kernel corn
4 dashes Tabasco
2 tablespoons sauterne wine
Salt to taste
3 tablespoons finely cut parsley

Bring water and salt to a boil. Add split peas, celery and onion and cook, covered, for about 1 hour, or until tender, adding more water if necessary. Don't drain but put mixture through a sieve. Remove legs from crabs and cut body into 4 pieces. Shell shrimp and clean; cut into small pieces. Heat oil in skillet; add all seafoods without their juices. Cook, covered, for 15 minutes.

Meanwhile bring above purée to a boil. Add sea-foods; bring to boil and skim off any foam. Cook over very low heat for 30 minutes, adding okra and corn the last 10 minutes of cooking. Add Tabasco, sauterne and salt to taste. Serve in bowls garnished with parsley. Serve with Melba toast, a white wine and a green salad. Yield: 5 portions (2 cups each).

PHILADELPHIA CLUB BLACK BEAN SOUP · PHILADELPHIA, PENNA.

1 pound black beans
2 tablespoons bacon
    drippings
1 cup minced onions
1 carrot, minced
2 tablespoons minced celery
3 sprigs parsley
⅛ teaspoon crushed thyme
Pinch of dried hot pepper
    seeds
1 bay leaf
2 tablespoons Worcestershire
    sauce
Salt and pepper to taste
6 cups ham stock or water
    with ham bone or bacon
    skin
¼ cup sherry wine

Cover beans with cold water and soak for at least 6 hours. Discard beans that float; drain and wash. Melt bacon drippings in skillet; add onions, carrot, celery, parsley and herbs. Sauté until vegetables are golden brown. Add Worcestershire sauce, salt, pepper, beans and stock. Simmer slowly, covered, 5 hours. Add more stock or water if soup becomes too thick. Cool overnight.

Place over low heat and bring to boil. Force through a sieve. Taste and add more salt, pepper or Worcester-shire sauce, if needed. Add sherry, stirring well. Serve with a slice of lemon or hard-cooked egg or 1 table-spoon chopped egg sprinkled over each cup. Yield: 6 to 8 portions.

BLACK BEAN SOUP WITH RED WINE AND FRANKFURTERS
MENGER HOTEL, SAN ANTONIO, TEX.

1 pound black beans
3 medium potatoes, diced
¼ cup diced celery
1 medium onion, chopped
2 small carrots, chopped
2 teaspoons salt
¼ teaspoon pepper
2 cloves garlic, chopped
½ pound frankfurters, diced
1 pint Burgundy wine
Tabasco to taste

Pick over beans carefully and wash; soak overnight. The following morning wash again and cook in just enough water to cover for 1½ hours. Add vegetables, seasonings and garlic. Add water to cover and cook until vegetables and beans are tender. Put through sieve. Add frankfurters, wine and Tabasco. Simmer until frankfurters are heated through. Yield: 6 to 8 portions.

DUTCH BEAN SOUP · MRS. CORNELIUS STOB, LISLE, ILL.

1 pound dried navy beans
2 quarts cold water
4 small smoked pork shanks
2 teaspoons salt
2 cups finely chopped onion
2 cups finely chopped celery
1 cup catsup

Soak beans in water to cover overnight. Combine with cold water and remaining ingredients. Cover and simmer until meat falls from bones, about 2 hours. Add boiling water as needed to keep liquid at 2 quarts.

Yield: 6 to 8 portions.

DRIED LIMA BEAN SOUP · MRS. ROBERT EUGENE OTTO, KEY WEST, FLA.

2 cups dried lima beans
4 tablespoons oil
2 tablespoons butter or
    margarine
Chunks of leftover baked
    ham, plus ham bone
4 onions, peeled and
    quartered
1 cup canned tomatoes
1 clove garlic
1 cup finely chopped celery
2 quarts boiling water
1 teaspoon salt
1 tablespoon Worcestershire
    sauce
Dash of freshly ground black
    pepper

Soak beans overnight and leave in water in which they were soaking. Rub off skins (with hands under water). Put in 4-quart kettle with oil, butter, chunks of ham, ham bone, onions, tomatoes, garlic and celery. Pour in boiling water and add salt, Worcestershire sauce, and black pepper. Bring to a boil and cook, covered, over low heat for 3 to 4 hours. Stir from time to time to prevent scorching and add additional boiling water if needed to prevent sticking. Don't strain, serve as is, and garnish with croutons, if desired.

Yield: 8 to 10 portions.

U.S. SENATE BEAN SOUP · WASHINGTON, D.C.

1 pound marrow beans
3 quarts cold water
3 medium potatoes, cooked
    and mashed
6 celery stalks, finely cut
¼ cup chopped parsley
2 medium onion, minced
2 cloves garlic, minced
2 pounds ham hock
Salt and pepper

Soak beans in water overnight; drain. Cook beans in fresh water to cover for about 1 hour, or until beans are tender; drain. Add the 3 quarts water and remaining ingredients. Season to taste, depending on saltiness of ham hock. Cook slowly for 2 hours, stirring occasionally to prevent scorching. Remove hock. Remove meat from bones and cut in small pieces. Add meat to soup. Serve in individual earthenware pots with garlic bread. Yield: about 2 quarts.

RED BEAN SOUP · MRS. R. E. PIGFORD, TULSA, OKLA.

1¼ cups dry red kidney beans
1 quart water
3 cups canned tomatoes
½ cup diced carrots
6 tablespoons finely chopped
    onion
6 tablespoons finely chopped
    celery leaves
Salt and pepper
Minced parsley
4 slices cooked bacon,
    crumbled

Cook beans in water until tender. Drain, reserve liquid. Combine beans, tomatoes, carrots, onion, celery leaves, and 3 cups of the reserved liquid. Simmer gently 1 hour. Put mixture through a fine sieve. Add salt, pepper to taste. Reheat to boiling point. Sprinkle with parsley and bacon. Yield: 4 to 5 portions.

NOTE: If desired, 2 cans (10½ ounces) condensed cream of tomato soup may be used in place of the canned tomatoes. The soup will have a thicker consistency and will serve 5 to 6.

POTATO SOUP WITH CHEESE · MRS. FRANK SCHIESSER, NEW GLARUS, WISC.

4 medium potatoes
1 large onion
1 quart boiling water
2 tablespoons butter or
    margarine
1 tablespoon flour
½ cup cold water
Salt and pepper to taste
Dash of nutmeg
2 tablespoons heavy cream
4 teaspoons grated hard
    Swiss cheese
Minced parsley

Peel and dice potatoes and onion. Simmer in boiling water until tender. Melt butter in skillet, add flour and heat slowly until cream-colored. Stir in cold water and mix well; stir into potato onion mixture. Season to taste with salt and pepper. Add a dash of nutmeg and cream. Heat. Pour over a teaspoon of grated cheese placed in each soup dish. Garnish with parsley.
    Yield: 4 portions.

HOLLAND PEA SOUP · MRS. CORNELIUS STOB, LISLE, ILL.

1 cup dried green split peas
1½ quarts cold water
½ pound lean pork shoulder,
    cut in ½-inch cubes
1½ teaspoons salt
12 peppercorns
½ teaspoon capers (optional)
½ cup minced onion
1½ cups finely chopped celery

Soak peas in water to cover overnight. Combine with cold water, meat, salt, peppercorns, and capers. Cover and simmer for 3 hours. Add boiling water to keep liquid at 1½ quarts. Add onion and celery; cook 30 minutes. Yield: 6 portions.

FRENCH-CANADIAN HABITANT SOUP · NORTHERN NEW ENGLAND

½ pound salt pork
1 pound dried split peas
3 onions, sliced
1 carrot, diced
⅛ teaspoon pepper
Salt to taste

Place salt pork in pot; cover with water. Simmer 1 hour. At the finish there should be three quarts of liquid and into this go the peas, their latent goodness loosened by overnight soaking. Add onions, carrot and pepper. Cover and simmer 4 hours; add salt to taste. A soup not soupy, but thick, a meal in a dish, its loving companion hot Johnny cake served brown and crisp.

LEEK AND POTATO SOUP · MRS. LEOPOLD ARNAUD, NEW YORK CITY

12 leeks
6 medium potatoes
6 cups water
4 beef bouillon cubes
Salt and pepper

Remove roots, outer leaves and green tips, then cut leeks in half lengthwise and slice finely crosswise; wash thoroughly. Pare potatoes and cut into pieces. Cook leeks and potatoes separately (the leeks in an extra-large pot) and add to each pot 3 cups water and salt. Cook about 20 minutes or until tender. Place a strainer over the leek pot, pour in contents of potato pot and mash potatoes through strainer. Add bouillon cubes, pepper and more salt if necessary. Add more water if too thick. Simmer 5 minutes. Add a little butter if desired. Yield: 6 portions.

LEEK AND PIG TAIL SOUP · MRS. LEOPOLD ARNAUD, NEW YORK CITY

6 pig tails
2 quarts water
12 leeks
6 small potatoes
4 tablespoons olive oil
Salt and pepper

Wash pig tails; slice off excess fat from large end; discard tip if discolored. With a cleaver and mallet, chop the tails into one-inch pieces. Boil in 1½ quarts of the water, salted, for about 1½ hours.

Remove roots, outer leaves and green tips from leeks. Cut in half lengthwise, then slice finely crosswise; wash thoroughly. Pare potatoes and cut into small dice. Place vegetables in pot with oil and just enough water to cover. Sprinkle with salt and pepper; cover. Cook, stirring occasionally, until vegetables are nearly done. Add remaining ½ quart water and boil until vegetables are thoroughly cooked. If necessary, skim off excess fat from the broth in which tails cooked. Add broth and tails to vegetables; add water if necessary. Simmer for 5 minutes. This is a main dish rather than a first-course soup; it should be eaten with French bread. Yield: 6 portions.

TOMATO SOUP · MRS. EZRA TAFT BENSON, SALT LAKE CITY, UTAH

1 can (1 pound, 13 ounces)
    tomatoes
2 whole cloves
1 large slice onion
½ teaspoon salt
¼ teaspoon sugar
1½ tablespoons butter or
    margarine
1½ tablespoons flour
1 teaspoon baking soda
3 cups milk, warmed

Press tomatoes through sieve. Add cloves, onion slice, salt, and sugar; bring to a boil. Simmer for 5 minutes. Remove onion and cloves. Cream butter and flour, and mix a little of the tomato mixture into it; then blend this into the large tomato mixture; mix until smooth. Bring to a boil again and add soda. Add tomato mixture to warm milk; reheat. Dot each portion with whipped cream, if desired. Yield: 6 to 8 portions.

TOMATO BOUILLON · MISS SUE TOKES, WINCHESTER, VA.

1 quart cut-up fresh tomatoes
    (about 6 large)
1 cup chicken stock
1 teaspoon salt
⅛ teaspoon black pepper
Dash of red pepper

Cook tomatoes in chicken stock until soft. Press through sieve. Heat liquid and seasonings. Serve hot. Yield: 6 portions.

GUMBO D'ZERB · MRS. RAY SAMUELS, NEW ORLEANS, LA.

½ pound mustard greens
1 bunch watercress
½ small head green cabbage
½ head lettuce
½ pound turnip greens
1 bunch radish tops
1 pound beet tops
½ bunch roquette or parsley
1 pound spinach
2 quarts water
2 onions
1 pound pickled pork or
    ham pieces, diced
2 slices bacon, diced
2 tablespoons shortening
2 tablespoons flour
Salt and pepper to taste
1 bay leaf

Pinch marjoram
Pinch thyme
1 whole clove
9 whole allspice
Dash of Tabasco
¾ cup cooked rice

Wash greens and boil together in water. Tear coarse stems off greens. Reserve water in which greens cooked. Finely chop or grind greens with onions. Brown the meats in shortening. Remove and add chopped greens and cook 10 minutes, stirring frequently. Blend in flour. Return meat to pot and add reserved cooking water (about 2 quarts). Season with salt and pepper to taste, add herbs, spices, and Tabasco. Cook for 1 hour. Serve with 2 tablespoons cooked rice in each portion.

Yield: 6 portions.

CHICKEN GUMBO · MRS. DELAWARE VOLLRATH, FRANKLIN, LA.

*2 3½- to 4-pound fryers, cut
   up*
Seasoned flour
Chicken or other fat
Hot water
*1 green pepper, finely
   chopped*
*4 stalks celery, finely
   chopped*
2 large onions, minced
*1 pound okra, finely chopped
   (optional)*
Salt and pepper
1 tablespoon filé powder
1½ to 2 cups cooked rice

Dredge chicken lightly in flour. Melt fat in heavy frying pan (about ¼-inch fat). Lightly brown chicken. Add enough hot water to cover. Add vegetables and season to taste. Cover pan tightly and cook slowly until meat is tender, about 30 to 45 minutes, adding more water if necessary. (The meat should taste like stewed chicken but have enough liquid to serve as a soup sauce.) Place filé powder in bowls, about ½ teaspoonful to each, add chicken. Ladle in soup and rice. A favorite way in the deep South is to serve the gumbo from a soup tureen, the rice in a covered dish, the filé powder in a shaker. Warning: filé powder makes soup stringy if overheated. Add it to the bowl or soup tureen, but never to the boiling soup. Yield: 8 portions.

NOTE: This is a basic dish for Louisiana cooks. More often than not they add shellfish before the dish is done—15 minutes for crab, shrimp or 10 minutes for oysters.

This is a meal-in-a-dish. Serve with green salad. For dessert fruit—pears, apples and grapes with Camembert or Gruyère, the right ending.

Gumbo blends to perfection when it is stored overnight in the refrigerator. Like many stews it is better the second day. Cook the rice just before serving.

MRS. HEBERT'S CREOLE GUMBO · MRS. ALLAIN HEBERT, LOUISIANA

1 tablespoon fat
1½ tablespoons flour
2 teaspoons salt
1 4½- to 5-pound fowl, cut up
1 large onion, diced
2 quarts water
3 dozen oysters
7 tablespoons minced parsley
Red pepper
1½ tablespoons filé powder
¾ cup cooked rice

Melt fat in heavy pot. When hot, stir in flour and let brown. Salt the chicken. Brown pieces in the roux. Add onion and sauté until transparent. Add water, cover pot. Cook over low heat 2 to 3 hours, or until chicken is tender. Add oysters, parsley and pepper to taste. Cook until oysters curl at edges. Remove from heat. Add the filé powder; do not reheat. Serve with 2 tablespoons cooked rice in each portion. Yield: 6 servings.

This to remember—filé powder is so delicate and gummy it should never be cooked or even warmed over. It must always be added to the dish just before serving, and it must be added gradually while the mixture is still boiling. Filé might be called an indigenous American curry powder, along with chili, its opposite number on the Tex-Mex border.

CRAB OR SHRIMP GUMBO WITH OKRA · NEW ORLEANS, LA.

12 crabs, or 3 pounds shrimp
25 okra pods
1 large onion, minced
¼ pod hot red pepper,
    or ½ pod green pepper
2 tablespoons butter or
    margarine
1½ cups canned tomatoes,
    chopped
2 quarts water
Salt
1 cup cooked rice

Scald crabs, remove shells and clean. If shrimp are used, cook them in the 2 quarts water; peel shrimp; reserve water. Cut okra pods crosswise and chop finely, seeds and all. Combine with onion and pepper. Sauté in butter for a few minutes only, being careful not to let the okra scorch. Stir in tomatoes and cook a few more minutes. Gradually add water and the crabs or shrimp. Simmer slowly for 2 hours. Season with salt. Serve with 2 tablespoons cooked rice in each portion. Yield: 8 generous servings.

NOTE: There is no objection, of course, to making a crab-shrimp gumbo as above, by using 6 crabs with 1½ pounds shrimp. The contrasting seafoods yield an even more sprightly gumbo. But you must not mix okra and filé in the same dish.

Since okra is easier to come by than filé in any place except New Orleans, this simple sort of seafood gumbo is recommended for beginners. The slippery, mucilagenous quality of okra simulates the gumminess of filé, but the flavor is more mild and bland.

NEW ENGLAND CLAM CHOWDER · SANDWICH, MASS.

2 dozen large clams
¼ pound salt pork
2 medium sized onions, thinly
    sliced
6 medium sized potatoes,
    diced
2½ cups boiling water
⅛ teaspoon pepper
1 quart scalded milk
Hard round water crackers
¼ cup cold milk

Steam clams from shells and look over well to see that no pieces of shell are left on them. Put into a saucepan with their own liquor and bring to a boil. Strain out clams, chop them and save the liquor. Cut salt pork into small cubes and fry out in a heavy frying pan; add onions and sauté until fat is well seasoned. Strain fat into kettle; add potatoes, clams, boiling water and pepper, cook 10 to 15 minutes more. Add hot clam liquor. Pour over split crackers which have been soaked in cold milk to soften them slightly.

Yield: 8 to 10 portions.

LONG ISLAND CLAM CHOWDER · JEANETTE RATTRAY, EAST HAMPTON, N.Y.

3 slices salt pork
3 large onions
12 potatoes, quartered
3 tablespoons finely chopped
    parsley
½ cup diced celery
½ cup diced green pepper
Water
1 can (1 pound, 4 ounces)
    tomatoes
Salt and pepper to taste
2 quarts hard-shelled clams,
    shucked

Fry out salt pork in large kettle. Remove slices, dice and return to pot. Add onions and fry until golden. Add potatoes, parsley, celery and green pepper with water to cover. Simmer until potatoes are tender. Add tomatoes, cook 10 minutes, season. There should be 2 quarts of liquid remaining. Run clams through grinder, strain off juice, add to mixture and bring to a boil. Add clams and simmer 30 minutes. This chowder tastes best if left standing overnight to be reheated the next day. Yield: 6 whopping bowls.

HOWARD FRYE'S CLAM CHOWDER · DORCHESTER, MASS.

½ peck soft-shell clams
1 cup water
¼ pound salt pork, diced
3 large onions, diced
1 quart clam juice
4 large potatoes, diced
2 quarts milk
¼ cup flour

Scrub soft clams and place with water in cooking pot over low heat; cover and steam 20 minutes. Try out salt pork in chowder kettle, add onions and cook until golden. Add clam juice. Toss in potatoes and when almost tender add clams. Prepare this part of the chowder the day before the dinner. The following day add 1¾ quarts milk; heat; do not boil. Make paste of one cup milk and the flour. Add to chowder and cook until thickened. It should be on the thin side but thicker than milk.
Yield: 10 portions.

BRUNSWICK CLAM CHOWDER · MRS. PAUL MORTON, BRUNSWICK, GA.

2 slices salt pork or bacon,
    diced
1 onion, sliced
Clam liquid
1 cup water
3 large potatoes, peeled and
    diced
1½ dozen clams, drained
1 teaspoon salt
Pepper to taste
1 quart milk
2 tablespoons flour

2 tablespoons butter or margarine
Crackers
1 teaspoon chopped parsley

Fry salt pork and onion slices until golden. Add clam liquid, water and potatoes. Cover and cook until potatoes are just tender. Finely chop clams and add with salt, pepper and milk. Blend together butter and flour; blend in a little of the soup liquid, then add to chowder. Cook until slightly thickened. Place crackers in tureen. Pour over chowder; sprinkle with chopped parsley. Yield: 6 to 8 portions.

CONCH CHOWDER · THELMA STRABLE'S COOK, BESSIE, KEY WEST, FLA.

6 conches in shell
Juice of 2 small or 1 large
    lime
1 green pepper, diced
1 onion, diced
2 cloves garlic, minced
4 tablespoons oil
1 can (6 ounces) tomato paste
1½ quarts water
Salt
Pepper
4 potatoes, pared and diced

Cook conches in boiling water until shells open, about 10 minutes. Remove meat from shell and beat with the edge of a plate until meat falls apart into pieces. Squeeze lime juice over meat and allow to stand for 2 hours. Sauté green pepper, onion and garlic in oil until golden brown. Add tomato paste and simmer 10 minutes. Add water and salt and pepper to taste. Bring to a boil. Add potatoes and simmer until about half done. Add conch meat and cook until potatoes are tender. Season further to taste. Yield: 6 main dish portions.

NOTE: about ¾ pound frozen ready-cooked conch meat may be used instead of conch in shells.

CORN CHOWDER · MARION FITCH AND JANE POOR, LINCOLN, MASS.

⅛ pound salt pork in ¼-inch
    dice
1 pound potatoes
1 medium onion
2 cups water
1 No. 2 can cream style corn
2½ teaspoons salt
⅛ teaspoon white pepper
1 pint light cream

Try out salt pork in heavy frying pan until brown and crisp. Grind potatoes and onion together. Add water, corn, pork fat and seasonings. Pour into a 2-quart casserole; cover tightly. Bake at 350°F. for one hour, just to thicken, and until the potatoes and onions are tender. Heat cream. Add to chowder mixture. Serve in small casseroles with toast sprinkled with grated cheddar. Run under broiler until cheese melts. Yield: 2 quarts.

SPITE HOUSE FISH CHOWDER · SAMUEL AND NARCISSA CHAMBERLAIN, MARBLEHEAD, MASS.

¾ pound finely diced salt pork
6 large onions, sliced
6 small potatoes, pared and
    diced
2 pounds haddock fillets
2 tablespoons flour
1 quart milk
Worcestershire sauce
Salt and pepper

Fry salt pork in a skillet until pieces are golden brown; drain thoroughly on absorbent paper. Brown onions in the fat remaining in skillet. Meanwhile, in a soup kettle, boil potatoes in just enough water to cover, for 10 minutes. Cut haddock into 1-inch pieces and add to kettle. Remove browned onions from fat and spread over fish. Discard all but 1 tablespoon of fat remaining in skillet. Blend in flour and slowly stir in milk. Season to taste with Worcestershire, salt and pepper. Pour seasoned milk into kettle. Cover and simmer over the lowest possible heat for 3 hours, without stirring. Twenty minutes before serving, heat the browned salt pork in a slow oven until crisp. Stir the chowder, taste for additional seasoning, and serve in soup bowls with chowder crackers and a sprinkling of the crisp pork.

Yield: 6 to 8 portions.

THOMAS TEW'S BLACKFISH CHOWDER · MRS. JOHN HOWARD BENSON, NEWPORT, R.I.

3 4-pound blackfish
3 quarts water
¼ pound salt pork, sliced
1 quart onions, coarsely ground
1 quart peeled diced potatoes (8 to 10)
1 quart canned tomatoes
1 lemon
1¼ teaspoons poultry seasoning
½ teaspoon powdered cloves
1 teaspoon sugar
Pinch of cayenne pepper
½ teaspoon black pepper
Salt to taste
1 cup red wine
1 tablespoon butter or margarine

Clean and scale fish leaving head on, as head contains good gelatin. Wrap fish in cheesecloth, put in a deep pot and cover with water; simmer over low heat until fish is tender enough to flake from the bones, allowing 12 minutes to the pound. Remove fish, save the stock—there should be 3 quarts. Flake fish from bones. In heavy iron skillet fry salt pork until golden, add pork to fish stock, retaining fat. Add onion to fat and fry until limp and pale gold and add to stock. Take a half cup of stock and rinse out frying pan to get every last bit of the flavor, then pour into chowder. Add potatoes and tomatoes. Simmer until potatoes are tender.

Wash a lemon and thinly slice, discarding tough ends. Quarter the slices and place in saucepan; cover with water; simmer slowly. After 10 minutes (do not let boil or the flavor will be bitter), add seasonings, stir a few times and add to chowder. Next add the flaked fish. If you think more lemon is needed, add juice to taste; cook 10 minutes. Just before serving, add wine and butter. Heat until very hot but do not boil. Serve in deep bowls with pilot crackers. Yield: 10 portions.

GROUPER CHOWDER · TRADE WINDS RESTAURANT, KEY WEST, FLA.

2 pounds grouper, or red snapper, or yellowtail or sea bass, filleted
1½ cups tomato juice
1¼ quarts water
¼ cup chopped green pepper
1 Bermuda onion, chopped
¼ cup chopped celery
½ clove garlic, minced
2 tomatoes, chopped
Salt, pepper and thyme
¼ cup sauterne wine

Cut fish into ½-inch pieces. Combine tomato juice, water, green pepper, onion, celery, garlic and tomatoes. Cook about 10 minutes or until vegetables are two-thirds done. Add the cut-up fish. Continue cooking 5 minutes, or until fish is tender. Beat the mixture with a wire whisk until fish is flaked and the vegetables softened. Add seasonings and sauterne. Serve hot. Yield: 6 portions.

Second-day Chowder: Reheat. Add 1 cup heavy cream and 1 cup tomato juice. Mix 2 tablespoons flour and some of the chowder to make a smooth paste. Add to soup and cook, stirring for 5 minutes.

BROWN OYSTER CHOWDER · WARREN POSEY, NEW ORLEANS, LA.

1 cup butter or margarine
1 large onion, minced
1 small carrot, minced
3 stalks celery, minced
2 cloves of garlic, minced
1 small green pepper, minced
2 bay leaves
Sprig fresh thyme
2 quarts oyster liquor (about)
¼ cup flour
1 scallion including top,
   minced
½ cup minced parsley
5 dozen oysters, drained
Water
Salt
Pepper
Tabasco

2 tablespoons grated lemon rind
1 hard-cooked egg, minced

Melt ½ cup of the butter in frying pan. Add vegetables and herbs; sauté until deep brown. Place in soup pot with oyster liquor. Bring to boil and cook 5 minutes. Drain, reserve stock; measure. Put cooked vegetables through sieve or grinder, using finest blade. Melt remaining ½ cup butter; blend in flour, stirring constantly. Cook until brown. Faster, faster with the stirring; it burns easily in the last minute or two. Gradually add reserved stock and puréed vegetables. Bring to a boil. Add scallion, parsley and oysters. Add water to make 4 quarts. As oysters' edges curl, season to taste with salt, pepper and Tabasco. Serve immediately, topped with grated lemon rind and minced hard-cooked egg.

Yield: 8 to 12 portions.

SUMMER COLD SOUP · MRS. R. E. PIGFORD, TULSA, OKLA.

3 cans (16 ounces each)
   tomatoes or 5 cups
   tomato juice
½ cup finely chopped celery
3 scallions, minced
1 tablespoon soy sauce
2 teaspoons Worcestershire
   sauce
Few drops Tabasco

Salt to taste
Thin cucumber slices

If canned tomatoes are used, put through sieve. Combine tomato liquid or tomato juice with celery, scallions, and seasonings. Chill thoroughly. Top each serving with slices of cucumber. Serve with hot toast points.

Yield: 4 to 5 portions.

ICED BROCCOLI SOUP · MRS. HAROLD HOLCOMB, PHOENIX, ARIZ.

1 cup finely sliced onion
½ cup diced celery
¼ cup diced carrots
2 cups water, about
1 package chopped, frozen
    broccoli
3 cups chicken stock or
    bouillon
1 teaspoon salt
¼ teaspoon cayenne pepper
2 tablespoons rice flour (or
    cornstarch)
1 cup light cream
1 tablespoon chopped chives
1 teaspoon chopped rosemary

Simmer onion, celery and carrot in water to cover until soft, about 15 minutes. Cook broccoli 5 minutes and drain; add to onion mixture. Add stock, salt and cayenne. Simmer until broccoli is tender, about 5 minutes. Add rice flour mixed with a little water. Bring to a boil, stirring constantly. Put through fine strainer or food mill, or mix in blender. Chill. Add cream with chives and rosemary.

Yield: 6 portions.

LOUIS DIAT'S VICHYSSOISE · NEW YORK CITY

4 leeks
½ cup chopped onion
1 tablespoon butter or
    margarine
1 quart boiling water
5 medium potatoes, peeled
    and chopped
1 tablespoon salt
2 cups milk
2 cups light cream
1 cup heavy cream
Chopped chives

Clean and chop the white part of the leeks, or enough to make 1½ cups and combine with onion. Melt butter in saucepan and add leek and onion mixture. Cook gently until soft but not brown. Add boiling water, potatoes, and salt. Cook until potatoes are well done, about 30 minutes. Strain through a fine sieve or food mill. Return the purée to the pan and add milk and light cream. Bring back to a boil and then strain through a very fine sieve. Cool, stirring occasionally. When cold, strain again and add heavy cream; mix well. Chill before serving. For a bright garnish and more flavor sprinkle with chopped chives.

Yield: 9 to 10 cups.

NOTE: Serve in a large bowl set in a bed of ice, or "simply in a cup set in a wide soup plate filled with ice cubes," to use Mr. Diat's suggestion for home service.

COLD CHERRY SOUP · MRS. JOHN VAN HEES, VERA COMMUNITY, WASH.

1 quart pitted fresh pie cherries
1½ quarts cold water
⅓ cup cornstarch
Dash of almond extract
Sugar to taste
Macaroons

Combine cherries and cold water. Simmer for a few minutes, or until cherries are cooked. Drain cherries; return juice to saucepan. Make a paste of cornstarch and water; stir into hot juice and cook, stirring constantly, until mixture is smooth. Add almond extract. Add cherries and sugar. Chill. Serve in soup plates with tiny macaroons sprinkled over each portion. Yield: 6 portions.

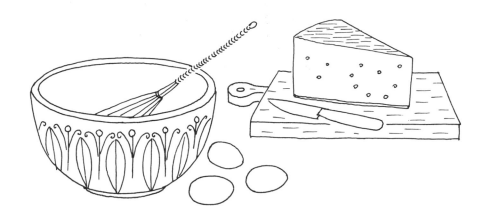

Eggs and Cheese

OMELETTE ESPAGNOLE · ANTOINE'S, NEW ORLEANS, LA.

1 can (1 pound, 4 ounces)
*   tomatoes*
3 tablespoons butter or
*   margarine*
1 teaspoon salt
Few grains pepper
Few grains cayenne
1 sprig thyme
1 tablespoon minced parsley
1 bay leaf
2 cloves garlic, minced
1 tablespoon flour
6 chopped shallots, or ½ cup
*   minced onion*
5 tablespoons chopped green
*   pepper*
½ cup white wine
½ cup cooked peas

½ cup canned button mushrooms
4 eggs
1 tablespoon olive oil

Combine tomatoes and 1 tablespoon butter; simmer 10 minutes, stirring occasionally. Add salt, pepper, and cayenne; cook 10 minutes, or until sauce is thick. Melt 1 tablespoon butter, blend in flour; cook until brown. Add shallots, green pepper; brown slightly. Add wine, stirring constantly until slightly thickened. Add mushrooms and peas. Beat eggs until well blended; add tomato mixture. Heat remaining butter and olive oil in skillet. Pour in egg mixture. Shake skillet until eggs begin to set, lifting edges of omelet to allow uncooked mixture to flow under omelet. When cooked, fold over. If desired, garnish with chopped parsley. Yield: 4 portions.

CHERRY OMELET · MRS. JOHN VAN HEES, VERA COMMUNITY, WASH.

6 whole eggs
6 eggs, separated
12 tablespoons flour
12 tablespoons milk
Salt and pepper to taste
3 cups pitted fresh pie
*　cherries, sugared to taste*

Combine the 6 whole eggs and the 6 egg yolks; beat until blended. Add flour, milk, salt, and pepper; mix until smooth. Beat the 6 egg whites until stiff but not dry. Heat an 8-inch iron skillet; butter lightly. For each omelet, pour in $\frac{1}{12}$ of the batter (about $\frac{1}{4}$ cup), tilting the pan to cover bottom. (Batter should be thin. If it thickens, thin with milk.) Let brown over medium heat about a minute. Spread $\frac{1}{12}$ of egg whites (about $\frac{1}{2}$ cup) on half of pancake. On other half sprinkle $\frac{1}{4}$ cup of cherries. Fold egg-white area over cherries and bake over medium heat $\frac{1}{2}$ minute; turn and bake $\frac{1}{2}$ minute longer.
Yield: 12 portions.

OEUFS SARDOU · ANTOINE'S, NEW ORLEANS, LA.

8 artichokes
16 anchovy fillets
8 poached eggs
1 cup Antoine's Hollandaise
*　Sauce*
½ cup chopped cooked ham
1 tablespoon glacé de viande
*　or meat glaze*
4 slices truffle

Cook artichokes in boiling salted water until tender. Remove petals and choke; reserve bottoms. Place bottoms on baking pan. Place 2 anchovy fillets on each. Run under low broiler heat to keep warm. Have poached eggs ready and warm on the side. Have Hollandaise at hand, this lukewarm. Now assemble the dish: on each artichoke, over the anchovy fillets, place poached egg. Cover with Hollandaise Sauce. Sprinkle chopped ham over, and a few drops of the glacé de viande over ham and sauce. Place one slice of truffle on the very top. Serve immediately.
Yield: 4 portions.

HOLLANDAISE SAUCE:
1 cup clarified butter
2 tablespoons tarragon
*　vinegar*
1 tablespoon water
1 tablespoon minced onion
3 peppercorns
4 egg yolks
Juice of ¼ lemon

To clarify butter: slowly melt butter. Let stand until clear part can be skimmed off easily and reserve. In saucepan place vinegar, water, onion, and peppercorns. Cook over very low heat to reduce liquid to 1 teaspoon. Remove peppercorns. Cool. Add egg yolks; beat slightly. Gradually add reserved melted butter, beating constantly. Add lemon juice. Serve immediately.
Yield: 4 portions.

CHILI RELLENOS · MRS. HUGH B. MC DUFFEE, LONG BEACH, CALIF.

2 cans little green chilis,
　already roasted and
　peeled (4 chilis in each
　can)
4 slices, halved, Jack or
　Cheddar cheese
5 eggs, separated
1 tablespoon salad oil

Split and remove seeds from chili peppers. Put a thin strip of cheese in cavity. Fold chili over cheese. Beat egg yolks until fluffy. Beat egg whites until stiff but not dry. Fold whites into yolks. Dip the chili bean into the egg mixture, coating as well as possible. Pick out with spoon along with a bit of the mixture. Heat salad oil in skillet. Sauté chilis gently until brown on underside. Turn quickly—it takes a dextrous twist of the wrist. Each chili looks like an individual omelet. Brown each side until done.

Surround the "omelets" with sauce, saving just enough to garnish the Spanish rice. This must be cooked quite dry so each kernel is separate as a solitaire.

Yield: 4 portions.

SAUCE:

1 can (1 pound, 4 ounces)
　tomatoes, chopped fine,
　plus juice
½ cup minced onion
Salt and pepper to taste

Combine tomatoes, juice, onion, and seasonings. Cook over low heat until onions are tender. Let gently simmer while the omelets are made.

BREAD CHEESE SOUFFLÉ · MRS. FRANK SCHIESSER, NEW GLARUS, WIS.

4 slices buttered bread, cubed
1 cup grated Swiss cheese
2 cups milk
2 eggs, slightly beaten
1 teaspoon salt

Turn bread into greased 1½ quart baking dish and cover with cheese. Combine milk, eggs and salt, mixing well. Pour over cheese and bread. Bake at 350°F. about 1 hour, or until top is browned.

Yield: 4 portions.

SWISS CHUCHEL · MRS. FRANK SCHIESSER, NEW GLARUS, WIS.

2 eggs
6 tablespoons sifted flour
1½ cups milk
½ teaspoon salt
2 tablespoons shortening

Combine eggs, flour, milk and salt; blend well. Heat shortening in skillet; add mixture and let brown slightly; stir until cooked, about 10 minutes. Cut with spoon or knife. Serve topped with fruit sauce or syrup.

Yield: 3 portions.

NOTE: This is used frequently as a hearty breakfast dish, also as a main dish at supper.

HUEVOS RANCHEROS · MRS. GEORGE D. SEARS, MEDINA, TEX.

¼ pound bacon
2 large cloves garlic, sliced
    paper thin
2 medium jalapeños or hot
    peppers, chopped
1 can (1 pound, 13 ounces)
    tomatoes
4 eggs
Salt and pepper
4 slices toast

Cut bacon into small pieces; fry slowly until almost crisp. Add garlic and brown. Add hot peppers and tomatoes. Simmer, stirring constantly, pressing and breaking tomatoes. Add salt to taste. When mixture is smooth and not too thick, drop in eggs one at a time; season with salt and pepper. Cover and poach for 3 to 5 minutes. Top toast with egg and sauce.

Yield: 4 portions.

INFALLIBLE SOUFFLÉ · TERRANCE HANOLD, MINNEAPOLIS, MINN.

½ cup butter or margarine
¾ cup sifted flour
1 teaspoon salt
¼ teaspoon dry mustard
⅛ teaspoon onion salt
1½ cups milk
1½ cups grated sharp cheese
¼ teaspoon Worcestershire
    sauce
6 egg yolks
6 egg whites stiffly beaten

Melt butter and sift in flour and seasonings. Add milk gradually and cook over low heat, stirring constantly, until mixture is thick and smooth. Add cheese, stirring until it is melted; remove from heat. Add Worcestershire sauce. Blend in egg yolks one at a time. Fold in egg whites. Pour into ungreased 2-quart casserole. Place in a pan of hot water. Bake at 350° F. for 45 to 55 minutes or until firm to touch. Serve with Shrimp-Tomato Sauce. Yield: 8 portions.

SHRIMP-TOMATO SAUCE:
2 pounds fresh or frozen
    shrimp
¼ cup butter or margarine
2 tablespoons finely chopped
    onion
1 can (1 pound, 4 ounces)
    whole tomatoes
1 bay leaf
½ teaspoon salt
½ teaspoon thyme
Dash of cayenne pepper
1 teaspoon sugar

1 can (10½ ounces) condensed mushroom soup
½ cup sherry wine
2 pimientos, cut into strips

Remove shell and clean shrimp. Melt butter; add onion and cook until yellow. Add tomatoes, seasonings, sugar, and soup diluted with sherry. Simmer 1 hour or until sauce has lost ¼ of its original volume, stirring occasionally. Add pimientos and shrimp. Boil briskly for 5 minutes.

Yield: 8 portions.

CHEESE MUFF · MRS. MILDRED M. RUTHERFORD, SOUTH WOODSTOCK, VT.

8 slices buttered white bread
¼ pound American cheese
Salt
Pepper
4 eggs, beaten
1 quart milk

Place four slices of bread on bottom of casserole, cutting to fit neatly. Cover bread with thin slices of cheese, sprinkle with salt and pepper. Cover with remaining buttered bread, cutting as before to fit dish. Add a second layer of sliced cheese, sprinkle with salt and pepper. Stir eggs into milk and pour over bread and cheese. Bake at 350°F. for 40 minutes or until the top browns and the dish is bubbly hot. Yield: 6 portions. Serve with a green salad for a light luncheon.

FATHER'S WELSH RABBIT · HARRY L. FINCH, SALT LAKE CITY, UTAH

½ pound sharp Cheddar
    cheese, grated
1 cup stale beer
1 egg, beaten
¼ teaspoon dry mustard
Cayenne
Salt to taste
8 slices buttered toast

Melt cheese in top of double boiler over hot water. Add beer, stirring in slowly. Mix in egg, mustard, cayenne and salt. Stir until thickened. Pour over hot buttered toast. Place under broiler until toast topping turns golden brown. Yield: 4 portions.

NOTE: This is thinner than the usual rabbit—more like a fondue.

OLIVE RABBIT · MRS. STAFFORD WENTWORTH, PALERMO, CALIF.

1 tablespoon butter or
    margarine
1 tablespoon flour
½ cup milk
2 cups diced Cheddar cheese
½ teaspoon salt
¼ teaspoon dry mustard

¼ teaspoon Worcestershire sauce
Dash of pepper
½ cup pitted olives

Melt butter over hot water and blend in flour. Add milk and cheese; stir until cheese melts. Add seasonings and olives. Serve over toast. Yield: 4 portions.

CHEESE FONDUE · MRS. GUY ROCKWELL, EAST CLEVELAND, OHIO

¼ pound milk Cheddar
    cheese, diced
1 cup milk, scalded
1 cup soft bread crumbs
1 teaspoon butter or
    margarine
½ teaspoon salt
3 eggs, separated

Melt cheese in milk. Add crumbs, butter, salt, and lightly beaten egg yolks. Fold in egg whites, stiffly beaten. Pour into deep, buttered casserole. Place in pan of hot water. Bake at 350°F. for 50 minutes or until knife, when inserted, comes out clean. Yield: 4 portions.

Cereals, Pasta and Rice

GNOCCHI · TOSCANINI'S COOK, ANNA, NEW YORK CITY

3 cups mashed potatoes
1 cup all-purpose flour
2 egg yolks
¼ cup grated Parmesan
*   cheese*

Turn hot mashed potatoes onto pastry board. Work in flour, egg yolks, and cheese with hands. Roll into ropes, each about as thick as the thumb. Cut into one-inch lengths and press with the floured tines of fork. Drop dumplings into boiling salted water. Boil until dumplings float to top, then remove with slotted spoon. Serve with melted butter and dust with grated Parmesan cheese. Yield: 4 portions. Or serve this tomato sauce as the accompaniment.

TOMATO SAUCE:
½ cup butter or margarine
1 small onion, chopped
¼ cup chopped celery
2 tablespoons chopped
*   carrots*
1¼ cups canned tomatoes
1 8-ounce can tomato sauce
Salt and pepper to taste

Heat butter or margarine in pan, add onion, celery and carrots. Cook a few minutes but do not brown the vegetables. Add tomatoes and tomato sauce. Cover and cook slowly until thick, about 45 minutes. Strain; season to taste. Pass with gnocchi. Yield: 4 portions.

41

MACARONI AND CHEESE · MRS. CARL STEWART, DES MOINES, IOWA

1½ cups scalded milk
1 cup soft bread crumbs
1½ cups grated Cheddar
    cheese
1 cup cooked macaroni
3 eggs, separated
¼ diced pimiento
1 tablespoon chopped parsley
1 tablespoon grated onion
1 teaspoon salt
3 tablespoons melted butter
    or margarine

Pour milk over soft bread crumbs; add cheese. Cover and let stand until cheese melts. Add macaroni. Combine and add beaten egg yolks, pimiento, parsley, onion, salt, and melted butter. Beat egg whites until stiff but not dry and fold into mixture. Pour into greased casserole. Bake at 350°F. for about 35 minutes. Serve with mushroom sauce as a luncheon main dish.

Yield: 6 portions.

COPY-CAT NOODLES · MRS. STANLEY H. WATSON, CLEVELAND, OHIO

1 pound medium noodles
1 pound creamed cottage
    cheese
1 small onion, grated
2 teaspoons salt
¼ teaspoon freshly ground
    pepper
Dash cayenne pepper
1 pint commercial sour
    cream

Cook noodles until tender but still firm. Drain. Place in casserole. Mix in cheese and grated onion. Season with salt, pepper and cayenne pepper. Mix in sour cream. Bake at 350°F. for 30 to 45 minutes, or until top is nicely browned. Yield: 6 portions.

RITA'S SPAGHETTI · MRS. THOMAS HART BENTON, KANSAS CITY, MO.

2 tablespoons olive oil
1 onion, chopped
1 pound pork tenderloin or
    pork chops, finely cut
½ pound mushrooms, sliced
1 can (6 ounces) tomato
    paste
1 can water
1 bay leaf
Salt and pepper
1 pound spaghetti
1 cup grated Parmesan
    cheese

Heat oil in heavy-bottomed skillet. Add onions and brown. Add meat cut by hand (not ground), mushrooms, tomato paste, water, and seasonings. Cover pan and simmer 30 minutes or until pork is tender. Cook spaghetti in boiling salted water 8 to 10 minutes. Drain. Pour on sauce and stir to blend. Serve with cheese.

Yield: 4 portions.

MR. YATKIN'S SPAGHETTI SAUCE · ARTHUR A. YATKIN, HARTFORD, CONN.

1 cup olive oil
2 cloves garlic, chopped
1 large onion, chopped
3 cans (1 pound, 4 ounces
*   each) tomatoes*
2 cans (6 ounces each)
*   tomato paste*
1 teaspoon salt
¼ teaspoon pepper

Heat olive oil to smoking point; add chopped garlic and cook until almost black; then remove garlic. Add chopped onion to smoking olive oil and cook until almost black. In a separate pan, simmer tomatoes and tomato paste 1 hour. Add tomato mixture, salt and pepper to olive oil mixture. Simmer, covered, 4 to 5 hours (adding water if necessary as the sauce cooks down), or until round black spots appear on the surface of mixture. Pour over cooked, thin Italian spaghetti.

Yield: 3 cups sauce.

SPAGHETTI SAUCE · DR. WILLIAM M. MANN, WASHINGTON, D.C.

½ cup olive oil
2 large onions, sliced
2 cloves garlic, chopped
1 pound hamburger
2 cans (4 ounces each)
*   tomato paste*
1 teaspoon salt
1 teaspoon dry mustard
1 teaspoon oregano
1 can (4 ounces) mushrooms,
*   pieces and stems*
Parmesan cheese, grated

Good

Heat olive oil in heavy frying pan. Brown onion, garlic and hamburger. Add tomato paste, salt, mustard, oregano and mushrooms. Cover and simmer 3 to 4 hours. Add a little water from time to time to keep moist. Pour over spaghetti cooked *al dente* (meaning not too soft). Pass Parmesan cheese.

Yield: 6 portions.

PIZZA · CAROL JEAN BYMA, DENVER, COL.

DOUGH MIXTURE:
1 package active dry yeast
2 tablespoons warm, not hot,
*   water*
1 cup boiling water
1 tablespoon shortening
1 teaspoon salt
½ teaspoon sugar
3 cups sifted flour
Olive oil

Soften yeast in warm water. Add boiling water to shortening, salt, and sugar, stirring until blended. Cool to lukewarm and add yeast. Add about half the flour and beat until smooth. Add enough of the remaining flour to make a soft dough. Knead on a lightly floured surface until smooth. Pat or roll about half of the dough to a ¼-inch thickness. Shape to fit a 9-inch round layer pan, allowing dough to extend up sides of pan. Press dough into place so it will not shrink. Brush with olive oil. Let rise 15 minutes. Use extra dough for garlic bread or another pizza. (*continued*)

PIZZA FILLING:

6 ounces Provolone cheese,
    cut in ½-inch squares ¹⁄₁₆-
    inch thick
1½ cups drained canned
    tomatoes
⅓ cup finely chopped onion
Cayenne
Oregano
Basil
Black pepper

2 tablespoons favorite-spaghetti sauce or 2-table-
    spoons tomato paste
4 to 8 anchovy fillets, or Italian or pork sausage, or
    small cubes of chicken, veal or ham

Arrange cheese squares to completely cover dough. Break up tomatoes and place on top of cheese. Add onion. Sprinkle with seasonings to suit your taste. Pour on spaghetti sauce. Place anchovies or other choice on top. Bake at 425°F. for 25 minutes. Cut into pie-shaped wedges and serve hot.

Yield: 6 portions.

RAVIOLI · MRS. ANTHONY J. CELEBREZZE, CLEVELAND, OHIO

6 cups sifted flour
¾ teaspoon salt
4 eggs
1 cup warm water (about)
Grated Parmesan cheese
Tomato sauce

Sift flour and salt onto board. Make a deep impression in the mound, put in eggs and beat lightly with finger tips. Then mix eggs into flour with a folding-in-and-lifting motion of the hands until they are well absorbed. Add water gradually and start shaping into a large ball. Knead dough just a few minutes and add just a bit more water if it seems too dry. Cover with a warm bowl for 15 minutes. Knead again until dough gains more smoothness and air pockets disappear. Cover with warm bowl. Repeat kneading process two more times. Keep dough covered until it is used for ravioli squares. Roll all or half of dough on lightly floured surface until very thin. Drop teaspoonfuls of filling about 2 inches apart on half of dough. Cover with other half. With finger tips, gently press around each mound of filling to form little filled squares. Cut squares apart with pastry wheel. Cook by dropping squares into boiling salted water in a very large pot. Ravioli must have ample room so they can be stirred occasionally while boiling. Water will stop boiling for a while when squares are dropped in but stir regardless, so they will not settle in pan. After water resumes boiling, continue to stir occasionally and cook until desired tenderness is reached, 15 to 25 minutes. Drain and place one at a time on a serving platter; sprinkle each layer with cheese and cover with tomato sauce.

Yield: 4 dozen ravioli.

RAVIOLI FILLING:
1 pound Ricotta cheese
2 eggs, slightly beaten
½ cup grated Parmesan
cheese
1 tablespoon finely chopped
parsley root
Salt and pepper to taste

Break up and mash Ricotta with fork. Add remaining ingredients and mix until smooth.

HOMINY GRITS · DR. GEORGE SELLECK, SAN FRANCISCO, CALIF.

1 quart milk
1½ cups hominy grits
1 teaspoon salt
⅛ teaspoon pepper
2 egg yolks
3 tablespoons grated
Parmesan cheese
3 tablespoons butter or
margarine

Heat milk to boiling. Pour slowly over hominy grits, stirring well to make a thick batter. Add salt and pepper. Cook, covered, over low heat for 35 minutes. Remove from heat. Beat in egg yolks. Add 2 tablespoons of the cheese. Pour into a greased 10 x 0 x 2-inch baking pan. Chill. Unmold on baking sheet. Cut into 2½ x 1½-inch squares. Sprinkle with remaining cheese; dot with butter. Bake at 250°F. for 30 minutes or until cheese browns and butter melts. Yield: 16 pieces.

NANCY RUSSELL'S GRIT PUDDING · AVERY ISLAND, LOUISIANA

1 cup hominy grits
2 cups boiling salted water
2 tablespoons butter or
margarine
1 cup milk
1 egg
Few drops Tabasco
Salt

Stir grits into water. Cover and cook over low heat for 20 minutes, stirring frequently. Stir in butter and milk. Add egg and beat. Add Tabasco, and salt, if needed. Turn into a greased 1-quart casserole. Bake at 375°F. for 30 minutes or until top is nicely brown. Serve with vegetables and meat.
Yield: 4 to 6 portions.

CHICKEN PILAF · MRS. A. L. DE GUIRE, DALLAS, TEX.

3 cups chicken broth
Salt and pepper to taste
1 cup uncooked white or
brown rice
1 tablespoon lemon juice

Bring chicken broth to a boil; add salt and pepper. Stir in rice and continue stirring for a couple of minutes. Reduce heat, cover pan and cook on very low heat until rice is tender. Midway, add lemon juice. Don't stir. Slowly cook until all the broth is absorbed and each rice grain stands alone.
Yield: 6 portions.

PINK RICE · MRS. J. KELL BRANDON, SIMSBURY, CONN.

½ pound butter or margarine
3 cups raw rice
⅔ cup finely chopped onion
½ cup peeled tomatoes,
    chopped
2½ cups tomato juice
2 cups consommé Madrilène
1 teaspoon salt
¼ teaspoon pepper

Melt butter in heavy iron frying pan. Add rice and cook until butter bubbles briskly. Add onion, tomatoes, tomato juice and Madrilène. Stir once; add seasonings. Cover. Bake at 375°F. for 30 minutes. Separate rice with fork, cover and bake 20 minutes more or until the rice is tender but not mushy.

Yield: 8 to 10 portions.

RICE MEXICAN · TICO TACO CAFE, SCOTTSDALE, ARIZ.

2 cups uncooked rice
6 cups chicken or meat stock
Peanut oil
Secret Sauce for rice

This is the only Mexican restaurant we have visited ever to feature rice on its menu. Here's how it's done. Clean and wash rice and add to boiling chicken stock in a gallon-size pot. Reduce heat and cook 20 minutes or until broth is absorbed. Cool, but while still warm pour into a large jar and shake around. Let stand in refrigerator overnight. The following morning use peanut oil to cover bottom of skillet ⅟₁₆-inch deep. Heat to bubbling; add rice stirring constantly for 2 or 3 minutes. Lower heat; let cook 15 minutes. Yield: 6 cups rice.

Serve on a plate with beans, tomatoes and enchiladas. The filled plate should go into the oven at 500°F. for 3 to 4 minutes, then out. Garnish with more chili sauce or tomatoes, more Secret Sauce over the rice. Then a garnish of chopped lettuce, tomato and ripe olives.

SECRET SAUCE FOR RICE:
2 cups chopped green
    peppers
2 cups finely chopped fresh
    green tomatoes
2 cups finely chopped ripe
    tomatoes
½ cup chopped onion
1 tablespoon salt

Pinch oregano
Garlic juice to taste

Combine all ingredients and simmer 1 hour. Serve warm over hot cooked rice. This is good any time, Mexican supper or not. Yield: about 2½ cups sauce.

BAKED SOUTHERN GRITS · MRS. EWING ELMORE, BIRMINGHAM, ALA.

1½ teaspoons salt
3 cups water
1 cup grits
1 cup milk
4 eggs, slightly beaten
¼ pound butter or margarine
½ cup grated Cheddar cheese

Add salt to water; bring to a boil. Sprinkle in grits, just a few at a time. Cook slowly, covered, for 1 hour, or until grits are soft, stirring occasionally. If the grits cook stiff add a little boiling water, stirring in well. Remove from heat. When lukewarm, add milk, eggs and butter, blending thoroughly. Pour into greased casserole. Bake at 350°F. for about 45 minutes. Ten minutes before the dish is done, sprinkle over grated cheese and let melt and brown. Insert knife and if it comes out clean, the grits are ready.

Yield: 6 portions.

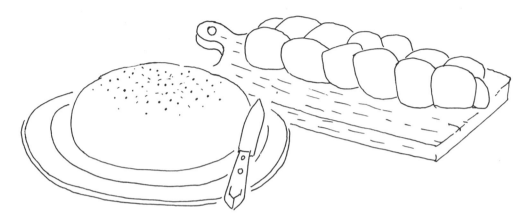

Breads

BINNIE DICK'S PANCAKES · LIBERAL, KANSAS

2 tablespoons bacon
   drippings
1 egg, beaten
1 cup milk
1 cup sifted flour
¾ teaspoon salt
2 tablespoons baking powder
2 tablespoons sugar

Mix bacon drippings, egg, and ½ cup of the milk. Add sifted dry ingredients and mix. Add remaining milk and blend; do not overbeat. Drop onto a hot griddle from the end of a spoon. Bake over medium-low heat. Turn pancakes only once, when the bubbles begin to break on the unbaked side and the edges are dry. Yield: 12 to 14 pancakes.

OLD-STYLE WHEAT CAKES · LIBERAL, KANSAS

1 cup milk
1 egg
1 teaspoon baking powder
¾ teaspoon salt
1¼ cups sifted flour

Combine milk and eggs. Sift dry ingredients together and add to egg mixture. Beat until smooth. Bake on ungreased hot griddle. Yield: about 10 cakes.

BUTTERMILK READY-MIX PANCAKES · LIBERAL, KANSAS

½ teaspoon baking soda
2¼ cups buttermilk
1 egg
2 tablespoons melted
    shortening
2 cups pancake mix

Dissolve soda in buttermilk. Add with unbeaten egg and shortening to pancake mix, stirring lightly. (For thinner pancakes add about ¼ cup more buttermilk.) Somewhat lumpy batter makes light, fluffy pancakes. Pour ¼ cup batter for each pancake onto a hot, lightly greased griddle. Bake to a golden brown, turning but once. Serve with butter and honey or syrup. Yield: 14 to 16 pancakes.

FLANNEL CAKES WITH CHICKEN HASH · HELEN RUCH, PITTSBURGH, PA.

2 cups sifted flour
¾ teaspoon baking soda
1 teaspoon salt
2½ cups buttermilk
2 tablespoons melted butter
    or margarine
2 eggs, separated
Chicken hash

Sift together flour, soda and salt into bowl. Beat in buttermilk and melted shortening. Beat in egg yolks. Fold in stiffly beaten whites. Bake on hot griddle. When brown, place a generous tablespoon of hash on cake, roll cake and fasten with toothpick. Place in rows on baking pan. Heat in a 350°F. oven or under low broiler. Yield: 12 cakes.

CHICKEN HASH:
3 tablespoons butter or
    margarine
2 tablespoons minced onion
3 tablespoons flour
1 cup chicken or turkey
    broth
⅓ cup minced celery
2 teaspoons minced parsley
⅓ cup light cream

2 cups cold chicken or turkey, cut in small pieces
Salt and pepper

Melt butter. Add onion and sauté until tender. Add flour and cook 4 minutes, stirring constantly. Add broth, celery and parsley and simmer for 5 minutes. Add cream and stir well. Add chicken. Heat to boiling point and season. Set aside to thicken while Flannel Cakes are baking.

OSA NICHOLS'S FLAPJACKS · LIBERAL, KANSAS

1¾ cups sifted flour
1 teaspoon baking powder
½ teaspoon salt
1 teaspoon baking soda
½ cup sour milk or buttermilk
1 cup milk
1 small egg, well beaten

Sift flour, baking powder, and salt together. Add soda to sour milk; add milk and egg and beat. Combine with dry ingredients. Bake on a hot bacon-greased griddle. Yield: 12 pancakes.

PALACSINTA (PANCAKES WITH COTTAGE CHEESE) · MRS. ALEX MIKO, ELYRIA, OHIO

2 cups sifted flour
2 teaspoons sugar
1 teaspoon salt
4 eggs, well beaten
2 cups milk
Confectioners' sugar
Sour cream
Preserves

Mix flour, sugar, and salt. Combine eggs and milk. Add gradually to flour mixture, beating to a thin smooth batter. Spoon 3 tablespoons of batter onto hot greased 6- to 7-inch skillet, tilting pan so batter is distributed to edges (cakes will be very thin). Brown lightly on both sides. Continue making cakes until batter is used up. Stack on warm plate. Spread with cottage-cheese filling. Roll up. Place in buttered baking dish. Sprinkle with confectioners' sugar. Heat thoroughly in a 300°F. oven. Serve topped with sour cream and preserves. Yield: about 24 pancakes.

CHEESE FILLING:
1 pound dry cottage cheese
1 egg, well beaten
¼ to ½ cup sugar
Few drops vanilla extract

Mix all ingredients thoroughly.

SWISS APPLE PANCAKES · MRS. FRANK SCHIESSER, NEW GLARUS, WIS.

1½ cups sifted flour
¼ teaspoon salt
1 cup milk
4 eggs, well beaten
2 tablespoons melted butter
    or margarine
¾ cup applesauce

Sift flour and salt into bowl. Combine milk, eggs, butter and applesauce, and add to dry ingredients. Drop onto hot greased griddle and brown on both sides as for pancakes. Serve with sugar or with sugar mixed with cinnamon (1 teaspoon cinnamon to 1 cup sugar).
Yield: 6 to 8 pancakes.

MR. OTTEN'S POTATO PANCAKES · GEORGE OTTEN, PORTLAND, ORE.

6 Oregon potatoes (1 quart
    grated)
3 eggs, beaten
1½ teaspoons salt (about)
3 tablespoons bacon fat
3 tablespoons butter or
    margarine

Peel potatoes—choose the long ones, handy to handle; grate on medium grater. Mix potatoes with eggs, add salt to taste. Heat bacon fat and butter in skillet. Turn in half of potato mixture, press thin, fry until brown on one side, turn with spatula and fry the down side until crisp and well browned. Add more fat if needed. Remove to platter, one big potato cake. Now fry the remaining half of the mixture. Dill pickles are a must as an accompaniment. Yield: 4 portions.

HAZEL WHITITH'S FLANNEL CAKES · AVERY ISLAND, LA.

1 egg, beaten
1½ cups milk
1½ cups sifted flour
½ teaspoon salt
2 tablespoons melted butter
*   or margarine*

Combine egg and milk. Add flour and salt; beat well. Blend in butter. Bake on ungreased griddle. Serve rolled with filling of grape jelly, brandy-spiked. Pass a brandied whipped-cream sauce to spoon over the cakes. Yield: 4 10-inch pancakes.

PHIL'S SOURDOUGH PANCAKES · PHIL KERR, KETCHIKAN, ALASKA

2 packages active dry yeast
1 quart warm, not hot, water
6 cups sifted flour
2 teaspoons salt
1 teaspoon baking soda
3 tablespoons molasses
½ cup hot water
5 eggs, beaten

Dissolve yeast in warm water. Stir in flour. Cover and let stand 24 hours at room temperature. Add salt, soda, molasses, and hot water. Add eggs; don't beat but mix well. Let stand ½ hour and the batter is ready.
Yield: about 40, 5 inch pancakes

PANCAKES WITH BLUEBERRIES · LUCY CORBETT, GROSSE ILE, MICH.

Sunday breakfast starred pancakes made paper-thin and the width of a dinner plate. The batter was the same as that used for the Crêpes Suzette of the French cuisine. Fresh blueberries were spooned across the middle of the buttered hot cake, then sour cream spooned over, next a sprinkle of sugar, the cake was rolled using fingers or fork. A bowl of currant jelly for those who might prefer a filling more sweet. Next came a platter of crisply fried bacon.

Here is the way Lucy made the pancakes: four whole eggs were broken into the mixing bowl and ¾ teaspoon salt added, a pinch of sugar, then as Sid said, "beat the 'be-jeepers' out of them with a rotary egg beater." Next she sifted in about ½ cut of all-purpose flour and continued beating until smooth. Slowly whole milk was added, just enough to thin the batter to heavy-cream consistency (about ¼ cup). Two tablespoons of melted butter were stirred in and the cakes were ready to bake.

The baking was done one cake at a time in an 8-inch heavy iron frying pan. In went one tablespoon butter, the heat high so the butter came to a quick sizzle and turned golden brown. At this moment Lucy poured in about three tablespoons of batter, she tilted the pan to and fro so it spread quickly over the pan bottom. After a moment she lifted the edge and peeked. We have been taught not to peek at a pancake's down side, but Lucy did. When golden brown she flips it over. The cakes were served directly from pan to plate, soft, never crisp.

APPLE MUFFINS · MRS. KENNETH BIXLER, CASHMERE, WASH.

1½ cups sifted flour
½ cup sugar
1 teaspoon salt
1¾ teaspoons baking powder
½ teaspoon nutmeg
1 egg, beaten
¼ cup milk
⅓ cup salad oil
½ cup grated apple, firmly
    packed
¼ cup butter or margarine,
    melted
½ cup sugar
1 tablespoon cinnamon

Sift first 5 ingredients. Combine egg, milk and oil, and add to flour mixture. Mix just until moistened. Add grated apple. Fill greased and floured muffin pans two-thirds full. Bake at 400°F. for 20 to 25 minutes. Dip muffin tops in melted butter, then roll in sugar-cinnamon mixture. Serve warm.

Yield: 9 medium muffins.

MINCEMEAT MUFFINS · MRS. ANNA BRYAN, CAMELBACK INN, PHOENIX, ARIZ.

½ cup shortening
⅓ cup sugar
1½ teaspoons salt
1 egg, beaten
1 cup milk
2 cups sifted flour
1 tablespoon baking powder
½ cup mincemeat

Cream together shortening, sugar and salt. Combine egg and milk; add to creamed mixture. Sift flour and baking powder. Add to creamed mixture; mix only until blended. Fold in mincemeat. Pour into greased muffin pans. Bake at 400°F. for 20 to 25 minutes.

Yield: 1 dozen medium muffins.

BREAKFAST CORN BREAD · NANCY FINCH, SALT LAKE CITY, UTAH

2 cups white or yellow corn
    meal
2 cups boiling water
2 teaspoons salt
2 tablespoons butter,
    margarine or bacon
    drippings
2 eggs
2¼ cups milk
2 teaspoons baking powder

Heat a 10-inch heavy iron skillet in a 425°F. oven. Combine corn meal, water, salt and butter; stir until thoroughly mixed. Beat eggs and combine with milk. Stir gradually into corn-meal mixture (it will be milk thin). Beat in baking powder. Pour at once into the heated skillet which has been greased. Bake at 425°F. for 20 minutes. Reduce heat to 350°F. and bake 40 minutes longer, or until firm. Cut into wedges and serve immediately with hot sausage. Yield: 6 portions.

MISSISSIPPI CORN BREAD · MRS. PHIL MAYHALL, GREENVILLE, MISS.

½ cup stone-ground corn meal
1½ teaspoons baking powder
1 teaspoon salt
1 teaspoon sugar
1½ cups milk
1 egg
4 tablespoons shortening

Combine corn meal and dry ingredients in mixing bowl. Add milk and beat in egg. Put 1 teaspoon shortening in each of 12 medium muffin cups. Place in a preheated 425°F. oven. When shortening is smoking hot, remove and add batter to half fill each cup. Return to oven and bake 25 to 30 minutes. Serve piping hot. Yield: 12 muffins.

TEXAS CORN BREAD · MRS. A. L. DE GUIRE, DALLAS, TEX.

½ cup fine white corn meal
½ cup sifted flour
½ teaspoon salt
1½ teaspoons baking powder
1 teaspoon sugar
1 egg, beaten
½ cup buttermilk (about)
1 teaspoon bacon drippings

Sift together dry ingredients. Add egg and mix with enough buttermilk to make a soft batter. Grease a 10-inch skillet with bacon drippings and heat. Pour in corn-meal mixture and cook over low heat on top of range. When brown around the edges, turn like a pancake (don't cover pan or bread will sweat). Brown on other side. Serve with turnip greens and ham hocks or pork jowls with blackeye peas. Yield: 3 portions.

HUSH PUPPIES · BEN MC INTOSH, SEA ISLAND, GA.

½ cup sifted flour
2 teaspoons baking powder
½ teaspoon salt
1½ cups white corn meal
½ cup canned whole kernel
    corn
½ cup diced onion
1 egg, beaten

½ cup milk
3 tablespoons vegetable oil

Sift flour, baking powder and salt into mixing bowl. Add corn meal, canned corn, onion, egg and milk; stir well. Beat in oil. Drop by teaspoonfuls into hot fat (350°F.) and fry until browned. Yield: 42 small-size pups.

HUSH PUPPIES · MRS. W. A. SAUNDERS, WHITE SPRINGS, FLA.

2 cups corn meal
1 tablespoon flour
1 teaspoon baking powder
1 teaspoon salt
½ teaspoon baking soda
1 cup buttermilk
1 egg, beaten

3 tablespoons finely chopped onion (optional)

Combine dry ingredients. Add onion, buttermilk and egg. Mix well. Drop by tablespoonfuls into deep hot fat (375°F.) and fry to a golden brown. (Fish and hush puppies may be fried at the same time.) Drain on absorbent paper. Serve very hot. Yield: about 30 hush puppies.

HUSH PUPPIES · MRS. MYRTLE EDMONDS, ST. LOUIS, MO.

2 cups boiling water
⅔ cup yellow corn meal
½ cup sifted flour
1 teaspoon salt
½ teaspoon black pepper
⅛ teaspoon cayenne pepper
1 egg, slightly beaten
2 tablespoons heavy cream
3 tablespoons minced onion
1 tablespoon minced parsley

Gradually pour boiling water over corn meal, stirring to prevent mixture from lumping. Cook in top of double boiler over boiling water 10 to 15 minutes or until very thick, stirring frequently. Cool slightly. Add flour sifted with salt, black pepper, and cayenne. Blend well into corn-meal mixture. Add egg, cream, onion and parsley; mix thoroughly. The onion gives added flavor, the parsley, color and more interesting texture. Dip by tablespoons into hot drippings in which catfish was cooked and fry until brown on all sides. Serve very hot with the fish.

Yield: 4 portions.

SPOON BREAD · TAYLOR FAMILY, BROWNSVILLE, TENN.

1 cup corn meal
1 teaspoon salt
1 cup milk, scalded
1 cup boiling water
2 teaspoons double-acting
    baking powder
2 eggs, well beaten
3 tablespoons shortening,
    melted

Combine corn meal and salt; gradually stir into the combined scalded milk and boiling water in top of double boiler over hot water. Cook until thick and smooth, stirring occasionally; cool slightly. Stir in baking powder, eggs and melted shortening. Bake in square pan 9 inches × 9 inches at 350°F. for 30 to 35 minutes, until golden brown.

Yield: 6 portions.

MARY AYE'S SPOON BREAD · MANHATTAN, KANSAS

1 quart milk
1 cup yellow corn meal
1 cup butter or margarine,
    melted
2 tablespoons sugar
1 teaspoon salt
4 eggs, separated

Heat milk in top of double boiler over hot water. Add corn meal gradually, stirring constantly. Cook, stirring, until mixture becomes thick and mushy. Remove from heat. Blend in butter, sugar, and salt. Beat egg yolks; stir small amount of hot mixture into yolks; combine with remaining hot mixture. Beat egg whites until stiff; fold into corn meal mixture. Pour into greased 2-quart baking dish. Set dish in pan of hot water. Bake at 325°F. for 1 hour, or until firm.

Yield: 6 portions.

JAMIE'S SPOON BREAD · MRS. FLOYD L. RHEAM, TULSA, OKLA.

1 cup corn meal
½ teaspoon salt
1 cup water
½ cup butter or margarine
1½ cups milk, scalded
1 egg, well beaten

Combine corn meal, salt, and water. Cook over low heat, stirring occasionally, for 15 minutes. Remove from heat. Melt butter in scalded milk. Add to corn-meal mixture and blend until smooth. Slowly stir beaten egg into hot mixture. Pour into a greased 1-quart casserole. Bake at 350°F. for 35 minutes.

Yield: 10 small portions.

RHODE ISLAND JOHNNYCAKE

3 cups johnnycake meal
2 tablespoons sugar
2 teaspoons salt
1 quart boiling water
½ cup milk, about

Sift meal with sugar and salt into mixing bowl. Scald thoroughly with boiling water. Thin with milk, using more or less of the quantity specified as needed for a thin batter. Drop by spoonfuls to hot well-greased griddle. Cook slowly on both sides. Frying time is about 20 minutes for each griddleful of cakes—each cake three inches in diameter. Yield: 22 johnny-cakes. What to eat with a johnnycake at the breakfast hour? Sausage the first round, maple syrup the second.

JOHNNYCAKE TOAST · VIOLET HIGBEE, KINGSTON, R.I.

Rhode Islanders never waste leftover johnnycake.

The cold cakes are split in half, laid in a spider or baking dish, dotted with butter or margarine and covered with milk or cream. Heat thoroughly on top of range or in oven. Have a care not to bring the milk to a boil. Salt to taste and serve like cream toast. Some families like johnnycake toast so much they make fresh cakes, let them cool, then toast just to serve in this fashion.

Johnnycakes are good any meal with meat, fish or fowl. And try them with beefsteak fried in beef fat. Good all by themselves with a big spread of butter or margarine and swimming in syrup.

CORN PONE · BIRMINGHAM, ALABAMA

1 teaspoon salt
3 tablespoons bacon fat,
  melted
3 cups white corn meal
5 cups boiling water (about)

Add salt and fat to corn meal. Add boiling water until meal absorbs all it can hold, bringing it to the consistency of a thick batter. Drop from spoon in stick shapes to greased baking sheet. Bake at 400°F. for 40 minutes. Yield: about 24 pones.

CRACKLING BREAD · MRS. HENRIETTA DULL, ATLANTA, GA.

2 cups cracklings
½ teaspoon baking soda
1 cup buttermilk (more if
    very thick)
2 cups corn meal
2 tablespoons fat

Render salt pork to make cracklings. Mix baking soda with buttermilk and add to corn meal a little at a time, stirring until smooth. Stir in cracklings and fat. Form pones, molding between palms. Bake at 350°F. for 12 to 20 minutes. Serve at dinner with vegetables or dunk in buttermilk to enjoy as a noontime snack. Yield: 6 portions.

FARINA DUMPLINGS · ANNA MARIA SCHWARZENBURG, BETHEL, VT.

2 eggs
⅔ cup farina
¼ cup butter or margarine
½ teaspoon salt
Boiling stock or boiling
    salted water

Beat ingredients together until batter is smooth. Let stand 1 hour. Drop from spoon into boiling stock. Cook, covered, 25 to 30 minutes. Yield: 6 portions. This batter can be made the day before and held in the refrigerator, then cooked just before serving.

CORN MEAL DUMPLINGS · VERMONT

1 cup sifted flour
1 cup corn meal (coarse
    grind)
2 teaspoons baking powder
1¼ teaspoons salt
1 egg
¾ cup milk

Mix and sift dry ingredients. If shortening is desired, cut in one tablespoon of fat, but greens cooked with salt pork need no added richening. Combine and stir in egg and milk quickly to make a soft batter. Drop by tablespoonfuls to rest on top of greens; cover pot tightly, steam 15 minutes.
Yield: 6 portions.

BASIC BISCUIT RECIPE · MRS. ROBERT CONOVER, MANHATTAN, KAN.

1½ cups sifted flour
4 teaspoons baking powder
3 tablespoons non-fat dry
    milk
2 teaspoons sugar
½ teaspoon salt
¾ cup lukewarm milk
¼ cup salad oil

Sift dry ingredients together. Combine lukewarm milk and salad oil; add. Stir lightly until just blended (about 10 strokes). Turn onto floured surface and knead gently 10 times. Pat out ½-inch thick. Cut with a floured biscuit cutter. Place on greased baking sheet. Bake at 400°F. for 10 to 12 minutes.
Yield: 12 2-inch biscuits.

CHEESE BISCUITS:

Add ⅔ cup finely grated cheese to dry ingredients; then add liquids. Roll very thin. Cut in tiny rounds; make an indentation in top with thumb or thimble; fill hole with additional grated cheese, or make cheese sticks or tiny triangles. Yield: about 2 dozen.

"NIFF-NIFF":

This is Mrs. Conover's word for knickknacks, or trifles. Add 1 teaspoon celery seed or 2 teaspoons chopped parsley to dry ingredients. Cut into 2-inch squares and use as dumplings on chicken broth, stew or meat pie. Yield: 6 portions.

CINNAMON CRUMB COFFEE CAKE:

Add ¼ cup sugar, dash of nutmeg to dry ingredients. Beat 1 egg slightly; add ¼ teaspoon lemon extract and liquids in basic recipe. Add to dry ingredients, beating until just blended. Pat into a greased and floured 8-inch square pan. Mix together ¼ cup sugar, 2 tablespoons flour, 2 teaspoons cinnamon, and ¼ cup melted butter or margarine. If desired, add finely cut nuts, currants, or small seedless raisins. Spread over top. Bake at 375°F. for 30 minutes. Serve hot. Yield: 4 to 6 portions.

APPLE DELIGHT:

Add ½ teaspoon grated lemon or orange rind to dry ingredients. Pat dough into 2 greased and floured 8-inch pie pans. Peel and core 4 large baking apples. Slice thinly, as for pie, and press wedges close together in dough. Pour over a syrup made by combining 2 tablespoons melted butter or margarine, dash of salt, ¼ cup dark corn syrup, and 1 teaspoon cinnamon. Bake at 375°F. for 45 minutes or until tender. Yield: 8 portions.

BUTTERMILK BISCUITS · MRS. HOWARD S. WILLIAMS, HATTIESBURG, MISS.

1½ cups sifted flour
1 teaspoon baking powder
½ teaspoon baking soda
½ teaspoon salt
2 tablespoons shortening
½ cup buttermilk

Measure 2 heaping tablespoons of the flour and use for flouring surface. Put remaining flour in a bowl. Make a hole in center of flour and into this add baking powder, baking soda and salt. Add shortening and pour in buttermilk. Use fingertips gradually to mix flour and liquid into a soft dough. Turn onto floured board and pat gently to ½-inch thickness. Cut into small-size biscuits. Place on a greased pan. Bake at 400°F. until brown on bottom, about 10 minutes, then place under a preheated broiler for a minute to brown tops. Yield: 16 2-inch biscuits. Allow at least 3 to a portion.

CLARA'S BUTTERMILK BISCUITS · MRS. DUNCAN HINES, BOWLING GREEN, KY.

2 cups sifted flour
1 teaspoon baking powder
¾ teaspoon salt
¼ teaspoon baking soda
¼ cup shortening
¾ to 1 cup buttermilk

Sift together flour, baking powder, salt and baking soda. Cut in shortening until mixture resembles corn meal. Add enough buttermilk to make soft dough. Roll out ½ inch thick on lightly floured surface. Cut with 2-inch cutter. Place on baking sheet. Bake at 450°F. for 15 minutes. Serve immediately. Yield: about 14 biscuits. In Duncan Hines's opinion that will serve 2.

OSSIAN HALL BISCUITS · MELANIE DE BEN, PASS CHRISTIAN, MISS.

3 cups sifted flour
5 teaspoons baking powder
2 teaspoons salt
1 cup vegetable shortening
1 cup milk (about)

Sift flour, baking powder and salt into a mixing bowl. Cut in shortening until particles are the size of fine beads. Add milk and mix until a smooth ball is formed. Roll out dough on lightly floured surface to ½-inch thickness. Double dough over and roll again to ½-inch thickness. Cut with a 2-inch cutter. Place on ungreased baking sheet. Bake at 450°F. for 10 to 12 minutes. Yield: 30 2-inch biscuits.

SOUR MILK DROP BISCUITS · MRS. HAROLD HOLCOMB, SCOTTSDALE, ARIZ.

2 cups sifted flour
1 teaspoon baking soda
1 teaspoon salt
¼ cup shortening
2 cup sour milk or buttermilk

Sift dry ingredients together. Cut in shortening until mixture resembles fine meal. Add sour milk, mixing lightly. Drop one tablespoonful at a time onto a hot greased iron skillet. Have Dutch oven over coals in fireplace. Put the pan in the hot oven, close oven lid and place a shovelful of coals on the top; leave ten minutes and remove coals; keep oven lid closed and bake 20 to 35 minutes or more depending on size of the biscuit. Yield: 10 large biscuits.

NOTE: To bake in a regular oven, drop mixture on greased baking sheet. Bake at 450°F. for 15 to 20 minutes.

CORNISH SCONES · MINERAL POINT, WISCONSIN

2 cups sifted flour
3 teaspoons baking powder
1 teaspoon salt
4 tablespoons sugar
2 tablespoons shortening
2 eggs
⅓ cup milk (about)
½ teaspoon lemon extract

Sift together flour, baking powder, salt and 2 tablespoons of the sugar. Cut in shortening. Beat together eggs and ⅛ cup milk; stir in lemon extract. Add to flour mixture; stir to make a soft but not sticky dough. Add a few drops of milk to dough if necessary. Knead dough lightly on lightly floured surfaces for a few seconds. Roll into 8 × 6-inch rectangle. Cut into 2-inch squares to form triangles. Place on greased baking sheet. Moisten edges and pinch together so that triangles hold shape. Brush lightly with milk. Sprinkle with remaining sugar. Bake at 400°F. for 18 to 20 minutes, or until light golden brown.

Yield: 12 scones.

EBLESKIVERS (DANISH FRIED CAKES) · MRS. A. G. ANDERSON, FRANKSVILLE, WIS.

1½ cups sifted flour
½ teaspoon baking soda
1 teaspoon baking powder
¼ teaspoon salt
2 cups thick sour milk or
    sour cream
2 eggs
Fat

Sift together dry ingredients. Stir in 1 cup of the sour milk slowly until batter is a thin paste. Add eggs and remaining cup of sour milk and beat until smooth. Place one teaspoon fat in each hole of skiver pan. Heat until sizzling. Spoon in batter to half-fill. When very delicately browned, turn with fork and let the other side fry. Keep heat low to prevent over-browning before the inside is thoroughly done. Serve with granulated sugar or brown sugar, jam or jelly. Yield: 24 ebleskivers.

MRS. McKAY'S COFFEE CAKE · MRS. DOUGLAS MC KAY, SALEM, ORE.

¼ cup butter or margarine
1 cup sugar
2 eggs, beaten
1½ cups sifted flour
2 teaspoons baking powder
Pinch of salt
½ cup milk
2 tablespoons butter or
    margarine
1 cup walnuts, chopped
1 cup brown sugar
2 tablespoons flour
1 tablespoon cinnamon

Cream butter and sugar thoroughly. Beat in eggs. Sift together flour, baking powder, and salt. Add alternately with milk to the creamed mixture. Prepare filling. Melt 2 tablespoons butter in 8 × 12 × 2½-inch baking pan. Pour the melted butter over combined nuts, brown sugar, flour and cinnamon. Wipe the pan with waxed paper and it's greased and ready for baking. Pour in half of the cake batter, add half the nut mixture, then the remaining batter and finish with remaining nut mixture. Bake at 375°F. for 30 minutes.
    Yield: 6 large portions.

SUGAR CAKES · EDNA HELLER, BUENA VISTA, PENNA.

½ cup lard
1¾ cups sugar
3 eggs, beaten
3 cups flour, not sifted
1 teaspoon baking soda
1 teaspoon cream of tartar
1 cup thick sour milk
    (soured naturally)
3 tablespoons sugar for
    topping

Cream lard and sugar thoroughly. Mix in eggs. Sift dry ingredients and add alternately with milk to creamed mixture. Pour into 3 greased 8-inch pie pans. Sprinkle 1 tablespoon sugar on top of each. Bake at 350°F. for 25 minutes.
    Yield: 3, 8-inch cakes.

EAST HAMPTON CRULLERS · JEANNETTE RATTRAY, EAST HAMPTON, N.Y.

7 cups sifted flour
8 teaspoons baking powder
½ teaspoon baking soda
½ teaspoon salt
2 teaspoons nutmeg
⅛ teaspoon ginger
1 cup egg yolks
1 cup buttermilk or sour milk
1 cup light cream
1¾ cups sugar

Sift flour, baking powder, baking soda, salt, and spices. Beat yolks; mix with buttermilk and cream. Add sugar and stir until well blended. Add sifted dry ingredients and beat until almost smooth. Turn a portion at a time onto a lightly floured surface and roll or pat out to ¼-inch thickness. Cut with doughnut cutter. Fry in deep fat (365°F.) until golden brown. Drain on absorbent paper.

Yield: 4 dozen doughnuts.

PINEAPPLE SOPAIPILLAS · TICO TACO CAFE, SCOTTSDALE, ARIZ.

2 cups sifted flour
1 tablespoon baking powder
1 teaspoon salt
1 tablespoon peanut oil
¾ cup water (about)
3 cups drained,
    crushed pineapple
Cinnamon
Sugar

Sift dry ingredients. Blend in oil. Stir in enough water to make a soft dough. Divide into four parts. Roll one part at a time to ⅛- to ¼-inch thickness. Cut into pieces 2½ by 4 inches. Fry in hot peanut oil (385°F.). Agitate oil until the biscuits puff like little pillows. Turn to brown on both sides. Remove from fat and place on paper to drain. Heat pineapple. Open sopaipillas at sides while hot, lift up top and fill each little puff with the warmed fruit. Sprinkle with a mixture of cinnamon and sugar. Spoon more pineapple over the finished product, add another sprinkle of cinnamon-sugar. Serve warm.

Yield: 20 puffs.

TORTILLAS · TICO TACO CAFE, SCOTTSDALE, ARIZ.

Mix 1 cup prepared biscuit mix and ¼ cup water. Knead 1 minute on board lightly dusted with more mix. Shape into 8 balls and roll each into 5-inch circle. Fry on ungreased griddle a few seconds on each side until *very* lightly browned.

Yield: 8 tortillas.

ENCHILADAS · TICO TACO CAFE, SCOTTSDALE, ARIZ.

Take a tortilla and dip into hot peanut oil (200°F.) for a few seconds to soften, then quickly dip in chili sauce. Place grated cheese on one side and roll. Pour chili sauce over roll and sprinkle with more cheese, a combination of longhorn (a Cheddar) and Mexican white cheese, the Mexican made from skimmed milk.

CROQUIGNOLLES · MRS. LEOTA CLAUDEL, AVOYELLES, LA.

1 cup sugar
2 tablespoons water
2 eggs
2¾ cups flour
1 teaspoon baking powder
½ teaspoon nutmeg
Hot deep fat

Combine sugar and water; mix well. Beat in eggs, singly. Sift flour, baking powder and nutmeg together. Add dry ingredients to creamed mixture in halves, blending after each addition. Roll dough on floured surface to ¼-inch thickness. Cut rounds with 2½-inch doughnut cutter. Fry rounds in deep hot fat (370°F.) until light golden brown. Drain. Yield: about 2 dozen.

APRICOT BREAD · MRS. ARTHUR B. LANGLIE, OLYMPIA, WASH.

½ cup dried apricots
1 large orange
Boiling water
½ cup raisins
2 tablespoons butter or
    margarine
1 cup sugar
1 teaspoon vanilla extract
1 egg
½ cup chopped nuts
2 cups sifted flour
2 teaspoons baking powder
½ teaspoon baking soda
¼ teaspoon salt

Soak apricots in water to cover for ½ hour; drain. Squeeze juice from orange and add enough boiling water to make 1 cup. Cut skins into pieces.

Put drained apricots, cut-up orange skins and raisins through a food chopper twice. Cream butter and sugar. Add vanilla; beat in egg. Add fruit mixture and nuts. Stir in sifted dry ingredients, alternating with orange-juice mixture. Pour into a greased and floured 9×5 ×3-inch loaf pan. Bake at 350°F. for 50 to 60 minutes. Yield: 1 loaf.

APRICOT NUT BREAD · LILLIAN JOHNSON, HOLLISTER, CALIF.

¾ cup dried apricots
¾ cup warm water
2 cups sifted flour
1 cup sugar
3 teaspoons baking powder
¾ teaspoon salt
¼ teaspoon baking soda
1 egg, slightly beaten
2 tablespoons melted
    shortening
½ cup water, apricot water,
    orange juice or milk
1 cup finely chopped walnuts

Wash apricots and let them soak in water about half an hour to soften. Drain apricots and chop fine. Sift together flour, sugar, salt and soda into mixing bowl. Add remaining ingredients and mix lightly, just until well blended. Pour into a 9×5×3-inch loaf pan, the bottom lined with waxed paper. Bake at 350°F. about 1 hour, or until done. Remove from pan and cool on rack. For best slicing, store 24 hours before cutting. Yield: 1 loaf.

BANANA BREAD · MRS. HOWARD S. WILLIAMS, HATTIESBURG, MISS.

½ cup butter, or
  margarine
1 cup sugar
2 eggs
2 cups sifted flour
1 teaspoon baking soda
½ teaspoon salt
1 cup mashed and sieved
  bananas (about 3)
½ cup finely chopped nuts

Cream butter and sugar thoroughly. Add eggs, one at a time, and beat well. Sift flour, baking soda and salt. Add to creamed mixture alternately with banana purée. Fold in nuts. Pour into a greased 9×5×3-inch pan. Bake at 350°F. for 55 to 60 minutes. Allow to cool thoroughly before slicing.
  Yield: 1 loaf.

BANANA BREAD · CAROL JEAN BYMA, DENVER, COLO.

½ cup butter or margarine
1 cup sugar
1 egg
1½ cups sifted flour
1 tablespoon baking powder
¾ teaspoon baking soda
½ teaspoon salt
3 large bananas, mashed

Cream butter and sugar thoroughly. Beat in egg. Blend in sifted dry ingredients and mashed bananas. Pour into greased and floured 8×4×2½-inch loaf pan. Bake at 350°F. for 50 to 60 minutes.
  Yield: 1 loaf
  NOTE: Chopped nuts and lemon juice may be added also.

BANANA WALNUT BREAD · MAXINE THORPE, HOLLYWOOD, CALIF.

⅔ cup soft butter or
  margarine
1 cup sugar
2½ cups sifted flour
1 teaspoon baking powder
1 teaspoon baking soda
½ teaspoon salt
2 eggs, beaten
1⅓ cups mashed ripe bananas
½ cup sour cream or
  buttermilk
1½ cups chopped walnuts

Cream butter and sugar thoroughly. Sift flour with dry ingredients, not once but 4 times. Place bowl with butter and sugar under electric mixer. Add 1 beaten egg with about 1 tablespoon of the sifted flour mixture, beat until smooth at low speed. Add second beaten egg with 1 tablespoon sifted flour mixture and beat again until smooth. Add mashed bananas and beat again. Add sour cream alternately with the balance of the sifted flour. Remove bowl from electric mixer and stir in the chopped walnuts. Place batter in 2-pound loaf pan or in 2 pans of 1-pound size, these oiled and lined with waxed paper. Bake at 350° F., about 1¼ hours for the 1 large loaf or 1 hour for 2 loaves. Let cool slightly before removing. Yield: 1 2-pound loaf or 2 of the 1-pound size.

BISHOP'S BREAD · MRS. FRANK ROBINSON, LAKE CHAUTAUQUA, N.Y.

2 cups brown sugar
½ cup melted butter or
    margarine
1 egg
2½ cups sifted flour
2 teaspoons baking powder
½ teaspoon baking soda
½ teaspoon salt
1 teaspoon cinnamon
¾ cup buttermilk or
    sour milk

1 cup chopped dates
Sugar and cinnamon for topping

Blend sugar and butter. Add egg and beat until smooth. Sift flour with dry ingredients. Add to creamed mixture alternately with the milk. Fold in dates. Pour into greased 9×9-inch pan. Bake at 375°F. for 35 to 40 minutes. Sprinkle with sugar and cinnamon. Serve hot as a dinner bread.
    Yield: 12 squares.

MAPLE GRAHAM BREAD · MISS SADIE F. HARD, VERMONT

2 cups sour milk or butter-
    milk
½ teaspoon baking soda
1 cup maple syrup
1 teaspoon salt
½ cup sifted white flour
3½ cups sifted graham flour
1 cup raisins
2 teaspoons baking powder

Combine sour milk, soda and maple syrup. Stir in salt, then flour and raisins. Add baking powder and mix well. Turn into loaf pan. Bake at 325°F. for 1½ hours.
    Yield: 1 large loaf.

EDITH'S WHOLEWHEAT BREAD · EDITH CRUMB, DEARBORN, MICH.

½ cup dark brown sugar
½ cup dark molasses (and a
    trifle more)
1 egg
¾ teaspoon baking soda
2 tablespoons hot water
1 cup milk
3 cups wholewheat flour
2 teaspoons baking powder
1 teaspoon salt
1 cup nuts, chopped
1 cup raisins

Measure sugar into cup and add molasses to fill. Let it seep through sugar, then pour in enough more for level-cup measure. Turn into bowl. Add egg and soda, which has been dissolved in hot water, and stir well. Add milk, stirring constantly. Sift flour with baking powder and salt, saving out 2 tablespoonfuls to dust nuts and raisins. Add flour to batter a bit at a time, stirring in well between each addition. The batter will be on the runny side, and so it should be. Dredge nuts and raisins in flour and add to mix. Pour into a well-greased 9×5×3-inch loaf pan. Bake at 375°F. about 1 hour.
    Yield: 1 loaf.

MRS. BOYD'S NUT BREAD · MRS. MAUD BOYD, BRUNSWICK, GA.

6 cups sifted flour
6 teaspoons baking powder
1 teaspoon salt
2 cups sugar
1 cup chopped pecans
1 cup ground pecans
2 eggs, beaten
2 cups milk

1 tablespoon shortening, melted and cooled

Sift together flour, baking powder, salt and sugar. Add nuts and blend. Combine eggs, milk and shortening and add to dry ingredients, stirring quickly until well blended. Turn into 2 greased 8½ × 4½ × 2½-inch loaf pans. Bake at 350°F. 50 to 60 minutes. Yield: 2 loaves.

ORANGE NUT BREAD · THE NUT TREE, VACAVILLE, CALIF.

¾ cup sugar
3 tablespoons butter or
    margarine
2 eggs
1 cup orange rind
1 cup chopped walnuts
2½ cups sifted flour
2 teaspoons baking powder
1 teaspoon salt
1 cup milk

Cream butter and sugar thoroughly. Beat in eggs one at a time. Continue to beat, adding orange rind and nuts. Sift flour, baking powder, and salt. Add alternately with milk to creamed mixture while continuing to beat. Pour into a greased 8 × 8 × 2-inch pan. Bake at 350°F. 40 to 50 minutes. Yield 1 loaf.

Waffle Nut Bread: Cut Orange Nut Bread into ½-inch thick slices. Place in waffle iron and heat until toasted.

HAMAN TASCHEN · MRS. NORMAN LESS, CLEVELAND, OHIO

DOUGH:
2½ cups sifted flour
½ teaspoon salt
½ pound butter (room
    temperature)
3 egg yolks
3 tablespoons white distilled
    vinegar
3 tablespoons cold water

Combine 1½ cups of the flour, salt and butter, rubbing butter into flour with fingers. Mix egg yolks with a fork. Add vinegar and water. Add the remaining 1 cup flour, sifting it into the egg mixture, mixing together lightly. Combine the mixtures and blend well with a fork. Store, covered, in refrigerator overnight.

When ready to use, pinch off dough the size of a walnut and roll on a floured surface into a 2½-inch round. Place a level teaspoon of one of the fillings in the center. Pinch the sides together, forming a closed triangle over the filling. Cut the pinched edges about ¼ inch deep at ½-inch intervals to give a scalloped top when baked. Place on an ungreased baking sheet. Bake at 400°F. for 20 minutes or until browned.

Yield: 30 turnovers.

POPPY-SEED FILLING:

1 pound ground poppy seeds
2 cups milk
1 cup honey
½ cup chopped pecans
½ cup sugar
¼ teaspoon cinnamon

Place seeds in a fine strainer and run water through it again and again. Place in top of double boiler with milk and cook over hot water until milk is absorbed. Add honey, pecans, sugar, and cinnamon. Cook a few minutes, stirring until sugar is dissolved and honey is blended. Cool, cover, and store in refrigerator. Yield: about 1 quart filling.

APRICOT FILLING:

1 pound dried apricots
3 cups water
3 cups sugar

Wash apricots. Add water and cook over low heat until very soft, adding more water if necessary. Add sugar and heat, stirring constantly until fruit comes to a boil. Cool, cover, and store in refrigerator.
Yield: about 3 pints filling.

PLOW LINES · MRS. VIOLA MILLER, KUTZTOWN, PENNA.

2 eggs
1 cup light cream
4 cups sifted flour, about
2 teaspoons salt
Molasses

Beat eggs and cream. Combine flour and salt and blend into egg mixture. Knead well. Roll out on floured surface to a rectangle ¼-inch thick. Cut into pieces 4 to 5 inches wide and 6 inches long. Using a pastry wheel, cut ½-inch strips in each piece, leaving a ½-inch border. Fry one or two at a time in deep hot fat (375°F.) until light brown. Dip in molasses. Serve as bread for supper.
Yield: 8 pieces.

BASIC LIGHT BREAD · MRS. PHIL MAYHALL, GREENVILLE, MISS.

1 cup milk
1 cup water
3 tablespoons shortening
1 tablespoon salt
2 envelopes active dry yeast
3 tablespoons sugar
1 cup warm, not hot, water
8 cups sifted flour

Scald milk and water; pour over shortening and salt; cool to lukewarm. In a separate bowl dissolve yeast and sugar in warm water. Add to milk mixture. Add 4 cups flour, mixing well with wooden spoon, then add remaining flour mixing thoroughly (the mixture should not be sticky). Cover and let rise until double in bulk, 1½ to 2 hours. Turn onto floured surface and knead. Make 3 bread loaves, pound size, or 5 round French-style loaves. Let rise in pan until double in bulk, 45 minutes for large loaves, ½ hour for small. Bake at 425°F. for 25 to 30 minutes for large, 15 to 20 minutes for small loaves. (continued)

LIGHT BREAD VARIATIONS:

The same dough may be used to make a coffee cake, cinnamon rolls, or apfel kuchen, the latter always served for Christmas breakfast at the Mayhalls' home.

CINNAMON ROLLS:

Take ¼ of the dough; turn onto a floured surface and roll ½ inch thick in rectangular shape. Spread with soft butter, sprinkle with cinnamon and sugar. Add 1 cup seedless raisins; now roll as a jelly roll and cut in 1-inch-thick slices. Set cut side down in a greased pan, roll beside roll. Let rise until double in bulk, about ½ hour. Bake at 400°F. for 25 minutes. Yield: 12 rolls.

APFEL KUCHEN:

Roll ¼ of dough ½ inch thick in rectangle; butter. Peel, core, slice 3 tart apples and lay over dough, edges of slices overlapping. Sprinkle with ½ cup sugar, dust with nutmeg. Fold dough in thirds the long way; form crescent on greased sheet, sealing edges well. Let crescent rise until double in bulk, about ½ hour. Bake at 400°F. for 25 minutes. Decorate with candied cherries (cut in half) and pecans. Bring crescent to the table on a breadboard. Yield: 6 large wedges.

WHITE BREAD · MRS. GREYTON TAYLOR, HAMMONDSPORT, N.Y.

4 packages active dry yeast
1 cup warm, not hot, water
2 cups milk
2 tablespoons lard
2 tablespoons butter or
*   margarine*
2 tablespoons sugar
4 teaspoons salt
2 cups warm water
12 to 14 cups sifted flour

Dissolve yeast in the 1 cup water. Scald milk; add lard, butter, sugar and salt; stir until dissolved. Add the 2 cups water and cool to lukewarm. Stir in yeast mixture. Add flour gradually, beating well at first as it stiffens. Add more flour and knead while turning bowl. Use enough flour to make a medium-soft dough. Turn into a greased bowl; cover and put in a warm place to rise until doubled in bulk, about 1½ hours. Knead for 2 minutes. Return to greased bowl to rise a second time until doubled in bulk, about 30 minutes. Cut into 4 pieces. Form into balls; cover and let rise about 10 minutes. Shape into loaves. Place in greased 9 by 5 by 3-inch loaf pans. Cover and let rise until dough is rounded above edge of pan, about 50 to 60 minutes. Bake at 400°F. for 40 to 45 minutes. Turn out on racks. For a soft crust, rub with butter; cover with waxed paper and towel; let cool. Yield: 4 loaves.

OATMEAL BREAD · DARTMOUTH COLLEGE, HANOVER, N.H.

2 cups boiling water
1 cup rolled oats
2 tablespoons shortening
½ cup dark molasses
2 teaspoons salt
1 package or cake yeast
    (active dry or
    compressed)
½ cup warm water (lukewarm
    for compressed)
5 to 6 cups sifted flour

Pour boiling water over rolled oats. Add shortening; cool. Add molasses and salt. Dissolve yeast in water and add to oatmeal mixture. Add flour, beating in gradually. Turn onto floured surface and knead until smooth and satiny. Turn into a greased bowl. Cover. Leave in a warm place 1 hour or until doubled in bulk. Shape into 2 loaves. Place in greased bread pans. Cover and let rise until doubled. Bake at 350°F. for about 50 minutes, or until well browned. Yield: 2 loaves.

SALLY LUNN BREAD · WILLIAMSBURG, VA.

1 package active dry yeast
¼ cup warm, not hot, water
¾ cup warm milk
3 tablespoons shortening
1½ tablespoons sugar
2 eggs
3½ cups sifted flour
1¼ teaspoons salt

Dissolve yeast in warm water; add warm milk and set aside. Cream shortening and sugar. Add eggs and mix well. Sift flour and salt and add to shortening mixture alternately with yeast mixture. Knead lightly and let rise in a warm place until doubled in bulk. Punch down, knead lightly again and put into a well-greased Sally Lunn mold. Let rise again for about 1 hour. Bake at 300°F. for 1 hour.

NOTE: 1 9-inch angel food pan or a 10-inch ring mold may be used.

Yield: 1 loaf bread.

KENTUCKY'S SALLY LUNN · KATE MEGIBBEN, CORAL GABLES, FLA.

2 cups milk
2 tablespoons butter or
    margarine
3 tablespoons sugar
1 teaspoon salt
8 to 9 cups sifted flour
    (about)
1 package active dry yeast
¼ cup warm, not hot, water
3 eggs

Scald milk. Pour over combined butter, sugar and salt in a bowl. Add 3 cups flour and yeast which has been dissolved in the warm water. Blend thoroughly. Cover and let rise in warm place for 2 to 3 hours or until light. Beat in eggs. Add flour enough to make a stiff dough (about 5 to 6 cups). Do not knead, but roll out on lightly floured surface and divide dough in half. Press lightly in a ¼-inch layer on the bottoms of 2 greased shallow 9×12×2-inch pans. Brush tops with melted butter or margarine and let rise again about 1 hour. Bake at 375°F. for 25 to 30 minutes.

Yield: 36 squares.

RAISIN BROWN BREAD · MRS. GREYTON TAYLOR, HAMMONDSPORT, N.Y.

2 tablespoons lard
1 tablespoon butter or
    margarine
1 cup brown sugar
2 teaspoons salt
2 cups hot water
1 cup molasses
½ cup water (to rinse out
    molasses cup)
4 packages active dry yeast
½ cup warm, not hot, water
9 to 10 cups sifted flour
2 teaspoons cinnamon
1 teaspoon allspice
2 cups raisins

Dissolve lard, butter, sugar and salt in the 2 cups hot water. Add molasses and ½ cup rinsing water; let cool to lukewarm. Dissolve yeast in the ½ cup warm water. Add to first mixture. Mix flour and spices and beat into liquid mixture. Stir in raisins. Knead lightly. Place in greased bowl; cover and let rise in a warm place until doubled in bulk, about 1½ hours. Knead again and let rise a second time until doubled in bulk, about 30 minutes. Cut into 3 pieces. Shape into loaves. Place in greased 9 by 5 by 3-inch loaf pans. Cover and let rise until dough is rounded above edge of pan, about 50 to 60 minutes. Bake at 400°F. for 35 to 40 minutes. Yield: 3 loaves.

FRENCH BREAD · CAROL JEAN BYMA, DENVER, COLO.

1 package active dry yeast
½ cup warm, not hot, water
2 cups lukewarm water
1 tablespoon salt
7 cups sifted flour
Corn meal
1 egg white
1 tablespoon water

Dissolve yeast in the ½ cup water. Add the 2 cups water, salt, and 2 cups of the flour. Beat. Add 4 more cups of the flour and blend well. Turn out on a cloth covered with remaining cup flour and let rest for 10 minutes. Knead in flour. Place in a greased bowl and let rise in a warm place 1½ hours. Punch down and let rise again for 1 hour. Turn out on floured surface and divide in half; let rest 10 minutes. Roll each half to a 15×12-inch rectangle. Roll tightly and seal well. Grease 2 large baking sheets and sprinkle with corn meal. Place loaves on sheets and slit every 2½ inches. Beat egg white with water and brush over top of loaves. Let rise 1½ hours. Bake at 375°F. for 20 minutes. Brush again with egg and bake another 20 minutes, turning cornerwise on the cooky sheet. Yield: 2 loaves.

NUT TREE BREAD · THE NUT TREE, VACAVILLE, CALIF.

1 cup warm, not hot, water
1½ tablespoons sugar
1 package active dry yeast
3 cups sifted flour (about)
1½ teaspoons salt

Place water in a warmed mixing bowl. Add sugar and yeast and stir until dissolved. Add 1½ cups of the flour and the salt; beat hard with a spoon for about 2 minutes. Gradually add remaining flour, mixing first with spoon, then with hands to make a smooth, springy

NOTE: Dough may be divided into 4 individual loaves and baked in 5 × 2½ × 1½-inch pans at 400°F. for 20 minutes.

ball of dough, about 5 minutes. Cover with a towel and allow to stand in a warm place until doubled in bulk, about 45 minutes. Flatten dough out on an oiled board. Shape into a loaf and put into a greased 9 × 5 × 3-inch pan. Again cover and let rise in a warm place until tripled in bulk, about 30 minutes. Bake at 425°F. for 25 to 30 minutes, or until golden brown. Turn out and cool on rack. Yield: 1 loaf.

SWISS PEAR BREAD · MRS. ELSIE GERBER, MONROE, WIS.

½ pound dried pears
½ pound dried apples (sweet)
½ pound currants
1 pound seedless raisins
½ pound prunes
⅛ pound citron, finely diced
¼ cup butter or margarine
1 cup sugar
1 tablespoon anise seed
½ teaspoon cloves
1 teaspoon cinnamon
1 teaspoon nutmeg
1 cup walnuts, whole or
    chopped
1 package active dry yeast
1 quart warm, not hot, water
1½ teaspoons lard
1½ teaspoons salt
8 to 10 cups sifted flour

Cook dried pears and apples in water until very tender. Combine while hot with currants and raisins. Cook prunes in water to cover until soft; pit; add to hot, cooked fruit mixture. Add citron, butter and ¼ cup of the sugar and spices while mixture is still hot. Let stand overnight.

The following morning add nuts to the fruit mixture. Dissolve yeast in ¼ cup of the warm, not hot, water and let stand 5 minutes without stirring. Then mix thoroughly and add lard, salt, the remaining ¼ cup sugar and the rest of the warm water. Let stand until the mixture bubbles. Mix in enough flour to make a stiff dough. Keep stirring in additional flour as long as it's possible (about 8 cups). Turn dough out on floured surface and work in enough more flour to prevent sticking (it might take 2 cups). Let dough rise until doubled in bulk. Pinch off 3 pieces, each the size of an English walnut; set aside. Add fruit-nut mixture to remainder of dough. Work fruit into dough by kneading until there are no strings of white left. The dough is quite sticky at this point, a little like fruit-cake dough. Divide into 3 portions, about 2 cupfuls in each. Shape into narrow loaves. If fruit dough is too sticky, add more flour, work in well. Roll each of the small pieces of dough you set aside into very thin sheets. Wrap a sheet of plain dough around each loaf. Make it uneven so that the dark fruited roll shows in spots. Let rise in a warm place until nearly doubled in bulk, about 1 hour. Bake for 1½ hours. Start oven at 375°F. and when dough has come up, reduce heat to 325°F.
Yield: 3 loaves.

MARY DUNN'S LOST BREAD · AVERY ISLAND, LOUISIANA

10 slices 2-day-old bread
3 eggs, beaten
½ cup milk
1 cup sugar
½ teaspoon vanilla extract
Nutmeg and sugar

Remove crusts from bread and cut each slice into 4 pieces. Combine eggs, milk, sugar and vanilla. Soak bread in egg mixture for 5 minutes. Fry on a hot greased griddle until brown on both sides. Sprinkle with nutmeg and sugar. Serve hot with mid-morning coffee. Yield: 40 squares.

HAIRNHUTTER BOODER SEMMEL (MORAVIAN BUTTER ROLLS)
LANCASTER, PENNA.

1 package active dry yeast
¼ cup warm, not hot, water
1 cup scalded milk
5½ cups sifted flour
½ cup sugar
¾ teaspoon salt
½ teaspoon nutmeg
1 egg, well beaten
¼ cup butter, melted
¼ cup lard, melted
Butter
1 egg white
1 tablespoon water
Poppy seeds

Dissolve yeast in water. Add milk that has been cooled to lukewarm. Stir in 2½-cups of the flour. Place in greased bowl. Grease top of dough. Cover and set in warm place to rise until doubled in bulk. Mix sugar, salt and nutmeg. Work into dough along with egg, butter and lard. Add enough flour to make a soft but easily kneaded dough (about 3 cups). Knead for 5 minutes until smooth and elastic. Place in greased bowl, grease top of dough, cover and set to rise in warm place until doubled in bulk. Turn out onto lightly floured surface and let rise 5 minutes. Roll, or pat with hands, until ½-inch thick. Spread generously with softened butter. With hands, form into 1-inch rolls, buttering generously as they are shaped. Place on buttered baking sheet about ½ inch apart. Beat egg white and water until foamy (not stiff) and brush on tops of rolls. Sprinkle with poppy seeds. Let rise until doubled in bulk. Bake at 400°F. for 15 to 20 minutes. Yield: about 36 rolls.

ORANGE ROLLS · MRS. MAX HINRICHS, PULLMAN, WASH.

Plain roll dough (based on recipe using 3 to 3½ cups flour)
Melted butter or margarine
¾ cup sugar
Grated rind of 2 oranges
1 cup confectioners' sugar
¼ cup orange juice

Roll dough out on lightly floured surface to a rectangle about ¼-inch thick. Spread with melted butter. Combine the ¾ cup sugar and orange rind and sprinkle over dough. Roll up as for jelly roll. Cut into 1-inch slices. Place cut-side down in greased small muffin pans. Cover and let rise until doubled in bulk, 30-45 minutes. Bake at 350°F. for 20 to 25 minutes. Mix confectioners' sugar and orange juice. Pour over hot rolls. Yield: 16 rolls.

MOM'S JAM SURPRISE ROLLS · MRS. JULIUS KASSER, EDISON PARK, ILL.

1 package active dry yeast
¼ cup warm, not hot, water
½ cup and 1 tablespoon sugar
¼ cup scalded milk
4 cups unsifted flour
1½ teaspoons salt
1 teaspoon grated lemon rind
1½ teaspoons vanilla extract
¼ teaspoon finely crushed
　　cardamom seed
3 egg yolks
1¼ cups commercial sour
　　cream
½ cup apricot jam (about)
¼ cup butter
¼ cup margarine
¼ pound walnuts or pecans,
　　ground
2 tablespoons sugar
1 cup confectioners' sugar
¼ cup light cream
½ teaspoon vanilla extract

Dissolve yeast in water. Add the 1 tablespoon sugar and milk, stirring until blended. Add ½ cup of the flour, beating in well. Cover bowl; set in warm place and let rise 15 minutes. Meanwhile, sift remaining 3½ cups flour, ½ cup sugar and salt. Add lemon rind, 1½ teaspoons vanilla, cardamom seed, egg yolk, and sour cream. Pour mixture into risen sponge and beat 5 minutes or until very smooth. Turn sponge into a large greased bowl and cover, but not too tightly. Set in a warm place to rise for 2 hours. (Mrs. Kasser sometimes coaxes the rising ahead 30 minutes by heating the oven to 70°F.; then off with the heat and in goes the sponge.) After its full rising the dough is divided into two parts; half may be refrigerated if desired and the rolls made up a day or two later. Turn dough onto well-floured surface and roll to ¼-inch thickness. Cut into 3-inch squares. Place 1 teaspoon apricot jam in center of each square. Pinch four corners together over jam. Now pinch protruding four corners together to form a ball, rounding smoothly with the hands. Melt butter and margarine; cool to lukewarm. Dip each roll into the shortening, then into ground nuts combined with 2 tablespoons sugar. Place rolls cut-side down into 10 × 2-inch pie plates.

Cover rolls and allow to rise in a warm place 1½ hours or until more than double in bulk. Bake at 375°F. for 15 minutes; reduce heat to 350°F. and bake 25 to 30 minutes longer. While still warm drizzle on sugar icing in a spiral starting at center of cake-like array, working outward. To make frosting, combine confectioners' sugar with cream and add remaining half-teaspoon vanilla. Around the border there should be a double drizzle as the rolls tend to over-brown at the outside edge. Yield: 32 rolls.

Mrs. Kasser makes this apricot jam for the filling: Soak 1 pound dried apricots for 2 hours in cold water, drain, cover with fresh water; cook until tender. Sieve fruit and add 1½ to 2 cups sugar. Cook over low heat until sugar is dissolved. Yield: about 3 cups jam.

PAPPY'S SOUTHERN ROLLS · PAPPY AND JIMMIE'S LOBSTER SHACK, MEMPHIS, TENN.

1 envelope active dry yeast
⅓ cup warm, not hot, water
3 eggs
½ cup shortening, melted
⅓ cup milk (room
    temperature)
1 tablespoon sugar
1 teaspoon salt
3 cups sifted flour
⅓ pound butter or margarine

Dissolve yeast in water. Combine eggs, melted shortening, milk, dissolved yeast, sugar and salt. Beat well and begin working in the flour. Knead continuously in the bowl until it's a good dough, smooth and elastic. Cover and let rise in warm place, about 45 minutes, or until doubled in bulk. Punch down dough. Cut off small pieces about the size of a walnut. Place in greased muffin pans. Let rise in a warm place until roll is high as the pan. Bake at 400°F. for 8 to 12 minutes. Hot from the oven brush over butter to give extra flavor. Yield: 2 dozen rolls.

CINNAMON ROLLS · MRS. T. H. GIGNILLIOT, SAVANNAH, GA.

1 package active dry yeast
¼ cup warm, not hot, water
1¼ teaspoons salt
½ cup melted shortening
¼ cup sugar
3 eggs, well beaten
¾ cup lukewarm milk
4 cups sifted flour
Melted butter or margarine
2 tablespoons confectioners'
    sugar
1 tablespoon cinnamon

Dissolve yeast in water. Add salt, shortening, sugar, eggs and milk. Add flour, a little at a time, beating thoroughly after each addition until dough is stiff and smooth. Cover with damp cloth, set in warm place and allow to rise until doubled in bulk. Work down with spoon, cover and allow to rise until doubled in bulk. Punch down, beat with spoon until shiny (do not knead). Fill well-oiled large muffin pans half-full. Cover and let rise until doubled in bulk. Brush with butter. Sprinkle liberally with mixture of confectioners' sugar and cinnamon. Bake at 450°F. for 12 to 15 minutes. Yield: 16 to 18 rolls.

BUTTERHORN ROLLS · MRS. ORVILLE BURTIS, ASHLAND BOTTOMS, TEX.

1 envelope dry granular yeast
    or 1 cake compressed
    yeast
¼ cup warm water
¾ cup scalded milk
½ cup melted shortening
½ cup sugar
1 teaspoon salt

3 eggs, beaten
4½ cups sifted all-purpose flour
Melted butter

Dissolve dry yeast in warm, not hot, water (lukewarm for cake yeast) for 10 minutes. Combine milk, shortening, sugar, and salt; cool to lukewarm. Stir in dissolved yeast and eggs. Gradually add flour, stirring with wooden spoon after each addition. Knead in last portion of flour with hands, if necessary. Knead continuously in bowl to a smooth elastic dough. Cover and let rise until double in bulk, about 1 hour. Punch dough down; divide in two. Roll each half on lightly floured board to a 12-inch circle of ¼-inch thickness. Brush with melted butter. Cut each circle into 16 wedge-shaped pieces; roll each wedge, starting with rounded edge and rolling to point. Arrange far apart on greased baking sheet with points underneath. Brush with melted butter. Cover and let rise until light (45 to 50 minutes). Bake in hot oven at 400°F. for 12 to 15 minutes.

Yield: 32 rolls.

MARTHA WASHINGTON'S LIGHT POTATO ROLLS · WILLIAMSBURG, VA.

2 large potatoes
3 tablespoons butter or
  margarine
2 tablespoons sugar
1 teaspoon salt
1½ cups water drained from
  potatoes
1 package active dry yeast
¼ cup warm, not hot, water
½ cup lukewarm milk
7 cups sifted flour, about

Peel and cook potatoes in rapidly boiling salted water until tender. Drain, saving water. Add butter, sugar and salt to hot potatoes, beating well. Add potato water. Dissolve yeast cake in water. Add to potato mixture. Beat in milk. Add 4 cups of the flour, beating well. Add enough remaining flour to make a stiff dough. Knead on floured surface until smooth and elastic. Brush top with melted butter and place in large bowl. Cover and let rise slowly, until doubled in bulk, about 5 hours. Place on floured surface and pat out flat, but do not knead again. Shape into small rolls. Place in greased pan. Let rise until very light. Bake at 400°F. for 20 minutes or until done. Yield: 4 dozen rolls.

MRS. WRIGHT'S ROLLS · MRS. CLEO WRIGHT, UTAH

1 large potato, pared
6 packages active dry yeast
1½ cups warm, not hot, water
¾ cup butter or margarine
1½ cups sugar
2 tablespoons salt
6½ cups milk, scalded

6 eggs, beaten
30 cups sifted flour

Cook potato and mash in cooking water to make about 1 pint potato mixture. Dissolve yeast in warm water. Combine butter, sugar, salt, and milk, and stir until butter is melted; cool to lukewarm. Add eggs and mix well. Stir in potato mixture. Make a hole in the center of the flour; add milk mixture and mix thoroughly. Knead dough until smooth and elastic. Place in a greased bowl, cover with a damp cloth, and let rise in a warm place until double in bulk, 1½ to 2 hours. Punch dough down and let rise again until double in bulk, 30 to 45 minutes. Cut off small pieces and form into rolls. (For festive occasions the dough is rolled into a rectangle about ½ inch thick, well buttered, sprinkled with brown sugar and cinnamon, folded 3 times, and cut into squares.) Place on a greased baking sheet. Let rise until light, 15 to 30 minutes. Bake at 400°F. for 10 to 15 minutes.

Yield: 80 to 100 large rolls.

FASTNACHTS · PENNSYLVANIA DUTCH

3 medium potatoes, peeled
    and quartered
2 cups salted water
¾ cup sugar
1 teaspoon salt
7 to 8 cups sifted flour
1 package active dry yeast
¼ cup warm, not hot, water
½ cup butter or margarine,
    softened
2 eggs
½ teaspoon nutmeg

Boil potatoes in salted water until tender. Drain; reserve 1 cup water and pour into large mixing bowl. Stir in sugar, salt and 1 cup of the flour. Beat until smooth. Dissolve yeast in the ¼ cup water; beat into batter. Cover bowl with a cloth and let rise in a warm place free from draft until bubbly (about 4 hours). Mash hot potatoes, measure 1 cup into a mixing bowl and beat in butter, eggs and nutmeg. When the batter is full of bubbles, stir in potato mixture and remaining flour, or enough to make a stiff dough. Turn out on a lightly floured surface and knead 8 to 10 minutes, or until smooth and elastic. Place in a greased bowl, brush top with melted shortening, cover and let rise in a warm place free from draft, until doubled in bulk, about 2 hours. Punch dough down, cover bowl, and store in refrigerator until 2 hours before serving time. Remove from refrigerator and cut in half. Roll each half ⅓-inch thick on floured surface. Cut with doughnut cutter or into 2-inch squares with a sharp knife. Place doughnuts on floured surface. Cover with a cloth and let rise in a warm place until doubled in bulk. Slip doughnuts into deep hot fat (365°F.). When they rise to the top, turn with a long-handled fork to brown the other side. Drain on absorbent paper toweling and sprinkle with sugar. Yield: about 4 dozen.

BUTTERSCOTCH RING AROUND · MRS. ROBERT E. BOGUE, WICHITA, KAN.

¼ cup milk
¼ cup sugar
2 tablespoons shortening
¾ teaspoon salt
1 package or cake yeast, dry
    or compressed
¼ cup warm water (lukewarm
    for compressed yeast)
1 egg, beaten
2½ cups sifted flour
⅓ cup butter or margarine
⅔ cup brown sugar
⅔ cup pecans
2 tablespoons butter or
    margarine, melted
⅔ cup brown sugar

Scald milk; stir into ¼ cup sugar, shortening and salt; cool to lukewarm. In large bowl sprinkle or crumble yeast into water; stir until dissolved. Stir in lukewarm milk mixture and egg. Add half the flour; beat until smooth. Add enough more flour to make a soft dough. Cover; let rise in a warm place until doubled in bulk, about 1 hour.

Meanwhile, cream ⅓ cup butter and ⅔ cup brown sugar thoroughly. Spread in bottom of 9-inch tube pan. Sprinkle pecans over mixture.

Punch dough down. Turn onto a floured surface. Roll into an oblong ¼-inch thick and 8 inches wide. Brush with one-half of the melted butter and sprinkle with remaining brown sugar. Roll up from short side, jelly roll fashion; seal edge. Cut into 1-inch slices. Place slices, cut side down, in single layer in prepared tube pan. Brush lightly with remaining melted butter. Cover; let rise in a warm place until doubled in bulk, about 1 hour. Bake at 375°F. for 20 to 25 minutes. Let stand 1 minute then turn out of pan. Yield: 8 rolls.

GRANDMA ANDERSON'S KRINGLE · MRS. A. G. ANDERSON, FRANKSVILLE, WIS.

1 package active dry yeast
½ cup warm, not hot, water
4 cups sifted flour
3 tablespoons sugar
1 teaspoon salt
1 cup shortening
3 eggs, separated
1 cup lukewarm milk
Filling (see below)

Dissolve yeast in water. Sift flour, sugar, and salt into a large bowl. Cut in shortening, as for pie crust, blending well. Beat egg yolks; add to yeast with milk, and stir into flour mixture. Cover bowl with towel and chill overnight. The dough is thin when it goes into the refrigerator; it comes out thick enough to knead on a lightly floured surface. Divide dough into three or four parts. Roll each piece 14 inches long and about 8 inches wide. Beat egg whites and spread over dough. Spread choice of filling over dough and sprinkle with brown sugar. Bring sides over filling; pinch edges together. Place on greased baking sheet. Let rise until double in bulk, about 2 hours. Bake at 400°F. for about 30 minutes. Cover with confectioners' sugar icing while hot. Yield: 3 or 4 kringles.

Filling: The filling may be chopped dates or seedless raisins or chopped nuts, preferably pecans. Sometimes a prune or raspberry jam is used.

MISS SUE'S PUFFS · MISS SUE TOKES, WINCHESTER, VA.

2 cups sifted flour
½ teaspoon salt
1 teaspoon shortening
1 teaspoon active dry yeast
¼ cup warm, not hot, water
1 cup lukewarm milk, about

Mix flour and salt, cut in shortening. Dissolve yeast in water and add to flour along with enough milk to absorb the flour. Knead on lightly floured surface until dough is smooth and rounded. Roll about ¼ inch thick. Cut with a 3-inch cutter. Cover and let rise in a warm place until doubled in bulk, about ½ hour. Fry on a hot lightly greased griddle, one side then the other until brown. Serve with butter.

Yield: 2 dozen puffs.

CALAS · NEW ORLEANS, LA.

½ cup uncooked rice
3 cups boiling water
½ package dry or compressed
    yeast
2 tablespoons warm, not hot,
    water (lukewarm for
    compressed)
3 eggs, well beaten
¼ cup sugar
½ teaspoon salt
⅛ teaspoon nutmeg
¼ cup sifted flour, about
Hot deep fat for frying

Add rice to the boiling water. Simmer, covered, until rice is very soft. Drain. Mash rice; cool. Dissolve yeast in warm water. Add to rice; mix thoroughly. Cover. Let rise overnight. In the morning, add egg, sugar, salt and nutmeg; blend. Add flour to make a thick batter. Cover. Let rise in warm place for 20 minutes. Drop batter by tablespoonfuls into hot deep fat (360°F.). Fry until golden brown. Drain. Sprinkle with sugar and serve hot. Yield: 20 calas.

APPLE BUTTERHORNS · PEACH RIDGE, MICHIGAN

¼ cup butter or margarine
¼ cup lard
¼ cup sugar
1 egg, beaten
Pinch of salt
1 teaspoon grated lemon rind
¼ cup lukewarm milk
1 package active dry yeast
¼ cup warm, not hot, water
2 cups sifted flour
Soft butter or margarine
1 cup finely chopped apples
½ cup finely chopped dates

Melt butter and lard; add sugar and cool to lukewarm. Mix in egg, salt, lemon rind, milk, and yeast dissolved in water. Beat in flour. Cover and refrigerate overnight. Divide dough into three parts. Roll each part on floured surface into a 9-inch circle. Spread each round with butter; sprinkle with apples and dates. Cut into 8 pie-shaped pieces. Beginning at rounded edge, roll up. Place on baking sheet, point underneath. Let rise in a warm place for 2½ hours. Bake at 375°F. for 12 to 15 minutes. Frost horns while still warm with a thick frosting of confectioners' sugar and warm water.

Yield: 24 horns.

FRENCH COFFEE CAKE · MRS. F. W. GLANTZ, FOX POINT, WIS.

4 cups sifted flour
¼ cup sugar
1 teaspoon salt
½ pound butter or margarine
1 cup warm milk
3 eggs, separated
1 package active dry yeast
¼ cup warm, not hot, water
2 teaspoons cinnamon
1 cup sugar
1 cup chopped nuts
1¼ cups confectioners' sugar

Sift together flour, sugar, and salt. Cut in butter until size of small peas. Add warm milk and well-beaten egg yolks, stirring until a soft dough is formed. Add yeast, dissolved in warm water. Beat. Let stand in cool place overnight. Divide dough into two parts. Roll each half on a floured surface into a rectangle ¼-inch thick. Spread with egg whites, stiffly beaten. Sprinkle with a mixture of cinnamon, sugar, and nuts. Roll as for a jelly roll and place in 2 greased loaf pans. Let rise until loaves double in bulk. Bake at 350°F. for 45 minutes. Frost while warm with confectioners' sugar icing, blending confectioners' sugar with enough water or milk or cream for a thin spreading consistency.

Yield: 2 loaves.

GERMAN COFFEE CAKE · MRS. HATTIE THIE, CINCINNATI, OHIO

1 package active dry yeast
½ cup warm, not hot, water
4 cups sifted flour
1 cup milk
¾ pound butter or margarine, melted
⅔ cup sugar
1 teaspoon salt
6 egg yolks

CRUMB MIXTURE:
2 cups sifted flour
¼ pound confectioners' sugar
¼ cup brown sugar
Pinch of salt
¼ teaspoon cinnamon
¼ cup butter or margarine, melted
¼ cup shortening, melted

Dissolve the yeast in warm water. Sift 2 cups of the flour into bowl. Scald and cool the milk. Make a hole in the flour—pour in milk along with the dissolved yeast. Stir into a smooth batter. Cover and let rise in warm place until doubled in bulk. Add ½ pound of the melted butter, sugar, salt and egg yolk. Stir in balance of flour until well blended. Place ½-inch layer of dough into two 8×8-inch pans. Cover and let rise in warm place until doubled in bulk. Sprinkle coffee cake with remaining melted butter and cover with the streusel or crumb mixture.

To make streusel, sift flour with dry ingredients, add melted butter and shortening until little balls or crumbs are formed. Sprinkle over coffee cakes. Bake at 350°F. for 25 minutes. Yield: 2 cakes.

NOTE: German butter cake is made with the same basic dough but omit the crumb mixture. Instead, sprinkle cakes with melted butter, then drop lumps of butter over surface of batter and lightly cover with powdered sugar. Let stand until it rises. Bake at 350°F. for 25 minutes.

HUNGARIAN KIFLI (CRESCENTS) · ELYRIA, OHIO

3 cups sifted flour
½ pound butter or
    margarine
3 egg yolks, beaten
1 package active dry yeast
¼ cup warm, not hot, water
¼ cup warm cream or milk
1 tablespoon sugar
⅛ teaspoon vanilla extract

Blend flour and butter thoroughly, using a pastry blender if desired. Add egg yolks, yeast which has been dissolved in water, and cream. Add sugar and vanilla. Knead thoroughly on well-floured surface. Chill dough if it is too soft to roll easily. Divide into 2 parts and roll each into a 12-inch circle. Cut into 16 pie-shaped pieces. Place a small amount of nut filling on each wedge and, beginning at the rounded edge, roll up. Place on greased baking sheet, point underneath. Let stand for 20 minutes. Brush top of crescents with beaten egg. Bake at 350°F. for 15 to 18 minutes or until light brown.
Yield: 32 crescents.

NUT FILLING:
Combine 1 pound ground walnuts, 6 tablespoons sugar and grated rind of ½ lemon. Stir in ½ cup hot milk.

APRICOT PINWHEELS · MRS. ROY BRADEN, DALLAS, TEX.

1 package active dry yeast
¼ cup warm, not hot, water
¾ cup milk, scalded and
    cooled to lukewarm
½ cup sugar
1½ teaspoons salt
3 eggs, beaten
4½ cups sifted flour
¼ cup shortening,
    melted and cooled
1½ teaspoons grated
    lemon rind
1 pound butter or margarine
½ cup apricot jam
¼ teaspoon cinnamon
1 egg white
1 tablespoon cold water

Dissolve yeast in water; add milk. Blend in sugar and salt, stirring until dissolved. Add eggs. Add half the flour, beating until smooth and elastic. Beat in shortening and lemon rind. Gradually work in remaining flour. Turn onto a lightly floured surface; cover and let rest 15 minutes. Roll out into an oblong ⅛-inch thick. Cover ⅔ of the dough with the butter cut into bits. Fold the uncovered portion over one-half of the buttered portion, then fold over the buttered part, making 3 layers. Repeat 2 or 3 more times, rolling and folding. The greater number of times, the flakier it will be. Chill overnight. Divide dough into 3 pieces. Roll out very thin into an oblong about 15 inches wide. Spread thinly with apricot jam; dust lightly with cinnamon. Roll up as for jelly roll (about 1½ inches thick). Cut into ½-inch slices; place on greased baking sheet. Beat together egg white and water; brush over dough. Allow to rise at room temperature to about one-third its original size. Bake at 400°F. about 15 minutes. Yield: 6 dozen pinwheels.

BUNDKUCHEN (GERMAN FORM CAKE) · MRS. HATTIE THIE, CINCINNATI, OHIO

1 package active dry yeast
1 teaspoon sugar
½ cup warm, not hot, water
1 cup warm milk
2 cups sifted flour
½ pound butter or margarine
1 cup sugar
⅛ teaspoon salt
12 egg yolks
6 tablespoons sifted flour
Almond halves

Dissolve yeast and the 1 teaspoon sugar in warm water; let stand until mixture bubbles. Add milk and the 2 cups flour, beating well. Let stand in warm place until light and bubbly. Cream butter and sugar; add salt. Then add egg yolks, two at a time, beating well. Add a tablespoon of flour between each addition of yolks. Combine with yeast mixture and beat thoroughly. The dough should be stiff enough to hold a spoon upright. If necessary, add more flour. Thickly butter a 9-inch tube pan and line with almond halves. Turn in dough. Cover and let rise in a warm place until doubled in bulk. Bake at 275°F. for about 1 hour and 45 minutes. Yield: 1 9-inch cake.

OLD-TIME STOLLEN · MRS. ROSE IMIG, SHEBOYGAN, WIS.

3½ cups milk
2 packages active dry yeast
½ cup warm, not hot, water
10 cups sifted flour, about
1 teaspoon salt
2¼ cups butter or margarine,
    melted and cooled
1½ cups sugar
2 teaspoons grated
    lemon rind
5 egg yolks
2 ounces brandy
1 pound raisins, chopped
1 pound citron, chopped
1 pound nuts (hickory or
    pecan) chopped
½ pound glacéed cherries,
    chopped
½ pound dates, chopped
½ cup confectioners' sugar

Scald milk and cool to lukewarm. Dissolve yeast in water, add to milk. Add 6 cups of the flour, sifted with salt, to make a soft batter. Let rise until doubled in bulk. Add 1½ cups of the butter, sugar, lemon rind, egg yolks, and brandy, mixing thoroughly. Add remaining 4 cups flour, slowly working it in until the mixture loosens from the bowl. Now knead in fruits and nuts, working in well. Divide mixture into 5 parts. Shape into long ovals and place in greased loaf pans. Slash tops making two rows of slanted slashes down length of oval. Let rise until doubled. Bake at 350°F. for 1 hour.

(The old home way of preparing the stollen, should you prefer, is to divide the dough in half, then roll each piece to about 1-inch thickness, flop one side over to cover half the top.)

When bread is out of the oven and partially cooled, but still warm, spoon over remaining 1 cup melted butter, letting it soak into the loaves. Sprinkle with confectioners' sugar. This bread needs two to three days in cool storage to mellow.

Yield: 5 stollens.

PHILADELPHIA CINNAMON BUNS · HARRIET WORRELL, PHILADELPHIA, PENNA.

1¼ cups milk
¼ cup warm, not hot, water
1 package active dry yeast
5 cups sifted flour, about
1½ teaspoons salt
1 tablespoon sugar
½ cup shortening
¾ cup sugar
2 eggs
¼ cup butter or margarine
½ cup brown sugar
2 teaspoons cinnamon
½ cup chopped walnuts
½ cup raisins or currants
1 cup corn syrup

Scald milk; cool to lukewarm. Dissolve yeast in water and combine with milk. Make a sponge by adding 2 cups of the flour, salt and the 1 tablespoon sugar, beating until smooth. Set aside in a warm place. Beat shortening until light. Whip in the ¾ cup sugar. Add eggs, one at a time, beating each in thoroughly. When the sponge is bubbly gradually beat in shortening mixture. Stir in remaining flour, or enough to make a soft dough. Cover and let rise in a warm place until doubled in bulk.

Divide dough in half and roll each portion to ¼-inch thickness. Spread with softened butter. Sprinkle with mixture of brown sugar and cinnamon. Scatter on the nuts and raisins and dribble with a part of the syrup. Roll as for a jelly roll and cut in 1½-inch lengths. Stand buns in 2 deep 9-inch pans that have been well buttered and filled with corn syrup to a depth of ¼-inch. Cover and let rise until doubled in bulk. Bake at 350°F. about 45 minutes, or until brown. Turn out of pans immediately. Yield: 2 dozen buns.

NEWPORT RAISED DOUGHNUTS · MRS. ELIZABETH LA ROSE, NEWPORT, VT.

¾ cup milk
½ package or cake yeast
    (active dry or
    compressed)
¼ cup warm water (luke-
    warm for compressed)
1 cup sugar
1 teaspoon salt
3 cups sifted flour (about)
⅓ cup shortening
1 egg, beaten
½ teaspoon nutmeg

Scald milk, place in mixing bowl and cool to lukewarm. Dissolve yeast in water, then add to milk. Make a sponge by adding ½ cup sugar, salt and 1 cup flour, beating until smooth. Cover and let rise in a warm place until double in bulk. Melt shortening, cool and add to sponge. Add egg and remaining sugar with nutmeg, mixing well. Add remaining flour (more if necessary) to make a dough stiff enough to roll but not too floury. Let rise in warm place until double in bulk. Turn out on floured board and knead until smooth and elastic. Roll out on lightly floured surface to a rectangle about ½-inch thick. Cut with floured doughnut cutter. Cover and let doughnuts rise on board until double in bulk. Fry in deep fat (350°F.) turning frequently until golden brown. Yield: 24.

Mrs. LaRose uses an old-fashioned wire egg beater to turn the doughnuts; a wooden spoon with slots is a good utensil if you haven't a wire frying basket. Drain on absorbent paper. When almost cold sprinkle with sugar. Leave plain if you plan to dunk in syrup.

Fish and Seafood

CATFISH · MISSOURI

Heads off, insides out. Wash first in salt water, then dry. Dip in milk, dredge in seasoned flour and fry in shallow fat about ½ inch deep, drippings preferred; fry slowly until golden. Remove from fat, place in a warm oven while hush puppies fry.

STUFFED CLAMS · JOHN B. RUSSEL, TREADWAY INN, NORTH FALMOUTH, MASS.

Combine two cups of ocean clams, cleaned and chopped, with two cups coarsely ground dry bread crumbs. Add one teaspoon paprika, two tablespoons grated Swiss cheese (Parmesan, he thinks, is too strong for the delicate flavor of clams) two tablespoons melted butter, a sprinkle of salt. The sweetness of the clam, John tells us, needs a salty touch; now a dash of pepper. Mix in two ounces of dry white wine and the juice of one-fourth lemon. Toss together well and spoon into the washed, dried clam shells. Oven bake at 350°F. for 15 minutes. Add a dot of butter just before serving. A little onion or garlic could be added, but don't overdo on these or you lose the sweet flavor of the clam.

MRS. GEORGE OTTEN'S CLAM FRITTERS · PORTLAND, ORE.

1 cup ground clams,
  fresh or canned
2 tablespoons cracker crumbs
1 egg
Salt
Pepper
½ cup bacon fat

Combine clams and cracker crumbs. Add egg, stirring to mix thoroughly. Season with salt and pepper. Form clam mixture into thin cakes 4 inches wide. Melt fat in skillet. Place cakes in fat and fry each side until golden. Serve immediately, preferably with dill pickles. Yield: 2 portions.

LONG ISLAND CLAM PIE · JEANETTE RATTRAY, EAST HAMPTON, N.Y.

1 cup cubed pared potato
½ large onion,
    coarsely chopped
1 tablespoon butter or
    margarine
1 tablespoon flour
1 tablespoon milk
2 teaspoons lemon juice
1 tablespoon minced parsley
24 large clams,
    finely chopped

1 9-inch pastry shell with top crust

Cook potato and onion in small amount of water until tender; drain. Add butter; stir until melted. Add flour, milk, lemon juice and parsley; mix lightly. Combine with clams. Pour into pastry shell. Cover with top crust. Bake at 450°F. for 15 minutes. Reduce heat to 350°F., bake 20 minutes, or until golden brown. Yield: 6 portions.

CLAM PIE · MRS. JOHN T. RUSSELL, JR., CHATHAM, MASS.

¼ pound salt pork,
    finely diced
5 onions, cut in rings
3 potatoes, peeled and diced
5 pounds clams, minced
3 tablespoons cornstarch
¼ cup cold water
Salt
Clam pie crust

Fry salt pork until crisp. Add onion rings and sauté until dark brown. Add potatoes, which have been boiled just tender in salted water, to clams. Add onion mixture. Make a smooth paste of the cornstarch and water. Stir into clam mixture. Season to taste. Turn mixture into 3 9-inch pie pans and cover with clam piecrust. Flute edges and slit top to allow steam to escape. Bake at 375°F. for 25 to 30 minutes. Yield: three 9-inch pies.

CLAM PIE CRUST:

4 cups sifted flour
1 teaspoon salt
½ teaspoon baking powder
⅔ cup vegetable shortening
⅔ cup butter or margarine
½ cup milk, about

Sift flour, salt and baking powder into bowl. Cut in shortening and butter until mixture resembles coarse meal. Add milk and stir just until dough holds together. Roll out on floured board. Yield: three 9-inch top crusts.

GRANDMA'S FISH BALLS · MILDRED BURRRAGE, WISCASSET, ME.

2 cups salt codfish,
    picked from bones
2 cups sliced raw potatoes
2 eggs, beaten
Salt, pepper
Fat for frying

Cover codfish with cold water and let stand overnight. Drain. Cut fish into mouth-sized pieces. Combine fish and potatoes and cover with water. Simmer until potatoes and fish are cooked. Drain and mash. Add eggs and beat until the mixture is smooth; no lumps should remain. Taste and add salt if needed.

Add pepper to your pleasure. Drop mixture by table-spoonfuls into deep hot fat, 365°F. and cook until light brown, about 1 minute. Cook a few at a time. Drain on absorbent paper. Yield: 18 balls about 2 inches in diameter, or, as Mildred says, "It's fish balls for a family of six: Mother, Dad, two brothers and two little girls all eating their heads off."

PICKED COD DINNER · PARKER HOUSE HOTEL, BOSTON, MASS.

3 pound salt cod fillets
18 white onions
8 small beets
8 carrots
8 potatoes
½ pound salt pork, diced
4 cups egg sauce
2 lemons, sliced
1 tablespoon finely minced
    parsley
¼ teaspoon paprika

Cover fillets with cold water and soak 8 hours, changing water twice. When ready to cook, drain cod and cover with fresh cold water. Bring to boiling point, reduce heat and simmer 30 minutes. Drain, add fresh boiling water and boil 5 minutes. While the cod is cooking, prepare vegetables. Boil each in separate pot so individual flavors are left unimpaired. Cook until just tender; drain, season to taste, dress with butter or margarine. Sprinkle carrots with brown sugar and lightly glaze. Roll the potatoes in parsley. Fry salt pork until crisp and brown. Heat a large platter, one turkey-size. Place fish in the center. At one end arrange hot beets, sliced, and the boiled onions. At opposite end place potatoes and carrots. Over the fish pour the Egg Sauce. On either side of fish lay a row of lemon slices sprinkled with minced parsley. At the last a rosy halo of paprika over the sauce. Pass with the crisply fried salt pork in a gravy boat along with the fat. Yield: 8 portions.

This is an enormously hearty dish, something to stick to your ribs and help keep you young long beyond your time. Day after picked dinner comes the hash to use up the leftovers. Here's the way of the sauce:

EGG SAUCE:
½ cup butter or margarine
½ cup flour
4 cups hot milk
6 hard-cooked eggs
2 teaspoons salt
½ teaspoon pepper
⅛ teaspoon nutmeg

Melt butter and blend in flour. Add milk gradually, stirring constantly, and cook until thick and smooth. Chop eggs, saving one yolk for garnishing. Add chopped eggs and seasonings. Yield: 4 cups sauce.

COD HASH SUPPER · BOSTON, MASS.

4 slices salt pork
3 cups shredded cooked cod
1 onion, finely minced
2 cups chopped cooked beets
Chopped cooked vegetables
Salt and pepper to taste

Fry salt pork until crisp. Remove from pan and reserve pieces to garnish the finished dish. Combine fish and vegetables, and season well. Spread mixture smoothly over the bottom of skillet in which salt pork was fried. Brown slowly. When a crust forms, turn as an omelet. Serve on a hot plate garnished with slices of crisply fried salt pork. Yield: approximately 6 portions. Serve with poached eggs.

GLOUCESTER CODFISH BALLS · MASSACHUSETTS

1 cup dry shredded codfish
2½ cups peeled and
*   diced potatoes*
½ tablespoon butter or
*   margarine*
⅛ teaspoon pepper
1 egg, or 2 egg yolks,
*   slightly beaten*

Soak codfish in cold water for 12 hours. The following morning pour off water, shred fish by placing pieces on cutting board and using fork. Steam, rather than boil, potatoes until tender; drain thoroughly and return to pot in which they were cooked. Shake over heat until dry; mash thoroughly. Add butter and pepper and beat until very light. Add dry flaked codfish and egg and continue beating until mixture is light and fluffy. Add more salt if necessary. Dip with tablespoon and drop into hot deep fat (380°F.) and cook until light brown—about 1 minute. Cook a few at a time. Drain on absorbent paper. Serve with catsup or tartar sauce. Yield: 9 balls, 2 ounces each.

CRAB MEAT LORENZO · CARROLL CORNISH, DALLAS, TEX.

1½ cups cooked crab meat,
*   flaked*
Salt and pepper
Lettuce
½ cup mayonnaise
½ cup heavy cream, whipped
¼ cup catsup
1 teaspoon Worcestershire
*   sauce*
2 tablespoons chopped chives
Paprika
3 hard-cooked eggs, sliced
6 lemon slices

Season crab meat with salt and pepper to taste. Chill. Place on a bed of lettuce. Combine mayonnaise, whipped cream, catsup and Worcestershire sauce. Pour mixture over crab meat and sprinkle with chives and paprika. Garnish with egg and lemon slices. Serve chilled. Yield: 6 portions.

DEVILED CRAB · WINN BRINDLE, WARD'S COVE, ALASKA

1 can (6½ ounces) crab meat,
    drained and flaked
1½ cups small bread cubes
½ cup cream
½ cup milk
½ teaspoon salt
¼ teaspoon dry mustard
⅛ teaspoon pepper
¼ teaspoon Worcestershire
    sauce
1 pimiento, chopped

2 teaspoons butter or margarine
Bread crumbs

Combine all ingredients except butter and bread crumbs. Fill four 5-inch crab-shell casseroles or 6-ounce baking dishes with crab mixture. Dot with butter and sprinkle lightly with bread crumbs. Bake at 375°F. for 20 to 25 minutes.
    Yield: 4 portions.

CREAMED DUNGENESS CRAB AU GRATIN · WINN BRINDLE, WARD'S COVE, ALASKA

2 tablespoons butter or
    margarine
2 tablespoons flour
½ teaspoon salt
⅛ teaspoon pepper
1 cup milk
1 can (6½ ounces) Dungeness
    crab meat, drained and
    flaked
½ cup grated cheese
Bread crumbs

Make a cream sauce from butter, flour, seasonings and milk. Add crab meat. Place in a small greased casserole and cover with cheese and bread crumbs. Bake at 425°F. for 10 minutes or until mixture is hot and crumbs are browned. Yield: 2 to 3 portions.

CRAB MEAT "SNUG HARBOR" · L. S. AYRES CO., INDIANAPOLIS, IND.

½ cup hot medium
    cream sauce
2¼ teaspoons onion juice
1½ teaspoons Worcestershire
    sauce
½ cup cubed fresh bread
½ cup mayonnaise
2 teaspoons lemon juice
Salt and pepper to taste
1¼ pounds fresh lump
    crab meat
2 tablespoons browned butter

Blend cream sauce, onion juice, Worcestershire sauce and bread cubes. Cool. Fold in mayonnaise, lemon juice, salt and pepper. Gently toss crabmeat with butter. Add cream-sauce mixture and fold in lightly. Place in shells or ramekins and brown in a hot oven (450°F.) for 10 to 15 minutes. Serve at once.
    Yield: 8 portions.

CRAB BURGERS · MRS. GORDON S. CLINTON, SEATTLE, WASH.

1 cup flaked crab meat
¼ cup diced celery
2 tablespoons chopped onion
½ cup shredded processed
    Cheddar cheese
½ cup mayonnaise (about)
4 hamburger buns, halved

Combine crab meat, celery, onion, and cheese. Add mayonnaise. Spread on buttered halved hamburger buns. Broil until hot and browned. Yield: 8 burger halves.

DEVILED CRAB · PIRATE HOUSE, SAVANNAH, GA.

1 pound crab meat
1 cup bread crumbs
2 eggs, lightly beaten
½ cup minced celery
½ cup minced green pepper
2 tablespoons lemon juice
1 tablespoon vinegar
1 teaspoon dry mustard
½ teaspoon salt
½ teaspoon black pepper
½ teaspoon hot sauce

1 tablespoon Worcestershire sauce
1 cup butter or margarine, melted

Mix ingredients thoroughly. Stuff into 8 crab shells or ramekins. Bake at 375°F. for 10 to 12 minutes or until piping hot.
    Yield: 8 deviled crabs.

CRAB TIMBALE · MRS. JOHN MINOR WISDOM, NEW ORLEANS, LA.

1 cup cooked crab meat
½ cup minced celery
2⅔ tablespoons chopped
    ripe olives
2⅔ tablespoons minced
    pimiento
2⅔ tablespoon minced
    green pepper
2 envelopes unflavored
    gelatin
1 cup cold milk
1 cup mayonnaise
1 teaspoon onion juice
1 teaspoon Worcestershire
    sauce
¼ teaspoon Tabasco
¾ teaspoon salt
Pinch of pepper

Watercress
6 medium-thick slices tomato
1 cup commercial sour cream
1 tablespoon minced chives
1 2½-ounce jar caviar (optional)

Combine crab meat with celery, olives, pimiento and green pepper. Soften gelatin in cold milk and place over hot water until dissolved; add to mayonnaise. Season with onion juice, Worcestershire, Tabasco, salt and pepper. Combine with crab meat mixture. Pour into six individual molds first rinsed with cold water. Place in refrigerator five hours. Unmold; serve on bed of watercress on tomato slice. Dress with sour cream; garnish with chives or—feeling rich —top each with a spoonful of caviar.
    Yield: 6 portions.

CASEROLE OF BAKED CRAB IMPERIAL · MARY E. TURNER, WASHINGTON, D.C.

¼ cup butter or margarine
¼ cup flour
2 cups milk
1 teaspoon salt
⅛ teaspoon pepper
½ teaspoon celery salt
Dash of cayenne
1 egg yolk, beaten
2 tablespoons sherry wine
1 cup soft bread crumbs
1 pound crab flakes
1 teaspoon minced parsley
1 teaspoon minced onion
¼ cup buttered crumbs
Paprika

Melt butter; add flour and blend. Gradually add milk and seasonings and cook over low heat, stirring constantly, until thickened. Gradually add egg yolk and cook 2 minutes more. Remove from heat and add sherry, soft bread crumbs, crab meat, parsley and onion; mix gently. Pour into well-greased 1½-quart casserole. Top with buttered crumbs and sprinkle with paprika. Bake at 400°F. for 20 to 25 minutes.

Yield: 6 portions.

CRAB SAVANNAH · MRS. R. C. PIGFORD, TULSA, OKLA.

17 to 18 ounces
    frozen crab meat, thawed
4 slices toasted white bread,
    crumbled
5 tablespoons butter or
    margarine, melted
1 tablespoon Worcestershire
    sauce
Few drops Tabasco
¼ teaspoon salt
Dash of pepper
½ cup light cream, about
¼ cup dry bread crumbs

Drain crab meat thoroughly, cut into smaller pieces; mix with crumbled bread. Combine 4 tablespoons of the butter, Worcestershire sauce, Tabasco, salt and pepper. Mix with crab meat. Add enough cream to make a soft mixture. Turn into greased 1½-quart casserole. Combine dry bread crumbs and remaining one tablespoon butter. Sprinkle over casserole. Bake at 325°F. for 30 minutes.

Yield: 6 portions.

MRS. BRADLEY'S SOFT SHELL CRABS · FREDERICK STIEFF, BALTIMORE, MD.

12 small soft-shell crabs
Salt and pepper
Flour
½ pound butter or margarine
Tartar sauce

Clean crabs thoroughly, wash and wipe dry. Season highly with salt and pepper. Dust with flour. Have butter in pan at boiling point. Place crabs in pan and turn frequently until nicely browned, allowing 3 to 4 minutes cooking time on each side. Serve at once with tartar sauce.

Yield: 6 to 12 portions.

CRAB CUSTARD · DUNCAN HINES

1 teaspoon grated onion
4 tablespoons butter or
    margarine
4 tablespoons flour
1 teaspoon salt
Few grains pepper
4 cups milk
½ cup light cream
1 dash Tabasco
1 teaspoon A-1 sauce
4 eggs
1 tablespoon sherry wine

3 cups crab meat
1 cup buttered crumbs

Cook onion in butter in top of double boiler. Blend in flour, salt and pepper. Add milk, cream, Tabasco and A-1 sauce. Cook, over boiling water, stirring constantly, until thickened. Beat eggs. Add sherry and milk mixture, stirring constantly. Put crab meat into greased, 1½-quart casserole. Add sauce. Sprinkle with buttered crumbs. Bake at 325°F. for 1 hour, or until inserted knife comes out clean. If desired, garnish top with avocado slices and ripe olives. Yield: 6 portions.

CRAB-CHEESE DELIGHT · BRUNSWICK, GA.

2 tablespoons butter or
    margarine
2 tablespoons minced green
    pepper
2 tablespoons flour
½ teaspoon dry mustard
½ teaspoon salt
1 cup strained, stewed
    tomatoes
1 cup grated American
    cheese
1 egg, slightly beaten

¾ cup milk
1 cup flaked, cooked crab meat
Toast triangles

Melt butter. Add green pepper and sauté until almost tender. Add flour, mustard and salt and blend thoroughly. Add tomatoes, cheese and egg. Cook slowly, stirring constantly, until cheese is almost melted. Gradually add milk, mixing well, then crab meat. Cook over low heat until thickened, stirring constantly. Serve on toast triangles. Yield: 4 portions.

CRAB OMELET · MRS. R. C. PIGFORD, TULSA, OKLA.

2 cans (6½ ounces) crab meat
6 scallions, minced
½ cup minced celery
2 tablespoons minced parsley
⅛ teaspoon salt
Dash of pepper
Few drops Tabasco
7 eggs, separated

Drain crab meat, flake; remove bony tissue. Add scallions, celery, parsley, salt, pepper and Tabasco. Mix. Beat egg yolks well, stir into fish mixture. Beat egg whites until stiff peaks are formed; fold into fish mixture. Melt butter in a 9-inch skillet. Add omelet mixture. Cook over low heat until omelet is set, about 10 minutes. With spatula or knife release omelet from sides of pan. Broil until top is puffy and light golden

2 tablespoons butter or
 margarine

brown, about 5 minutes. Remove. Continue cooking over low heat 5 minues. Serve immediately. Yield: 6 portions.

 NOTE: Crab mixture may be prepared in the morning and chilled in refrigerator until a half hour before mixing with beaten eggs.

CRAYFISH A LA CREOLE · VICTORIA TOUCHTONE, AMITE, LA.

1 large onion, chopped
2 cloves garlic, minced
½ cup oil
1 can (6 ounces)
 tomato paste
1 can (1 pound, 4 ounces)
 tomatoes
3 cups hot water
Salt to taste
Dash of cayenne
2 pounds fresh crayfish or
 shrimp, or rock lobster
 (boiled and peeled)

 Fry onion and garlic in oil until soft and yellow. Add tomato paste and tomatoes, crushing the whole tomatoes into the sauce. Cook until the fat spreads over top of sauce, about 30 minutes. Add water and seasonings, then crayfish (or shrimp or rock lobster cut into small chunks). Simmer until sauce is medium-thick, 1 to 1½ hours. Serve hot with dry cooked rice.
 Yield: 4 portions.

CRAWFISH NEWBURG · MRS. ROBERT EUGENE OTTO, KEY WEST, FLA.

2 pounds crawfish or
 rock-lobster tails
Boiling water
12 whole allspice
1 bay leaf
1 teaspoon salt
¼ teaspoon pepper
3 tablespoons butter or
 margarine
2 tablespoons flour
1 cup light cream
½ cup milk
3 tablespoons tomato catsup
2 teaspoons Worcestershire
 sauce
¼ teaspoon paprika
¼ teaspoon garlic salt
3 tablespoons sherry wine

 Place crawfish in 3-quart kettle; half cover with boiling water. Add allspice, bay leaf, salt and pepper. Cover. Cook 20 minutes. Cool in cooking water. Shell by splitting crawfish tail down the back; remove meat; cut lengthwise three times, then cut crosswise and remove meat in small pieces. Melt butter in top of double boiler over direct heat. Stir in flour and mix to a paste. Gradually stir in cream until smooth and add milk. Stir until medium thick. Add catsup and Worcestershire sauce. Set aside over boiling water. Add meat to cream sauce with paprika and garlic salt. Reheat just before serving, adding sherry. Serve on mound of One-One Fried Rice. (see next page)
 Yield: 4 portions.

ONE-ONE FRIED RICE

4 tablespoons oil
1 cup rice
1½ teaspoons salt
2½ cups boiling water

Pour oil into large frying pan, tipping pan to cover entire surface. Add unwashed rice and place over low heat, stirring from time to time, until all kernels are opaque, about 20 to 25 minutes. Add salt. When all kernels are white, increase heat and let the rice cook until golden brown, stirring constantly. Again, reduce heat low and add boiling water. Increase heat and bring to a boil for 1 minute. Reduce heat and cook about 20 minutes longer. The rice comes out, each grain 'one-one' as the Key Westers say, meaning each kernel separate. Yield: 4 portions.

HALIBUT WITH ONION AND BACON · GENERAL FRANK DORN, SAN FRANCISCO, CALIF.

¼ pound butter or margarine
1 cup white wine
6 boned halibut steaks, or
    whitefish, shark,
    barracuda or similar fish
6 slices large Bermuda onion
12 half slices of bacon
Salt and pepper

Melt butter in roasting pan. Add wine and bring mixture to a boil. Form fish steaks into patties about 3 inches thick and 3 inches in diameter; secure with a pick if necessary. Place patties in wine sauce. On each patty place a slice of onion and cross with two slices of bacon. Salt and pepper to taste. Bake, uncovered, at 400°F. for 15 minutes. Then cover and cook at 350°F. for 20 minutes, or until fish is tender. Serve with the pan juices and tartar sauce. Yield: 6 portions.

ROCKLAND LOBSTER NEWBURG · MRS. JOHN M. RICHARDSON, ROCKLAND, ME.

9 egg yolks, slightly beaten
3 cups heavy cream
¾ cup milk
¼ cup flour
¾ cup butter or margarine
3 cups lobster meat or
    cooked meat of 3 fresh
    lobsters (1½ pounds each)
1 teaspoon salt
3 tablespoons sherry wine

Combine egg yolks, cream and milk and heat to scalding in top of double boiler, stirring occasionally. Blend flour and soft butter to a paste and gradually add to egg-yolk mixture, stirring until well blended. Add lobster meat and salt. Cook, stirring constantly until thickened, about 10 minutes. Add sherry. Serve on toast points. Yield: 8 portions.

CROWN OF LOBSTER · "21" CLUB, NEW YORK CITY

4 lobsters, 2½ pounds each
2 cups thick cream sauce
4 egg whites, stiffly beaten
¼ cup brandy, sherry, or
*   white wine*
Salt
Pepper
Dash of Worcestershire sauce
Cayenne pepper
Red food coloring
2 or 3 truffles, sliced thin
White of 1 hard-cooked egg

Parboil lobsters for 3 minutes. Cool. Remove meat and run 3 times through fine grinder. Press or pound through fine sieve to form paste-like substance. Place in bowl buried to the rim in another bowl of chopped ice. Add cream sauce slowly; mix well. Fold in egg whites gradually. Blend in brandy. Season with salt and pepper, Worcestershire and cayenne. Add a dash of food coloring to give a rosy color.

Butter 2-quart metal mold and chill. Decorate bottom with sliced truffles cut in any desired shape, arranging alternately with pieces of egg white cut as desired. Pour lobster mixture into mold. Place in refrigerator and chill 3 hours. Then cover mold with buttered wax paper; fasten tightly.

Place mold in a container, just large enough to receive it comfortably, in which there is an inch of *boiling* water. Bake at 375°F. for 35 minutes or until firm. Turn mold upside down on a hot platter, unmold. Slice and serve with Sauce Cardinal or any other sauce you may prefer.

Yield: 8 portions.

SAUCE CARDINAL

1 boiled lobster, 2½ pounds
¼ cup diced truffles
¼ cup butter or margarine
1 full Delmonico glass of
*   brandy*
3 cups Fish Velouté*
1 cup heavy cream
3 tablespoons Lobster Butter
*   (recipe below)*

Remove meat from lobster and dice. Combine with truffles. Sauté in butter a few minutes. Add brandy and flame. Add Fish Velouté and cream. Cook slowly until sauce is of medium thickness. Add lobster butter and mix well. Serve hot.

LOBSTER BUTTER:

Melt about 1 pound butter over hot water; skim top, let rest. Pound lobster shells and add to butter with lobster lungs. Simmer for 3 hours. Strain. Leftover butter may be frozen if desired. Yield: about 1½ cups.

* Fish Velouté is a strong fish stock slightly thickened with flour.

FRIED OYSTERS · MRS. SMITHERS, EASTERN SHORE, MD.

3 dozen fresh shelled oysters
  and juice
1 pound lard
2 eggs, beaten
¼ cup oyster juice
½ teaspoon salt
½ teaspoon coarsely ground
  black pepper
Cracker meal

Be sure oysters have some juice. When ready to cook them strain the liquid through cheesecloth, and save ¼ cup of it. Wash oysters and drain well. In a deep iron frying pan or deep fat fryer, melt lard but do not bring to the smoking point. To the beaten eggs add the reserved oyster juice, salt and pepper. Place a generous pile of cracker meal on a sheet of waxed paper. At this point heat the lard until it becomes smoky hot, or registers 350°F. to 375°F. Roll a few oysters at a time first in the cracker meal, then into the egg mixture, again in the cracker meal and then into the hot fat. Watch out, for they may splatter a bit. Cook 3 to 4 minutes or until a rich, golden brown. Remove from pan with 2-pronged fork and drain on absorbent paper. Keep warm until all oysters are fried, then serve at once on a hot serving platter accompanied by homemade mustard pickle, if desired. Yield: 6 to 8 portions.

OYSTERS À LA ROCKEFELLER · MRS. WILLIAM KENT, MEMPHIS, TENN.

2 pounds fresh spinach
1 head Boston lettuce
2 bunches scallions
2 bunches Pascal celery
1 bunch parsley
Water
1 pound butter or
  margarine
1 cup dry bread crumbs
Salt to taste
1 teaspoon Tabasco
1 tablespoon anchovy paste
1½ pounds rock salt
3 dozen oysters, half-shell
½ cup grated Parmesan
  cheese
6 lemon quarters

Wash and clean vegetables, removing ribs and stem ends of spinach. Cut tops from scallions leaving 2 inches of green; remove strings from celery; pick parsley leaves from stem. Chop vegetables together very fine. Add just enough water to cover, butter, ½ cup crumbs, salt, Tabasco and anchovy paste. Cook until thick, about 1½ hours. Make beds of rock salt in 6 shallow 8-inch metal pie pans. Place in 450°F. oven until salt is crackling hot. Place 6 oysters, half-shell, in each pie pan and run under broiler 5 minutes or until edges start curling. At this point cover each bivalve with a generous serving of sauce. Sprinkle on remaining ½ cup crumbs combined with Parmesan cheese and run under broiler until topping is browned. Serve at once, a pan of 6 to a guest with a quarter of lemon. Yield: 6 portions.

OYSTERS À LA ROCKEFELLER · ANTOINE'S, NEW ORLEANS, LA.

5 tablespoons butter or
  margarine
5 tablespoons finely minced
  spinach
2 tablespoons finely minced
  onion
1½ tablespoons minced
  cooked lettuce
2 teaspoons minced celery
3 tablespoons fine dry bread
  crumbs
¼ teaspoon herb blend
  (for fish)
¼ teaspoon anchovy paste
¼ teaspoon salt
Few grains pepper
24 oysters on half shell

Heat butter. Add spinach, onion, lettuce, celery, crumbs, herb blend, anchovy paste, salt and pepper. Mix well. Remove oysters from shell. Scrub oyster shells; boil to be sure every particle of sand has been washed away. Set 6 shells on each of 4 pie plates holding rock salt. Place oysters in each shell. Broil slowly 5 minutes. Place spoonfuls of spinach mixture on each oyster. Broil until thoroughly heated. Serve immediately. Yield: 4 portions.

CAPTAIN CHRIS OYSTER PIE · CAPTAIN CHRIS JENSEN, GREENPORT, N.Y.

1 cup sliced mushrooms
3 tablespoons butter or
  margarine
3 tablespoons flour
1 cup milk
½ teaspoon salt
¼ teaspoon celery salt
Dash of pepper
1 teaspoon lemon juice
1 pint bluepoint oysters
Biscuit dough

Cook mushrooms in butter until partially tender. Stir in flour. Add milk gradually and cook until thickened, stirring constantly. Add seasonings, lemon juice and oysters. Line bottom and sides of 1-quart casserole with about ⅔ biscuit dough, rolled ⅛-inch thick. Fill with oyster mixture and cover with remaining dough. Press edges of dough together with fork dipped in flour. Make slits in top to allow escape of steam. Bake at 450°F. for 15 minutes, then reduce heat to 350°F. and bake 10 to 15 minutes longer. Yield: 4 portions.

BISCUIT DOUGH:

1 cup sifted flour
1 teaspoon baking powder
¼ teaspoon salt
3 tablespoons shortening
6 tablespoons milk

Sift together flour, baking powder and salt. Cut in shortening. Add milk gradually, stirring until a soft dough is formed. Turn out on lightly floured surface and knead about 30 seconds.

NEW YORK'S OYSTER PIE · GRAND CENTRAL STATION OYSTER BAR, NEW YORK CITY

6 tablespoons diced salt pork
1 tablespoon grated onion
2 tablespoons chopped
    green pepper
6 tablespoons sliced
    mushrooms
3 cups milk
3 cups oyster liquor
6 tablespoons flour
¼ cup butter or margarine
Salt to taste
3½ dozen oysters, cleaned
12 whole small onions,
    cooked
30 potato balls,
    cooked just tender
½ recipe biscuit dough

Cook salt pork until lightly browned. Add onion, green pepper, and mushrooms; sauté 10 minutes. Heat milk and oyster liquor over hot water. Make a smooth paste of flour and butter. Add to milk mixture a little at a time, stirring constantly, until sauce comes to a boil and is slightly thickened. Add vegetable mixture and salt. Add oysters and heat until edges curl. In each of six individual serving dishes arrange seven oysters, two onions, five potato balls and one cup sauce. Cover each casserole with biscuit crust. Bake at 425°F. for 15 to 20 minutes, or until brown.

Yield: 6 pies.

OYSTERS BROCHETTE · ANTOINE'S, NEW ORLEANS, LA.

10 bacon slices
36 shucked raw oysters
Seasoned flour
⅔ cup butter or margarine
⅓ cup olive oil
12 toast triangles
1 teaspoon chopped parsley
1 teaspoon lemon juice

Cut bacon in 1-inch pieces. Sauté until partially cooked, turning to cook both sides and draining off fat as it accumulates in skillet. On each of 6 skewers string 6 pieces of bacon alternating with 6 oysters (sticking skewer through eye of oyster). Roll in flour. Heat butter and olive oil; add skewered food. Sauté, turning to cook on all sides. Lay each skewer on 2 toast triangles. Add parsley and lemon juice to butter in skillet; pour over each portion. Yield: 6 portions.

OLD SOUTHERN BAKED OYSTERS · MARY MC KAY, VICKSBURG, MISS.

2 quarts oysters, drained
½ cup finely chopped parsley
½ cup finely chopped
    shallots or onions
Salt and pepper
Tabasco
1 tablespoon Worcestershire
    sauce
2 tablespoons lemon juice
½ cup melted butter or
    margarine

2 cups fine cracker crumbs
Paprika
¾ cup half and half (milk and cream)

Place a layer of oysters in bottom of greased shallow 2-quart baking dish. Sprinkle with half of parsley, shallots, seasonings, lemon juice, butter and crumbs. Make another layer of the same ingredients. Sprinkle with paprika. Just before baking, pour the milk into evenly spaced holes, being careful not to moisten crumb topping all over. Bake at 375°F. for about 30 minutes or until firm. Yield: 12 to 15 portions.

KING'S ARMS TAVERN ESCALLOPED OYSTERS · WILLIAMSBURG, VA.

1 quart oysters
½ cup butter or margarine
¾ cup flour
1 tablespoon paprika
1 teaspoon salt
½ teaspoon black pepper
¼ cup chopped onion
¼ cup finely chopped
    green pepper
½ teaspoon chopped garlic
2 teaspoons lemon juice
1 tablespoon Worcestershire
    sauce
2 tablespoons cracker crumbs

Pick over oysters and heat in enough oyster liquor and water to make 1½ cups. Melt butter, add flour; cook for 5 minutes, stirring constantly. Add paprika, salt, pepper; cook for 3 minutes. Add onion, green pepper, garlic; cook slowly for 5 minutes. Remove from heat. Add lemon juice, Worcestershire, oysters and liquor; blend. Transfer to a 1½-quart baking dish. Sprinkle crumbs on top. Bake at 400°F. for 30 minutes.
    Yield: 6 to 8 portions.

LONG ISLAND OYSTER FRITTERS · GREENPORT, L. I.

2 cups sifted floor
1 tablespoon baking powder
1 cup milk
2 eggs, beaten
1 tablespoon chopped parsley
1 teaspoon chives
Salt and pepper to taste
1 dozen large oysters,
    chopped
Butter or margarine for
    frying

Sift flour and baking powder. Mix milk and eggs. Add to dry ingredients, mixing well. Blend in parsley, chives and seasonings. Add chopped oysters, blending in thoroughly. Melt butter in skillet. Drop batter by tablespoonfuls in pan to form small pancakes. Brown well on both sides. Serve very hot. Yield: 4 portions.

MRS. JENSEN'S PAN ROAST OF OYSTERS · GREENPORT, N.Y.

4 tablespoons butter or
    margarine
¼ teaspoon Worcestershire
    sauce
½ teaspoon salt
Dash of pepper
1 pint oysters
½ cup chili sauce

½ cup heavy cream
4 slices toast

Combine butter, Worcestershire sauce, salt and pepper in saucepan. Add oysters and simmer gently until edges of oysters begin to curl. Add chili sauce and cream and heat thoroughly. Serve at once on hot buttered toast. Yield: 4 portions.

CURRIED OYSTERS · GREENPORT, N.Y.

3 dozen oysters
2 tablespoons butter or
*   margarine*
2 tablespoons flour
Oyster liquor
Light cream
1 cup milk
½ teaspoon salt
½ teaspoon curry powder
Cayenne pepper
1 bay leaf
4 cups hot cooked rice
Chopped parsley
Chutney

Pat oysters dry with absorbent paper. Melt butter and blend in flour. To oyster liquor add enough cream to make 1 cup liquid. Add to flour mixture with milk, and cook, stirring constantly, until mixture thickens. Reduce heat. Add seasonings and simmer 15 minutes. Place pan over hot water and add oysters. Season rice to taste, if desired, with salt and pepper, melted butter and a little grated onion. Place in a circle on hot platter. Pour oyster mixture in center. Garnish with chopped parsley. Serve with chutney. Yield: 6 portions.

OYSTER PAN ROAST · GRAND CENTRAL STATION OYSTER BAR, NEW YORK CITY

4 dozen oysters, cleaned
½ pound butter or margarine
6 tablespoons chili sauce
2 teaspoons Worcestershire
*   sauce*
1½ tablespoons lemon juice
1½ cups oyster liquor
½ teaspoon celery salt
1 teaspoon paprika
¼ cup light cream
Salt to taste

Place oysters in a deep pan. Dot with butter. Add sauces, lemon juice, oyster liquor, and seasonings; bring to boiling point and cook 1 minute, stirring constantly. Add cream and bring to boiling point. Salt to taste. Serve over toast squares in soup plates. Yield: 6 portions.

POMPANO OR FLOUNDER AU GRATIN · MRS. CHARLES HOWELL, JR.
JACKSONVILLE, FLA.

2 pounds pompano or
*   flounder*
1 quart cold water
1 bay leaf
Few allspice berries
1 teaspoon salt
Few grains pepper

Have market man fillet the fish. Ask to have head, tail, skin and bones; cover these with cold water. Add bay leaf, allspice, salt and pepper. Bring to a boil; simmer, uncovered, reducing stock to 1½ cups. Strain stock. Reserve pieces of fish that flake off the bones. Place fish fillets in buttered, shallow baking dish or platter. Sprinkle with lemon juice and salt, and dot

2 tablespoons lemon juice
4 tablespoons butter or
    margarine
3 tablespoons flour
½ cup cream
1½ cups fish stock
2 egg yolks
2 tablespoons cold butter or
    margarine
2 teaspoons finely chopped
    parsley
2 dozen small boiled shrimp
2 tablespoons grated
    Cheddar cheese

with 2 tablespoons butter. Cover with waxed paper. Bake 425°F. for 7 to 10 minutes. Melt remaining 2 tablespoons butter; blend in flour. Gradually add cream, mixing to smooth paste. Add stock. Simmer over low heat 10 minutes, stirring occasionally. Beat egg yolks; add sauce gradually. Add cold butter, fish bits saved from stock pot and parsley. Pour sauce over cooked fillets. Garnish with shrimp and sprinkle with cheese. Return to oven until cheese is browned.

Yield: 6 portions.

POMPANO EN PAPILLOTTE · ANTOINE'S, NEW ORLEANS, LA.

3 medium-sized pompano
3 cups water
1 chopped shallot, or
    2 tablespoons chopped
    onion
5 tablespoons butter or
    margarine
2¼ cups white wine
1 cup crab meat
1 cup diced cooked shrimp
½ clove garlic, minced
1½ cups chopped onion
Pinch thyme
1 bay leaf
2 cups fish stock
2 tablespoons flour
2 egg yolks
Salt and pepper to taste

Clean pompano; cut into 6 fillets, removing head and backbone. Combine head, bones, and water; simmer until there are two cups stock. Sauté shallot and fillets in 2 tablespoons butter. Add 2 cups wine. Cover. Simmer gently until fillets are tender, about 5 to 8 minutes. Sauté crab meat, shrimp and ¼ clove garlic in 1 tablespoon butter. Add onion, remaining ¼ clove garlic; cook 10 minutes. Add thyme, bay leaf and 1¾ cups fish stock. Simmer 10 minutes. Blend together 2 tablespoons butter and flour; gradually add remaining ¼ cup fish stock. Add to crab meat mixture with wine stock drained from fillets. Cook, stirring constantly, until thickened. Beat egg yolks; add hot sauce and ¼ cup wine. Mix thoroughly. Place in refrigerator to chill until firm. Cut 6 parchment-paper hearts 8 inches long and 12 inches wide. Oil well; place spoonfuls of sauce on one side of heart; lay poached fillet on sauce. Fold over. Hand-seal edges. Lay sealed hearts on an oiled baking sheet. Bake at 450°F. for 15 minutes, or until paper hearts are browned. Serve immediately in paper hearts. Yield: 6 portions.

NOTE: Fresh salmon, sea trout, or striped bass may be used instead of pompano.

FRESH POACHED SALMON · CONNECTICUT

3 quarts water
3 tablespoons vinegar
2 medium onions, minced
2 small carrots, minced
8 peppercorns
2½ teaspoons salt
4 celery leaves
6 sprigs parsley
1 sprig thyme
1 bay leaf
4 pounds fresh salmon
2 hard-cooked egg yolks,
    sieved
Parsley for garnish

Pour water into a large pot. Add vinegar, onions, carrots, peppercorns (slightly bruised), and salt. Tie herbs in cheesecloth bag, add to pot. Bring water to boiling, then simmer 30 minutes. Wipe salmon with a clean damp cloth. Wrap in a square of cheesecloth to keep shape during cooking and place in bouillon. Cover. Cook slowly, allowing 8 to 10 minutes to the pound. Take fish from pot; remove cloth, place on hot platter. Sprinkle with egg yolks and garnish with parsley. Serve with a side dish of egg sauce.

Or, serve salmon cold if you like, with a garnish of watercress and lemon slices. Pass with a sauce made of sour cream blended with finely cut scallions.

Yield: 8 to 12 portions.

CREAMY EGG SAUCE:

4 hard-cooked egg yolks
¼ teaspoon salt
¼ teaspoon paprika
½ cup butter, or margarine,
    creamed
2 tablespoons heavy cream
2 teaspoons lemon juice

Rub egg yolks to a paste. Blend in salt and paprika. Gradually work in creamed butter, cream, and lemon juice. Yield: about 1 cup sauce.

SALMON PATTIES · ASTORIA, ORE.

1 can (1 pound) salmon,
    drained and flaked
4 eggs
2 tablespoons cream
⅓ to ½ cup bread crumbs
½ teaspoon salt
Pinch of pepper
2 tablespoons cold water
Bread crumbs for coating
Butter or margarine
2 cups medium white sauce
½ cup finely cut celery

Combine salmon, 2 of the eggs slightly beaten, cream, bread crumbs, salt and pepper. Mix and shape into 12 flat cakes. Beat slightly remaining 2 eggs with water. Dip cakes into egg and coat lightly with crumbs. Sauté in butter until well browned on both sides. Serve on hot toast with sauce to which celery is added.

Yield: 4 portions.

SALMON IN DILL · CONNECTICUT

1 salmon steak (2 pounds)
¼ cup butter or margarine
⅓ cup minced fresh dill
¼ teaspoon salt
½ cup water
⅓ cup dry white wine
1 tablespoon lemon juice
1 tablespoon flour
1 cup light cream

Wipe salmon with damp cloth and cut into 1-inch cubes. Melt 2 tablespoons of the butter. Add salmon, sprinkle with dill and salt. Add water, and lemon juice. Simmer 15 minutes, stirring gently once or twice. Melt remaining butter, add flour and stir to a smooth paste. Gradually add cream and cook over low heat heat until smooth and slightly thickened, stirring constantly. Add to fish and heat through but do not boil. Serve at once. Yield: 6 portions.

BAKED STUFFED SALMON · MRS. DAVID GAISER, SPOKANE, WASH.

1 (10- to 12-pound) salmon
1 tablespoon salt
3 tablespoons lemon juice
1 cup chopped celery
1 cup chopped celery leaves
2 small onions, finely
*   chopped*
¼ cup butter or margarine
½ pound mushrooms, sliced
1 loaf whole-wheat bread,
*   crumbed*
2 teaspoons poultry seasoning
1 teaspoon salt
⅛ teaspoon pepper
1 bottle (8 ounce) stuffed
*   olives, chopped*

Ask the fish man to clean, bone and scale salmon. Rub fish well inside and out with salt; sprinkle with lemon juice. To prepare stuffing: sauté celery, leaves, and onions in butter until onion is transparent. Add mushrooms; cook 5 minutes longer. Combine with crumbs. Add seasonings and olives. Place stuffing in one side of salmon; sew fish together. Lay fish on greased baking sheet. Bake at 425°F. allowing 10 minutes per pound. Baste frequently. The fish should be tender but not dry. Serve with a rich white sauce combined with hard-cooked egg slices.

Yield: 15 to 20 portions.

SALMON SOUFFLÉ · ASTORIA, ORE.

1 cup medium cream sauce
2 tablespoons minced parsley
¼ teaspoon Worcestershire
*   sauce*
1 tablespoon sherry wine
Onion juice to taste
2 eggs, separated
1 can (1 pound) salmon,
*   drained and flaked*

Prepare cream sauce. Mix in parsley, Worcestershire, sherry and onion juice. Remove from heat immediately and add beaten egg yolks. Return to heat and cook 1 minute. Gently fold in flaked salmon followed by the stiffly beaten egg whites. Pour into greased 1½-quart baking dish. Bake at 350°F. for 45 minutes.

Yield: 4 portions.

SALMON BOX · ASTORIA, ORE.

2 cups cooked rice
2 cups thin white sauce,
    seasoned with ¼ teaspoon
    Worcestershire sauce
1 can (1 pound) salmon,
    drained and flaked
½ cup buttered bread crumbs

Line the bottom of a greased 1½-quart baking dish with rice. Then layer white sauce and salmon alternately, ending with sauce. Cover with crumbs. Bake at 350°F. about 20 minutes or until crumbs are browned.

Yield: 4 portions.

BAKED SHAD · MRS. HELEN DUPREY BULLOCK, WASHINGTON, D.C.

1 5- or 6-pound roe shad
1 extra shad roe
1 tablespoon mild vinegar
½ teaspoon salt
1 bay leaf
2 or 3 sprigs parsley
¼ cup butter or margarine
1 mild onion, finely minced
½ cup flour
1 cup milk
1 cup chopped parsley
¼ cup white wine (optional)
3 eggs, separated
1 teaspoon salt
Juice of 1 lemon
Salt
Paprika
Lemon juice
Butter or margarine
Flour

Have the market prepare the shad by splitting open (not dividing in half) and removing the spine and bones. Oil the outside well and place flat, skin down, on the broiler on a piece of aluminum foil. In the meantime prepare the roe by parboiling very gently in water to cover to which has been added the vinegar, salt, bay leaf and parsley. When the roe becomes firm, drain. Remove membrane. Melt the ¼ cup butter in a heavy frying pan; add onion and cook until clear. Add roe, breaking it gently with a fork, and cook until the small eggs are separated and well coated with butter. Add the ½ cup flour and milk. Cook and stir until thickened. Remove from heat. Add chopped parsley, wine and 3 egg yolks, slightly beaten (stir some of the warm mixture into yolks before adding to prevent curdling). Add salt, lemon juice and fold in the 3 egg whites which have been stiffly beaten.

In the meantime, sprinkle the shad with salt, paprika, lemon juice, dot generously with butter and sprinkle lightly with flour. Bake at 350°F. about 12 minutes to the pound. Remove from oven, spread the roe mixture over the inner portions of entire fish; dot with butter and paprika. Return to over for about 10 minutes. Place under the broiler until the soufflé is delicately browned. Yield: 10 to 12 portions.

NOTE: If you are one who must keep a strict eye on the budget, substitute buck shad for the roe shad or use any large white fish. Buy fresh herring roe to pinch hit for the shad roe. Roe of herring comes in 12-ounce tins; drain well. Prepare as recipe directs after the parboiling.

MEXICAN RICE WITH SHRIMP · MRS. HOWARD S. WILLIAMS, HATTIESBURG, MISS.

1 cup raw long grain rice
4 tablespoons shortening
1 medium onion, chopped
¼ cup chopped green pepper
1 can (1 pound) tomatoes,
    sieved
1 cup water
1 teaspoon salt
Dash of cayenne
2 dozen cooked shrimp,
    shelled

Wash rice and dry on towel. Heat shortening in heavy pan; add rice and stir constantly until a deep golden brown. Add onion and cook until transparent. Add green pepper, stirring for a few seconds. Add tomato purée, water, salt and cayenne. Cover and cook over low heat, without stirring, until every grain is separate (15 to 20 minutes). Add shrimp a few minutes before serving. Heat.

Yield: 6 portions.

SHRIMP JAMBALAYA · MRS. DELAWARE VOLLRATH, FRANKLIN, LA.

2 pounds raw shrimp
Salt and pepper
3 tablespoons fat
1 tablespoon flour
3 to 4 cups stock (shrimp,
    ham or chicken)
1 green pepper, finely
    chopped
6 scallions, finely chopped
4 stalks celery, finely
    chopped
2 dozen oysters
1½ cups diced, cooked ham

1 cup diced, cooked chicken (pieces about the size of half a medium shrimp)
4 to 6 cups cooked rice

Shell and clean shrimp. Cover with cold water; season with salt and pepper. Cook until shrimp are tender, about 5 minutes; drain, saving stock. Melt fat in pan, stir in flour, blend in hot stock. Add vegetables and oysters and simmer a few minutes until tender. Add shrimp, ham, chicken and rice. Stir until piping hot. Turn onto a hot platter and decorate with parsley, hearts of celery, radishes and scallions. Brandied peaches are good with this. Jambalaya is usually served with an aspic salad. Yield: 6 to 8 portions.

MISSISSIPPI RIVER JAMBALAYA · HELEN RUCH, PITTSBURGH, PENNA.

½ cup finely diced onion
2 cloves garlic, minced
2 tablespoons shortening
½ cup shredded raw ham
1 dozen shrimps, cleaned
½ cup diced tomatoes (or
    condensed tomato soup)
3 cups meat stock or hot
    water
½ cup raw rice
1 tablespoon minced parsley

1 tablespoon minced celery tops
¼ teaspoon thyme
½ bay leaf
Salt and pepper

Sauté onion and garlic in shortening until tender. Add ham strips and shrimps and brown slightly. Add tomatoes and stock. Heat mixture and when boiling add rice and remaining ingredients. Simmer gently until rice is almost dry, about 20 minutes. Yield: 4 portions.

KEY WEST SHRIMP SAUTÉ · TRADE WINDS RESTAURANT, KEY WEST, FLA.

48 raw jumbo shrimp
½ cup butter or margarine
1 garlic clove
3 tablespoons finely chopped
*   parsley*
½ cup sherry wine

Peel and clean shrimp. Heat butter; add garlic and cook 2 minutes, then remove garlic. Add shrimp, sauté 5 minutes over medium heat or until shrimp are pink. Remove shrimp to hot platter. Now add parsley and sherry to butter; increase heat and sauté 30 seconds. Serve sauce over shrimp.

Yield 6 portions.

ADELAIDE VAN WEY'S SHRIMP-AVOCADO · NORTH CAROLINA

5 medium avocados
¾ cup French dressing
3 pounds cooked shrimp,
*   cleaned*
¼ cup butter, melted
1¾ cups cornflakes, finely
*   rolled*
5 slices bacon
2 cups rock salt

Cut avocados into halves and remove pits. With fingers rub inside of fruit with French dressing, pressing gently not to bruise the flesh. (The French dressing should be made with cider vinegar, pure olive oil, seasoned with salt, paprika, a dash of catsup and freshly ground pepper.) Pack shrimp into avocado halves and dribble one tablespoon of the dressing over each "cradle." Pour over melted butter. Cover with cornflakes, tucking these around and over the shrimp. Now lay on one-half slice of raw bacon to a shell. Spread rock salt on bottom of baking pan. Place filled avocado halves on salt. Bake at 350°F. for 15 minutes. Run under a broiler for two minutes to brown bacon.

Yield: 10 portions.

STEWED SHRIMP À LA CREOLE · MRS. CAROLINE WEISS, KISKATOM, LA.

2 tablespoons butter or
*   margarine*
1 tablespoon flour
2 onions, finely chopped
2 pounds peeled raw shrimp
6 tomatoes or 1¼ cups canned
1 cup water
1 green pepper, diced
1 teaspoon fresh thyme or ½
*   teaspoon dried*
2 teaspoons fresh parsley,
*   chopped, or 1 teaspoon*
*   dried*

1 bay leaf or ½ teaspoon powdered
½ teaspoon garlic salt
Salt and pepper to taste
1½ cups cooked rice

Melt butter, add flour gradually and cook to light brown. Add onions and sauté until golden. Add shrimp and mix well. Let cool slightly. Add tomatoes, water, green pepper and seasonings. Cook, stirring frequently, 10 minutes. Serve over rice in soup plates. Yield: 6 portions.

SHRIMP MULL · THE CLOISTER, SEA ISLAND, GA.

3 bacon slices
1½ cups diced onion
1 green pepper, diced
2 stalks celery, finely
    chopped
1 quart uncooked, cleaned
    shrimp
1 quart water, about
1 cup catsup

1 teaspoon Worcestershire sauce
Salt to taste
Tabasco to taste

Fry bacon slices until cooked. Add onion and sauté until golden. Add green pepper and celery. Cover. Simmer for 5 minutes. Add shrimp, water to cover. Add catsup, black pepper, Worcestershire, salt and Tabasco. Simmer until thickened, 30 minutes. Yield: 4 portions.

POPHAM SHRIMP PIE · MRS. WILLIAM S. POPHAM, CHARLESTON, S.C.

1 cup shortening
½ pound onions, finely grated
1 quart canned tomatoes
2 to 3 pounds raw shrimp,
    cleaned
1 teaspoon Worcestershire
    sauce
½ teaspoon paprika
Pinch of red pepper
Pinch of mace
Salt to taste

1 quart cooked rice
6 strips bacon

In a heavy saucepan melt shortening. Add onions, tomatoes, shrimp, Worcestershire sauce and seasonings. Cook over low heat, stirring occasionally, for about 30 minutes. Add rice (must be dry and fluffy). Turn into a greased baking dish. Arrange bacon strips on top. Bake at 375°F. about 25 minutes or until bacon is crisp. Yield: 8 to 10 portions.

SHRIMP, SAUCE PIQUANTE · ETIE TRAHAN, AVERY ISLAND, LA.

3 cups salad oil
1 cup flour
4 onions, chopped
6 tomatoes, cut in pieces
5 cans (6 ounces each)
    tomato paste
7 pounds shelled, cleaned,
    raw shrimp
½ bunch onion tops, chopped
4 stalks celery, chopped
2 green peppers, chopped
Salt
Tabasco

Blend oil and flour in large pot over low heat. Add onions and cook until brown. Add tomatoes and tomato paste. Cover; cook over low heat for 45 minutes, stirring occasionally. Add shrimp; cook 30 minutes, stirring occasionally. Add onion tops, celery and peppers. Season to taste with salt and Tabasco. Let cook very, very slowly until flavors are blended. Serve with garlic bread or with rice.
Yield: 10 to 12 portions.

MARION BUGBEE'S SHRIMP · MANHATTAN, KANSAS

2 tablespoons butter or
    margarine
2 small cloves garlic, pressed
2 tablespoons flour
2 tablespoons catsup
4 teaspoons chili powder, or
    to taste
2 cups milk
2 tablespoons sherry wine
2 teaspoons minced parsley
2 cups shelled, cleaned
    shrimp
Cooked white or brown rice

Melt butter; add garlic; brown slightly. Blend in flour. Add catsup and chili powder; mix well. Add milk. Cook over low heat, stirring constantly until mixture comes to a boil and thickens. Blend in sherry and parsley. Add shrimp. Pour into a 1-quart casserole. Bake at 325°F. for 30 minutes. Serve over hot rice.

Yield: 4 portions.

SHRIMP, SAUCE ARNAUD · ARNAUD'S RESTAURANT, NEW ORLEANS, LA.

French Dressing (recipe
    below)
1 tablespoon prepared creole
    mustard
1 teaspoon prepared creole
    horseradish
6 shallots, chopped, or chives
    with tops
¼ teaspoon garlic salt
¼ teaspoon paprika
1½ pounds cooked shrimp,
    peeled

Make French dressing. Add remaining ingredients, except shrimp, stirring each one in separately. Pour mixture over shrimp: mix thoroughly. Chill in refrigerator 30 minutes to 2 hours before using so the shrimp flavor permeates the sauce. Yield: 6 portions.

FRENCH DRESSING:

1 tablespoon vinegar (prefer-
    ably tarragon or basil)
1 teaspoon salt
¼ teaspoon finely ground
    pepper
3 tablespoons olive oil
1 teaspoon prepared creole
    mustard

Mix vinegar, salt, and pepper thoroughly, beating with fork until of uniform solution. Blend oil with mustard, adding oil first drop by drop, then in small quantities, beating constantly. Add the vinegar, salt and pepper solution, a few drops at a time, as the dressing appears to be curdling. When the last of the oil and the last of the vinegar mixture have been whipped in, the dressing is ready to use as a base for the Arnaud sauce—also called Rémoulade.

Yield: about ¼ cup dressing.

FISH STEW · MRS. HAROLD F. DOWNING, LEBANON, OHIO

2 cups water
2 cups white wine
½ lemon, sliced
2 sprigs parsley
1 tablespoon salt
¼ teaspoon pepper
2 raw lobster tails
2 pounds shrimp
3 pounds red snapper,
    entrails removed
¼ cup butter or margarine
4 medium onions, finely
    chopped
1 small green pepper, finely
    chopped
1 tablespoon minced parsley
2 cloves garlic, minced
½ teaspoon crushed, dried red
    peppers
2 tablespoons flour
3 pounds boned bluegill (5 to
    6 fish)
2 packages (12 ounces each)
    frozen oysters
1 tablespoon saffron

Combine water, wine, lemon, parsley, salt and pepper; bring to a boil. Add lobster tails and simmer, covered, 7 to 8 minutes or until tender. Add shrimp, shelled and cleaned, the last 3 minutes of cooking. Remove lobster and shrimp from stock. Cut lobster meat into large pieces. Add red snapper to stock and simmer, covered, 5 to 7 minutes or until tender. Remove from stock; skin and bone the fish and break into large pieces. Strain fish stock and reserve. Melt butter in large skillet; add onions, green pepper, parsley, garlic, and red peppers and sauté until tender but not brown, about 4 minutes. Blend flour with ¼ cup fish stock to make a paste; add to remainder of stock and pour into skillet. Cook, stirring constantly, until thickened, 3 to 5 minutes. Add bluegill, and oysters. Simmer 3 to 5 minutes or until bluegill are tender and oysters plump. Add lobster, shrimp and red snapper and cook 1 minute longer, or until fish is well heated. Stir in saffron. Serve immediately with hot garlic bread and a green salad. Yield: 8 portions.

OTRANTO CLUB PINE-BARK STEW · GOOSE CREEK, S.C.

1 pound bacon
12 potatoes, sliced
12 medium onions, sliced
Boiling salted water
18 bigmouth bass, bream or
    red breast, cleaned
2 teaspoons curry powder
Cooked rice

Cook bacon in a large, deep iron saucepan. Remove and reserve. In the bacon fat place a layer of ⅓ of the potatoes and a layer of ⅓ of the onions. Just cover with boiling salted water. Simmer gently for 10 minutes. Add a layer of whole fish; sprinkle with 1 teaspoon curry powder, then place a second layer of potatoes, onion and fish and sprinkle with remaining curry powder. Add boiling salted water to cover. Top with third layer potatoes and onions. Cover. Cook very slowly until top layer of potatoes is cooked. Pour sauce (see next page) over stew. Arrange cooked bacon on top. Serve with rice. Yield: 12 portions.

SAUCE:
1 cup butter or margarine
½ cup Worcestershire sauce
2 cups catsup
1 tablespoon curry powder
½ teaspoon red pepper
½ teaspoon black pepper
2 cups stew broth

Melt butter in saucepan. Add Worcestershire sauce, catsup, curry powder, red pepper and black pepper. Add stew broth and mix well.

GEFÜLLTE FISH · MRS. WILLIAM STURT, ALBANY PARK, ILL.

Bones and head of fish
    (see fish balls)
3 cups water
1 teaspoon salt
½ teaspoon pepper
2 medium onions, quartered

Have fishman bone and fillet fish and package back and head bones, minus eyes and skin. Combine bones, water, salt, pepper, and onions. Cover and simmer 10 minutes. Add the fish balls.

FISH BALLS:
1½ pounds pike
1 pound lean trout or white
    fish
1 tablespoon fine dry bread
    crumbs
1 medium onion, grated
1 carrot, grated
1 egg, beaten
2 teaspoons salt
¾ teaspoon pepper

Grind fish once with fine blade or twice with coarse one. Add bread crumbs, onion, carrot, egg, and seasonings. Mix thoroughly, adding just a little water if necessary to make a moist mixture. Wet hands and form fish into 8 balls, not too tightly packed. Simmer in stock for 1¾ hours; after 1 hour, taste to see if stock has enough seasoning. Arrange balls on a platter around a dish filled with horseradish-beet sauce. Serve with baked beets. Yield: 8 fish balls.

HORSERADISH-BEET SAUCE:
¼ pound fresh horseradish,
    finely grated
1 fresh beet, finely grated
Juice of 1 lemon
½ cup water
1 teaspoon sugar
¼ teaspoon salt

Combine all ingredients. Yield: 2 cups sauce.

SEAFOOD CASSEROLE · MRS. ELEANOR O'SHEA, ST. PETERSBURG, FLA.

¾ pound butter or margarine
3 tablespoons flour
3 cans (14½ ounces each)
    evaporated milk
1½ teaspoons salt
¼ teaspoon pepper
1 tablespoon Worcestershire
    sauce
1 tablespoon capers
6 tablespoons grated
    Parmesan cheese
1 teaspoon paprika (about)
1 pound medium raw shrimp
1 pint scallops
2 quarts boiling water
2 tablespoons salt
1 pound fillet of flounder
½ pound crab meat, canned
    or fresh
2½ cups cooked lobster meat
2 tablespoons sherry wine

½ cup dry bread crumbs
Dash of paprika

Melt butter in top of double boiler over boiling water; gradually stir in flour to a smooth thin paste. Add 1 can evaporated milk and cook, stirring constantly, until mixture begins to thicken. Gradually add remaining evaporated milk and cook 5 minutes longer, stirring occasionally. Add salt, pepper, Worcestershire sauce, capers, 2 tablespoons Parmesan cheese and enough paprika to give a pale pink color. Wash shrimp, shell and clean; cook with scallops (washed) in boiling water and salt for 5 minutes; add fillet of flounder the last 3 minutes of cooking time and drain. Flake scallops, fillet of flounder, crab meat and lobster into large-size pieces. Combine with shrimp and add to cream sauce; stir in sherry. Pour mixture into a 3-quart casserole; refrigerate until 40 minutes before dinner. Top with bread crumbs and remaining cheese; sprinkle with paprika. Bake at 300°F. for 40 minutes.
Yield: 6 to 8 portions.

PHILADELPHIA CLUB SNAPPER STEW · PHILADELPHIA, PENNA.

2 3-pound baby snappers
1½ cups butter or margarine
1 cup sherry wine
6 egg yolks, slightly beaten
2 cups light cream
½ teaspoon salt
Dash of cayenne

Plunge snappers into boiling salted water to take off the horny skin. Cook 10 minutes, drain and cover with cold water. Pull out nails and rub dark skin from legs. Cover again with boiling salted water and simmer, covered, 30 to 45 minutes, or until shell separates easily and the legs can be dented. Cool in water. Place turtle on its back, and working from the tail end, loosen and remove under-shell. The gall bladder, the sac near the head, and intestines should be carefully removed and discarded. Reserve eggs and cut meat in pieces of serving size. Melt ⅝ cup of the butter, add sherry and meat and simmer until meat is tender and liquid nearly evaporated. Combine egg yolks and cream and blend with cooked mixture. Add remaining butter, salt, cayenne and snapper eggs, stirring very carefully until mixture thickens. Serve at once with sherry wine on the side, if desired. Yield: 6 portions.

MR. CAREY'S CIOPPINO · R. A. CAREY, SAN ANSELMO, CALIF.

¼ cup olive oil
1 cup butter or margarine
2 onions, chopped
2 green peppers, diced
2 cloves garlic, minced
2 cans (1 pound, 4 ounces
    each) solid-pack tomatoes
1 can (6 ounces) tomato
    paste

2 cups canned tomato sauce
1 bay leaf
1 teaspoon paprika
Salt and pepper to taste
6 peppercorns
1 cup white wine
¼ cup sherry wine
1 tablespoon grated orange rind

THE FISH:
2 pounds striped bass, rock
    cod or any flaky fish,
    cleaned, boned, and cut
    in 2-inch pieces
1 pound small shrimp or
    prawns, cooked and
    cleaned
1 pound cooked crab meat
1 pint raw clams
1 pint raw oysters
2 small lobsters, cooked and
    removed from shell
2 tablespoons chopped
    parsley

Heat olive oil and butter in large skillet. Add onions, green peppers and garlic, and sauté until golden. Add tomatoes, tomato paste, tomato sauce, bay leaf, paprika, salt and pepper to taste, and peppercorns. Cook covered, for 1 hour, very, very slowly. Add white wine, sherry, and orange rind. Layer the fish in deep pot, the seafood on the bottom, then the shellfish, kind by kind. Pour over sauce. Cover. Simmer for 20 minutes. Sprinkle with parsley. Serve in deep soup dishes.

Yield: 10 portions.

Sauces

TARANTINO'S CIOPPINO · SAN FRANCISCO, CALIF.

4 cloves garlic, minced
1 medium onion, finely diced
1 green pepper, finely diced
1 leek with leaves, finely
    diced
3 green onions, finely diced
1 can (1 pound, 4 ounces)
    solid pack tomatoes,
    chopped fine, with juice
    from can
1 can (8 ounces) tomato
    purée sauce

Pinch of thyme
1 bay leaf
Salt and pepper to taste
2 cups white wine

Sauté garlic, onion, green pepper, leek, and green onion in oil until golden. Add tomatoes, tomato sauce, thyme, and bay leaf. Cover. Cook slowly 2 to 3 hours, stirring frequently. Add salt and pepper to taste. Add wine; cook 10 minutes longer. Pour over layered Shellfish Assortment.

SHELLFISH ASSORTMENT:
*16 Little Neck clams in the
    shell, uncooked*
*4 medium oysters in the shell,
    uncooked*
*2 small lobsters, or 1 large,
    cooked*
*2 medium West Coast crabs
    or the East Coast hard-
    shelled crabs, cooked*
*8 large shrimp, shelled,
    uncooked*

Allow clams and oysters to stand in fresh water for one hour to remove sand. Scrub shells thoroughly. Split lobsters in half in shell. Split the crabs in half; disjoint the legs. Place all the ingredients in layers in a deep saucepan. Cover with the sauce and simmer, covered, for 15 minutes, adding water if necessary.

Heap into soup plates, garnish with garlic-toast fingers and serve from the kitchen. See that each bowl has some of each kind of fish and a big helping of the piping sauce. Yield: 4 generous portions.

MIGNONETTE SAUCE · SHERRY NETHERLAND HOTEL, NEW YORK CITY

½ cup white wine vinegar
*3 teaspoons coarsely cracked
    pepper*
3 shallots, finely chopped

Combine ingredients. Store in covered glass jar and allow to stand 3 days in the refrigerator before serving as an oyster dunk. The sauce grows better with age; hold corked and stored in a cool place. Yield: about ¾ cup sauce. For oysters.

COCKTAIL SAUCE · MRS. CARL WOODWARD, NEW ORLEANS, LA.

1 cup mayonnaise
Pepper to taste
Tabasco to taste
1 tablespoon anchovy paste
2 tablespoons catsup
1 tablespoon tarragon vinegar

Combine mayonnaise, pepper, and Tabasco. Blend in remaining ingredients. Use over shrimp or crabmeat. Yield: 1¼ cups or 5 portions.

COCKTAIL SAUCE · GRAND CENTRAL STATION OYSTER BAR, NEW YORK CITY

1½ bottles (14 ounce) catsup
½ bottle (12 ounce) chili sauce
*6 tablespoons Worcestershire
    sauce*
1 cup horseradish
Few dashes of Tabasco

Mix ingredients well. Let stand to blend flavors one day before using. Yield: 1 quart. For oysters.

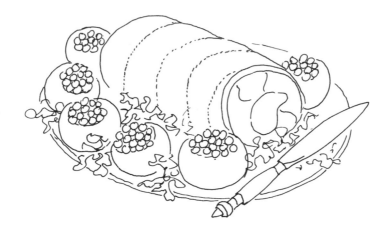

Meat

NEW ENGLAND BOILED DINNER · HERMAN SMITH

4 pounds corned beef
½ pound salt pork
3 quarts boiling water
½ cup sugar
3 bay leaves
1 clove garlic
9 potatoes
3 yellow turnips
8 carrots
8 white onions
6 parsnips
1 small head cabbage
9 small beets

Wash beef in cold water, and if very salty, soak 30 minutes. Place beef and salt pork in pot with boiling water. Add sugar, bay leaves and garlic. Simmer 4 hours. A half hour before completion of cooking add peeled potatoes, also turnips peeled and thickly sliced, the carrots scrubbed until their faces shine. Next the onions neatly peeled and follow with parsnips scrubbed and scraped. At this time dip out 2 cups of cooking liquor and add boiling water to cover cabbage cored and cut into 6 wedges. Cook in separate pot until just tender. Cook the beets separately.

Arrange the dinner on your biggest platter, corned beef and salt pork in the center, the pink and white slices alternating. Carrots, beets and parsnips are sliced while hot to ring around the meat. Next the potatoes left whole and the pale green cabbage wedges. The yield: 6 big helpings, then pass again.

Accompaniments: English mustard, also horseradish for the corned beef; sweetened vinegar for the cabbage and beets. By all means a dish of green tomato pickle. Pass golden corn bread squares, split and buttered. No salad, but a big bowl of cottage cheese instead, sprinkled with caraway.

BOILED BEEF WITH HORSERADISH SAUCE · NANCY FINCH, SALT LAKE CITY, UTAH

4½ pounds rump beef
Water
1 cup sliced onion
1 small carrot, sliced
1 bay leaf
2 tablespoons salt
Pepper, freshly ground
1 tablespoon flour

Cook beef a day in advance of serving. Place meat in kettle and add just enough water to cover. Add onion, carrot and seasonings. Cover and simmer 3 to 4 hours or until meat is tender. Let meat stand in broth 24 hours to absorb flavor. Remove fat from top. Melt 1 tablespoon of the fat; stir in flour to make a smooth paste. Add 1 cup of broth; cook until thickened. Reheat meat in remaining broth. Serve with gravy and horseradish sauce. Yield: 8 portions.

HORSERADISH SAUCE:
1 cup sour cream
1 teaspoon prepared
    horseradish
1 teaspoon vinegar
Pinch of sugar
Dash of Tabasco sauce
Salt

Combine cream, horseradish, vinegar and sugar. Add Tabasco and salt to taste. Yield: 1 cup sauce.

BEEF À LA MODE · ROSETTA CLARKSON, MEDFORD, CONN.

1 pound stewing beef, cubed
½ cup flour
1½ teaspoon salt
¼ teaspoon pepper
3 tablespoons bacon fat
4 carrots, sliced
1 large onion, sliced
6 potatoes, quartered
1 can (1 pound, 13 ounces)
    tomatoes
1 tablespoon No. 1 herb
    mixture*

Roll meat cubes in mixture of flour, salt and pepper. Brown cubes in bacon fat. Arrange meat in deep baking dish. Add carrots, onion, potatoes and the pulp drained from the canned tomatoes. (Reserve tomato juice.) Stir remaining seasoned flour into fat left in pan. When mixture bubbles add gradually reserved tomato juice, stirring constantly. Cook until slightly thickened. Add herb mixture. (If you dislike seeing herb flecks in the liquid it may be tied in a square of cheesecloth.) Pour liquid over meat and vegetables, adding, if necessary, enough water to come one inch from top of casserole. Cover. Bake at 325°F. for 1½ to 2 hours. The longer the cooking the better the dish. Serve over rosemary biscuits. (Add 1 teaspoon finely chopped or powdered rosemary to a regular biscuit dough.) Yield: 6 portions.

* No. 1 herb mixture: 1 tablespoon each, summer savory, sweet marjoram, chervil, basil.

SWISS STEAK · MARIAN SCHLEICHER, INDIANA

3½ pounds round steak, cut
   1 inch thick
½ cup flour
1 teaspoon salt
½ cup bacon drippings
¼ cup chopped onion
¼ cup chopped celery
1 tablespoon finely chopped
   green pepper
1 can (1 pound, 13 ounces)
   tomatoes
1 can (14 ounces) tomato
   juice (optional)

Place meat on board, sprinkle half of the combined flour and salt on one side and pound with a meat hammer for 1 minute. Turn over, sprinkle with the remaining flour and pound for 1 minute. Heat drippings in heavy skillet, and add meat; brown on each side until golden brown. Add onion and let cook for about 1 minute, then add remaining ingredients, except tomato juice. Cover pan, reduce heat and cook slowly for 1½ hours. If liquid isn't sufficient, open a can of tomato juice and add as needed.

Yield: 6 portions.

FRIED BEEFSTEAK

For all their barbecue apparatus Western women still like to fry beefsteak. It sounds sort of awful but the stuff tastes marvelous. One of the best cooks I met in Albuquerque, Mrs. A. H. Beirne, told me she takes a two-inch steak, pounds in flour with pepper and salt. Meanwhile, she heats vegetable oil in an iron skillet and gets that good and hot, then adds one teaspoon Worcestershire sauce, and in with the steak. One side to fry and then the other, to rare, medium, or well-done as you like it. Serve with a baked potato and a green vegetable and you won't ever turn up your nose again at folks who fry steak.

BANKAKEN · MRS. EZRA TAFT BENSON, UTAH

3 to 4 pounds round steak,
   cut 1 inch thick (suet
   and meat)
1 cup sliced onions
2 tablespoons flour
1½ quarts boiling water
   (about)
1 bay leaf
1 tablespoon salt
½ teaspoon pepper

Render suet in large, heavy 2-quart skillet. In half of the rendered fat, brown steak on both sides. Remove meat to saucepan and add onions to fat; fry until golden. Add onion to meat. Add second half of rendered suet to pan. Add flour and brown well. Add water almost to fill skillet, making gravy. Stir until it is smooth and bring to boiling. Pour this over meat and onions; add bay leaf and seasonings. Cook covered over low heat until meat is tender, about 1½ hours. Serve with mashed potatoes, a green vegetable, and a fruit salad.

Yield: 6 to 8 portions.

BRAISED BEEF · MRS. RICHARD S. WRIGHT, PIEDMONT, CALIF.

2 pounds lean stew beef,
*   cubed*
Flour
1 medium onion, minced
1 clove garlic, minced
2 tablespoons salad oil
1 ounce dried mushrooms
1 cup water
2 cans (8 ounces each)
*   tomato sauce*
½ cup red wine
½ teaspoon oregano

1 teaspoon monosodium glutamate
Salt and pepper to taste

Dredge meat in flour. Sauté meat, onion, and garlic in oil until brown. Combine mushrooms and water in saucepan and bring to a boil. Cut mushrooms fine, using scissors. Add with liquid to meat. Add remaining ingredients. Cover. Simmer gently, or put in 325°F. oven, for 2 hours until tender, stirring frequently. If necessary add more water or wine when the sauce cooks down. Serve in a macaroni ring.

Yield: 4 to 6 portions.

ORVILLE BURTIS RANCH STEW · KANSAS

5 pounds beef round, cubed
4 pounds potatoes, peeled
*   and diced*
2 pounds carrots, scraped
*   and diced*
2 large onions, grated
Salt and pepper to taste

Brown meat in its own fat in a large kettle. Add 2½ quarts (10 cups) water. Cover and simmer 2 to 2½ hours, or until meat is tender. The last 30 minutes, add vegetables and continue to simmer until tender but not mushy. Season to taste. Yield: 10 to 12 generous portions.

This stew at first glance is so simply done, you wonder why it's wonderful. The answer is that it tastes like meat, good meat, plainly seasoned, and no tomatoes to detract from the flavor.

FARM POT ROAST · MRS. THOMAS E. DEWEY, PAWLING, N.Y.

4- to 6-pound piece of beef,
*   round or boneless chuck*
¼ cup flour
1 tablespoon salt
¼ teaspoon pepper
3 tablespoons shortening
1 clove garlic
2 large onions, sliced
2 large carrots, sliced
1 cup diced tomatoes
½ cup water
2 tablespoons flour
¼ cup cold water

Dredge meat in the ¼ cup flour, season with salt and pepper. Brown slowly on all sides in hot fat with garlic clove in a heavy kettle. Watch that garlic— when it's brown lift it out! Add vegetables, return garlic, season to taste. Add ½ cup water. Simmer covered until tender, about 3½ hours. Turn the pot roast occasionally, adding more water if needed. Remove meat, strain and measure broth in pot and add enough meat stock to make 2 cups. Blend and add the 2 tablespoons flour and the ¼ cup cold water. Cook, stirring constantly, until thickened. Season to taste, strain and pour over meat. Yield: 6 portions.

KEY WEST POT ROAST · MRS. ROBERT EUGENE OTTO, FLORIDA

4 to 6 pounds beef (top,
   bottom, eye or heel of
   round)
3 cloves garlic, cut into
   thin strips
1 teaspoon salt
½ teaspoon freshly ground
   black pepper
3 tablespoons oil
2 tablespoons butter or
   margarine
2 cups sliced onions
2 cups sliced celery
½ cup coarsely cut celery
   leaves
1 can (1 pound, 4 ounces)
   tomatoes
½ cup sliced green peppers
   (1 inch wide)
2 bay leaves
2 pinches of oregano
1 cup boiling water

Cut 6 long gashes in the roast and in each insert a strip of garlic. Rub meat with salt and pepper. Heat oil and butter in a skillet. Add meat and brown quickly on all sides. Add onions, celery, celery leaves, tomatoes, green peppers, bay leaves, and oregano. Cook for about 10 minutes, mixing lightly. Place remaining pieces of cut garlic in a roasting pan, put meat on top and cover with vegetables; add boiling water. Cover. Roast slowly at 300°F. for about 5 hours or until tender.

Yield: 8 to 12 portions.

POT ROAST WITH FRESH DILL · EDWARD HEITH, WALES, WIS.

4 pounds beef pot roast
Bacon fat
Salt and pepper
1 tablespoon prepared
   mustard
3 onions, finely chopped
½ lemon, juice and rind
1 bay leaf
12 peppercorns
12 allspice
6 sprays fresh dill
¼ cup water
½ cup red wine

Brown one side of pot roast in fat; season unbrowned side with salt and pepper, spread with mustard. Turn roast, season, spread with mustard; brown. Add onions, lemon juice and rind, bay leaf, peppercorns, and allspice. Lay on dill. Add water, cover tightly and simmer 3 hours or until tender. Add more water only if needed. Add wine during last 15 minutes of cooking. Strain gravy, thicken slightly. Slice meat thin. Serve with tiny dumplings. Yield: 8 portions.

SCHWARZENBERG VIENNESE POT ROAST · ANNA MARIA SCHWARZENBERG, BETHEL, VT.

4 pounds top round beef, rolled
2 teaspoons salt
⅛ teaspoon pepper
4 strips of bacon (if the meat is very lean)
1 carrot
1 stalk celery
8 small sprigs parsley
Pinch of marjoram
Pinch of sage
1 bay leaf
2 tablespoons butter or margarine
1 medium onion, sliced
3 shallots
2 tomatoes, peeled and quartered
1 cup bouillon
1 cup white or red wine
¼ cup cognac or whiskey
2 tablespoons sherry wine

1 large head cabbage, quartered
3 tablespoons flour
3 tablespoons water
1 tablespoon heavy cream

Wipe meat with clean cloth, sprinkle with salt and pepper. If very lean, cover with bacon strips. Place in Dutch oven with carrot, celery, parsley and herbs. In a separate pan melt butter. Add onion and shallots and sauté until golden. Add to meat with tomatoes, bouillon, wine, cognac and sherry. Cover with tight-fitting lid and bring to slow simmer; cook 3 hours. About 20 minutes before finished, remove cover, add cabbage and replace the cover. When done remove meat to warm platter, arrange cabbage around meat. Strain liquid left in pan and boil down to 2½ cups. Thicken with flour blended to a smooth paste with water. Add cream and stir well. Yield: 8 portions.

GAME SAUERBRATEN · MRS. JESSIE SPRAGUE CLAYCOMB, GATEWAY, COLO.

3 to 4 pounds roast, rump, chuck or any meaty part of the game
2 cups sliced onions
1½ cups wine vinegar
3 cups water
2 teaspoons salt
⅛ teaspoon pepper
3 bay leaves
15 allspice berries
12 whole cloves
6 to 10 tablespoons fat

Wipe meat with damp cloth. Place in earthenware crock with onions, vinegar, water, salt, pepper, bay leaves, allspice, and cloves. Marinate the meat in this mixture for 24 hours. Remove from marinade, wipe dry. Melt fat in 4-quart pressure cooker. Sear meat on all sides. Strain the marinade liquid and pour over meat. Cover and cook at ten pounds pressure for 1½ hours. Reduce pressure and remove meat. Thicken the broth in the cooker for gravy. Cut meat into thick slices and serve with gravy.

Yield: 6 to 8 portions.

SAUERBRATEN · PENNSYLVANIA DUTCH

1½ cups cider vinegar
½ cup red wine
1 cup water
12 peppercorns
2 tablespoons sugar
2 large onions,
    peeled and sliced
4 bay leaves
12 whole cloves
1 teaspoon mustard seed
2 teaspoons salt
4 pounds round or
    rump of beef
2 tablespoons flour
1½ teaspoons salt
Dash pepper
¼ cup shortening
1 onion, sliced
½ teaspoon mustard seed
6 whole cloves
½ teaspoon peppercorns
⅓ cup flour
⅓ cup crushed gingersnaps

Two to four days before serving, combine the first 10 ingredients in a large bowl. Place beef in this mixture and let stand for two to four days covered, in refrigerator, turning each day. At the end of this marinating period remove meat, dry on paper toweling.

Combine 2 tablespoons flour, salt and pepper. Coat meat on all sides with seasoned flour. Brown on all sides in shortening in Dutch oven. Strain marinade and add to meat with sliced onion, mustard seed, cloves and peppercorns. Cover. Simmer 3½ to 4 hours or until meat is tender. Remove meat to heated platter, slicing beforehand, if desired. Strain liquid. Mix the ⅓ cup flour and crushed gingersnaps in Dutch oven. Slowly add liquid. Simmer, stirring constantly until thickened. Pour some of this gravy over meat. Serve remainder at table. Yield: 6 portions.

MADER'S SAUERBRATEN · MILWAUKEE, WIS.

4 pounds beef round or
    chuck
    or sirloin
1½ teaspoons salt
1 onion, sliced
10 peppercorns
3 bay leaves
3 cloves
1 cup vinegar
Water
⅛ pound unsmoked bacon
2 tablespoons drippings or
    lard
2½ tablespoons flour

2 tablespoons sugar
5 to 6 small gingersnaps, crushed
Salt and pepper to taste
½ cup red wine
Sweet or sour cream

Wipe meat with damp cloth and trim off gristle; rub with salt. Place in an earthenware crock or a glass bowl. Pour over a pickling brine made with the onion, spices, vinegar, and enough water to cover meat. Allow to marinate 48 hours, turning the meat twice daily. Remove meat from liquid, reserving 2 cups of brine. Cut bacon into strips ⅛-inch thick and 2½- to 4-inches long. Pierce meat with a pointed knife and insert bacon. Heat drippings in skillet and lightly brown meat on all sides. Remove meat from skillet and place in roasting pan. Pour over the following sauce: Brown flour in skillet with the drippings, add sugar, gingersnaps, salt and pepper to taste, and 2 cups brine; boil until smooth and creamy. Bake meat at 400°F. allowing 20 to 30 minutes to the pound. Baste frequently during roasting. Add the red wine ½ hour before end of roasting time. Strain gravy. If too thick or sour, add water; or if not sour enough, add vinegar to taste. Sweet or sour cream may be added to gravy before serving. Potato dumplings are the best accompaniment to the dish.

Yield: 8 portions.

POTATO DUMPLINGS:

4 cups seasoned, mashed
   potatoes
1 cup flour
1 egg
2 slices white bread, toasted

Cool mashed potatoes. Add flour and egg, blending well. Cut toast into small dice. Form potato mixture into balls about twice the size of golf balls, flatten in center, add a teaspoonful of croutons, form into ball shape again. Drop into boiling salted water and boil for 10 minutes. Yield: 10 dumplings.

HAIRNHUTTER RINSFLAISH MIT DOONKES · LANCASTER COUNTY, PENNA.
(Moravian Beef with Gravy)

1 teaspoon sage or
   poultry seasoning
1½ teaspoon thyme
1 teaspoon salt
⅛ teaspoon pepper
2 teaspoons whole cloves
2 teaspoons whole allspice,
   crushed
2 bay leaves, crumbled
2 cans beef bouillon
2 tablespoons grated
   lemon rind
   (or finely slivered)
3 tablespoons lemon juice
2 tablespoons fat
1 medium carrot, quartered

1 4-pound pot roast (chuck or round)
1 medium onion, sliced
½ cup sour cream (optional)

Combine seasonings, bouillon, lemon rind and juice. Heat but do not boil. Pour over meat. When cold, place in refrigerator and marinate 24 hours, turning several times. Remove meat from marinade. Melt fat in Dutch oven or other heavy pan. Add meat and vegetables. Brown meat on all sides. Add marinade, cover and simmer until meat is tender, 2 to 3 hours. Meat may be baked, covered, in 350°F. oven if desired. Remove meat and strain gravy. Thicken with flour. Gradually stir in sour cream and serve immediately. Do not boil gravy after sour cream is added. Yield: 8 to 10 portions.

CHIPPED CREAMED BEEF WITH MUSHROOMS · ARECE ANDERSON, COATESVILLE, PA.

½ pound dried beef,
*   shredded*
3 tablespoons butter or
*   margarine*
3 tablespoons minced onion
3 tablespoons minced
*   green pepper*
¼ cup flour
2 cups milk
1 tablespoon chopped parsley
¼ teaspoon paprika
2 tablespoons sherry wine
2 cans (4 ounces each)
*   mushrooms, drained*

Sauté beef in butter until light brown. Add onion and green pepper, and cook until tender. Blend in flour. Add milk slowly, stirring constantly. Simmer until thickened. Add parsley, paprika, sherry and drained mushrooms. Serve immediately over hot waffles. Yield: 6 portions or topping for 12 waffles.

ROAST-BEEF HASH · HAWTHORN ROOM, INDIANAPOLIS, IND.

1 quart cooked, diced
*   roast beef*
1 cup chopped onions
1 cup diced, raw potatoes
¼ cup chopped green pepper
1 cup beef stock
½ teaspoon salt
¼ teaspoon pepper

Combine ingredients in a 1½ quart casserole. Heat thoroughly on top of range. Then bake at 300°F. for 1½ hours. Yield: 6 portions.

RED FLANNEL HASH · HERMAN SMITH, NEW ENGLAND

6 slices salt pork
1 cup chopped cooked
*   corned beef*
¼ cup milk
3 cups chopped boiled
*   potatoes*
1 cup chopped cooked beets
1 cup chopped leftover
*   vegetables*
1 onion, minced

Fry salt pork until crisp. Remove pieces and retain as garnish for meat dish. Combine meat, milk, and vegetables. Spread mixture smoothly over the bottom of skillet in which salt pork was fried. Brown slowly. When a crust forms, turn as an omelet. Serve on a hot plate garnished with the slices of crisply fried salt pork. Yield: 6 portions.

SOUTHERN-STYLE BEEF HASH · RICH'S, ATLANTA, GA.

½ cup diced green pepper
½ cup diced white onions
2 tablespoons butter or
    margarine
1 cup diced raw potatoes
2 cups finely diced cold
    roast beef
1 cup beef stock
Salt to taste
Black pepper to taste
2 tablespoons minced parsley

Sauté pepper and onion in butter over low heat in covered skillet 10 minutes. Add all other ingredients except parsley. Cook slowly 40 minutes. Add water as needed. When potatoes are tender fold in one tablespoon parsley. Remove hash to serving dish and garnish with remaining parsley. For a back-yard supper, serve hash right from the iron skillet, resting it on a large wooden plate or iron griddle. Yield: 6 portions.

CORNISH PASTY · MARY ROGERS NEAL, WISCONSIN

6 cups sifted all-purpose
    flour
1 tablespoon salt
⅔ pound shortening
½ to ⅔ cup water
Cornish pasty filling

Sift together flour, salt. Cut in shortening with pastry blender or two knives, until half the mixture resembles coarse corn meal, and half the particles are the size of small peas. Add enough water to hold the dough together when it is pressed lightly. Roll out on a large, lightly floured board to a circle 18 inches in diameter. Carefully slip onto greased baking sheet. Turn Cornish pasty filling onto half of the circle; moisten edges of pasty with water. Fold uncovered side over covered side of pasty to form a semi-circle. Pinch the edges together. Make 8 slashes on the top of the pasty with the point of a knife. Bake in a moderate oven (350°F.) about 2 hours. Yield: 8 to 10 portions.

CORNISH PASTY FILLING:
3½ pounds shoulder steak
1½ cups coarsely chopped
    onion
6 cups thinly sliced raw
    potatoes
½ cup finely cut kidney suet
2 tablespoons salt
1 teaspoon black pepper

Remove tendons, membrane and bone from steak; trim off excess fat, but not all. There should be at least 2 pounds of meat left. Cut in bite-size pieces; combine with onion, potatoes, kidney suet, seasonings. Fill pasty with mixture.

NOTE: To be truly Cornish, the pasty will go long on the potatoes and short on the meat. Just a touch of the onion and no other vegetable as it is so frequently met on other folks' tables.

MRS. JAMES RAFERTY'S CHILI · MIAMI, FLORIDA

2 pounds ground beef
2 cans (1 pound, 4 ounces
    each) tomatoes
1 can (6 ounces) tomato
    paste
2 green peppers, diced
2 medium onions, diced
2 celery stalks, diced
2 tablespoons chili powder

1 clove garlic
2 cans (1 pound, 4 ounces each) kidney beans, drained
Salt and pepper

Brown meat. Add remaining ingredients; mix well. Cover. Simmer for 1½ to 2 hours. Season to taste. Remove garlic. Serve with rice. Good also on scrambled eggs, delicious on hot fried mush.
    Yield: 2 quarts chili.

CARNE CON CHILI · ANA BEGUE DE PACKMAN, CALIF.

2 pounds beef chuck
1 teaspoon salt
2 tablespoons fat
1 cup ripe black olives
Dash of black pepper

Cut chuck into 1-inch pieces. Season with salt and pepper. Fry in hot fat until well browned. Simmer in Chili Sauce until tender. Serve garnished with olives.
    Yield: 4 to 6 portions.

CHILI SAUCE:
¼ pound dry red chilis
1 quart boiling water
2 tablespoons fat
1 tablespoon flour or
    2 tablespoons toasted
    bread crumbs
1 clove garlic
1 teaspoon salt
1 tablespoon vinegar

Remove stems and cut open chilis; wipe clean. Cook in water until pulp is separated from hulls. Rub through a sieve (this should make about 1½ cups purée). Heat fat in skillet; add flour and garlic mashed with salt; stir until flour is light golden color. Combine with the chili purée and vinegar.

MRS. GEORGE HAYDU'S HUNGARIAN MEAT BALLS · PLAINFIELD, N.J.

2 pounds ground chuck
1 teaspoon salt
¼ teaspoon pepper
1 onion, grated
1 clove garlic, crushed
¾ cup tomato juice
1 egg
1 cup finely ground bread
    crumbs

Combine ingredients, reserving ½ cup of bread crumbs; mix well. Form into 1½-inch balls and roll in remaining crumbs. Fry in hot shallow fat 3 to 4 minutes, or until balls are brown and cooked. Yield: about 40 1½-inch balls, or 6 to 8 portions.

SMETANA HAMBURGER · MRS. FLOYD L. RHEAM, TULSA, OKLA.

1 pound ground beef
1 teaspoon salt
⅛ teaspoon pepper
½ cup commercial sour cream
1 tablespoon finely chopped
    fresh dill or ½ teaspoon
    crushed dill seeds
Paprika

Combine beef, salt and pepper. Shape into 16 patties. Broil patties about 3 inches from heat, turning once, until done. Meanwhile combine sour cream and dill. Place topping of sour cream mixture over each patty. Return to broiler for few minutes to heat cream. Sprinkle with paprika. Serve at once.

Yield: 16 small patties.

NORWEGIAN MEAT BALLS · MRS. ORREN SANFORD, MINNEAPOLIS, MINN.

1 pound round steak
½ pound pork
½ cup dry bread crumbs
½ cup milk
1 egg
¾ cup minced onion
1 teaspoon salt
1 teaspoon sugar
¼ teaspoon ginger
¼ teaspoon nutmeg
¼ teaspoon allspice
¼ cup butter or margarine
1 tablespoon flour
1 cup milk

Have meat man grind steak and pork together very fine. Soak bread crumbs in the ½ cup milk. Combine with meat. Mix in egg, onion, salt, sugar, and spices; blend and knead mixture thoroughly. Shape into small balls. Brown in butter, shaking the skillet to turn balls and brown evenly on all sides. Easy does it for the balls should hold to their shape. Remove to serving dish. Add flour to pan and brown well. And milk with just enough water to make a medium-thick gravy. Salt to taste. Return balls to pan and gently cook, covered, for 15 minutes. Serve in a wild-rice ring. Yield: 6 portions.

PLANTATION GOULASH · MRS. C. WESLEY FRAME, YEMMASSEE, S.C.

1 pound bacon
2 cups diced green peppers
2 pounds onions, finely
    chopped
1 quart diced celery
7 pounds round beef, ground
2⅓ tablespoons salt
1 teaspoon pepper
3 cans (1 pound, 4 ounces
    each) tomatoes
1 tablespoon sugar
1 teaspoon crushed bay
    leaves

Cut ½ pound bacon into small pieces and sauté with peppers, onions and celery until bacon is crisp. In a second pan, fry ½ pound bacon in strips. Remove strips and crumble. Season meat with salt and pepper. Add crumbled bacon. Form into balls about 2 inches in diameter. Brown quickly in hot bacon fat. Add balls to the sautéed vegetables. Add tomatoes, sugar and bay leaves. Cover. Cook until sauce is medium thick.

Yield: 35 portions. Can be frozen and stored.

GROUND BEEF DINNER · MRS. HOLLIS BECKER, IDAHO

1½ pounds ground beef
2 teaspoons salt
1 teaspoon pepper
3 tablespoons fat
2 medium onions, sliced
7 medium potatoes,
    thinly sliced
1 quart canned tomatoes
1 teaspoon salt

Combine meat with the 2 teaspoons salt and pepper. Shape into 7 or 8 patties. Brown well on both sides in hot fat. Arrange in the bottom of a baking dish. Pour over fat. Layer with onions and potatoes. Combine tomatoes with remaining salt and pour over top of potatoes. Cover. Bake at 400°F. for 1 hour. Remove cover and cook 30 minutes longer. Yield: 4 portions.

MEAT LOAF · SUSANNE COOLEY, ARKANSAS

1½ pounds ground beef
¼ pound ground veal
¼ pound ground pork
2 eggs
1 cup cocktail
    vegetable juice
½ cup tomato juice
2 cups dry bread crumbs
¼ cup minced onion
¼ cup minced green pepper
2 teaspoons salt

½ teaspoon black pepper
¼ teaspoon dry mustard
¼ teaspoon sage
½ cup catsup

Combine meats. Add next 10 ingredients and mix well. Pack in 9 × 5 × 3-inch loaf pan. Bake at 350°F. for 1½ hours. Spread top with catsup. Bake 15 minutes longer. Yield: 8 to 10 portions.

MEAT LOAF SUPREME · CHEF MILANI, LOS ANGELES, CALIF.

1¾ pounds ground beef
¼ pound ground veal
1 cup dry bread crumbs
½ cup sherry wine
3 tablespoons minced parsley
2 eggs
2¼ teaspoons salt
Pepper
½ pound Swiss cheese, grated
¼ pound cooked ham,
    minced
¾ cup chopped onion
3 tablespoons olive oil
2 cans (8 ounces each)
    tomato sauce

Mix beef, veal, bread crumbs, sherry, and 2 tablespoons of the parsley, eggs, 2 teaspoons of the salt, and a good pinch of pepper. Then mix separately the Swiss cheese, ham, 1 tablespoon parsley, onion, ¼ teaspoon salt, and pinch of pepper. Oil a 10½ × 5½ × 3½-inch loaf pan. Line bottom and sides well with half of meat mixture; fill with cheese combination. Top with remaining meat mixture. Seal edges so cheese filling is enclosed inside loaf. Brush top with oil. Bake at 325°F. for 1 hour. Pour tomato sauce over. Bake 45 minutes longer. Yield: 8 portions.

APPLESAUCE MEAT LOAF · PEACH RIDGE, MICH.

1½ pounds ground meat
2 eggs, beaten
2 tablespoons chopped onion
2 teaspoons salt

½ teaspoon allspice
¾ cup rolled oats
1 cup strained applesauce

TOPPING:
1 pared apple,
    cut in thin rings
¼ cup brown sugar
⅛ teaspoon cloves
1 tablespoon water

Combine all ingredients for meat loaf. Pack firmly into a greased 9 × 5 × 3-inch loaf pan. Press apple rings into top of loaf. Brush with glaze made by mixing sugar, cloves, and water. Loaf may be made early and refrigerated before baking, if desired. Bake at 350°F. for 1 hour and 15 minutes. Let stand 5 minutes before serving. Yield: 8 portions.

MEAT LOAF · MRS. JOHN POWELL, CALIFORNIA

3 slices fresh bread,
    crusts removed
½ cup milk
3 pounds ground beef
3 slices bacon, cut fine
1 tablespoon grated
    orange rind
1 tablespoon salt
½ teaspoon pepper

½ teaspoon garlic salt
¼ teaspoon sweet basil
½ cup chopped onion
¼ cup minced parsley

Soak bread in milk for 10 minutes. Combine with remaining ingredients. Shape into loaf. Place in a greased pan. Bake at 350°F. for 1 hour. Garnish with orange slices and stuffed olives. Yield: 6 portions.

FRENCH-CANADIAN LUMBERJACK PIE · NORTHERN NEW ENGLAND

3 pounds fresh pork shoulder
3 pounds chuck beef
5 large onions
⅛ teaspoon thyme
⅛ teaspoon oregano
5 peppercorns
Salt to taste
1 tablespoon cinnamon
1 teaspoon sage
3 cups mashed potatoes
Pastry for 4 double-crust
    9-inch pies

Place pork and beef in deep pot. Add one onion, chopped, cover with water and cook 2 hours. Add thyme, oregano, peppercorns and salt to taste. Continue cooking 4 hours, or until the meat is tender enough to fall from the bones. Cool, remove fat from meat; grind lean meat, adding back a little of the fat (not the orthodox way, but Isabel's preference). Run four onions through the grinder and mix well with meat. Add cinnamon and sage. Mix in mashed potatoes, adding enough of the meat stock (about 2½ cups) to give a consistency not dry, not mushy, just in between. Season with salt to taste. Use as filling for double crust pies. Bake at 375°F. for 1 hour. Yield: four 9-inch pies.

SOUTHWEST TAMALE PIE · DUNCAN HINES

1 onion, minced
1 clove garlic, minced
1 green pepper, minced
2 tablespoons fat or salad oil
1 pound ground beef
¼ pound ground pork
1 can (1 pound, 12 ounces)
    tomatoes
½ cup chopped ripe olives
Few grains salt, pepper,
    cayenne
½ cup grated Cheddar cheese
2 tablespoons yellow
    corn meal
1 teaspoon chili powder
1 cup yellow corn meal
3 cups boiling water
1 teaspoon salt

Sauté onion, garlic and green pepper in fat until light brown. Add beef and pork; brown lightly. Add tomatoes, olives, salt, pepper and cayenne. Cook slowly 1 hour. Add cheese, two tablespoons corn meal and chili powder. Cook until cheese melts, stirring occasionally. (Mixture should be consistency of baked hash.) Gradually add 1 cup corn meal to water, stirring constantly; cook until thickened. Add the 1 teaspoon salt. Pour corn meal mixture into greased 2-quart casserole. Add meat mixture. Bake at 375°F for 20 minutes. Yield: 8 portions.

KENTUCKY BURGOO · CISSY GREGG, LOUISVILLE, KY.

2 pounds pork shank
2 pounds veal shank
2 pounds beef shank
2 pounds breast of lamb
1 4-pound hen
8 quarts water
1½ pounds potatoes, diced
1½ pounds onions, diced
1 bunch carrots, diced
2 green peppers, diced
2 cups diced okra
1 cup diced celery
2 cups chopped cabbage
2 cups whole corn,
    fresh or canned
2 cups lima beans
2 pods red pepper
1 quart tomato purée
Salt and cayenne

Tabasco
A-1 Sauce
Worcestershire sauce
Chopped parsley

Put all the meat into cold water and bring slowly to a boil. Simmer until meat is tender enough to fall from the bones. Remove meat from stock. Cool and chop the meat. Return meat to stock. Add all the vegetables. Simmer until thick. (Burgoo should be very thick, but still "soupy".) Season along but not too much until it is almost done. Add chopped parsley just before stew is served. Stir frequently with a long-handled wooden paddle or spoon during the first part of the cooking and almost constantly after it gets thick.
    Yield: about 25 portions.

BEEF PICADILLO · MENGER HOTEL, SAN ANTONIO, TEXAS

½ pound ground beef
½ pound ground pork
1 teaspoon salt
¼ teaspoon pepper
1 can (6 ounces) tomato paste
3 medium potatoes, diced
Dash of oregano
¾ cup diced pimiento
¾ cup seedless raisins
¾ cup toasted whole almonds

4 medium tomatoes, peeled and diced
2½ cloves garlic, finely chopped
3 green onions, finely cut
2 jalapeno (or hot) peppers, chopped

Cover meat with water. Add salt and pepper. Simmer, covered, for ½ hour. Add remaining ingredients. Cook, covered, until potatoes are done. Yield: 4 to 6 portions.

BRUNSWICK STEW · MRS. JOHN SNIVELY, FLORIDA

1½ pounds ground beef
1½ pounds ground lean pork
3 cans (16 to 17 ounces)
    whole kernel corn
3 cans (1 pound, 4 ounces)
    tomatoes
2 medium onions, chopped
⅓ cup catsup
Juice of 1 lime
3 tablespoons vinegar

½ teaspoon Tabasco
1½ teaspoons salt
2 cups bread cubes

Brown meats in heavy skillet, breaking up into small pieces with fork. Add undrained corn, tomatoes and onion. Combine catsup, lime juice, vinegar, Tabasco and salt; stir into stew. Add bread cubes. Bring to a boil; reduce heat. Cover and simmer 45 minutes to 1 hour. Yield: 9 to 12 portions.

STUFFED CABBAGE · MRS. LOUIS IGNATZ, ELYRIA, OHIO

1 large head cabbage
1 large onion, minced
3 tablespoons shortening
¾ pound ground pork
¾ pound ground beef
2 tablespoons salt
1 tablespoon paprika
1 teaspoon black pepper
¾ pound rice, washed well
1 can (1 pound, 4 ounces)
    sauerkraut
1 can (1 pound, 4 ounces)
    tomato juice
½ pint commercial sour cream

Core cabbage and place in enough boiling water to cover. With a fork in one hand and a knife in the other, keep cutting off the leaves as they become wilted. Drain. Trim thick center vein of each cabbage leaf. Brown onion in shortening. Add meat, seasonings, and rice; mix well. Place a heaping tablespoon of filling on each cabbage leaf; roll up. Place in a pot and cover ⅔ full with water. Arrange sauerkraut on top. Add tomato juice. Cook and cook slowly for about ½ hour. Pour on sour cream; cook 5 minutes.
Yield: 6 to 8 portions.

BOLICHE · MRS. ELIOT FLETCHER, TAMPA, FLA.

3½ pounds eye of round beef
4 strips cooked salt pork
4 strips cooked ham
32 ripe pimiento-stuffed
   olives
1 clove garlic, crushed
4 tablespoons oil
¼ cup lime juice
½ cup white wine
2 tablespoons chopped
   parsley
¾ cup coarsely chopped
   onions
1 cup beef consommé,
   (about)

Remove skin and fat from beef and wipe with damp cloth. Take a sharp slender knife and make 4 deep punctures almost through the meat from end to end. Fill punctures with strips of salt pork. Make 4 more punctures through meat and fill with strips of ham. Fill 4 more punctures with olives. Force fillings in with fingers. Mix garlic with 1 tablespoon oil, rub over meat. Place in shallow pan. Squeeze lime juice over meat; add wine, parsley and onion. Let meat stand, covered, in this marinade 2 to 6 hours or overnight. Turn the meat occasionally so that all sides have a turn in the marinade.

Remove from marinade, reserving marinade, and brown on all sides in 3 tablespoons of oil, in deep saucepan with tightly fitting lid. Pour marinade over meat, adding beef consommé (enough to cover meat about halfway). Cover tightly. Cook over low heat for 3 hours, turning occasionally. Remove meat to hot platter, strain gravy into bowl or else purée and serve thickened by vegetables. Yield: 8 to 10 portions.

DOLMADES · MRS. A. L. DE GUIRE, DALLAS, TEXAS

1 pound lean round steak,
   ground
1 pound pork shoulder,
   ground
2 medium onions,
   finely chopped
4 teaspoons salt
⅞ teaspoon pepper
1 tablespoon minced parsley
1 teaspoon minced fresh
   mint or ¼ teaspoon dried
½ cup uncooked rice
2 medium heads cabbage or
   28 grape leaves
3 cups lightly salted water
   (about)

Combine meats and onions. Mix in pepper, parsley, mint and rice. Place a tablespoonful of the mixture on a grape or cabbage leaf. (To prepare cabbage leaves, drop cabbage head into boiling water for 3 to 5 minutes; separate leaves, cut out the heavy rib.) After filling is laid on, fold over the ends so mixture cannot spill out. Roll and fasten with a toothpick. Place in a pot layer upon layer. Add just enough water to cover. Cover pot and cook for 1½ hours or until rice is tender and meat is done. Serve hot as a main dish or well chilled as a first course.

Yield: 28 rolls.

SPICY LAMB SHANKS · MRS. HAROLD HOLCOMB, SCOTTSDALE, ARIZ.

4 lamb shanks
¼ cup flour
1 teaspoon salt
½ teaspoon pepper
1 cup dried prunes, cooked
1 cup dried apricots, cooked
½ cup sugar
½ teaspoon cinnamon
½ teaspoon allspice
½ teaspoon cloves

¼ teaspoon salt
1 cup water
3 tablespoons tarragon vinegar

Dredge lamb shanks in flour seasoned with salt and pepper. Place pieces in well-greased baking dish. Cover. Bake at 350°F. until tender, about 2 hours. Combine remaining ingredients; simmer 5 minutes. Drain fat from shanks. Add fruit mixture. Cover. Bake at 400°F. for 30 minutes. Yield: 6 to 8 portions.

BARBECUED SHOULDER OF LAMB · MRS. ROBERT NAYLOR, EMMETT, IDAHO

1 shoulder of lamb
1 medium onion, chopped
2 tablespoons butter or
    margarine
Salt
Cayenne
1 cup catsup
1 cup water
2 tablespoons brown sugar
4 tablespoons lemon juice
3 tablespoons Worcestershire
    sauce
2 tablespoons vinegar

Have meat man bone shoulder and roll. Force the sharpened end of an iron rod through the center of rolled shoulder and place over a good bed of coals. Turn every half hour, brushing with barbecue sauce. Cook slowly for 4 hours.

Sauce: Brown onion in butter; season with salt and cayenne. Add remaining ingredients. Cover and simmer 30 to 40 minutes.

Yield: 1 cup sauce.

LAMB SHOULDER WITH RICE STUFFING · MRS. ROBERT NAYLOR, EMMETT, IDAHO

Square cut lamb shoulder
Salt and pepper
1½ tablespoons minced onion
¾ cup uncooked rice
1 tablespoon fat
2 cups stock
1 teaspoon salt
½ teaspoon curry powder

Have meat man bone square cut shoulder and sew on two sides with one side left open to insert stuffing. Season shoulder inside and out with salt and pepper. To make stuffing, sauté onion and rice in fat until rice is golden. Add stock, salt, and curry powder. Cover and steam 20 minutes, or until rice is dry. Fill pocket of roast with stuffing and sew or skewer edges together. Place roast on rack in open roasting pan. Roast at 300°F. allowing 35 to 40 minutes per pound.

JIFFY LAMB DINNER · MRS. ROBERT NAYLOR, EMMETT, IDAHO

6 lamb patties
6 slices bacon
Salt and pepper
6 canned pineapple slices
6 large tomatoes
1 cup whole kernel corn
6 pared boiled potatoes
2 tablespoons grated cheese

Have ground lamb shaped into thick patties and wrapped around with bacon. Place seasoned patties on a broiling rack with pineapple slices. Broil until patties are browned. Turn patties, placing them browned side down on pineapple slices. Add the whole tomatoes, hollowed and filled with corn. Add potatoes, sprinkled with cheese. By the time the patties are done the tomatoes and potatoes will be heated and slightly browned. Yield: 6 portions.

LAMB AND CABBAGE · EDWARD HETH, WALES, WIS.

3 pounds lamb-stew meat
Fat (half butter, half bacon fat)
1 large cabbage, cut into eighths
4 large potatoes, diced
1 bunch green scallions
2 tablespoons salt
1 teaspoon caraway seeds
12 peppercorns
12 allspice
2 bay leaves
1 tablespoon white vinegar

Brown lamb in fat in a deep pot. Add cabbage and potatoes. Barely cover with water. Simmer, covered 1½ hours, or until meat is almost tender. Cut scallions into 1½-inch lengths and add with salt and spices. Cook about 30 minutes longer. Serve on large platter; sprinkle with vinegar. Yield: 8 portions.

ROBERT E. SMYLIE'S LAMB CURRY · BOISE, IDAHO

4 pounds boneless lean, lamb, cut in 1½-inch pieces (if meat is from shoulder or leg pieces, use bones for stock)
2 tablespoons fat or drippings
2 tablespoons curry powder
2 tablespoons flour
Small clove garlic, mashed, with 1 tablespoon salt
1 large onion, diced
1 small tart apple, peeled, cored, and sliced
Grated rind of 1 small orange
6 small sweet pickles, sliced
½ cup Mrs. Smylie's fresh purple plum chutney (page 292)
1½ cups tomatoes
2 cups water or stock

Brown lamb on all sides in fat until well browned. Sprinkle curry powder and flour over meat; stir until well coated. Add remaining ingredients; bring lamb to the boiling point. Cover tightly and cook until lamb is tender, about 2 hours. Stir occasionally and add more liquid if necessary Yield: 8 portions.

Serve with steamed rice, plum chutney, a salad of crisp greens. For dessert, fruit sherbet and cookies.

PHILADELPHIA CLUB LAMB KIDNEY IN CASSEROLE · PHILADELPHIA, PENNA.

3 tablespoons butter or
  margarine
½ cup minced onion
1 clove garlic, minced
1 tablespoon flour
½ cup claret wine
2 cups stock or consommé
1 can (8 ounces) tomato
  sauce
Salt and pepper to taste
2 pounds mushrooms, cut
  into 4 pieces each
¼ cup water
1½ teaspoons sugar
12 small white onions, peeled
18 lamb kidneys
Dash of salt
¼ cup shortening
½ pound salt pork, cooked
  and cut into 1-inch cubes

Melt 2 tablespoons of the butter in frying pan; add onion and garlic and sauté until golden. Add flour and cook, stirring constantly, over low heat until golden brown—careful, don't overbrown. Add wine, stock, tomato sauce and salt and pepper. Cook slowly, uncovered, for 30 minutes. Meanwhile sauté mushrooms. Combine remaining 1 tablespoon butter, water and sugar in skillet. Stir until butter is melted and sugar dissolved. Add onions and cook over low heat, stirring occasionally, until onions are brown and tender. Add the glazed onions and the sautéed mushrooms to the sauce.

Just before serving, slice kidneys into 4 or 5 pieces each and sprinkle with salt. Melt shortening in frying pan. Add kidneys and cooked salt pork and sauté until tender, about 3 to 5 minutes. Combine with sauce and garnish with chopped chives, parsley or fresh peas.

Yield 8 portions.

NOTE: To cook salt pork, place in kettle and cover with water; boil until tender. Cool, then dice.

CHALBER BÄLLELI (VEAL BALLS) · MRS. FRANK SCHIESSER, NEW GLARUS, WIS.

2½ pounds veal, ground
½ pound pork, ground
4 eggs
1 cup light cream
¼ cup milk
¼ cup finely chopped onion
1 teaspoon salt
½ teaspoon pepper
¼ teaspoon nutmeg
6 slices toasted bread, finely
  crumbled
6 tablespoons butter or
  margarine
1 tablespoon flour
1 cup milk or water

Mix veal and pork with eggs and cream diluted with the ¼ cup milk. Stir in onion. Season with salt, pepper, and nutmeg. Mix in toast crumbs thoroughly. Form meat mixture into balls about the size of an egg. Brown in butter. Turn balls and fat into casserole. Cover. Bake at 350°F. for 30 minutes. Uncover and let veal balls brown, about 10 minutes. Place balls on platter and keep warm. Combine flour and juice in bottom of casserole in a skillet and brown slightly. Add the 1 cup milk and stir until slightly thickened. Season to taste. Pour gravy over veal balls or serve in separate bowl.

Yield: 6 portions.

KALV SYLTA (AMERICAN STYLE) · MRS. WESLEY C. HEISE, TIGARD, ORE.

1 large veal shank
1 medium pork shank
2 cloves garlic
1 stalk celery with leaves
2 medium onions, quartered
2 tablespoons salt
1 teaspoon whole black
  pepper
1 teaspoon whole allspice
4 to 5 bay leaves
1¼ teaspoons ground allspice

Wash veal and pork shanks. Cover with cold water and bring slowly to a boil. Add garlic. Break celery into 4 pieces and add to pot with chopped leaves. Add onions, salt, pepper, whole allspice, and bay leaves. Simmer slowly 2½ to 3 hours or until meat falls from the bones. Cool in the stock. Remove meat from bones and run through food chopper using coarse blade. Strain stock into saucepan, add ground meat with more salt if desired and the ground allspice. Bring to a boil. Pour into mold; cool, then place in the refrigerator until the meat jellies. Slice to serve.

Yield: 15 portions.

PHILADELPHIA CLUB VEAL-AND-HAM PIE · PHILADELPHIA, PENNA.

2 pounds leg of veal, sliced
  very thin and flattened
1½ pounds tenderized, un-
  cooked ham, thinly sliced
3 thin strips salt pork
1 tablespoon Worcestershire
  sauce
½ cup sherry wine
2 envelopes unflavored
  gelatin
2 cups stock
Pastry for 2-crust 10-inch pie
Beaten egg
¼ cup minced onion
¼ cup minced celery
¼ cup minced green pepper
1 teaspoon minced parsley
Salt and pepper to taste

Roll pastry ⅛-inch thick. Place bottom crust in 3-quart baking dish. Brush edge of dish with beaten egg. With strip of dough, line sides having it go over edge ½ inch. Mix together onion, celery, green pepper, parsley, salt and pepper. Cut meat into 3- to 4-inch squares. Arrange a layer of veal on crust; then a layer of mixed vegetables over the veal; next a layer of ham. Repeat this until ingredients are used but place one layer of salt pork in the middle. Combine Worcestershire sauce and sherry and sprinkle over. Soak gelatin in ½ cup of stock for 5 minutes; add remaining stock. Pour ½ cup of this over pie. Cut hole in center of top crust, reserving cut-out for use as a plug. Adjust top crust, sealing edges. Replace plug, bake at 350°F. for 30 minutes.

(If crust browns before the time is up, cover with wet brown wrapping paper and continue baking the full period.) Remove from oven. Remove plug and pour in stock to fill, using funnel; replace plug. Continue baking for 30 minutes; repeat stock-filling process. Bake 30 minutes longer. If stock is reduced below crust level when pie is finished baking, add more stock. Cool, then chill in refrigerator. Slice in ½-inch-thick pieces and serve cold with a salad such as asparagus or sliced tomatoes. Yield: 8 portions.

CASSOULET · MRS. GEORGE M. GUEST, CINCINNATI, OHIO

1 pound dried kidney beans
1 medium onion
Salt and pepper to taste
4 slices bacon
½ pound sausage meat
1 pound boneless veal, cut
　　into small pieces
2 cloves garlic, crushed
1 teaspoon minced parsley
½ teaspoon crushed rosemary
1 cup dry red wine

Rinse beans and soak overnight in water to cover. Remove the floaters but do not drain. Add onion, salt, pepper, bacon, and more water, if needed to cover. Simmer, covered, 1½ to 2 hours, or until beans are tender but not broken. Stir occasionally, adding water as needed in small amounts. Meanwhile, form sausage into marble-size balls and brown in skillet. Remove sausage and all but 2 tablespoons of fat from pan. Turn veal into skillet. Add salt, pepper, garlic, parsley, rosemary and wine. Cook slowly, covered, for 1 hour. Remove from heat and add sausage balls. Place beans and meat with sauce in bean pot or 3-quart baking dish, in layers, using 3 of beans and 2 of meat. Cover. Bake at 350°F. for 1½ hours, removing cover last half hour of baking in order to form a brown crust on top. Yield: 6 to 8 portions.

AUNT DELL'S PORK CHOPS · EDWARD HETH, WALES, WIS.

6 pork chops, about ¾ inch
　　thick
Salt and pepper
2 carrots, thinly sliced
6 green onions, finely
　　chopped
Paprika
4 tablespoons commercial
　　sour cream
Butter or margarine

1 can (1 pound, 4 ounces) creamed corn
¼ cup finely crushed corn flakes

Brown chops; season with salt and pepper. Put a layer of carrots in the bottom of a casserole. Place browned chops over carrots. Cover with onion; douse with paprika. Add sour cream, then corn. Season again. Top with corn flakes; dot with butter. Cover. Bake at 350°F. for 45 minutes or until chops are tender.
Yield: 6 portions.

POOR MAN'S STEW · NORTHERN NEW ENGLAND

6 slices salt pork (6 inches
　　long, ¼ inch thick)
2 onions, minced
6 potatoes, peeled and sliced
2 tablespoons flour
2 tablespoons water
⅛ teaspoon salt
1 cup milk

Try out salt pork until brown and crisp. Add onions and potatoes. Blend flour and water, add salt and thin with milk. Add thickening to stew, blending well. Cover. Simmer until potatoes are tender. Raw sliced carrots may be added with potatoes, or sliced green beans. Yield: 6 portions.

ARROZ CON PUERCO · MRS. HARRY BEST, N. MIAMI, FLA.

2 tablespoons vegetable oil,
　heated
2 small cloves garlic, finely
　minced
1 pound lean pork shoulder,
　cubed
2 pounds square salt pork,
　cubed
1 medium onion, sliced
1 green pepper, sliced
1 cup raw rice
1 can (1 pound, 13 ounces)
　tomatoes

¾ cup cooked peas
¼ cup chopped peanuts

Heat oil in skillet. Add half the minced garlic and pork shoulder and brown slowly about ½ hour. In a separate skillet, render salt pork, add remaining garlic, onion and green pepper. Sauté until vegetables are golden. Pour off all but ½ cup fat. Add rice and cook until grains begin to brown. Add tomatoes and pork mixture. Cover tightly. Simmer until rice is tender, about 20 minutes. Just before the dish is done, add peas and peanuts. Yield: 4 portions.

CITRUS SPARERIBS · MRS. JOHN POWELL, CALIF.

4 pounds spareribs
1 large lemon
1 large orange
1 large onion
1 cup catsup
2 cups water
1 teaspoon chili powder
1 teaspoon salt
⅓ teaspoon Worcestershire
　sauce
2 dashes Tabasco

Cut ribs into serving size pieces. Place in a shallow roasting pan, meaty side up. On each piece arrange a slice of unpeeled lemon, unpeeled orange and onion. Bake at 450°F. for 20 minutes. Combine remaining ingredients, bring to boiling point and pour over ribs. Continue baking at 350°F. until tender, about 1 hour, basting twice. Yield: 4 to 6 portions.

BARBECUED SPARERIBS · JAMES R. DUNLAP, CHEVY CHASE, MD.

3 to 4 pounds ribs, cut in
　pieces
1 lemon
1 large onion
2 cups water
1 cup catsup
⅓ cup Worcestershire sauce
2 dashes Tabasco
1 teaspoon salt
1 teaspoon chili powder

Place spareribs in shallow pan meaty side up. On each lay a thin slice of unpeeled lemon and onion. Roast at 450°F. for 30 minutes. Combine remaining ingredients, bring to a boil and pour over ribs. Continue roasting at 350°F. until tender, about 1 hour. Baste ribs with the sauce every 15 minutes. If sauce gets too thick, add more water. Yield: 4 portions.

BARBECUED PORK · MRS. CARL STEWART, DES MOINES, IOWA

1 fresh pork tenderloin
Olive oil or salad oil
Clove garlic, cut
1 to 2 tablespoons crumbled
   fresh dried sage

Split tenderloin lengthwise almost through. Make parallel cuts an inch apart down to within 2 inches of the thin end. Take cleaver and pound thick end to about the thickness of the tail end (about half-inch thick). Rub cut surface with oil and the clove garlic. Sprinkle sage over tenderloin. Roll up and let stand for at least 2 hours. Unroll and grill over hickory coals, at least 5 to 6 inches from medium heat. This will take 35 to 45 minutes. To test for doneness cut through thickest portion. No blood must show. Pork may look pink but the meat must look dry. Serve with barbecue sauce: Yield: 2 to 3 portions.

NOTE: Surface of tenderloin may be rubbed with a little liquid smoke, if you lack the hickory.

BARBECUE SAUCE:
1 can (8 ounces) tomato
   sauce
1 can water
1 small clove garlic, minced
1¼ teaspoon prepared
   mustard
¼ teaspoon salt
⅛ teaspoon fresh ground
   pepper
⅛ teaspoon paprika
Juice of ½ lemon

1½ teaspoon Worcestershire sauce
2 tablespoons vinegar
1 sprig parsley
1 small onion, minced
Tabasco to taste

Combine all ingredients, except Tabasco, in saucepan. Cover and bring to boiling point. Reduce heat and simmer 30 minutes, stirring occasionally. Add Tabasco to the hotness desired. Yield: ¾ cup sauce.

BAKED HAM · WILLIAMSBURG, VA.

1 12-pound smoked ham
½ cup vinegar
½ cup brown sugar, firmly
   packed
3 cups dry bread crumbs
½ cup water from ham
¼ cup melted butter or
   margarine
½ cup finely chopped
   chow-chow
Cucumber pickle to garnish

Wash ham. Cover with cold water. Add vinegar and sugar. Simmer 4 hours or until tender. Remove skin. Score fat in diamond shapes. Combine bread crumbs, water from ham, butter and chow-chow, making a thick paste. Pat this into cuts of fat, and make a layer over it. Garnish with slices of cucumber pickle. Cover. Bake at 375°F. for 2 hours. Yield: 24 portions.

COLONEL FREEMAN'S MARYLAND STUFFED HAM · FREDERICK STIEFF, BALTIMORE, MD.

1 15-pound smoked ham
3 pounds spinach
3 pounds kale
1 large handful shallots,
    chopped, or 2 onions,
    chopped
1 teaspoon celery seed
Salt and pepper

If ham is strongly cured, soak overnight in cold water. Then add fresh cold water to cover and simmer for 1 hour. Wash spinach and kale thoroughly; remove all stems and chop leaves fine. Combine vegetables and celery seed; season to taste. After the 1 hour of cooking remove ham but leave skin on. With a long sharp knife make incisions in the ham as deep and as many as possible. Dampen the stuffing (greens and seasonings) with liquor in which ham boiled and fill the incisions with just as much as you can get in. Spread remaining stuffing over top of ham. Wrap ham tightly in a large piece of cheesecloth; sew together well. Return to pot and simmer until tender, about 15 minutes per pound. Remove from liquid and refrigerate, leaving the covering on for a day, or until ready to use. Yield: about 30 portions.

FRUITED BAKED HAM · MRS. FRANCES MC CLUER, FULTON, MO.

1 smoked ham, 10 to 12
    pounds
½ cup brown sugar, firmly
    packed
2 teaspoons dry mustard
½ teaspoon paprika
Whole cloves
1 cup pineapple juice

Soak well-scrubbed ham overnight in cold water to cover and then rinse. Add boiling water to cover; simmer, partially covered, for 25 to 30 minutes per pound, or until meat is tender. Cool ham slightly in stock, then drain. Remove rind and score fat into diamonds. Rub mixture of brown sugar, mustard, and paprika into surface; stud with cloves in diamond formation. Bake, uncovered, at 400°F. about 30 minutes, basting several times with pineapple juice. Yield: 25 to 30 portions.

VICKSBURG STUFFED BAKED HAM · MARY MC KAY, VICKSBURG, MISS.

10- to 12-pound ham
1 tablespoon vinegar
2 tablespoons brown sugar
Steaming water

Cut off ham hock. Add vinegar and brown sugar to water and steam ham until meat is tender enough to feel loose at the bone. Remove bone and all fat. Reserve 1 cup of the fat. Fill bone cavity with dressing. Cover outside of ham about 2½ inches thick with remaining dressing. Wrap securely in cheesecloth and tie tightly with cord. Bake at 300°F. for 1½ hour. Chill 24 hours and slice thinly.

DRESSING:

1 cup ham fat, ground
1 pound toasted crackers,
    ground
1 small loaf toasted bread,
    ground
2 medium onions, ground
1 stalk celery, ground
2 tablespoons sugar
1 teaspoon mustard seed

1 teaspoon dry mustard
½ cup pickle relish
1 tablespoon chopped parsley
4 eggs, beaten
1 cup sherry wine
4 dashes Tabasco
Vinegar to make a paste-like consistency, not too soft.

Thoroughly combine all ingredients. Stuff ham as directed.

BAKED HAM WITH APPLES · MRS. CARL WOODWARD, NEW ORLEANS, LA.

1 12- to 14-pound hickory-
    smoked ham, uncooked
6 apples
Juice of 1 lemon
¼ cup whole allspice
¼ cup whole cloves
¼ cup black peppercorns
3 pepper pods
Few pieces fresh thyme
4 bay leaves
1½ cups vinegar
1 stalk celery, diced
1 bunch carrots, diced
Cloves to quilt ham
2 cups brown sugar
1½ cups sherry wine

Place ham in large kettle, cover with water. Peel apples, leaving ½ inch skin on stem end. Add peelings to ham pot. Sprinkle apples with lemon juice and hold for later use. Add spices, herbs, vinegar and vegetables to pot. Slowly simmer, allowing 15 minutes to a pound of meat, cooking until the small bone of the ham feels loose. Cool in stock overnight. Skin ham, leaving on 3 inches at hock end. Score fat in diamond pattern and quilt with whole cloves. Cover ½ inch thick with brown sugar. Sprinkle with sherry. Place in roasting pan with peeled apples around ham. Bake at 350°F. for 30 minutes or until crust browns. Serve just warm.

Yield: 18 portions.

HAM IN BEER · GENERAL FRANK DORN, SAN FRANCISCO, CALIF.

1 tenderized ham
1 cup brown sugar
½ cup dry mustard
4 tablespoons water (about)
Whole cloves
12 bay leaves
3 cans beer

Remove all but a thin layer of fat from the ham. Score surface of remaining fat. Place in roaster. Mix sugar, mustard, and water to the consistency of prepared mustard. Cover surface of ham with this mixture. Quilt with cloves, using them generously. Fasten bay leaves to ham with toothpicks. Pour in beer and cover pan. Bake at 450°F. for 20 minutes per pound of ham. Before serving decorate with quarter slices of pineapple and maraschino cherries, fastening in place with toothpicks. Use beer liquid as sauce for ham.

DUNCAN HINES' HICKORY-SMOKED HAM

1 hickory-smoked ham
6 medium onions, sliced
2¾ cups brown sugar
2 cups cider-vinegar
    or cooking wine
2 bay leaves
24 whole cloves
1 cup dry bread crumbs
2 teaspoons dry mustard
1 teaspoon ground cloves

Cover ham with cold water; soak 1 to 3 days, changing water frequently. Scrub ham, place on rack, skin side down in large kettle. Cover with cold water. Add onions, 2 cups brown sugar, vinegar, bay leaves and whole cloves. Bring to boiling; simmer 20 to 25 minutes per pound. When small bone at hock end can be twisted out, ham will be done. Let ham cool in water. Remove skin; cut off some of fat. Score fat. Mix remaining ¾ cup sugar, bread crumbs, mustard and cloves. Pat on ham, while fat is moist. Bake at 400°F. for 25 minutes or until ham is glazed and brown. Cut ham in very thin slices when serving.

HAM LOAF, BOILED · EDITH DAVISON, DES MOINES, IOWA

3 eggs, beaten
1½ pounds smoked ham,
    ground
1½ pounds fresh ham, ground
6 large soda crackers,
    crushed
2 quarts water
½ cup vinegar

Combine eggs, ham, and cracker crumbs. Form into a roll and tie loosely in cheesecloth. Combine water with vinegar and bring to a boil. Place ham roll in boiling liquid and simmer 1½ hours. Remove cloth and slice. Serve hot or cold with this horseradish sauce.
    Yield: 8 portions.

HORSERADISH SAUCE:
¼ cup grated and drained
    horseradish
½ tablespoon prepared
    mustard
¼ teaspoon salt
Few grains cayenne
Dash of paprika

1 tablespoon vinegar
½ cup heavy cream, whipped

Mix together all ingredients, except cream. Slowly stir mixture into cream. Chill. Serve cold. Yield: ⅔ cup sauce.

HAM LOAF · MADELINE LAMBERT, TULSA, OKLA.

1 egg beaten
½ cup milk
1 tablespoon onion juice
Dash of Worcestershire sauce
½ cup fine cracker crumbs
1½ teaspoons salt
¼ teaspoon pepper
1 pound ground beef

½ pound ground lean pork
½ pound ground cured ham

Combine egg, milk, onion juice, Worcestershire, crumbs, salt and pepper. Add to ground meats; mix thoroughly. Pack into 9×5×3-inch greased loaf pan. Bake at 350°F. for 1½ hours. Serve with horseradish sauce. Yield: 8 portions.

HORSERADISH SAUCE:
1 cup heavy cream, whipped
¼ cup prepared horseradish

Dash of salt
    Combine all ingredients; blend well.

PANTRY HAM LOAF · EDITH B. CRUMB, DEARBORN, MICH.

2 pounds finely ground ham,
    butt end
1 pound finely ground fresh
    pork
2 cups bread crumbs
¾ cup milk
2 eggs
¾ teaspoon salt
1½ teaspoons sugar

1 cup canned tomatoes
    Mix ham and pork with bread crumbs. Add milk and eggs, mixing well. Mold into loaf form and place in baking pan. Add salt and sugar to tomatoes and cook 10 minutes. Pour half of tomatoes over loaf. Save remainder to use for basting during baking. Bake, uncovered, at 350°F. for 30 minutes. Cover and bake 1 hour longer. Serve with hot mustard sauce.
    Yield: 8 portions.

EDITH'S MUSTARD SAUCE:
2 eggs
2 tablespoons flour
1 tablespoon dry mustard
1 cup brown sugar

1 cup vinegar
1 cup consommé
    Combine ingredients and cook in double boiler over hot water until thick. Yield: 1¼ cups sauce.

ENDIVE-HAM ROLLS · MRS. ABRAHAM ELKON, PURCHASE, N.Y.

12 small to medium stalks
    endive
6 slices boiled ham, ¼-inch
    thick
½ pound Swiss cheese, grated
2 cups medium cream sauce
Bread crumbs
Butter or margarine

Wash endive, place in kettle and cover with water. Cook until just tender, about 10 minutes. Drain well; trim root ends. Cut ham slices in half. Lay stalk of endive on ham; roll up. Fasten with toothpicks. Place in a shallow baking dish. Add cheese to sauce; heat in top of double boiler till cheese is melted. Pour sauce over ham rolls, cover with crumbs and dot with butter. Bake at 350°F. until mixture is bubbling and crumbs are browned, about 15 minutes. Yield: 6 portions.

SAUSAGE FRUIT SCRAPPLE · PENNSYLVANIA

1 cup wheat cereal
3½ cups boiling water
1 pound sausage meat
1 tablespoon chopped parsley
½ teaspoon salt
Flour
Fried bananas

Combine cereal and boiling water in top of double boiler. Cook over boiling water for 45 minutes. Fry sausage until browned. Add to cooked wheat mixture with parsley and salt. Pour into a loaf and chill. Cut into ¼-inch slices. Dredge with flour. Fry in hot fat until browned. Serve with fried bananas. Yield: 6 portions.

INDIANA SCRAPPLE · MARIAN SCHLEICHER

2½-pound soup bone with
    about 1½ pounds of meat
    on it
2 to 3 quarts boiling water
2 cups yellow corn meal
2 teaspoons salt
½ cup grated carrots
    (optional)
½ cup bacon or pork
    drippings

Cover soup bone with boiling water in heavy kettle. Cover kettle and bring to a boil; reduce heat and simmer until meat begins to fall away from the bone, about 2½ to 3 hours. Add water to bone as it cooks to keep it covered. When meat is done, remove from stock and dice into very small pieces. Reheat stock to boiling temperature (there should be about 8 cups) and slowly stir in corn meal and salt. Add diced meat and grated carrots. Cook, uncovered, until mixture is very thick, stirring several times. Pour mixture into two 9×5×3-inch loaf pans that have been rinsed with cold water. Press down with a spoon to form even, solid loaf. Cover with waxed paper and refrigerate overnight. Turn out of pan, slice about ½ inch thick and fry in hot bacon or pork fat, until golden brown on both sides. Serve as a main dish with syrup.

Yield: 36 ½-inch slices or about 12 "supper" portions.

CABBAGE AND SCRAPPLE · PENNSYLVANIA

1 small head cabbage
½ pound scrapple
1 teaspoon salt
2 tablespoons catsup
1 tablespoon chili sauce
½ cup minced cooked
    vegetables or meat
⅓ cup cream or milk, about
6 strips lean bacon

Line a greased, deep casserole with the outer leaves of cabbage head. Core and chop remaining cabbage with scrapple until quite fine. Add seasonings, vegetables or meat and moisten with cream. Fill center of casserole. Arrange bacon over top. Bake at 375°F. for 20 to 30 minutes, or until thoroughly heated and bacon is crisp. Yield: 6 portions.

OATMEAL SAUSAGE · MRS. DONALD DRAKE, INDIANAPOLIS, IND.

2 pounds pork shoulder
2 pounds beef-neck meat
1½ cups steel-cut rolled oats
1 tablespoon brown sugar
2 tablespoons salt
1 teaspoon poultry seasoning

½ teaspoon of each of the following: cinnamon, cloves, allspice, ginger, mace, nutmeg, pepper, paprika, salt

Wipe off pork shoulder and beef neck with damp cloth. Cover with water, bring to a simmer and cook until tender, about 3 hours. Put meats through food chopper. Cook oats in meat stock 25 to 30 minutes. Add ground meat to oatmeal; add sugar and seasonings. Turn into two 9×5×2½-inch loaf pans. Let stand in cool place until set. Slice to fry. Yield: 2 loaves.

Sauces and Marinades

ROAST BEEF SAUCE · MRS. WILLIAM KENT, MEMPHIS, TENN.

1 bunch watercress
1 bottle (12 ounces) chili
    sauce
¼ teaspoon Tabasco
1 tablespoon horseradish

Wash watercress, dry well and finely mince. Add the sauces and horseradish. Chill. Serve cold.
    Yield: 1½ cups sauce.

MARINADE FOR STEAKS · JAMES R. DUNLOP, CHEVY CHASE, MD.

9 tablespoons bourbon
    whiskey or red wine
6 tablespoons soy sauce
2 tablespoons garlic vinegar
2 tablespoons oil
½ teaspoon plain salt or
    smoked salt
½ teaspoon of almost any
    herb
½ teaspoon monosodium
    glutamate
½ teaspoon freshly ground
    pepper

Combine all ingredients and mix well. (The bourbon imparts a special flavor and the Dunlops prefer it to wine.) Yield: about 1 cup sauce.

STEAK MARINADE · BEN PROJAN, PHOENIX, ARIZ.

1 quart soya sauce
2 cups beef consommé
½ cup lemon juice
Liquid smoke to taste
3 cloves garlic

Combine ingredients, mixing well. Yield: sufficient to marinade six steaks, one pound each.

JEZEBEL SAUCE · MRS. ROBERT E. BOGUE, WICHITA, KAN.

1 cup apple jelly
½ cup pineapple preserves
¼ cup prepared mustard
1 to 2 tablespoons prepared
    horseradish
Salt and freshly ground
    pepper

Blend first 4 ingredients. Add salt and pepper to taste. Serve with baked ham or meat loaf.
    Yield: about 2 cups sauce.

BARBECUE SAUCE · JOHN SNIVELY, JR., FLORIDA

1 gallon cider vinegar
6 bottles catsup
¾ bottle Tabasco
1½ bottles (6-ounce) A-1
    sauce
1½ bottles (10-ounces)
    Worcestershire sauce
1½ bottles (8-ounce) beefsteak
    sauce
¼ cup black pepper
1 cup butter or margarine
1 cup sugar
½ medium-sized garlic head
    (about 4 buds), mashed

1 orange halved, juice and whole shells
1 grapefruit halved, juice and whole shells
Salt to taste
3 onions, diced
2 bay leaves
Oregano

Combine ingredients and bring to a boil. Remove from heat and let stand overnight. Strain before using. Fasten a new dish mop to a stick and swab the meat every 30 minutes over a 6 to 8 hour period. Yield: about 2 gallons.

NOTE: Leftover sauce keeps for weeks in the refrigerator.

GREAT SMOKY BARBECUE SAUCE · COLONEL JACK LAPHAM, BANDERA, TEX.

1 cup catsup
½ cup prepared mustard
½ cup Worcestershire sauce
½ cup salad oil
¼ cup grated horseradish
2 tablespoons brown sugar
1 tablespoon liquid smoke
2½ ounces crushed chili
    peppers
2 teaspoons cumin seed
2 teaspoons mixed spices
2 teaspoons salt
2 teaspoons paprika

3 quarts beef stock
3 tablespoons vinegar
1 medium onion, sliced
1 small clove garlic, cut up
½ cup cornstarch

Combine all ingredients, except cornstarch, and bring to a boil. Strain through a fine sieve. Return to kettle. Mix the cornstarch and enough water to form a smooth paste. Add gradually to hot liquid and cook about 10 minutes. Yield: 1 gallon sauce. Keeps and can be used in many ways.

LA SALSA DE TOMATE Y CHILI VERDE · ANA BEGUE DE PACKMAN, CALIF.

4 long green chili peppers
3 tomatoes
1 small onion, minced
½ teaspoon salt

Roast and blister peppers and tomatoes over flame or in a broiler. Remove skin and stems (if peppers are not soft, steam until tender). Finely chop the peppers and tomatoes; blend in onion and salt. A delicious sauce and ready to serve with barbecued and broiled meats.

Yield: 2 cups sauce.

BARBECUE SAUCE · MRS. GEORGE D. SEARS, MEDINA, TEX.

2 cups chili sauce
½ cup tarragon vinegar
½ cup brown sugar, firmly
    packed
2 tablespoons powdered
    mustard
3 tablespoons chopped young
    green onion
2 bay leaves
2 cloves garlic
2 dashes Worcestershire
    sauce
2 drops Tabasco
2 tablespoons butter or
    margarine

Combine ingredients. Simmer 1 hour or until mixture thickens, stirring occasionally. Remove garlic. Serve hot, thinned with water. Yield: 2 cups thick sauce.

Barbecued Spareribs: Spread spareribs with liquid smoke. Season with salt and pepper. Bake at 300°F. about 2½ hours, draining off fat when necessary, then baste with sauce.

SAVORY LEMON PATS · CAROL ACKLEY, CALIF.

½ cup butter or margarine
2 teaspoons grated lemon
    rind
3 tablespoons fresh lemon
    juice
teaspoon seasoned salt
2 tablespoons finely chopped
    parsley
⅛ teaspoon savory
⅛ teaspoon rosemary

Cream butter until soft. Add lemon rind and juice gradually, mixing until butter has absorbed juice. Stir in seasoned salt, chopped parsley, savory and rosemary. Place on waxed paper and mold into a roll. Chill until firm. Slice and serve on broiled steaks or hamburgers. Also delicious with chicken and fish.

Yield: 12 pats.

Poultry

CHICKEN BREAST ON SLICED HAM · WARREN POSEY, NEW ORLEANS, LA.

8 chicken breasts
¼ cup butter or margarine
3 scallions including tops,
    minced
½ cup minced parsley
1 clove garlic, minced
Pinch of thyme
1 bay leaf
2 cups fresh mushrooms,
    sliced
4 cups medium white sauce
2 egg yolks, slightly beaten

Salt and pepper
4, ½-inch thick slices cooked ham

Cook chicken breasts until tender. Meanwhile melt butter in frying pan; add scallions, parsley, garlic, thyme, bay leaf and mushrooms. Sauté until scallion is golden. Add to white sauce. Gradually add to egg yolks; season to taste with salt and pepper. In a greased baking pan, arrange slices of ham; top with chicken breasts; pour over sauce. Bake at 350°F. for 15 minutes or until piping hot.

Yield: 8 portions.

BROILERS SIMSBURY · MRS. J. KELL BRANDON, SIMSBURY, CONN.

3 1-inch-thick slices fresh
    smoked ham (about 2
    pounds)
½ pound butter or margarine
2 pounds fresh mushrooms
4 plump broilers, quartered
½ cup chicken stock

Cut ham into 1-inch cubes and brown in ¼ pound hot butter; remove and keep hot. Sauté mushrooms lightly in same hot butter. Place chicken pieces in large roasting pan. Pour ham, mushrooms and butter around chicken. Dot with remaining butter. Bake at 450°F. for 10 minutes. Pour off about ½ cup of the fat and add stock to pan. Continue baking for 45 minutes or until chicken is tender, basting birds every 15 minutes. Yield: 8 portions.

PICNIC BROILERS · MRS. WILLIAM D. MC MILLAN, ITHACA, N.Y.

6 broilers
½ cup vegetable oil
2 tablespoons lemon juice
¼ teaspoon salt
⅛ teaspoon marjoram

Day before the picnic, have the broilers dressed and cut into halves; keep the giblets for stew. Brush each half-broiler with mixture of oil, lemon juice, salt and marjoram. Lay halves in waxed-paper-lined enamel roaster, one over the other and cover with waxed paper. Store overnight in refrigerator. Before starting for the picnic spot, again brush chicken with oil mixture. When the outdoor fire is a smooth gray mass of coals, lay chicken on oiled broiler, skin-side down and quickly brown. Turn and brown other side. Place pieces in roaster, cover and allow to remain in a just-warm spot over fire, maybe 15 minutes, until flesh cooks down to the bone. Just before serving again, brush the bird with oil mixture and season to taste with salt and pepper. Yield: 12 portions.

CHICKEN BRAZIL · ROBIN WOODS, LITTLE ROCK, ARK.

1 5-pound stewing chicken,
    cut up
1 tablespoon salt
1 onion
⅛ lemon, sliced
3 celery tops
1 sprig parsley
1 bay leaf
1 cup light raisins
½ cup dry white wine
2 tablespoons butter or
    margarine
¼ cup flour
2 cups light cream
Salt to taste
Dash of cayenne pepper
Pinch of saffron
1 cup blanched almonds
Mace or allspice to taste
¼ cup finely chopped
    pimiento
¼ cup finely chopped green
    pepper

8 cups cooked rice

Cover chicken with cold water. Add 1 tablespoon salt, onion, lemon, celery tops, parsley, and bay leaf. Simmer, covered, 3 to 4 hours or until chicken is tender. Remove chicken from broth. Remove meat from bones; dice. Return bones to broth; continue cooking until broth is reduced to about 3 cups. Strain broth; skim off fat; reserve fat and broth. Allow raisins to stand in wine until plump, about 15 minutes. Heat butter and 2 tablespoons of the reserved chicken fat. Blend in flour. Add 2 cups of the reserved chicken broth and cream. Cook over low heat, stirring, until the mixture thickens and comes to a boil. Add salt, cayenne pepper and saffron. Blend in raisins and wine. Add chicken and almonds; mix. Add mace. Stir in pimiento and green pepper. Reheat. Serve over rice. Yield: 10 portions.

BRUNSWICK STEW · WILLIAMSBURG, VA.

1 5-pound chicken, cut into
   pieces
5 quarts cold water
2 teaspoons salt
2 cups cut fresh string beans
4 potatoes, pared and diced
2 cups cut okra
3 medium tomatoes,
   quartered
¼ cup flour

1 can (1 pound 4 ounces) corn kernels

Wash chicken. Place in large kettle with water. Bring slowly to a boil and simmer 1 hour or until meat is tender. Skim fat; reserve. Add salt and vegetables, except corn. Cover and simmer 30 minutes or until chicken is tender. Blend ¼ cup of the chicken fat with with flour and add to stew. Cook until thickened, stirring occasionally. Add corn and cook 5 minutes longer. Serve at once. Yield: 6 portions.

MOLLY McCREA'S BRUNSWICK STEW · MRS. ARCHIBALD MC CREA, CARTER'S GROVE, VA.

1 4- to 4½-pound stewing
   chicken, cut into pieces
3 quarts water
6 medium tomatoes, peeled
4 large potatoes, pared and
   cut into halves
4 medium onions
2 cups fresh okra
1 cup butter or margarine
2 cups fresh sweet corn (6
   medium ears)

Salt and pepper
4 tablespoons flour

Place chicken and water in large kettle or Dutch oven. Bring to a boil. Simmer, covered, for 1 hour. Add tomatoes, potatoes, onions, okra and butter. Simmer, covered, for 3 hours. Add corn and salt and pepper to taste. Make a paste with flour and a small amount of the hot liquid. Stir into stew. Simmer 10 minutes longer, stirring occasionally. Yield: 6 portions.

FRED'S BRUNSWICK STEW · CONRAD FREDERICK SMITH, TRENTON, TENN.

1 3- to 5-pound hen (stewing
   chicken) ready to cook
3 tablespoons salt
½ pound salt pork
Corn cut from 6 ears
5 medium onions, sliced
1 pound of okra
2 pounds lima beans, shelled
2 green peppers, chopped
5 large tomatoes, quartered
½ teaspoon pepper

1 pod red pepper or
   ⅛ teaspoon Tabasco

Wash hen in large pot and cover with water. Add salt. Slice pork down to the skin and put in pot. Simmer till meat separates from bones, about 3 hours. Remove bones and add all vegetables. Add seasonings. Reduce heat until mixture barely simmers, stirring often to prevent sticking. Stew is ready when it is thick and mushy. Add more seasonings if desired. Serve in warm bowls. Yield: 10 portions.

CHICKEN CACCIATORE · CHEF MILANI, LOS ANGELES, CALIF.

2 2-pound broilers
3 tablespoons olive oil
4 cloves garlic, minced
Salt to taste
Pepper to taste
Pinch of crumbled oregano
2 leaves basil, crumbled
1 can (1 pound, 4 ounces)
    solid pack tomatoes,
    mashed
1 can (4 ounces) button
    mushrooms, drained
2 tablespoons butter or
    margarine
¼ cup sherry wine
1 tablespoon minced parsley

Disjoint broilers. Heat olive oil in a deep frying pan. Add chicken and season with garlic, salt, pepper, oregano, and basil. Brown. Add tomatoes. In separate pan sauté mushrooms in butter, add to chicken. Cover, and cook 15 minutes. Remove cover and add sherry, cooking uncovered 10 minutes. Sprinkle with parsley
    Yield: 6 portions.

CHICKEN CACCIATORE · LARRY NICHOLS, DALLAS, TEX.

1 3½-pound chicken, cut up
1 cup cooking sherry
1½ cloves garlic, finely
    chopped
Salt and pepper
Flour
Fat for frying
2 cups finely chopped onion
1½ cups finely chopped green
    pepper
1 teaspoon salt
⅜ teaspoon white pepper
1½ teaspoons curry powder
1½ teaspoons powdered
    thyme
2 cans (16 to 17 ounces each)
    tomatoes
1 teaspoon chopped parsley
4 cups hot cooked rice
1 cup sliced toasted almonds
1 cup currants

Marinate chicken in mixture of sherry and 1 of the finely chopped garlic cloves for 2 hours in a cool place. Remove chicken pieces from sherry; season with salt and pepper, roll in flour. Fry in shallow hot fat (350°F.) until golden brown. Place in preheated roasting pan; cover and place in a warm oven. (This is the secret of success.)

To prepare sauce: Combine onions, peppers and remaining garlic. Sauté in about 4 tablespoons of the frying fat until tender, about 4 minutes, stirring constantly. Stir in salt, pepper, curry powder and thyme. Add tomatoes and parsley. Stir in sherry marinade. Heat. Pour sauce over chicken. Cover pan. Bake at 350°F. for 40 minutes or until tender. Remove chicken and keep warm. Add currants to sauce. Season further if desired. Put chicken in center of rice ring mold. Cover with sauce. Sprinkle almonds over top. Yield: 6 portions.

CHICKEN CASSEROLE · MRS. ROBERT E. BOGUE, WICHITA, KAN.

STEP 1: CHICKEN

(May be done one day in advance.)
1 4- to 5-pound stewing
   chicken, cut in pieces
1 carrot, sliced
1 onion, quartered
1½ teaspoon salt
Water

Place chicken, carrot, onion, and salt in deep kettle. Cover with water; bring to a boil. Simmer covered until meat is fork-tender, about 3 to 4 hours. Remove chicken from broth. When cool remove skin and meat from bones; put both through meat grinder. Strain broth. Refrigerate meat and broth until ready to prepare casserole.

STEP 2: STUFFING

1 medium onion, finely
   chopped
2 large stalks celery with
   tops, finely chopped
½ cup chicken fat, from broth
6 tablespoons chicken broth
1 teaspoon salt
1 teaspoon pepper
1 teaspoon sage or poultry
   seasoning
3 quarts soft bread crumbs
   or cubes

Sauté onion and celery in chicken fat 5 minutes. Add chicken broth, salt, pepper, and sage. Add to bread crumbs; mix lightly.

STEP 3: SAUCE

1 cup chicken fat, from broth
1 cup flour
2 teaspoons salt
4 cups hot chicken broth
1 cup milk
4 eggs, slightly beaten

If necessary, add butter to chicken fat to make 1 cup. Melt fat in large skillet. Add flour and salt; blend until smooth. Stir in broth and milk and cook until thick. Remove from heat. Cool slightly. Stir a little of mixture into eggs; combine with rest of mixture. Do not reheat.

STEP 4: CASSEROLE

1 cup dry bread crumbs
¼ cup butter or margarine,
   melted

Put stuffing in greased 4-quart casserole. Cover stuffing with ½ of the sauce. Add layer of chicken, cover with remaining sauce. Sprinkle with combined bread crumbs and butter. Bake at 375°F. for 30 minutes, or until crumbs brown. Yield: 20 portions.

CHICKEN CREOLE · ANTOINE'S, NEW ORLEANS, LA.

1 3½-pound frying chicken
¼ cup olive oil
1 can (1 pound, 4 ounces)
    tomatoes
2 tablespoons butter or
    margarine
1 teaspoon salt
Few grains pepper
Few grains cayenne
1 sprig thyme
1 tablespoon minced parsley
1 bay leaf
3 cloves garlic, minced
1 tablespoon flour
6 chopped shallots, or ½ cup
    minced onion
5 tablespoons chopped green
    pepper
½ cup white wine

Disjoint chicken. Wipe pieces with damp cloth. Sauté in olive oil, turning to brown both sides. Combine tomatoes and 1 tablespoon butter; simmer 10 minutes, stirring occasionally. Add salt, pepper, cayenne; cook 10 minutes. Add thyme, parsley, bay leaf, and garlic; cook 15 minutes or until sauce is thick. Melt 1 tablespoon butter; blend in flour; cook until brown. Add chopped shallots and green pepper; brown slightly. Add wine, stirring constantly, until slightly thickened. Add chicken. Cover; simmer 45 minutes, or until chicken is tender. If desired, place chicken on hot cooked rice; garnish with avocado slices and parsley sprigs.

Yield: 4 portions.

INDIAN CHICKEN CURRY · MRS. HAROLD HOLCOMB, PHOENIX, ARIZ.

1 4- to 5-pound fowl, cut up
5 cups boiling water
1 teaspoon salt
¾ cup finely chopped onion
3 tablespoons peanut oil
1 whole clove
1½ teaspoons curry powder
1½ teaspoons turmeric
1½ teaspoons ginger
1 teaspoon cardamom
1 teaspoon marjoram
⅓ teaspoon thyme
1 small bunch parsley, finely
    chopped
½ cup chopped carrot
¼ cup celery leaves

4 chili peppers, chopped
1½ cups chicken broth
1½ cups coconut water

Cook chicken in boiling salted water until tender; about 2 hours. Remove chicken pieces from pot and reserve broth. Sauté onion in oil until tender, being careful not to burn. Add all the seasonings and blend well. Add chicken broth and coconut water, stirring well. Remove chicken from bone and cut into small pieces. Add to sauce and simmer for 15 minutes. Serve with rice and pineapple chutney. Yield: 8 portions.

NOTE: Make coconut water by soaking 1 cup coconut in 1¾ cups water for several hours and drain; use water, not coconut milk.

CHICKEN CEROLA · MRS. ELIOT FLETCHER, TAMPA, FLA.

1 2- to 3-pound frying
    chicken, cut in pieces
1 clove garlic, minced
1 teaspoon salt
3 tablespoons lemon juice
¼ cup white wine
1 bay leaf
3 tablespoons oil
1 tablespoon flour
¼ cup chopped onion
¼ cup chopped green pepper
1 cup diced carrots
½ cup sherry wine

Rub pieces of chicken with cut garlic and sprinkle with salt. Arrange chicken in large pot. Mince the cut garlic and add with lemon juice, wine and bay leaf. Let stand about 2 hours. If pieces are not covered with this marinade, turn a few times. Remove chicken pieces from marinade, reserving marinade, and brown in oil. Remove chicken and add flour to drippings, stirring until smooth. Add onion, green pepper and carrots to pan and cook 1 minute. Add marinade and heat. Arrange browned chicken in casserole and pour contents of skillet over chicken. Add sherry. Cover. Bake at 350°F. for about 40 minutes or until no pink shows at the bone. If desired, potato balls can be added to the casserole to cook with the chicken. Yield: 2 to 4 portions.

FRIED CHICKEN · MARION FITCH AND JANE POOR, LINCOLN, MASS.

1 5- to 6-pound fowl, dressed
1 quart boiling water
1½ teaspoons salt
Butter or margarine
Pepper to taste

Place bird and water in pan; cover. Simmer 1 hour; add salt and cook 30 minutes longer. Cool bird in stock to room temperature. Remove, thicken stock and place in refrigerator. When thoroughly chilled, remove skin and bones. (Cooling helps set the meat and makes it easier to handle in frying.) Fry pieces in butter until browned, using just enough fat so that the meat doesn't stick. Add more salt if desired and pepper to taste. Yield: 6 portions.

MISSISSIPPI FRIED CHICKEN · MRS. PHIL MAYHALL, GREENVILLE, MISS.

2½-pound frying chicken
½ cup flour
1 teaspoon salt
Pepper
Vegetable shortening
1 cup water, milk or cream
1 tablespoon finely chopped
    parsley

Have butcher cut chicken into frying pieces. Combine flour, salt and pepper and coat chicken pieces one at a time. Drop into skillet in 1½ inches hot fat. Brown quickly on each side. Reduce heat to low and let chicken slowly brown on each side until tender, 15 to 20 minutes. Pour off all but 2 tablespoons of fat from the pan. Take 2 tablespoons of the flour left over after dredging the chicken, add to fat and brown. Add 1 cup liquid gradually, stirring constantly. Add salt and pepper to taste, and parsley.
Yield: 3 portions.

MISS CORA'S FRIED CHICKEN · MRS. CORA HANCOCK, GIRDLETREE, MD.

1 3-pound Delmarva chicken
1 tablespoon salt
⅛ teaspoon pepper
1 teaspoon baking powder
½ cup water
¼ cup milk
1 cup flour
¾ cup lard

Cut chicken up in individual serving pieces and put pieces in bowl. Combine salt, pepper and baking powder, mix well. Add water and milk and then the flour all at once. Stir thoroughly and mix until a batter is formed. Coat each piece of chicken with batter; place lard in a 10-inch frying pan and heat to the smoking point. Place chicken in hot fat and cover with a heavy lid, let cook over medium heat until golden brown. Turn and brown on other side. Entire cooking time is about 25 to 30 minutes. Remove from fat to serving dish. Serve hot or cold with hot rolls, salad and vegetables. This chicken carries well for a picnic, too. Yield: 4 portions.

SOUTHERN FRIED CHICKEN · ELIZABETH PARKER, ATLANTA, GA.

1 2½-pound broiler
1 teaspoon salt
½ teaspoon pepper
½ cup flour
1½ cups vegetable shortening
    or lard

Disjoint chicken, cut into pieces: drumsticks, thighs, wings; cut breast into the pulley-bone piece and 2 side portions; make 3 parts of the backbone. Lay aside wings, back parts and neck to steam, and remove meat from bones—tomorrow's chicken pie. Wash remaining chicken pieces thoroughly, pat dry with a clean cloth. Season with salt and pepper, dredge in flour. Melt fat to 1-inch depth in heavy frying pan. Keep heat just below smoking point. Lay in thick meaty pieces first—these take the longest to cook. Brown quickly on one side, then on the other. Cover pan, lower heat and cook until done; that is, until there is no pinkness of meat at the bone. Yield: 2 portions.

Gravy: Pour off all but 4 tablespoons fat, add 4 tablespoons flour to fat in pan and blend; slowly add 1 cup milk, 1 cup cream, salt and pepper to taste. Cook gravy until smooth and thick.

FRIED CHICKEN · KANSAS

For honest-to-goodness Kansas fried chicken take ⅓ butter to ⅔ lard and enough to stand ½ to ⅝ inches deep in a wide, thick-walled skillet of iron. When the fat is hot but not smoking, lay in the chicken, allowing plenty of turning room. Largest pieces first, you know, to give extra cooking time. Turn the pieces as soon as they are brown and keep the pan partly covered so the fat can't splutter, but not a tight cover, for the steam must escape. Use moderate heat throughout the frying and whenever a piece is done remove immediately to crock or pan with a rack in the bottom so the fat drains off.

When cold, lay the pieces in a big bread pan padded with paper towels. Cover with a tea towel, à la 1912. When the towel is lifted there is chicken in a golden pyramid, piece upon piece, crisp but not crackly, the soft meat finely grained under the coating. Thin slices of homemade yeast bread and plenty of butter are the thing to eat with fried chicken. And pass crisp chunks of watermelon pickle—it adds that something special. But so do quince preserves.

OLIVE CHICKETTI · MRS. STAFFORD WENTWORTH, PALERMO, CALIF.

1 5-pound stewing chicken
¼ cup olive oil
6 cups hot water
1 tablespoon salt
⅓ cup chopped onion
⅓ cup diced green pepper
2 cups sliced celery
¼ cup chicken fat
½ cup diced pimiento
1 pound spaghetti
1½ cups whole and halved
    olives
2 cups grated Cheddar cheese
Salt and pepper to taste

Disjoint chicken and brown pieces in hot oil. Add hot water and salt. Cover. Cook until tender. Cool. Skim off fat and reserve. Remove skin and bones from chicken, leaving meat in large pieces. Return chicken to broth. Cook onion, pepper, and celery in chicken fat until tender. Stir into chicken and broth; add pimiento. Heat to boiling. Add broken spaghetti and boil until spaghetti is tender, adding more water if necessary. Just before serving, stir olives and cheese into chicken mixture and heat slowly until cheese is melted. Season to taste. Yield: 6 portions.

CHICKEN PAPRIKAS · ELYRIA, OHIO

1 onion, chopped
¼ cup shortening
2 tablespoons salt
1 tablespoon paprika
1 teaspoon pepper
1 4- to 5-pound chicken,
    disjointed
1½ cups water
½ pint commercial sour cream
½ pint light cream (optional)

Brown onion in shortening; mix in seasonings. Add chicken and brown 10 minutes. Add water; cover and simmer slowly until tender. Remove chicken. Add sour cream to drippings in pan and mix well. If more gravy is desired, add the light cream. Add dumplings. Arrange chicken on top. Heat through and serve.

Yield: 4 to 6 portions.

DUMPLINGS NOKEDLI:

3 eggs, beaten
½ cup water
2½ cups sifted flour (about)
2 teaspoons salt

Blend ingredients together, adding more flour if necessary, to make a stiff batter. Drop by teaspoonfuls into boiling salted water. Cook 10 minutes; rinse with cold water; drain.

CHICKEN MOLE · MRS. HUGH B. MC DUFFEE, LONG BEACH, CALIF.

1 4-pound fowl, cut up
Celery tops
1 carrot
½ onion
1 slice dry bread
2 tablespoons seedless raisins
¼ ounce (¼ square)
    unsweetened chocolate
3 tablespoons blanched
    almonds
2 tablespoons minced onion
3 tablespoons salad oil
2 tablespoons flour
1 tablespoon chili powder
½ teaspoon salt
¼ teaspoon cinnamon
¼ teaspoon cloves
2½ cups chicken stock
½ cup canned tomato juice

Cover chicken with cold water. Add celery tops, carrot and onion. Cook until tender. Set aside and cool. Grind bread, raisins, chocolate and almonds. Sauté minced onion in oil until golden. Stir in flour and spices. Add bread mixture. Stir in chicken stock and tomato sauce. Cook until slightly thickened. Add chicken. Simmer over low heat for 3 minutes. Serve with Spanish rice.

Yield: 6 portions.

MEXICAN CHICKEN · GENERAL FRANK DORN, SAN FRANCISCO, CALIF.

1 5-pound chicken, disjointed
Salt and cayenne pepper
¼ cup fat
¼ cup blanched almonds
⅓ cup seedless raisins
½ cup pineapple chunks
⅛ teaspoon cinnamon
⅛ teaspoon ground cloves
1½ cups orange juice
2 tablespoons flour
¼ cup water
1 avocado
2 oranges
1 bunch water cress

Season chicken well by rubbing with salt and pepper. Brown on all sides in hot fat. Add almonds, raisins, pineapple, cinnamon, cloves, and orange juice. Cover and simmer over low heat for 1 hour, or until chicken is tender. Remove chicken, fruits, and nuts to serving platter. Make a smooth paste of flour and water and add to liquid in pan. Cook until thickened, stirring constantly. Pour over the chicken. Garnish with avocado wedges, orange sections, and water cress. Serve with rice and a green salad. Yield: 6 portions.

CHICKEN À LA KING · BRIGHTON BEACH HOTEL, LONG ISLAND, N.Y.

2 tablespoons butter or
    margarine
½ green pepper, shredded
1 cup thinly sliced
    mushrooms
2 tablespoons flour
Salt and pepper
2 cups light cream
3 cups cut-up cooked chicken
¼ cup butter or margarine,
    creamed
3 egg yolks
1 teaspoon onion juice
1 tablespoon lemon juice
½ teaspoon paprika

Cooking sherry
Shredded pimiento

Simmer the 2 tablespoons butter, green pepper and mushrooms 5 minutes. Add flour and seasonings. Stir and cook gently until frothy. Mix in cream and stir until sauce is thickened. Pour into top of double boiler. Add chicken; heat thoroughly over hot water. Beat the creamed butter into the egg yolks. Add onion juice, lemon juice and paprika. Add slowly to hot chicken mixture, stirring until thickened. Add sherry to taste. Add pimiento. Serve at once in noodle nests, patty cases or on hot buttered toast. Yield: 8 portions.

FRENCH CHICKEN LOAF · MRS. LAWRENCE ADAMS, JACKSONVILLE, FLA.

1 4-pound fowl, disjointed
2 bay leaves
1 clove garlic, crushed
¼ teaspoon oregano
2 quarts boiling water, salted
½ teaspoon salt
¼ teaspoon pepper
1 can (4 ounces) pimientos,
    finely chopped
2 envelopes unflavored
    gelatin
½ cup cold water
10 hard-cooked eggs,
    separated
Salt and pepper to taste

Put disjointed fowl in large saucepan with bay leaves, garlic, oregano and boiling water. Bring to a boil. Cover tightly. Simmer for about 1½ hours or until chicken is very tender and meat begins to separate from bones. Remove chicken and boil water down to 2 cups. While stock is reducing, put chicken through food chopper using coarse blade. Season with salt and pepper; add chopped pimientos. Soften gelatin in cold water for 5 minutes. Add 2 cups hot chicken stock from which the herbs have been strained. Lightly oil a 8×5×3-inch loaf pan. Pack ½ of the chicken into the bottom of the pan to a depth of 2 inches. Pour over ¼ of the gelatin stock mixture. While it is congealing, mash egg yolks and season with salt and pepper. Now scatter ½ of the yolks over the chicken; add the rest of the chicken and over this ¼ of the gelatin mixture. Allow to congeal slightly and then add the rest of egg yolks. Pour over another ¼ of the gelatin and allow to congeal slightly. Layer on top all of the mashed egg whites (to give the effect of icing) and add the remain ¼ gelatin mixture. Chill well. Slice like cake. Yield: 8 portions.

THE TAYLORS' CHICKEN PIE · MRS. GREYTON TAYLOR, HAMMONDSPORT, N.Y.

1 4-pound chicken, cut up
2 tablespoons salt
2 stalks celery, cut in 1-inch
    pieces
1 large onion, coarsely
    chopped
3 tablespoons butter or
    margarine
¼ cup flour
2 cups chicken stock
¼ cup heavy cream
Nutmeg
Salt and pepper
Paprika
Pastry for 1 crust pie
¼ cup sauterne wine

Place chicken pieces in pot; cover with cold water. Add salt, celery and onion. Cook over low heat until chicken is tender enough to slip from the bones, about 1½ hours. Let cool in stock. Remove chicken and take meat from bones in large pieces. Melt butter, blend in flour, gradually stir in stock (fat removed first) and cook until thickened. Add cream, cooked celery and onion, and seasonings to taste. Line the sides only of a deep 9-inch pie pan with part of pastry. Put chicken pieces in pan, using the white ones first. Add dark meat until pan is half filled. Pour over the sauce; add the sauterne. Cover with pastry; cut openings for escape of steam. Bake at 400°F. for 20 to 25 minutes or until brown. Yield: 6 portions.

CHICKEN PIE CREOLE · MRS. HAMILTON POLK JONES, NEW ORLEANS, LA.

1 5-pound stewing chicken,
    cut up

SAUCE:
2 tablespoons butter or
    margarine, melted
¼ cup flour
3 cups chicken stock
1 cup light cream
½ teaspoon salt
¼ teaspoon pepper

Simmer chicken 2 hours or more or until tender. Remove meat from bones and arrange in baking dish.

Sauce: Blend together melted butter and flour. Gradually add warm chicken stock, cream, salt and pepper. Cook, stirring constantly, until sauce comes to a boil. Pour 2 to 3 cups over chicken, reserving enough sauce for a gravy bowl. Simmer reserved sauce 15 minutes.

CRUST:
2 cups sifted flour
4 teaspoons baking powder
1 teaspoon salt
2 tablespoons butter or
    margarine, melted
1 egg, well beaten
¾ to 1 cup milk

Crust: Sift together flour, baking powder and salt. Combine melted butter, egg and milk, and add, stirring quickly to make a soft dough. Drop by spoonfuls over chicken and sauce in baking dish. Bake at 425°F. for 15 to 20 minutes. Serve with reserved sauce. Yield: 6 portions.

LIB'S CHICKEN PIE · LIB TAYLOR, BROWNSVILLE, TENN.

1 frying chicken, 3½ to 4 lb.
1½ teaspoon salt
1 recipe rich biscuit dough
⅛ teaspoon pepper
¼ cup butter or margarine

Have chicken cleaned and cut up in pieces. Place chicken in just enough water to cover, about 1 quart. Add 1 teaspoon salt. Cover. Cook until tender, about ½ hour; cool in broth. Roll half of biscuit dough to ⅛-inch thickness and rectangular in shape and line an 11×7×1½-inch baking dish with dough. Lay chicken pieces on dough. Add remaining salt and pepper and dot with butter. Cover with broth (the dough will absorb some of the broth during baking). Roll out remaining dough in rectangular shape to ⅛-inch thickness. Cover top of baking dish and seal edges; prick top with fork. Bake at 400°F. for 30 to 35 minutes or until top is brown. Yield: 6 portions.

CHICKEN GUILI · MRS. GEORGE D. SEARS, MEDINA, TEX.

3½-pound chicken, disjointed
Salt and pepper
½ cup butter or margarine
2 cups chopped celery
1 cup chopped onion
1 cup chopped green pepper
¾ cup finely chopped parsley
6 cloves garlic, chopped
2 tablespoons flour
2 cans (1 pound, 13 ounces each) tomatoes
4 bay leaves
4 eggs, hard-cooked and chopped
Hot cooked rice

Season chicken with salt and pepper. Melt butter in large frying pan. Brown chicken on all sides and set aside. Add all chopped ingredients to frying pan. Cook until onion becomes transparent. Add flour and stir slowly until mixture is smooth. Add tomatoes and bay leaves; season to taste. Add chicken sections. Cover and simmer until meat is tender, about ¾ hour. Add eggs and serve with rice. Yield: 4 to 5 portions.

CHICKEN PILAU · WHITE SPRINGS, FLA.

4 to 4½ pounds fowl, cut into pieces
Chicken liver and gizzard
1 large onion, sliced
2 teaspoons salt
Boiling water
1½ cups long-grain rice
¼ cup butter or margarine
1½ teaspoons salt
⅛ teaspoon pepper
Dash of cayenne pepper

Put chicken, giblets, onion and 2 teaspoons salt in large iron pot. Cover with boiling water. Simmer until chicken is tender, about 1½ hours. Remove chicken. Add rice to liquid in pot (be sure there are 3 cups of liquid). Add butter, remaining salt, pepper and cayenne. Cover and cook slowly until rice is tender and water absorbed, about 25 minutes. Return chicken to pot and heat, stirring gently so as not to break the rice. Yield: 6 portions.

POLLO CON ARROZ · ANA BEGUE DE PACKMAN, CALIFORNIA

1 3-pound chicken, cut up
2 tablespoons fat
1 cup uncooked rice
1 teaspoon salt
½ teaspoon pepper
1 onion, chopped
1 green chili pepper, chopped
1 large tomato, cut up, or ½
    cup canned tomatoes
1 clove garlic, minced
3 cups boiling water

Fry chicken in hot fat until golden brown on both sides. Add rice and stir with a fork until fat is absorbed. Add seasonings, onion, chili pepper, tomato and garlic. Fry for 5 minutes, stirring frequently. Add water, cover tightly. Bake at 350°F. for 45 minutes to 1 hour, or until chicken is tender and rice is cooked.
    Yield: 4 portions.

ARROZ CON POLLO · COLUMBIA RESTAURANT, YBOR CITY, FLA.

½ cup oil
1 frying chicken, quartered
1 onion, chopped
2 cloves garlic, minced
1 green pepper, chopped
¾ cup tomatoes
3 cups water
1 bay leaf
1 tablespoon salt
Pinch of saffron
1 cup raw rice

¼ cup small cooked green peas
2 pimientos, cut into strips

Heat oil in frying pan. Add chicken and brown well on both sides. Add onion, garlic and green pepper; cook 5 minutes. Add tomatoes and water; cook for 5 minutes. Stir in bay leaf, salt, saffron and rice. Cover. Bake at 350°F. for 20 minutes or until tender. Garnish with peas and pimiento.
    Yield: 4 portions.

CHICKEN RAPHAEL WEILL · LOUISE SAVIN, ALMADEN VINEYARD, CALIF.

3 2-pound broilers
½ cup butter or margarine
2 tablespoons shallots
½ cup white wine
2 cups heavy cream
4 egg yolks
Pinch sweet parsley
1 teaspoon minced chives
Dash of nutmeg
Cayenne
Salt to taste

Disjoint broilers as for frying and bone body, leaving wing and leg bones intact. Sauté in butter or margarine, a little at first, adding more until the chicken comes to a golden color; add shallots and sauté a few minutes more. Add white wine.
    Cover pan and cook slowly 10 minutes. Then add 1½ cups of the cream. Cook slowly, covered, 20 minutes. Beat egg yolks with remaining half cup of cream and add to chicken. Shake the pan to mix. Heat to just under boiling. Keep shaking the pan gently until the sauce thickens. Add parsley, chives, nutmeg, cayenne, and salt to taste.
    Yield: 6 servings.

CHICKEN RICE RING WITH MUSHROOM SAUCE · SUSANNE COOLEY,
LITTLE ROCK, ARK.

1 cup diced, cooked chicken
2 cups cooked rice
1 cup dry bread crumbs
1 teaspoon salt
½ teaspoon paprika
4 eggs, well beaten
¼ cup chopped pimiento
¼ cup butter or margarine,
*   melted*
2½ cups milk or chicken stock,
*   or half and half*

Combine ingredients in order given. Use ½ teaspoon salt if chicken stock is used instead of milk. Turn into a greased 1½-quart ring mold. Bake at 325°F. for 1 hour. Let stand for 15 minutes before unmolding onto a warm platter. Serve with Mushroom Sauce. Yield: 6 portions.

MUSHROOM SAUCE:
½ pound mushrooms, sliced
¼ cup butter or margarine
¼ cup flour
¼ teaspoon salt
2 cups chicken stock
2 egg yolks, slightly beaten
¼ cup light cream
1 teaspoon lemon juice
1 teaspoon finely chopped
*   parsley*

Sauté mushrooms in 2 tablespoons of the butter until lightly browned. In another pan melt remaining 2 tablespoons butter. Stir in flour and salt. Add chicken stock and cook, stirring constantly, over low heat, until mixture comes to a boil and thickens. Combine egg yolks and cream. Stir into hot sauce. Cook a few minutes longer. Remove from heat. Stir in lemon juice, parsley, and sautéed mushrooms. Reheat if necessary.

CHICKEN IN SHERRY SAUCE · MRS. CARLTON YATES, SALISBURY, MD.

1 3-pound Delmarva chicken
2½ cups water
2 teaspoons salt
⅓ pound flat egg noodles
1 tablespoon butter or
*   margarine*
Sherry Sauce
3 tablespoons grated
*   Parmesan cheese*

Cook chicken in deep pot with the water and salt until tender, about 1 hour. Take chicken out and when cool enough to handle discard skin and bones; reserve cooking liquid. Slice chicken. Cook noodles in boiling salted water until tender; drain. Pour boiling water over and drain again. Return noodles to pot, add butter and mix thoroughly. Spread buttered noodles in greased 8 × 11-inch baking pan, or in 2-quart casserole. Arrange chicken over noodles. Pour Sherry Sauce over chicken and noodles; sprinkle with Parmesan cheese. Bake at 425°F. for 30 minutes, or until delicate brown.

Yield: 4 portions.

SHERRY SAUCE:
1/4 cup butter or margarine
6 tablespoons flour
3 cups chicken stock
1/2 teaspoon salt
1/4 teaspoon paprika
1 can (4 ounces) sliced
    mushrooms, drained
2/3 cup sherry wine

Melt butter; add flour and blend well. Slowly add reserved chicken stock and cook until a creamy consistency. Add salt, paprika, mushrooms and sherry. Blend thoroughly.

TARRAGON CHICKEN · MRS. WILLIAM KENT, MEMPHIS, TENN.

1 3- to 3 1/2-pound frying
    chicken, cut in pieces
Seasoned flour
1/4 cup butter or margarine
1 jigger brandy
Small white onions (optional)
1/2 pound mushrooms, sliced
    (optional)
1/2 cup dry white wine
Bunch of fresh, or 1 teaspoon
    dried tarragon

Dredge chicken in flour. Melt 2 tablespoons of the butter in skillet; add chicken and brown lightly. Heat brandy; light and let burn about half a minute, then pour over chicken. Add wine and tarragon. Cover tightly. Cook slowly about 40 minutes, or until tender. Before serving, add remaining butter and melt.

Yield: 4 portions.

CHICKEN TCHAKHOKHBELLI · MRS. STUART COULTER, CALIFORNIA

2 4- to 5-pound frying
    chickens, skinned and cut
    into serving pieces
1/4 pound butter or margarine
2 large onions, sliced
3/4 cup sherry wine
1/2 cup tomato juice
1 can (8 ounces) sliced
    mushrooms
1 can (8 ounces) tomato sauce
2 teaspoons paprika
1/2 teaspoon monosodium
    glutamate
1 cup hot water or chicken
    stock

1 teaspoon salt
Pepper

Sauté chicken in butter until lightly browned. Remove pieces to baking pan. Sauté onion in frying-pan fat until yellow. Add remaining ingredients; bring to a boil. Pour over chicken. Bake at 400°F. for 30 minutes. Turn pieces and bake another 30 minutes, or until tender. Serve with rice.

Yield: 6 to 8 portions.

CHICKEN SOUFFLÉ · MRS. WILLIAM KENT, MEMPHIS, TENN.

2½ cups diced cooked white
    chicken meat
1 cup finely chopped cooked
    dark chicken meat
¼ teaspoon pepper
Salt to taste
1 teaspoon Worcestershire
    sauce
1 onion, grated
2 eggs, separated
1 cup heavy cream, whipped
1 pint chicken stock
3 tablespoons flour
¼ pound fresh mushrooms,
    halved
2 tablespoons butter or
    margarine

Combine dark- and white-meat chicken. Season with pepper and salt to taste. Add Worcestershire sauce, onion and beaten egg yolks. Beat egg whites until stiff but not dry and fold into mixture. Fold in whipped cream. Place in a greased 8½×2-inch ring mold. Bake at 325°F. for 40 minutes or until firm. Serve with sauce: thicken chicken stock with a paste made of flour blended with 3 tablespoons of the stock. Season with salt and pepper, cook 10 minutes or until thick, stirring constantly. Sauté mushrooms 5 minutes in butter; add to sauce.

Yield: 8 portions.

CHICKEN SOUTHWEST · MRS. FLORENCE MAHONEY, WASHINGTON, D.C.

1 3-pound frying chicken, cut
    in pieces
¼ cup fat
1 onion, chopped
1 cup tomato juice
3 tablespoons tomato catsup,
    or 1 cup tomato sauce
1 cup Burgundy wine
1 large bay leaf
Black pepper, to taste
White pepper, to taste
1 teaspoon sugar
4 cloves
1 tablespoon Worcestershire
    sauce
1½ teaspoon chili powder
¾ teaspoon paprika

Fry chicken in hot fat until three-quarters done and golden brown, about ½ hour; remove from pan. Fry onion in same fat until brown. Add remaining ingredients. Cover and simmer 30 minutes. Add chicken and cook 15 minutes longer. Remove bay leaf. Add a little more Burgundy to sauce just before serving. Yield: 4 portions. Note: Use the same recipe for Chicken Creole, using sherry or white wine in place of Burgundy, and omit chili powder.

TENNESSEE CLUB CHICKEN · MEMPHIS, TENN.

6 half breasts of chicken
6 tablespoons flour
6 tablespoons shortening
6 slices country ham
6 tablespoons ham fat
¼ cup butter or margarine
3 tablespoons flour
2 cups milk
½ cup sherry wine
6 toast circles
12 broiled fresh mushrooms

Carefully remove skin and bones from chicken breast; ask meat man to cut breasts, leaving wing bone to first joint. Dredge in flour, shake well to remove loose bits. Brown breasts in shortening in heavy-bottomed frying pan, but do not cook tender. In a separate pan, brown country-ham slices. Remove from pan, trim off and add fat back to pan with 2 tablespoons butter or margarine. Blend in flour, add milk and cook until thickened. Add sherry, stir well, season to taste. Place chicken pieces in sauce. Cover pan tightly. Bake at 300 to 325°F. until the chicken is tender. The sauce should have the grace of proper consistency, too thick to run, too thin to clot, just thick enough to cling to the meat. On toast rounds, one to a plate, lay on a slice of country ham, trimmed to fit toast, over the ham the chicken breast, wing tip up. Decorate each breast with 2 broiled mushroom caps. Pour over gravy. Place in oven until heated thoroughly. Serve immediately.

Yield: 6 portions.

BROILED LIVERS · GENERAL FRANK DORN, SAN FRANCISCO, CALIF.

1 pound livers (chicken,
    whitefish or duck)
1 cup dry white wine
½ cup brandy
2 dashes Tabasco
2 tablespoons Worcestershire
    sauce
8 whole cloves
1 teaspoon caraway seeds
1 teaspoon ginger
4 bay leaves
8 peppercorns
½ cup butter or margarine
Salt and pepper to taste
1 tablespoon flour

Combine all ingredients except livers and flour in saucepan; boil for 2 to 3 minutes. Pour over livers and place in refrigerator for at least 6 hours. Remove livers from sauce and drain; reserve sauce. Broil livers until golden brown. Make a thin paste of some of the sauce with the flour. Bring sauce to a boil and stir in paste gradually. Cook until thickened. Pour over livers. Garnish with white radishes.

Yield: 3 to 4 portions.

AUNT ALICE'S GIBLET STEW · MRS. WILLIAM D. MCMILLAN, ITHACA, N.Y.

1 cup diced celery
½ cup diced onion
2 quarts water
Giblets and necks of 6 broilers
1 cup raw rice
1 teaspoon salt
¼ teaspoon pepper
1 tablespoon minced parsley

Cook vegetables in water until tender. Add gizzards and necks and simmer until almost tender. Drop in livers and continue cooking 15 minutes. Add more water if needed. Trim gizzards of tough portions and slice. Cut each heart in half. Pick meat from necks. Measure liquid to make one quart including meat and vegetables. Bring to a lively boil. Add rice; season with salt and pepper. Bring to rolling boil, reduce heat and simmer slowly until rice absorbs liquid. The dish has a chop-suey look and flavor. Serve in deep bowls and garnish with minced parsley.

Yield: 6 portions.

Chicken Sauces and Stuffing

BASTING SAUCE FOR BROILERS · JAMES R. DUNLOP, CHEVY CHASE, MD.

2 tablespoons butter or
    margarine, melted
2 tablespoons sherry wine
Salt to taste
Paprika to taste

Combine ingredients. Brush over chicken every few minutes during cooking time. Yield: ¼ cup, enough for 1 broiler.

FLYING "L" CHICKEN BARBECUE SAUCE · BANDERA, TEX.

½ pound butter or margarine
2 cans (6 ounces each) tomato
    paste
1 cup catsup
1 cup vinegar
1 tablespoon brown sugar
3 tablespoons Worcestershire
    sauce
1 tablespoon red hot sauce
1 tablespoon steak sauce

Juice of 2 lemons
Salt and pepper to taste

Melt butter and blend in remaining ingredients. Simmer about 10 minutes.

Yield: 4 cups sauce.

BARBECUE SAUCE · THE CLOISTER, SEA ISLAND, GA.

1 quart vinegar
1 pint catsup
2 cups French mustard
Tabasco to taste
Black pepper to taste
Red pepper to taste
1 pound butter or margarine,
    melted

Combine vinegar, catsup, mustard and Tabasco. Bring to a boil and add other seasonings to taste. Blend in butter, and keep the mixture warm. Using a new dish mop, swab the chicken with sauce when it comes hot from the pit. Yield: 2½ quarts, sufficient for 25 servings.

WILD RICE STUFFING · PUMP ROOM, HOTEL AMBASSADOR EAST, CHICAGO, ILL.

1 cup wild rice
1 teaspoon salt
1 quart boiling water
2 egg yolks
¼ cup sherry wine
1 pound chicken livers, finely
    diced
Fat
2 medium onions, minced
½ pound fresh mushrooms,
    chopped
3 tablespoons butter or
    margarine
1 tablespoon flour
½ cup chicken stock
Salt to taste

Wash rice thoroughly. Add salt to boiling water, then add rice slowly so water continues to boil. Do not stir; shake pot to prevent rice from sticking. Cook until tender, 25 to 45 minutes. Beat egg yolks with sherry and add. Fry chicken livers in small amount of fat until tender; add to rice. In separate pan, sauté onions and mushrooms in butter. Add flour and blend; add chicken stock and bring to boil, stirring constantly. Add to rice mixture with salt to taste.

Yield: 5½ cups stuffing.

HERB-CELERY DRESSING · WILLIAMSBURG, VA.

1 1-pound loaf white bread
1 cup finely diced celery
½ cup minced onion
½ cup butter or margarine
1 tablespoon poultry
    seasoning
Butter, or chicken or turkey
    fat

Cut crusts from bread. Coarsely grate remaining part of loaf. Sauté celery and onions in butter over moderate heat. (This must not brown, merely simmer.) Add cooked vegetables and poultry seasoning to bread crumbs; mix well. Turn into a well greased 1½-quart baking dish. Dot with butter or poultry fat. Bake at 350°F. for 45 minutes. Yield: about 1½ quarts dressing.

NOTE: This is a dry, crumbly type stuffing that may also be used as a poultry stuffing.

BIGARADE SAUCE · PUMP ROOM, HOTEL AMBASSADOR EAST, CHICAGO, ILL.

3 cups thin brown drippings
    from roasting pan
1 cup currant jelly
3 oranges
2 lemons
1 jigger Burgundy
1 jigger Madeira
½ jigger Cointreau

Mix drippings with jelly and simmer slowly for 1½ hours. If necessary, skim from time to time. Peel rind from oranges and lemons without disturbing white pulp. Cut into fine strips; squeeze juice of fruit into separate pan; add strips. Simmer 15 to 20 minutes. Add fruit juice, strips, wines, and Cointreau to beef-jelly mixture and simmer 10 minutes. Strain through fine cheesecloth. Dip slices of bird into sauce prior to serving.

Yield: 2 cups sauce.

NOTE: 2 cans condensed bouillon plus enough water to make 3 cups can be substituted for drippings.

Duck, etc.

ROAST DUCKLING IN ORANGE JUICE · LONG ISLAND, N.Y.

1 5- to 6-pound duckling
Salt
1 onion
Salad oil
½ cup orange juice
2 tablespoons flour
1 cup water
Rind of 1 orange, blanched
    and finely shredded
Orange sections

To prepare duckling for roasting: Rub salt over surface and in cavity, and place onion inside; rub outside surface with oil. Place in roasting pan. Bake at 500°F. for 15 minutes, then reduce temperature to 350°F. and continue baking for 15 to 20 minutes longer. Baste frequently with orange juice. Take duck from pan and remove onion. Skim fat from drippings in pan. To 2 tablespoons of the fat add flour and blend. Add water, gradually stirring until mixture is smooth. Add remaining orange juice and rind. Do not boil. Cut duck for serving. Cover with sauce and garnish with orange sections. Yield: 4 portions.

FRIED DUCKLING · LONG ISLAND, N.Y.

1 5- to 6-pound duckling
1 egg, beaten
3 tablespoons milk
Salt and pepper
Fine dry bread crumbs
2 tablespoons water

Singe and wash duckling. Remove oil sac. Peel off skin and fat from body and legs. (It will not come readily from wings.) Split down back, and remove neck and backbone. Cut off legs, second joints and wings; divide breast into four pieces, removing rib bones. Cook gizzard, heart and neck with bones in seasoned water for gravy stock. Cut skin and fat into small pieces and fry out fat. Dip meat and liver halves into egg combined with milk and seasonings, then roll in seasoned crumbs. Brown in duck fat. Pour off excess fat and add water. Cover. Bake at 350°F. for 50 mining.

Yield: 4 portions.

DUCK WITH FLORIDA ORANGE SAUCE · MARY CALL COLLINS, TALLAHASSEE, FLA.

1 4- to 5-pound drawn
    duckling
2 tablespoons sugar
1 tablespoon cornstarch
1 teaspoon ginger
½ teaspoon salt
1⅓ cups orange juice
1 tablespoon lime juice
2 teaspoons slivered orange
    rind
⅔ cup hot water
1 orange, sectioned

Wash duck inside and out with cold water; dry carefully. Cut in quarters. Place pieces on rack in shallow roasting pan. (Do not cover or add water; do not prick skin.) Roast at 350°F. for 2 hours. While duck is baking, blend together sugar, cornstarch, ginger and salt in saucepan. Stir in fruit juices and orange rind. Cook, stirring constantly, until mixture thickens and comes to a boil.

Take roasting pan from oven; remove duck and rack. Pour off all fat; add hot water to pan and stir to dissolve brown particles. Stir into orange sauce. Return duck to pan; pour orange sauce over duck. Arrange orange sections over top. Reheat in a 350°F. oven 10 to 15 minutes longer.

Yield: 4 portions.

DOROTHY SMITH'S PHEASANT · MANHATTAN, KAN.

1 2½-pound pheasant, cut up
Salt
Pepper
Monosodium glutamate
2 cups milk
1 small clove garlic, pressed
¼ cup flour
2 tablespoons butter or
    margarine
2 cups commercial sour cream
½ teaspoon paprika

Sprinkle pheasant with salt, pepper and monosodium glutamate. Combine milk and garlic. Marinate pheasant in milk for 1 hour. Drain pheasant. Roll in flour. Brown pieces on both sides in butter. Bake at 325°F. for 1 hour, or until pheasant is tender, turning occasionally so meat will brown evenly. Remove pheasant; keep warm. Stir sour cream and paprika into drippings. Heat. Strain sauce and pour over pheasant. Yield: 4 portions.

PHEASANT CASSEROLE · MRS. DONALD C. DRAKE, INDIANAPOLIS, IND.

3 pheasants
1 cup seasoned flour
1 cup butter or margarine
3 cups commercial sour cream

Dress pheasant and cut into pieces as for frying chicken. Divide breast into three parts, the front as one piece, the back divided. Dredge pieces in seasoned flour. Brown in butter in heavy skillet, first one side, then the other, and remove to large oven-proof casserole. Add cream. Bake at 300°F. for 1 hour.

Yield: 8 portions.

PAVO PICANTE · DR. WILLIAM M. MANN, WASHINGTON, D.C.

2 turkey broilers, about 4
    pounds each, cut in
    serving pieces
½ cup butter or margarine,
    melted
2 cups beef stock (made with
    bouillon cubes)
1 tablespoon mole powder

Broil the turkey pieces until brown on both sides, basting with butter occasionally. Place in casserole with stock to which mole powder has been added; add broiler drippings. Cover and simmer for about 45 minutes or until tender. Serve with rice, Cuban-style black beans and a big guacamole salad.

Yield: 8 to 10 portions.

MRS. THOMAS BENTON'S GUINEA HENS · KANSAS CITY, MO.

2 2½- to 3-pound guineas
    (frozen)
½ cup flour
2 teaspoons salt
¼ teaspoon pepper
5 tablespoons olive oil
1 large onion, sliced
1 large green pepper, diced
1 clove garlic, minced
1 can (6 ounces) tomato paste
2 cans water
1 pound mushrooms, sliced
1 can (1 pound, 13 ounces)
    tomatoes
2 bay leaves
½ teaspoon thyme
Salt and pepper to taste
1 cup white wine

Defrost guineas and cut into quarters. Roll in seasoned flour. Fry in 4 tablespoons of the oil until golden brown on one side, then the other. Remove guineas from pan and place in Dutch oven. Add remaining 1 tablespoon oil to the oil in pan; add onion, pepper and garlic and cook over low heat (about 10 minutes) or until tender. Pour into Dutch oven. Turn tomato paste and water into frying pan to blend, then over the guineas. Add mushrooms, tomatoes, bay leaves and thyme, with salt and pepper to taste. Cover and simmer 1½ hours. Turn off heat and let the dish stand until 30 minutes before dinner. Add white wine and heat thoroughly. Serve with wild rice, or white rice or buttered noodles arranged in a copper dish, the guinea pieces laid over this and the sauce over all.

Yield: 4 portions.

Vegetables

ASPARAGUS CAESAR · MRS. STANLEY H. WATSON, CLEVELAND, OHIO

2 cans (1 pound, 4 ounces
    each) white asparagus
    tips
¼ pound butter or margarine,
    melted
3 tablespoons lemon juice
Dash paprika
½ cup grated Parmesan cheese

Drain asparagus and lay 1 layer deep in flat oven dish. Pour butter over asparagus; drizzle over the lemon juice; sprinkle with paprika and Parmesan cheese. Bake at 400°F. for 15 minutes or until the asparagus is crispy.

Yield: 6 portions.

MARGARET FISHER'S ASPARAGUS · TULSA, OKLA.

1 can (1 pound, 13 ounces)
    asparagus
1 cup fine, cheese-flavored
    cracker crumbs
1 can (10½ ounces) condensed
    cream of mushroom soup
1 tablespoon butter or
    margarine or 4 slices
    cooked bacon, crumbled

Drain asparagus; reserve liquid. Sprinkle ⅓ of the crumbs evenly in bottom of buttered 1½-quart casserole. Top with layer of asparagus. Spread ½ of soup evenly over asparagus; sprinkle with 2 teaspoons asparagus liquid. Repeat layering, ending with crumbs. Dot with butter or sprinkle with bacon. Bake, uncovered, at 350°F. for 20 minutes, or until crumbs brown slightly.

Yield: 8 portions.

ALASKA BAKED BEANS · KATCHIKAN, ALASKA

1 pound dried navy beans
¼ pound salt pork, diced
1 teaspoon dry mustard
½ cup brown sugar
2 teaspoons salt
Pepper
1 large onion, chopped
2 cloves garlic, minced

Wash and pick over beans; soak overnight. Drain and wash again. Put in pressure saucepan with salt pork and just enough water to cover. Add remaining ingredients. Cook at 15 pounds pressure for 45 minutes.

Yield: 6 to 8 portions.

BLACK BEANS CUBAN STYLE · DR. WILLIAM M. MANN, WASHINGTON, D.C.

1 pound black kidney beans
    or black-eyed beans
1 tablespoon salt
1 clove garlic, cut in half
½ cup oil
3 cloves garlic, mashed
3 green peppers, chopped
3 medium onions, chopped
½ teaspoon ground sage
2 bay leaves, crushed
3 tablespoons cider vinegar
1 teaspoon salt
Pepper

Wash and pick over beans. Cover with water and soak overnight. Drain and place in kettle with fresh water to cover. Add 1 tablespoon salt and garlic halves. Cook beans till tender, about 3 hours, adding more water as needed. Just before serving, heat oil in skillet. Add mashed garlic, green pepper, onion, sage and bay leaves. Cook until vegetables are soft. Add vinegar, salt and pepper to taste. Place beans in serving dish and pour vegetable mixture over all.

Yield: 4 to 6 portions.

HOME BAKED BEANS · MRS. MILDRED M. RUTHERFORD, SOUTH WOODSTOCK, VT.

4 cups dried pea or navy
    beans
1 teaspoon baking soda
½ cup sugar
½ cup maple syrup
1 tablespoon salt
1½ teaspoons ground ginger
1 teaspoon dry mustard
1 small onion
1 pound salt pork

Wash and pick over beans, soak overnight in water to cover. Parboil in the soaking water, adding the soda. Simmer until the skins ruffle when blown upon.

Drain off the water and turn beans into pot. Add sugar, maple syrup, salt, ginger and mustard and bury onion deep in the beans. Score and add salt pork, pressing in until only the rind shows. Fill pot with hot water. Cover. Bake at 200°F. for 8 hours. Keep covered until the beans are 1 hour from done, adding more water if necessary. Remove cover and allow beans to brown the last hour of baking.

Yield: 8 portions.

BOURBON BAKED BEANS · MRS. FLORENCE MAHONEY, WASHINGTON, D.C.

*6 cans (1 pound each) baked
    beans
½ cup bourbon
½ cup strong black coffee
1 can (1 pound, 4 ounces)
    sliced pineapple*

Three to four hours before serving time, empty beans into a baking dish. Stir in bourbon and coffee and let stand, covered, at room temperature. A little more than an hour before serving time, remove cover and bake at 375°F. about 1 hour. Cut pineapple slices in halves and stand around edge of beans. Bake another 15 minutes. Yield: 18 to 20 portions.

SPANISH BEANS WITH RUM AND SOUR CREAM · MRS. FLORENCE MAHONEY,
WASHINGTON, D.C.

*1 pound dried black beans
1 onion, finely chopped
3 stalks celery, finely cut
1 carrot, diced
1 tablespoon chopped parsley
1 tablespoon salt
¼ teaspoon pepper
3 tablespoons butter or
    margarine
2 jiggers dark rum
Cold sour cream*

Soak beans overnight; drain. Put in pot, cover with water. Add onion, celery, carrot, parsley, salt and pepper. Simmer until bean skins burst when blown upon, about 3 hours. Drain, if necessary. Put in bean pot with butter and 1 jigger of rum. Cover and bake at 325°F. until tender, about 1 hour. Stir in remaining jigger of rum. Serve with cold sour cream on top, or pass cream in separate serving bowl. Garnish cream with finely chopped chives, scallions or parsley, or sprinkle with freshly ground black peppercorn. Yield: 6 to 8 portions.

RED BEANS · MRS. HUGH B. MCDUFFEE, LONG BEACH, CALIF.

*½ pound red beans
1 tablespoon bacon drippings
Grated Parmesan cheese
1 tablespoon minced onion*

Cover red beans with salted water and cook until very well done. Drain thoroughly. In frying pan, warm bacon drippings over low heat and add a very few beans at a time, mashing each bean in the fat. Keep adding until all the beans are mashed. Sprinkle top with grated cheese. Add onion. Leave on top of range until cheese melts. Yield: 4 portions.

WALDO'S PINTO BEANS · TICO TACO CAFE, SCOTTSDALE, ARIZ.

Cook beans in pressure cooker according to manufacturer's directions. Chill overnight. Grind to a pulpy mass. Heat peanut oil (¼ cup to 1 quart beans) in a large pot. Add beans and stir quickly for 1 minute. Lower heat and simmer for 30 minutes, stirring every few minutes to give a smooth texture.

RED BEANS AND RICE · MRS. RAY SAMUELS, NEW ORLEANS, LA.

¾ pound large dried red
    kidney beans
½ pound salt pork, pickled
    pork or ham hock
1 tablespoon fat
1 tablespoon flour
1 large onion, chopped
1 carrot, sliced
3 pints beef stock or bouillon
3 sprigs parsley
1 bay leaf
Pinch of powdered thyme

Pinch of sage
2 stalks and leaves of celery
Salt and pepper to taste

Soak red beans overnight in cold water. Brown meat in fat. Remove meat from pan. Stir flour into fat in pan; brown lightly. Add onion and cook 3 minutes. Add beans, carrot slices, meat and stock. Cook slowly 1 hour. Then add herbs, celery, salt and pepper. Cook till gravy is thick and dark. Serve with rice.

Yield: 4 portions.

T-DART PINTO BEANS · T-DART RANCH, PHOENIX, ARIZ.

2 pounds pinto beans
2 pounds ground beef
2 cups chopped onion
1 clove garlic, mashed
2 teaspoons salt
Pinch of oregano
1 dried red pepper
¼ cup bacon fat
Salt to taste

Pick over beans and soak 12 hours in water to cover. Drain, add fresh cold water to cover and bring to a boil. Reduce heat, bringing beans to slow simmer. Mix meat with onion, garlic, salt and oregano. Wash pepper, finely crush and add meat. Melt fat in skillet. Add meat and fry until golden brown. Add to beans and simmer, partially covered, 4 hours. Add salt to taste.

Yield: 8 portions.

TEX KNECHT'S LAREDO RANCH BEANS · DALLAS, TEX.

2 cups pinto beans
8 cups water
½ pound salt pork, cut in
    pieces
2 onions, finely diced
1 green pepper, finely diced
1 can (17 to 18 ounces)
    tomatoes
1 clove garlic, finely diced
½ teaspoon monosodium
    glutamate
¼ teaspoon dry mustard

¼ teaspoon chili powder
Worcestershire sauce
Salt and pepper

Clean beans. Place in kettle with the water. Simmer for 2 hours. Drain. Add remaining ingredients. Boil slowly about 2 hours, or until tender, adding more liquid if necessary. Yield: 4 to 6 portions.

ELIZABETH'S PINTO BEANS · ELIZABETH SCHAFFER, ALBUQUERQUE, N.M.

2 cups pinto beans
4 cups cold water, about
½ pound salt pork cut in
    2-inch dice
1 garlic clove
3 teaspoons chili powder
Salt to taste
2 tablespoons flour

Wash beans and pick over well. Turn into a deep kettle and pour in the cold water to 2 inches above bean level. Simmer gently 4 hours, replacing water as it boils away. Add salt pork and garlic, pierced on a toothpick for convenience in removing. Add 1 teaspoon of the chili powder. Cook 30 minutes. Add salt as needed. Continue to simmer 3 hours, or longer, until beans have gorged themselves with fat and water and swelled like the fat boy in his prime. About 30 minutes before serving blend the remaining 2 teaspoons chili powder, flour and the water from the bean pot to make a smooth paste. Add paste to thicken gravy. Yield: 4 portions.

Note: Under pressure, pintos cook in a fraction of the usual time.

FRIJOLES CON QUESO · MRS. DOROTHEA DALTON, CALIFORNIA

1 pound pinto beans
5 trips bacon, diced
¼ cup Cheddar cheese, diced
Salt to taste

Wash and pick over beans. Cover with cold water and bring to a boil. Cook slowly 5 to 6 hours, adding more boiling water to cover as needed. Drain. Mash beans in pot. Fry bacon until crisp and add to bean mixture. Both beans and bacon must be hot. Add cheese and mix until melted. Add salt to taste. Yield: 1 quart beans.

CLARA'S BARBECUED BUTTER BEANS · MRS. S. A. MC CRACKEN, MANHATTAN, KAN.

¾ cup light brown sugar
½ cup catsup
⅓ cup dark corn syrup
2 to 3 teaspoons liquid smoke
2 to 3 drops Tabasco sauce
1 medium onion, diced
3 cans (1 pound, 4 ounces)
    large lima beans, drained
4 strips raw bacon

Combine brown sugar, catsup, syrup, liquid smoke, Tabasco and onion. Add beans; mix well. Turn into 1½-quart casserole. Arrange the bacon strips on top, and put in oven. Bake at 325°F. for 1 hour.

Yield: 6 portions.

LIMA BEAN CASSEROLE · MRS. J. KELL BRANDON, SIMSBURY, CONN.

3½ cups cooked lima beans
¼ pound salt pork, cut into
  strips
1 small onion, minced
1 tablespoon molasses
2 cups drained cooked
  tomatoes
1 tablespoon brown sugar

1 teaspoon salt
¼ teaspoon pepper

Combine all ingredients. Place in a 2-quart casserole. Bake at 375°F. for 45 minutes.

Yield: 4 to 6 portions.

GREEN-BEAN CASSEROLE · MRS. JOHN SNIVELY, SR., FLORIDA

2 packages French-style
  frozen green beans,
  thawed
1 cup water chestnuts, sliced
1 can bean sprouts, drained
½ pound fresh mushrooms,
  sliced
1 medium onion, chopped
2 cups medium cream sauce
Salt

Grated cheese
1 can French fried onions, crumbled

In a 2-quart casserole, layer half the beans with half the water chestnuts, half the bean sprouts, half the mushrooms and half the chopped onion. Cover with half the cream sauce; sprinkle lightly with salt and cheese. Repeat layering. Bake at 400°F. about 30 minutes or until bubbly hot, topping with fried onions the last 10 minutes of baking. Yield: 6 generous portions.

SCHNITZEL BOONA MIT TAMATS (SNAP BEANS WITH TOMATOES)

LANCASTER COUNTY, PENNA.

1 pound fresh string beans
4 strips lean bacon
2 large onions, chopped
2 cups chopped fresh
  tomatoes
1 teaspoon salt, about
1 teaspoon whole basil leaves
⅛ teaspoon pepper
1 cup hot water

String beans if necessary. Remove tips. Cut into 1-inch pieces. Fry bacon until crisp. Drain and put aside. Sauté onions in bacon fat until soft but not brown. Add remaining ingredients. Simmer, covered, for ½ to ¾ hour or until beans are very tender. Serve topped with the crumbled bacon.

Yield: 6 portions.

BAKED BEETS · MRS. WILLIAM STURT, ALBANY PARK, ILL.

Cut off all but about 2 inches of beet tops; wash thoroughly but do not peel. Place in a casserole, cover tightly. Bake at 300°F. for about 3 hours, or until tender. While beets are still warm, peel under running water. Cool; slice. Serve plain—no seasoning, no dressing.

MARY WEICHERT'S ORANGE BEETS · TULSA, OKLA.

1¼ cups light brown sugar
2 tablespoons cornstarch
1 can (6 ounces) frozen
    orange juice concentrate,
    thawed
¾ cup cider vinegar
¾ cup water
1 can (1 pound, 13 ounces)
    small whole beets,
    drained
1 tablespoon butter or
    margarine

Blend brown sugar and cornstarch thoroughly. Stir in orange concentrate, vinegar, water. Bring to full boil, stirring constantly. Add beets, butter. Reheat. Yield: 6 portions.

BROCCOLI CASSEROLE · MRS. RUTH MOSS CARROLL, FORT SMITH, ARK.

¼ cup finely chopped onion
6 tablespoons butter or
    margarine
2 tablespoons flour
½ cup water
1 jar (8 ounces) pasteurized
    process cheese spread
2 packages (10 ounces) frozen
    chopped broccoli, thawed
    and well drained
3 eggs, well beaten
½ cup soda cracker crumbs

Sauté onion in 4 tablespoons of the butter until soft. Stir in flour. Add water. Cook over low heat, stirring, until mixture thickens and comes to a boil. Blend in cheese. Combine sauce and broccoli. Add eggs; mix gently until blended. Turn into a greased 1½ quart casserole. Cover with crumbs. Dot with remaining butter. Bake at 325°F. for 30 minutes. Yield: 8 portions.

BROCCOLI CASSEROLE · MRS. RICHARD S. WRIGHT, PIEDMONT, CALIF.

2 cups chopped, cooked
    broccoli
½ cup thick white sauce*
½ cup mayonnaise
1 tablespoon onion juice
3 eggs, well beaten
Salt and pepper to taste

Combine all ingredients in order given. Pour into a well-greased 1-quart casserole. Set in a pan of hot water. Bake at 350°F. for about 45 minutes or until firm. Yield: 6 portions.

NOTE: Spinach, Swiss chard, artichoke hearts or asparagus may be substituted for broccoli with equally good results.

* ½ cup milk and 1½ tablespoons each of butter and flour

SOUR-CREAM CABBAGE · MRS. MYRTLE EDMONDS, ST. LOUIS, MO.

4 tablespoons butter or
    margarine
4 cups grated white cabbage
1 teaspoon salt
1 tablespoon sugar (optional)
½ cup sour cream

Melt butter in skillet. Add grated cabbage and cook over low heat 15 minutes, stirring every 3 minutes. Add salt, sugar, and sour cream. Stir cream through cabbage until thoroughly heated but do not let boil. Serve hot. Yield: 4 portions.

NOTE: Heavy cream may be made sour by adding ½ tablespoon vinegar or lemon juice to each ½ cup cream and allowing it to stand for about 5 minutes.

CLARA McCRACKEN'S SKILLET CABBAGE · MANHATTAN, KANSAS

4 cups shredded cabbage
1 green pepper, shredded
2 cups diced celery
2 large onions, sliced
2 tomatoes, chopped
¼ cup bacon drippings

2 teaspoons sugar
Salt and pepper to taste

Combine ingredients in large skillet. Cover. Cook over medium heat 5 minutes. Yield: 6 portions.

SWEET-SOUR RED CABBAGE · MRS. JOHN VAN HEES, VERA COMMUNITY, WASH.

1 cup vinegar
1 tablespoon salt
2 tablespoons butter or
    margarine
1 large head red cabbage,
    shredded
1 cup sugar
2 tart apples, grated

In a deep pot bring to a boil vinegar, salt, and butter. Add cabbage, cover and simmer 1½ hours. Add sugar and apples; simmer 30 minutes.
    Yield: 6 to 8 portions.

BAKED CARROT LOAF · WILLIAMSBURG INN, WILLIAMSBURG, VA.

12 medium carrots, pared
4 eggs
3 tablespoons sugar
1 teaspoon salt
3 tablespoons melted butter
    or margarine
1 tablespoon cornstarch
1 pint light cream

Cook carrots in boiling water until tender. Let cool slightly and put through food chopper or sieve. Beat eggs thoroughly. Add to carrot mixture together with sugar, salt and melted butter. Mix cornstarch with a little cold water to make a paste and add to the above mixture. Stir in cream; mix well. Pour into a greased 1½-quart baking dish. Place dish in a large pan of hot water. Bake at 350°F. for 45 minutes. Serve hot. Yield: 10 portions.

MRS. BECK'S CAULIFLOWER À LA POLONAISE · LONG ISLAND, N.Y.

1 large head cauliflower
1 teaspoon salt
1 quart water
3 tablespoons butter or
    margarine
6 tablespoons dry bread
    crumbs or cracker meal

Remove leaves and stalk of cauliflower. Wash well. Cook, covered, in 1 inch of boiling salted water for 20 to 30 minutes, or until just tender. Drain and place on warm platter. Melt butter in pan. Add crumbs and cook to a caramel color. Spread over cauliflower.
    Yield: 4 to 6 portions.

CORN PUDDING · PIRATE HOUSE, SAVANNAH, GA.

8 cups fresh or frozen cut
    corn
5 tablespoons sugar
1 tablespoon salt
1¼ tablespoons baking
    powder
3 eggs, lightly beaten
3 cups milk

6 tablespoons butter or margarine, melted
½ cup flour

    Mix together corn, sugar, salt and baking powder. Combine eggs with milk and butter. Add alternately with flour, a little at a time, to the corn mixture. Turn into a buttered 3-quart casserole. Bake at 350°F. for about 1 hour and 20 minutes. Yield: 12 portions.

AVERIL'S CORN PUDDING · MRS. EDMUND TAYLOR, BROWNSVILLE, TENN.

3 eggs
2 to 4 tablespoons sugar
¼ cup butter or margarine,
    melted
½ cup milk
2 cups whole-kernel corn

    Combine eggs and sugar and beat well. Stir in butter. Add milk and beat until smooth. Stir in corn. Refrigerate 30 minutes. Blend well and turn into a 1-quart greased casserole. Bake at 350°F. for 30 to 35 minutes or until set.
    Yield: 6 portions.

KING'S ARMS TAVERN CORN PUDDING · WILLIAMSBURG, VA.

3 eggs
2 cups fresh corn kernels
¼ cup flour
1 tablespoon sugar
1 teaspoon salt
½ teaspoon white pepper
2 tablespoons melted butter
    or margarine
2 cups light cream

    Beat eggs well; combine with corn. Mix flour, sugar, salt and pepper and add to corn mixture. Stir in butter and cream and mix thoroughly. Pour into a buttered 1½-quart baking dish. Place dish in a larger pan of hot water. Bake at 325°F. for about 1 hour or until firm and brown. Yield: 8 to 10 portions.

AUNT ELVIRA'S "CAWN PUDDIN" · MARY MC KAY'S COOK, VICKSBURG, MISS.

1 can (1 pound, 4 ounces)
    cream-style corn
1 tablespoon sugar
1 teaspoon salt
3 tablespoons butter, melted
5 eggs, well beaten
3 cups milk
1 tablespoon cornstarch
1 tablespoon cold water

Combine corn, sugar, salt, butter, eggs and milk. Dissolve cornstarch in water and stir into corn mixture. Pour into a greased shallow 2-quart baking dish. Bake at 350°F. for about 1 hour or until custard is firm.

Yield: 6 to 8 portions.

CORN FRITTERS · RICH'S DEPARTMENT STORE, ATLANTA, GA.

1 egg, separated
½ cup milk
½ cup canned cream-style
    corn
½ cup sifted flour
½ cup stone-ground corn meal
1 teaspoon baking powder
1 teaspoon sugar
½ teaspoon salt
3 tablespoons melted
    shortening

Beat together egg yolk and half the milk, mixing well. Add corn. Sift together flour, corn meal, baking powder, sugar and salt. Add to corn mixture and beat until light. Add remaining milk. Stir in, do not beat, melted shortening. Fold in stiffly beaten egg white. Drop fritters by tablespoonfuls into shallow fat and fry until golden brown and well done. (Fritters should be oval-shaped, about 2½-inches long.) Serve with fried country ham, crisp bacon or link sausage. Pass the cane syrup and a big pat of print butter. Garnish plate with glazed apple rings. Yield: 12 fritters.

VERMONT'S MESS O' GREENS

½ pound salt pork
1 peck dandelion greens
9 peeled potatoes, halved
Salt to taste

Place salt pork in pot, cover with water and boil 30 minutes. Wash and clean greens thoroughly; add to pot with pork. Lay in potatoes, cover and cook over low heat 15 minutes or until potatoes are partially tender. Lid off, drop in the dumplings. Cover and continue the cooking another 15 minutes. Yield: 6 portions.

GRON KAL · MRS. A. G. ANDERSON, FRANKSVILLE, WIS.

Ham bone or smoked ham
    butt
2 quarts boiling water
4 carrots, sliced

Simmer ham bone in boiling water, covered, for 1½ hours. Add carrots, onion and potatoes, and cook 15 minutes. Add parsley and kale; cook 15 minutes longer. Season with salt and pepper to taste. If the kale shows

1 onion, finely diced
4 potatoes, peeled and diced
2 sprigs parsley, minced
1 cup chopped kale (middle
   rib removed)
Salt
Pepper

a tendency to float, thicken the soup slightly by using 1 tablespoon flour blended to a smooth paste with 2 tablespoons water. This shouldn't be a thick soup, but thick enough that the kale stays suspended in the liquid. Cook until kale is tender.

Yield: 6 portions.

LEEKY PIE · COLORADO

12 leeks
1 teaspoon salt
2 cups boiling water
½ pound sliced fat bacon
Salt and pepper
½ recipe plain pastry (based
   on 2 cups flour)
2 eggs, separated
¼ cup cream

Wash and trim leeks. Cut into ½- to 1-inch slices. Add the 1 teaspoon salt and boiling water. Let stand for 10 minutes; drain. Cover bottom of 9-inch pie pan with part of the bacon slices. Add a layer of leeks and repeat until dish is filled. Season with salt and pepper. Cover with 9-inch pastry circle; cut steam vents but do not seal crust. Bake at 425°F. for 30 to 40 minutes, or until crust is golden. Remove crust carefully. Drain off liquid in pan. Beat egg whites until stiff. Beat egg yolks and cream; fold into egg whites. Add to leeks. Mix well. Replace crust. Return to 425°F. oven for 5 to 10 minutes, or until egg mixture has set. Serve hot or cold.

Yield: 6 portions.

LEEK AND CELERY ROOT · MRS. LEOPOLD ARNAUD, NEW YORK CITY

12 leeks
6 celery roots
1 cup milk
1 cup celery-root water
2½ tablespoons cornstarch
Salt and pepper

Remove roots, outer leaves and green ends from leeks. Cut in half lengthwise, then slice into 1-inch pieces; wash thoroughly. Cook in salted water for about 20 minutes, or until tender. Pare celery roots and cut into ½-inch dice. Cook separately from the leeks in enough salted water to cover for 20 minutes, or until tender. Drain vegetables, saving 1 cup celery-root water, and combine. Mix milk and celery water and bring to the boiling point. Add cornstarch which has been mixed with a small amount of cold water. Again bring to the boiling point. Add more salt and pepper if necessary. Add to vegetables; heat and serve.

Yield: 6 portions.

WILTED LETTUCE · MRS. JOHN MCDERMOTT, OTTUMWA, IOWA

Leaf lettuce from the garden row, one pound for six. Wash well, shake out excess moisture, place in bowl, shred with knife. Add a teaspoon of salt, four green scallions, finely cut, tops included. Into a frying pan go four strips of bacon cut crosswise into one-fourth-inch shreds. When the bacon is crisp, one-half cup cream is added with four tablespoons vinegar.

Heat and whip well to smooth curds. Pour over lettuce, cover bowl with plate ten minutes and hustle to the table.

MUSHROOMS À LA NEWBURG · MRS. EWING ELMORE, BIRMINGHAM, ALA.

1 pound fresh mushrooms
½ cup sherry wine
3 cups thick white sauce
½ cup blanched almonds,
    slivered
¼ cup bread crumbs
¼ cup butter or margarine

Wash mushrooms, drain in colander. Remove stems from caps and slice crosswise. Cut caps into 2 or 3 pieces according to the size. Cook mushrooms in small amount of salted water 10 minutes; drain. Add sherry to white sauce. Dip layer of sauce into 1½-quart casserole, add layer of mushrooms, a sprinkle of almonds. Repeat layers until ingredients are used (reserving 1 tablespoon of the nuts). End with a topping of white sauce. Sprinkle with crumbs; dot with butter; add the last sprinkle of almonds. Bake at 350°F. for 20 minutes or until lightly browned.

Yield: 6 portions.

FRESH MUSHROOMS SOUS CLOCHE · ANTOINE'S, NEW ORLEANS, LA.

1 pound fresh mushrooms
1 cup water
½ cup white wine
3 tablespoons butter or
    margarine
1 tablespoon flour
Juice of ½ lemon
1 egg yolk
¼ cup light cream
Toast

Scrub mushrooms. Combine water, wine and 1 tablespoon butter. Add mushrooms. Bring to boiling point. Cover. Simmer 10 minutes. Drain, reserving stock. Melt remaining 2 tablespoons butter; blend in flour. Add mushroom stock and cook, stirring constantly, until slightly thickened. Thinly slice mushrooms. Add to sauce with lemon juice. Cook 5 minutes. Beat egg yolk. Add cream. Gradually add mushroom mixture; mix well. Pour into heated glass bell. Seal bottom of bell with round piece of toast cut to fit. Turn bell over onto porcelain shirred-egg dish. Serve immediately.

Yield: 4 portions.

NOTE: Bell is removed at the table, or, the mixture may be served on toast, omitting the bell.

MRS. DAYTON'S GLAZED ONIONS · EAST HAMPTON, N.Y.

24 *small white onions*
1½ *cups sugar*
⅓ *cup water*
⅓ *cup butter or margarine*
¾ *teaspoon salt*

Parboil onions about 10 minutes, and drain. Combine sugar and water and cook until sugar has dissolved. Add butter and salt, stirring until melted. Cook 5 minutes. Arrange onions in pan and pour syrup over them. Place under broiler until lightly browned, basting frequently with the sugar syrup. Yield: 6 portions.

SWISS ONION PIE · MRS. JOSEPH A. GAMMA, MILWAUKEE, WIS.

2 *slices bacon, diced*
3 *cups chopped onion*
2 *eggs*
¾ *teaspoon salt*
1 *cup light cream*
1 *unbaked 9-inch pastry shell*
2 *tablespoons grated Swiss*
  cheese

1 *tablespoon butter or margarine*

Fry bacon until crisp. Add onions and cook until transparent. Cool. Add eggs one at a time, beating well after each addition. Add salt, stir in cream. Pour into pastry shell. Sprinkle with grated cheese, dot with butter. Bake at 350°F. for 30 minutes or until firm. Yield: 6 portions.

CREAMED ONIONS · MAXINE THORPE, HOLLYWOOD, CALIF.

The onions are cooked not quite done, drained and one tablespoon of butter added, then placed in a casserole and over this mushroom sauce. The sauce requires one cup condensed mushroom soup plus ¼ cup heavy cream and folded into this ½ cup English walnut meats; grated cheese is sprinkled on and again to the oven until the cheese melts.

BOLLOS CALIENTES (HOT BOLLOS) · MRS. MARIO MARTINEZ, HIALEAH, FLA.

1 *pound dried black-eyed*
  peas
1 *bulb of garlic, medium size*
2½ *teaspoons salt*
1 *teaspoon pepper*

Soak peas overnight. Drain and roll a few at a time on cloth-covered board with rolling pin to break peas and loosen skins. Fill a large bowl with cracked peas and wash with hands. Lift peas, let fall, lift, repeat. Float skins over side of bowl, add more water and keep at it until all skins are off. Put peas through food chopper using fine blade; grind a few at a time, alternating with a clove of garlic, and continue until all the peas are used. Place in large bowl. Add salt and pepper and beat until fluffy. Fry by teaspoonfuls in deep hot fat (375°F.) until brown. Drain. Between each batch beat peas to keep batter light. Yield: 4 dozen *bollos*.

GRANDMA'S AERTER · MRS. A. G. ANDERSON, FRANKSVILLE, WIS.

1 cup dried yellow split peas
¼ teaspoon salt
1 ham bone
3 quarts boiling water
3 carrots, diced
4 potatoes, diced
1 onion, chopped or whole
Salt to taste

Wash peas and pick over well. Cover with cold water, bring to a boil. Simmer gently 30 minutes; drain. Add salt, cook 5 minutes more. Cook ham bone in boiling water, covered, for 1½ hours. Add carrots, potatoes, onion and peas, and cook together 30 minutes or until vegetables are tender. Salt to taste. That's a full meal along with crackers or bread, a tossed green salad and a hearty dessert.

Yield: 6 portions.

RUTH THORNTON'S STUFFED PEPPERS · BROWNSVILLE, TENN.

6 large green peppers
1 cup boiling water
1½ teaspoons salt
1 pound ground beef
1 tablespoon bacon drippings
    or melted shortening
1 cup chopped fresh or
    drained canned tomatoes
1 small onion, minced
1 cup cooked rice
½ teaspoon salt
⅛ teaspoon black pepper
3 tablespoons grated sharp
    Cheddar cheese

Cut thin slice from stem end of pepers; remove seeds and membrane. Parboil in boiling water with the 1½ teaspoons salt about 6 minutes; drain. Brown beef in bacon drippings. Simmer tomatoes, juice and onion until onion is tender, about 5 minutes, stirring occasionally. Combine tomato mixture, browned meat and rice. Add the ½ teaspoon salt and pepper. Blend. Stuff mixture into peppers. Sprinkle top of each with ½ tablespoon grated cheese. Place in a baking dish. Bake at 350°F. for 20 minutes or until cheese melts and browns lightly. Yield: 6 portions.

STUFFED BELL PEPPERS, CREOLE · MARY MC KAY, VICKSBURG, TENN.

16 large peppers
2 cloves garlic, chopped
4 onions, chopped
½ cup butter or margarine
1 cup chopped ham
1 cup water
1 cup tomato juice
1 can (1 pound, 4 ounces)
    tomatoes
2 eggs, well beaten
4 cups cracker crumbs

Salt and pepper to taste
1 teaspoon sugar
Bread crumbs
Melted butter or margarine
Dash of paprika

Chop 4 of the peppers leaving in seeds. Sauté in butter with garlic and onions until tender. Add ham, water, tomato juice and tomatoes. Cook until liquid is absorbed. Stir in eggs and cracker crumbs. Season to taste. Cut off tops and remove seeds from remaining 12 peppers. Parboil with sugar until slightly tender. Stuff with the tomato mixture. Cover lightly with bread crumbs, butter, and a sprinkle of paprika. Bake at 350°F. for about 20 minutes or until peppers are piping hot.

Yield: 12 portions.

POTATO PUDDING · MRS. WILLIAM STURT, ALBANY PARK, ILL.

4 large baking potatoes,
    unpared
1 medium carrot, unpared
1 large onion, sliced
¼ cup butter or margarine
2 tablespoons dry bread
    crumbs
1 teaspoon salt
¼ teaspoon pepper

Medium shred potatoes and carrots. Sauté onion in butter until golden brown. Combine with potatoes, carrot, bread crumbs, salt, and pepper. Turn into a greased 1½-quart casserole; cover. Bake at 350°F. for 1 hour and 15 minutes. Yield: 6 portions.

POTATO WHIRLS · MRS. LILY W. HANSON, IDAHO FALLS, IDAHO

Pastry for one-crust 9-inch
    pie
½ cup grated Cheddar cheese
Mashed potato filling

When making pastry, add cheese with dry ingredients. Roll pastry to a 9-inch square. Spread with potato filling. Roll as for jelly roll. Cut into 6 slices and place cut-side up on a greased baking sheet. Bake at 450°F. for 25 minutes. Serve with creamed vegetables or left-over meat. Yield: 6 portions.

MASHED-POTATO FILLING:

1 cup mashed potatoes
1 teaspoon chopped parsley
½ teaspoon salt
¼ teaspoon pepper
1 egg, beaten
½ teaspoon onion juice

Combine ingredients and mix thoroughly.

BAKED POTATOES · MAXINE THORPE, HOLLYWOOD, CALIF.

Split across one side with a sharp pointed knife, fork-stir the potato to a light fluff, add a big lump of butter and stir it again. Sprinkle over ground walnuts and into the oven till piping hot.

POMMES SOUFFLÉS · ANTOINE'S, NEW ORLEANS, LA.

Peel Burbank, California, potatoes. Cut in ⅛-inch lengthwise slices. Place in wire basket and run cold water over to remove extra starch. Dry thoroughly. Have 2 frying kettles of fat, 1 at moderate temperature, the other very hot. Place several sliced potatoes in frying basket in moderately hot fat and cook until they rise to the surface of the fat and the edges show faint signs of puffing. (If the puff does not develop that is just too bad; start over from scratch.) If the faint puffing appears, then immediately transfer potatoes in basket to the very hot pot of fat; cook until fully puffed and browned. Drain on absorbent paper. Sprinkle with salt. Serve immediately. If desired, the potatoes may be put aside after the second cooking and given a final dip later in the very hot fat, then rushed to the table. If this is to be done, do not fully brown potatoes in second fat pot. Finish them off in the third cooking.

SELMA'S SCALLOPED POTATOES · SELMA BIRD, MIAMI, FLA.

6 medium potatoes
6 tablespoons butter or
    margarine
Salt and pepper
Flour
12 slices Cheddar cheese
2 cups milk

Pare potatoes; slice thin. Place ⅓ of slices in bottom of 2-quart casserole, dot with ⅓ of butter and season with salt and pepper, dust with flour and cover with 4 slices of cheese. Add second layer of potatoes, repeat with butter, seasonings, flour and cheese. Add third layer of potatoes, butter, seasonings. Add milk and top with cheese. Bake at 350°F. for 1 hour. Serve with fried chicken and mixed green salad. Yield: 4 to 6 portions.

GROOMBEERA FILLAS · LANCASTER COUNTY, PENNA.
(Potato Filling)

2½ cups hot mashed potatoes
2 eggs, well beaten
¼ cup melted butter or
    margarine
1 tablespoon dried parsley
    flakes
1 teaspoon garlic salt
2 teaspoons grated onion
1 teaspoon celery salt
¼ teaspoon pepper
4 cups coarsely crumbled dry
    bread*

Combine potatoes, eggs and butter. Combine remaining ingredients and fold into potatoes. Serve hot. Yield: 6 portions.

*Bread that has been dried lightly toasted in the oven is ideal for this. Crumble it coarsely with the hands so bread is consistency of kernels of corn.

POTATO FILLING · MRS. CLAUDE F. MOYER, ALLENTOWN, PENNA.

4 pounds potatoes
1 medium onion, diced
3 stalks celery, minced
½ pound butter or margarine
½ pound white bread
2 cups milk, about
2 eggs, beaten
1 cup chopped parsley

Cook potatoes in salted water until tender. Drain and mash. Sauté onion and celery in half of butter until celery is tender. Add to mashed potatoes along with the fat. Add bread which has been crumbled and soaked in milk. Add eggs and remaining butter, melted. Keep beating and add parsley. Turn into a 3-quart casserole. Bake at 350°F. for 30 minutes or until heated. Yield: 12 portions.

SWEET POTATOES AND APPLES · PEACH RIDGE, MICH.

4 medium sweet potatoes
4 medium apples
¾ cup light brown sugar
½ teaspoon salt
½ teaspoon cinnamon
1 teaspoon lemon juice
2 tablespoons butter or
  margarine
½ cup warm water

Cook potatoes until just tender; cool and peel; cut into 1-inch thick slices. Pare and core apples and slice into ½-inch rings. Arrange potatoes and apples in alternate layers in greased baking dish. Mix sugar, salt, and cinnamon. Sprinkle part of the sugar-cinnamon mixture and lemon juice over each layer. Dot with butter. Add water. Cover. Bake at 375°F. for 35 minutes. Remove cover; cook about 10 minutes.
Yield: 6 portions.

SWEET POTATO TIPSY · WARREN POSEY, NEW ORLEANS, LA.

8 medium sweet potatoes
⅓ cup butter or margarine
2 tablespoons brown sugar
⅓ cup light cream
2 tablespoons sherry wine

Cook sweet potatoes until tender. Peel, mash, then whip, adding butter, brown sugar, cream and sherry. Turn into greased casserole. Bake at 350°F. about 25 minutes or until top is browned.
Yield: 8 portions.

BRANDIED SWEET POTATOES · WILLIAMSBURG, VA.

2½ pounds sweet potatoes,
  unpared
¼ pound butter or margarine
½ cup light brown sugar
1 teaspoon cinnamon
½ teaspoon salt
¼ teaspoon nutmeg
½ cup brandy

Cook sweet potatoes until soft. Remove from water and cool. Peel and slice crosswise in 1½-inch-thick slices. Place in well-greased, shallow baking dish. Dot with butter. Mix sugar, cinnamon, salt and nutmeg. Sprinkle over potatoes. Pour brandy over. Bake at 375°F. for 30 minutes.
Yield: 6 portions.

OLD FASHIONED SWEET-POTATO PONE · MARY McKAY, VICKSBURG, MISS.

6 medium sweet potatoes
2 cups sugar
¼ cup butter or margarine
3 eggs, beaten
1 teaspoon cinnamon
1 teaspoon allspice
1 teaspoon nutmeg
1 teaspoon ground cloves
1 box (12 ounces) white
　　raisins

Cook potatoes until tender. Peel and place in single layer in casserole. Blend sugar and butter. Mix in the remaining ingredients. Pour over potatoes. Bake at 250°F. for 1 hour or until potatoes are hot.

Yield: 6 portions.

ELISE GERBER'S SPINACH · MONROE, WIS.

2 cups cooked spinach,
　　drained
1 tablespoon butter or
　　margarine
1 teaspoon finely minced
　　onion
1 tablespoon flour
Dash of nutmeg
Salt and pepper to taste

1 cup milk
1 tablespoon heavy cream

Chop spinach finely. Add butter and onion, and simmer 1 minute. Sprinkle with flour. Add nutmeg and salt and pepper, stirring well. Add milk and heat to a bubble boil. Add more seasoning, if desired. Just before serving, stir in cream. Yield: 4 portions.

SPINACH-RICE RING · MRS. HAROLD FABIAN, JENNY LAKE, WYO.

2 cups raw rice
6 cups water
2 teaspoons salt
3 packages frozen, chopped
　　spinach
1 clove garlic
3 cans (16 to 17 ounces)
　　baby beets

Cook rice in boiling salted water until very soft. Drain, but leave enough water so rice is moist. Cook spinach according to package directions, adding garlic after spinach is broken up. Drain; remove garlic. Combine spinach and rice and press into a heated 2½-quart ring mold. Turn out on a hot platter. Fill center with beets which have been heated, seasoned and sauced with butter. Yield: 8 to 10 portions.

SWEET-SOUR SPINACH · MRS. JOHN VAN HEES, VERA COMMUNITY, WASH.

1 cup vinegar
1 cup sugar (about)
½ cup plumped raisins
4 pounds spinach, cooked

Combine vinegar and sugar to taste. Add raisins. Simmer a few minutes. Add cooked spinach. Cover pan and turn off heat. Allow spinach to heat through before serving. Yield: 6 to 8 portions.

BAKED SPINACH · MRS. RICHARD S. WRIGHT, PIEDMONT, CALIF.

1 package frozen, chopped
    spinach, thawed
2 tablespoons butter or
    bacon fat
Nutmeg to taste
Salt and pepper to taste
2 eggs, slightly beaten
3 tablespoons fine, dry bread
    crumbs
4 raw bacon slices

Heat spinach in butter. Season with nutmeg, salt and pepper. Combine eggs and crumbs, add to spinach. Place in casserole and cover with bacon. Bake at 350°F. for 45 minutes. Yield: 4 portions.

NOTE: If desired ½ cup chopped nuts or chopped mushrooms or grated cheese may be mixed into the spinach with the bread crumbs and eggs.

SPINACH PUDDING · MENGER HOTEL, SAN ANTONIO, TEX.

3 cups cooked fresh spinach
½ small onion
½ green pepper
1½ cloves garlic
2 eggs
1 teaspoon salt
¼ teaspoon pepper
Dash of nutmeg
1½ cups fine bread crumbs
½ cup softened butter or
    margarine

Put spinach, onion, green pepper and garlic through a grinder, using a fine blade. Add eggs and seasonings, mixing well. Mix in 1 cup of the bread crumbs. Take a clean dish towel and spread the butter onto it, forming a 9- to 10-inch square. Sprinkle butter with remaining bread crumbs. Drop spinach mixture in center of crumbed area and form into a roll about 1½ inches thick. Wrap cloth loosely around roll. Tie ends and middle loosely with string. Steam 20 minutes.

Yield: 10 to 12 portions.

TOMATO SOUFFLÉ · MRS. J. KELL BRANDON, SIMSBURY, CONN.

2 tablespoons butter or
    margarine
2 tablespoons flour
2 cups milk
1 teaspoon salt
½ teaspoon garlic or onion
    salt
1 teaspoon Worcestershire
    sauce
Pinch sugar (optional)
1 bay leaf
6 tablespoons tomato paste
6 eggs, separated

Melt butter and blend in flour. Gradually stir in milk and cook over low heat until smooth and thickened. Add salt, garlic salt, Worcestershire sauce, sugar, bay leaf and tomato paste. Cook 5 minutes; remove bay leaf. Add a small amount of hot mixture to beaten egg yolks, then combine with remaining hot sauce. Fold in stiffly beaten egg whites. Pour mixture into ungreased 3-quart baking dish. Place in pan of hot water. Bake at 350°F. for 50 to 60 minutes. Serve immediately.

Yield: 6 portions.

TURNIP GREENS WITH GARDEN RELISH · MOUNTAIN BROOK CLUB, BIRMINGHAM, ALA.

*4 pounds young turnip
    greens
Coarse salt
1 quart water
1 2-inch square salt pork
1 dry pod hot pepper, or a
    pinch of cayenne*

Strip turnip leaves from stems leaving sides of leaf and top portion in one piece. If the greens are very young, merely pinch off stem end and leave the leaf intact. Put leaves in colander, sprinkle over a big handful of coarse salt and start dousing under running water. It takes several minutes of constant washing to get out the grit. When clean, drain well. Pour water into heavy-bottomed pot. Add salt pork, well washed. Bring to a boil and boil 10 minutes. Drop in the pepper pod, broken in half, now dump in the greens. Cover and in 10 minutes when the leaves have withered, taste, and add salt if necessary. If the greens are young, 15 to 20 minutes' cooking is sufficient. If old and on the tough side, cook 30 to 40 minutes. Drain, reserve pot liquor and serve as a bouillon, with a slice of lemon, to drink with the main course. Cut greens a few times across with knife, place in serving dish, top with broken pepper pod and pass with Garden Relish.
Yield: 6 portions.

GARDEN RELISH:
*2 tomatoes, chopped, ¼-inch
    dice
¾ cup chopped celery
1 large cucumber, peeled,
    chopped
1 green pepper, chopped
2 tablespoons finely chopped
    onion*

*1 tablespoon French dressing
2 to 3 tablespoons cider vinegar
Salt to taste
Black pepper to taste*

Mix ingredients thoroughly. Chill 2 hours or until flavors are blended. Yield: 2 cups relish.

ZUCCHINI SQUASH AND TOMATOES · MRS. ANTHONY J. CELEBREZZE, CLEVELAND, OHIO

*½ small onion, chopped
2 tablespoons oil
4 or 5 large fresh tomatoes
Salt and pepper to taste
2 basil leaves (optional)
1 large or 2 small zucchini
    squash*

Sauté onion in oil. Peel and cut up tomatoes; add to onion. Season to taste and add basil. Cover and simmer for about 20 minutes. Pare and cube squash. Add to tomatoes and simmer until squash is transparent and tender, about 15 minutes. If desired, cook further with egg and cheese dumplings (recipe below). Yield: 4 portions.

EGG AND CHEESE DUMPLINGS:

1 egg, slightly beaten
1 cup finely grated Parmesan
  cheese
Pepper to taste

Blend egg and cheese. Season with pepper. Drop by tablespoonfuls onto hot cooked squash and tomato mixture. Simmer, covered, until dumplings are firm, about 5 minutes.

Yield: about 12 dumplings.

STUFFED ZUCCHINI · MRS. RICHARD S. WRIGHT, PIEDMONT, CALIF.

6 small-to-medium zucchini
1 cup fine, soft bread crumbs
½ cup finely chopped, well-
  drained, cooked spinach
½ cup grated Parmesan
  cheese
1 tablespoon minced onion
2 eggs, slightly beaten
2 tablespoons oil
¼ teaspoon thyme
Garlic salt
Paprika

¼ teaspoon monosodium glutamate
Salt and pepper to taste

Wash zucchini; cut off ends. Parboil in boiling salted water for 15 minutes; remove and let cool. Cut in half lengthwise and scrape out pulp using a teaspoon. Drain pulp thoroughly; mash. Combine with other ingredients, putting aside part of the cheese. Fill half shells with mixture. Place in a greased, shallow baking dish. Sprinkle tops with remaining cheese, garlic salt, and paprika. Bake at 350°F. for 30 minutes.

Yield: 6 portions.

COLACHI · MRS. DOROTHEA DALTON, CALIFORNIA

3 strips bacon, diced
1 medium onion, sliced
1 clove garlic, minced
1 pound zucchini, cut in
  ½-inch slices
1 tomato, chopped
1½ cups corn niblets
1 teaspoon vinegar

1 cup cooked green beans, cut in pieces
1½ teaspoons salt
½ teaspoon sugar

Sauté bacon, onion and garlic. Add remaining ingredients. Cover. Cook over low heat 35 to 40 minutes.

Yield: 6 portions.

TORQUEMADO · GEORGE STICKNEY, FREDERICKSBURG, VA.

3 medium onions, sliced and
  separated into rings
2 tablespoons bacon fat
2 cups canned tomatoes
Salt and pepper to taste
2 eggs
3 to 4 slices buttered toast

Cook onions in fat until yellow. Add tomatoes and simmer about 20 minutes, or until onions are tender. Add salt and pepper. Remove from heat and add eggs, stirring them quickly in the tomato mixture. Serve over toast triangles. Yield: 3 to 4 servings.

GARDEN TORTA · DR. GEORGE SELLECK, SAN FRANCISCO, CALIF.

3 pounds spinach
1 cup water
4 medium zucchini squash,
*   unpeeled*
¼ cup olive oil
3 tablespoons Parmesan
*   cheese, grated*
4 eggs
2 slices bread, crusts
*   removed*
¼ cup light cream
⅛ teaspoon pepper
Pinch powdered thyme
Salt to taste
¼ cup chopped parsley
3 green onions, sliced

Wash and pick over spinach. Steam in water for 5 minutes; drain and finely chop. Slice zucchini in ¼-inch circles. Sauté in oil, with cover on pan, to steam slightly; do not cook thoroughly! Add cheese to spinach. Add eggs, one at a time, whipping thoroughly after each addition. Soak bread in cream; whip into mixture. Add seasonings and parsley. Fold in zucchini and green onions. (Be careful not to break the slices of squash.) Turn into greased 12×8×2-inch baking dish. Bake at 350°F. for about 45 minutes. Test for doneness with straw as in testing for cake. Can be served hot or cold.

Yield: 12 portions.

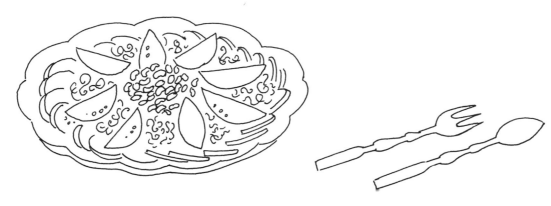

Salads

SWEET-SOUR BEANS · PENNSYLVANIA DUTCH

2 pounds fresh green beans
1½ tablespoons salt
3 tablespoons butter or
    margarine
½ cup cider vinegar
¼ cup water
½ cup sugar
1 medium onion, sliced

Slice beans diagonally ¼-inch thick. Cook until tender in a small amount of water, drain. While hot, add salt and butter. Cool. Add onion. Mix vinegar, water and sugar and pour over beans. Store in covered jar in refrigerator. These beans will keep for weeks. Yield: 6 portions.

PEPPER CABBAGE · MRS. CLAUDE F. MOYER, ALLENTOWN, PENNA.

1 cabbage, about 2 pounds
1 green pepper
1 sweet red pepper or carrot
1 stalk celery
1 cup sugar
2 tablespoons salt
½ cup water
½ cup vinegar, about

Grate cabbage finely. Chop peppers and celery; mix with cabbage. Combine sugar, salt, water and vinegar. Always taste to see if you have enough vinegar. Add to vegetables; toss. Yield: 6 portions.

GOURMET'S CAESAR SALAD · TERRACE-HILTON HOTEL, CINCINNATI, OHIO

Sprinkle salt with a generous hand over inside of wooden bowl. Rub with cut clove of garlic. Break 3 heads of washed and dried romaine into fair-sized lengths (about 2 inches), dropping into wooden bowl. Now come the additions. Have a small bowl ready with 5 fillets of anchovies mashed to a paste. Add to greens with ¼ cup garlic-flavored oil and mix well. Add a few drops of Worcestershire sauce. Add coarse-ground pepper to suit. Sprinkle over 3 tablespoons of grated Parmesan cheese. Break over a two-minute coddled egg.

Squeeze juice of 2 lemons directly over egg. Toss salad lightly and thoroughly, using wooden fork and spoon. Have bowl of hot croutons ready as the last addition. To make these, take 2 slices of sandwich bread, remove crust, cut each slice into 16 cubes; fry golden in oil well scented with garlic. Drop into salad. Mix again and serve. This provides 4 large portions.

CRAB SALAD, PACIFIC · KETCHIKAN, ALASKA

½ cup sour cream
¼ cup minced celery
2 tablespoons chopped olives
1 tablespoon grated onion
1 tablespoon chopped parsley
2 tablespoons chili sauce
¼ teaspoon salt
Shredded lettuce
2 large tomatoes, peeled and
    halved crosswise

1 can (6½ ounces) Dungeness crab meat, drained
    coarsely flaked and chilled
1 hard-cooked egg, sieved

Combine sour cream, celery, olives, onion, parsley, chili sauce, and salt. Chill to blend flavors. Arrange bed of lettuce on four salad plates; put tomato half on each. Pile crab meat on each tomato. Spoon sour cream dressing over top. Cover with egg. Yield: 4 portions.

THELMA BROWNFIELD'S FRUIT GELATIN SALAD · TULSA, OKLA.

1 package lime-flavored
    gelatin
1 package lemon-flavored
    gelatin
2 cups boiling water
1 cup evaporated milk
2 tablespoons lemon juice
1 pound creamed cottage
    cheese
2 cups drained, crushed
    pineapple
1 cup chopped nuts or celery

Combine lime and lemon-flavored gelatins; dissolve in boiling water. Cool. Stir in evaporated milk and lemon juice. Chill until slightly thickened. Fold in cottage cheese, pineapple and nuts or celery. Pour into 2-quart mold or two 8 × 8 × 2-inch pans. Chill until firm. Yield: 12 to 16 portions. Serve with mayonnaise topping.

Topping Recipe: blend 1 cup mayonnaise with 2 teaspoons prepared horseradish.

GARDEN COURT SALAD · SHERATON-PALACE HOTEL, SAN FRANCISCO, CALIF.

Salad base is shredded lettuce cut fine as fine—use the scissors. Make a half-inch thick mattress of the shreds to almost cover the plate. Center on this a thick slice of tomato, now a large heart of artichoke (these you buy canned), turn cup side up resting on tomato. Fill the cup with cooked crab meat, cooked shrimp, or diced white meat of chicken marinated in French dressing and very well drained. Build the tower spoonful by spoonful to a peak 5 inches tall from the base of the artichoke. Over this dip 3 or 4 tablespoons of the Thousand Island Dressing as it is made at the Palace. Add 2 tablespoons sieved yolk of hard-cooked egg to trim the base of the salad like a golden wedding band.

THOUSAND ISLAND DRESSING:

1 pint mayonnaise
1 cup catsup
½ cup chili sauce
¼ teaspoon paprika
1 tablespoon tarragon vinegar
1 tablespoon chopped parsley
2 teaspoons chopped chives
1 teaspoon chopped tarragon

Combine all ingredients; gently mix until thoroughly blended. Cover. Let stand in refrigerator overnight to blend the various flavors. Yield: 3¼ cups dressing.

MARY READ'S PEAR SALAD · SACRAMENTO, CALIF.

1 can (1 pound, 13 ounces)
    Bartlett pear halves
24 Maraschino cherries,
    approximately
2 packages (3 ounces each)
    cream cheese
5 tablespoons mayonnaise
1 cup pear juice
Romaine
½ cup heavy cream
5 tablespoons mayonnaise

Arrange pears, cavity up, in bottom of ring mold or deep ice-cube tray. Place cherries in cavity of pears and between pears. Blend cream cheese and 5 tablespoons of the mayonnaise; slowly beat in fruit juice. Pour over pears. Place mold in freezing compartment of refrigerator. Freeze until firm. Arrange romaine on serving dish. Unmold salad in center of plate. Whip cream until stiff; fold in remaining mayonnaise. Fill center of mold with the mayonnaise dressing.
    Yield: 10 portions.

GUACAMOLE SALAD · MRS. HARRY BEST, NORTH MIAMI, FLA.

4 cups thickly sliced avocado
1 cup fresh pineapple
    wedges
⅓ cup salad oil
⅓ cup vinegar
1 clove garlic, finely minced
Salt and Pepper

Combine fruits. Blend oil, vinegar, garlic, adding salt and pepper to taste. Pour over fruit and chill in refrigerator, turning occasionally. Serve on lettuce.
    Yield: 6 portions.

APPLE POTATO SALAD · PEACH RIDGE, MICH.

2 unpared red apples
7 large potatoes, cooked in
    skins
½ cup diced celery
9 hard-cooked eggs, chopped
24 stuffed olives, sliced
2 dill pickles, chopped
2 tablespoons chopped
    parsley

2 onions, diced
1½ pints salad dressing
Salt and pepper

Core and dice apples. Peel and dice potatoes. Place apples and potatoes in a large mixing bowl. Blend in celery, eggs, olives, pickles, parsley, and onions. Add salad dressing to moisten; salt and pepper to taste. Mix lightly. Yield: 3½ quarts salad.

CURRIED POTATO SALAD · SUSANNE COOLEY, LITTLE ROCK, ARK.

3 cups water
1½ teaspoons curry powder
1 teaspoon salt
4 cups diced, raw potatoes
3 tablespoons French
    dressing
2 tablespoons lemon juice
2 tablespoons grated onion
1½ teaspoons salt
¼ teaspoon black pepper
¼ teaspoon garlic powder
1½ cups diced celery

½ cup diced green pepper
3 hard-cooked eggs, diced
¾ cup mayonnaise

Combine water, curry powder, and 1 teaspoon salt. Add potatoes and cook, covered, until tender. Drain. Combine French dressing, lemon juice, onion, 1½ teaspoons salt, pepper, and garlic powder. Mix lightly with potatoes and let stand 30 minutes. Add celery, green pepper, and eggs; mix. Blend in mayonnaise.
Yield: 6 portions.

DONNA'S POTATO SALAD · DONNA HANSEN, IDAHO FALLS, IDAHO

6 medium potatoes, boiled
    and diced (2 quarts
    diced)
6 hard-cooked eggs, sliced
½ cup minced onion
1 tablespoon chopped parsley
¼ cup chopped dill or sweet
    pickle
1 tablespoon salt
¼ teaspoon pepper
1 tablespoon prepared
    mustard
1 tablespoon mayonnaise

1 tablespoon French dressing
1 tablespoon dill-pickle juice
¾ cup milk or light cream (about)
Paprika

Toss together lightly: potatoes, 5 of the sliced eggs, onion, parsley, pickle, salt, and pepper. Combine mustard, mayonnaise, French dressing, pickle juice, and enough milk or cream to make 1 cup dressing. Toss with potato mixture. Arrange in a bowl. Place remaining egg slices around top and sprinkle with paprika.
Yield: 2 quarts salad.

GENEVIEVE'S POTATO SALAD · MRS. JOHN MCDERMOTT, OTTUMWA, IOWA

12 potatoes, medium size
6 eggs hard-cooked
Salt to taste
1 teaspoon celery seed
¼ cup finely chopped
    scallions
1 cup (about) oil base
    mayonnaise

Wash potatoes well and boil unpeeled in the early morning. Chill until suppertime. Peel and cut into half-inch dice. Shell eggs and dice four of the six. Add to potatoes with salt, celery seed and scallion. Mix in mayonnaise. Add just enough that the salad will mound prettily. Never, never sloppy! Garnish with remaining two eggs, sliced. Sprinkle with parsley. Ring with young radishes and scallions alternating. Make a second ring of cold cuts.

NICHOLAUS POTATO SALAD · NICHOLAUS DELICATESSEN RESTAURANT, SCHENECTADY, N.Y.

8 large potatoes
1 cup thinly sliced celery
3 medium-sized onions,
    thinly sliced
3 tablespoons minced parsley
½ teaspoon celery seed
⅔ cup cider vinegar
⅓ cup water
¼ teaspoon prepared mustard
2 teaspoons salt
¼ teaspoon pepper
4 slices bacon

Boil potatoes in jackets 30 to 35 minutes in boiling salted water. As soon as they can be handled, peel and slice about ⅛-inch thick. Combine celery, onions, parsley and celery seeds with sliced potato in bowl. Heat and blend vinegar, water and mustard and pour while hot over potatoes. Add salt and pepper and mix well. Fry bacon until crisp; remove bacon and keep warm. Pour hot bacon drippings over potatoes, mixing thoroughly. Stir in the crumbled bacon. Place salad on platter; then let stand at room temperature for about 2 hours before serving. Yield: 6 portions.

SPECK'S POTATO SALAD · SPECK'S COFFEEHOUSE, ST. LOUIS, MO.

3 pounds potatoes
¼ cup finely diced bacon
¼ cup diced onion
1¼ tablespoons sugar
1 tablespoon flour
2 teaspoons salt
¼ teaspoon pepper
⅔ cup cider vinegar
⅓ cup water
½ teaspoon celery seed
3 tablespoons chopped
    parsley

Cook potatoes in jackets until tender. Cool and peel; thinly slice. Cook bacon until crisp. Add onion and cook 1 minute. Combine sugar, flour, salt and pepper; blend into bacon mixture. Stir in vinegar and water. Cook mixture 10 minutes, stirring well. Pour over sliced potatoes and add celery seed and parsley; toss lightly. Serve warm.
    Yield: 6 portions.

GREEN FROSTED POTATO SALAD · THE NUT TREE, VACAVILLE, CALIF.

4 pounds potatoes (about 12
    medium), cooked in
    jackets
½ cup chopped parsley
¼ cup chopped green
    pepper
¼ cup chopped celery tops
¼ cup chopped mustard
    greens (optional)
¼ cup chopped green
    onions
¼ cup chopped dill pickle
1 cup mayonnaise
¼ cup clear French
    dressing
2 to 2½ teaspoons salt
1 teaspoon dry mustard
½ teaspoon pepper

Coarsely dice peeled potatoes. Mix ¼ cup of the chopped parsley with the next 5 ingredients; take out about ½ cup of the mixture and add to rest of parsley; set aside. Toss remainder of chopped mixture with potatoes. Combine mayonnaise, French dressing and seasonings. Add to salad and toss to mix well. Pack into an 8×8×2-inch pan or shallow 2-quart baking dish. Sprinkle reserved parsley mixture over top. Chill. Lift out servings with a pancake turner. Garnish with sprigs of water cress or chopped celery tops.

Yield: 9 portions.

ADELE MILCZARCK'S POTATO SALAD · SALT LAKE CITY, UTAH

12 cups diced, cooked
    potatoes
12 hard-cooked eggs, diced
1 onion, finely chopped
⅓ cup French dressing
4 tablespoons cornstarch
1 cup water
1 egg
¾ cup salad oil
¼ cup vinegar
2 teaspoons prepared
    mustard
2 tablespoons sugar
3 teaspoons salt
¼ teaspoon paprika
1 cup evaporated milk
6 hard-cooked eggs

Combine potatoes, diced eggs, onion and French dressing. Chill. Make a smooth paste of cornstarch and water and cook over boiling water until clear, stirring constantly. In a bowl combine egg, oil, vinegar, mustard, 1 tablespoon of the sugar, 1 teaspoon of the salt and paprika. Mix well and add gradually to hot mixture; beat until smooth. Add evaporated milk, remaining tablespoon sugar and remaining 2 teaspoons salt. Beat until smooth. Cool. Combine with potatoes. Season further, if desired. Put half of potato mixture into serving bowl. Slice 3 of the hard-cooked eggs and lay over salad. Add rest of potatoes. Garnish top with 3 eggs cut into wedges. Chill.

Yield: 12 portions.

MOLDED SALMON · ASTORIA, ORE.

1 tablespoon unflavored
   gelatin
⅓ cup cold water
2 egg yolks, slightly beaten
1 teaspoon salt
1 teaspoon dry mustard
1½ tablespoons melted butter
   or margarine
¾ cup milk
2 tablespoons vinegar

1 can (1 pound) salmon, drained and flaked
½ cup sliced olives

Soften gelatin in water. Combine egg yolks, seasonings and butter in top of double boiler. Stir in milk gradually. Cook over hot water for 5 to 6 minutes or until thickened, stirring constantly. Add gelatin and stir until dissolved. Add vinegar, salmon, and olives. Pour into a 1-quart mold. Chill until firm. Serve on a bed of lettuce.

Yield: 6 to 8 portions.

WILLIMAE WHITE'S KING SALMON MOLD · TULSA, OKLA.

1 can (1 pound) salmon
½ cup finely chopped celery
¼ cup minced onion
2 packages unflavored gelatin
½ cup cold water
½ cup catsup
¼ cup vinegar
1 cup mayonnaise

Drain salmon; reserve liquid. Flake salmon; mix with celery and onion. Soften gelatin in water. Combine reserved salmon liquid, catsup, and vinegar; bring to a boil. Add softened gelatin; stir until dissolved. Gently blend hot liquid with salmon mixture. Stir in mayonnaise. Turn into 1-quart fish mold which has been coated with additional mayonnaise. Chill until firm. If desired sprinkle with paprika and use stuffed olive slices for eyes and a sprig of parsley for tail. Garnish with deviled eggs, tomato quarters, green onions, pickles, carrot sticks, olives, and pickled beets.

Yield: 6 to 8 portions.

U. S. SENATE SALAD · WASHINGTON, D.C.

1 cup bite-size pieces lettuce
1 cup bite-size pieces romaine
   or escarole
½ cup bite-size pieces water
   cress
1½ cups diced fresh lobster
   meat
1 cup diced celery
½ cup chopped green onions
   and stems

2 medium tomatoes, cubed
1 medium avocado, peeled and cubed
5 large stuffed olives, sliced
Sections from ½ grapefruit
Garlic salad-dressing mix

Place ingredients, except salad dressing, in large salad bowl. Toss lightly. Garnish salad top with lobster claws. Serve with salad dressing. Yield: 4 entree salads.

TODAY'S WALDORF SALAD · WALDORF HOTEL, NEW YORK CITY

1½ cups diced, tart, red
   apples, unpeeled
1 tablespoon lemon juice
1 cup diced celery
½ cup mayonnaise
Lettuce, chilled

1 cup walnuts, chopped

Sprinkle apples with lemon juice to keep from discoloration. Combine apple with celery. Add mayonnaise, mixing well. Arrange leaves of crisp cold lettuce on six salad plates and spoon in salad mixture. Just before serving, sprinkle with nuts. Yield: 6 portions.

HOLIDAY WALNUT SALAD · MAXINE THORPE, HOLLYWOOD, CALIF.

1 cup canned Bing cherries
2 cups orange juice
1½ cups sherry wine
2 tablespoons sugar
2½ tablespoons unflavored
   gelatin
Walnut meats, quartered

Drain cherries, reserve juice (about ¾ cup). Mix with 1½ cups of the orange juice, wine, and sugar. Bring to a boil and remove from heat. Soften gelatin in remaining ½ cup of orange juice and dissolve in hot fruit syrup. Chill until mixture begins to set. Add cherries, first stuffing each one with a quarter of a walnut. Turn into a ring mold. Chill until firm. Unmold and fill center with mayonnaise blended half and half with sour cream. Yield: 8 portions.

Dressings

GREEN-GODDESS DRESSING · SHERATON-PALACE HOTEL, SAN FRANCISCO, CALIF.

4 anchovy fillets, finely cut
2 tablespoons chopped onion
1 teaspoon chopped parsley
1 teaspoon chopped tarragon
2 teaspoons chopped chives
1 teaspoon tarragon vinegar

1½ cups mayonnaise

Combine anchovy, onion, parsley, tarragon, chives, and tarragon vinegar. Add mayonnaise; gently mix until blended. Serve over greens tossed together in a salad bowl rubbed with a cut clove of garlic. Yield: 1¾ cups.

MARY BOHN'S HOT SALAD DRESSING · PENNSYLVANIA

4 slices bacon
⅓ cup vinegar
⅔ cup water
1 tablespoon flour
2 tablespoons sugar
½ teaspoon dry mustard

Pinch of salt
1 egg, beaten

Fry bacon until crisp. Remove bacon and add vinegar and water to fat; bring to a boil. Mix flour, sugar, mustard and salt. Add to liquid and blend to a smooth paste. Stir in egg and heat for a minute. Use as a warm dressing for potato salad. Yield: 1¾ cups or enough for 6 portions.

CELERY SEED DRESSING · MRS. MAX HINRICHS, PULLMAN, WASH.

2½ cups sugar
4 teaspoons salt
4 teaspoons dry mustard
1 medium onion, grated
1½ cups vinegar
1 quart salad oil
¼ cup celery seeds

Combine sugar, salt, mustard, onion, and one-half the vinegar; beat thoroughly. Gradually add oil and continue beating. Beat in remaining vinegar in small amounts. Add celery seeds and beat until mixture is thick. Store in refrigerator.

Yield: 2 quarts.

NOTE: A superb sweet dressing, perfect to use on a fresh fruit salad.

BLEU CHEESE DRESSING · MRS. MAX HINRICHS, PULLMAN, WASH.

6 egg yolks
¾ teaspoon salt
¾ teaspoon paprika
½ teaspoon dry mustard
6 cups salad oil
9 tablespoons vinegar
½ cup sugar
½ teaspoon salt
6 ounces bleu cheese,
    crumbled
1 teaspoon minced garlic
¾ cup catsup
3 tablespoons vinegar

¾ teaspoon celery salt
¾ teaspoon onion salt

Beat egg yolks; add salt, paprika, and mustard. Add part of the oil slowly and continue beating until mixture is thick. Add the 9 tablespoons of vinegar a little at a time, alternating with remaining oil. Mix remaining ingredients thoroughly. Blend into oil mixture.

Yield: about 6½ cups dressing.

ROQUEFORT CHEESE DRESSING · TENNESSEE CLUB, MEMPHIS, TENN.

6 egg yolks
¼ cup olive oil
¼ cup vegetable oil
¼ cup lemon juice
Dash of Tabasco
½ teaspoon Worcestershire
    sauce
1 teaspoon salt
¼ teaspoon paprika
1 cup crumbled Roquefort
¼ cup light cream

Beat egg yolks until thick. Slowly add blended oils and continue the beating until the mass starts to thicken. Keep thinning with lemon juice, adding a dribble at a time. When thoroughly smooth, add Tabasco, Worcestershire sauce, salt and paprika. Crumble in cheese. Add cream and beat until smooth. The dressing should be thick but not too thick to pour. Serve over greens or a Chef's Salad; delicious sauce for shrimp cocktail; a love match with the avocado.

Yield: 3 cups dressing.

Desserts

BRANDIED FRUIT · MRS. HELEN DUPREY BULLOCK, WASHINGTON, D.C.

2 cans (1 pound each) whole
apricots or peaches with
pits and juice
Brandy

Drain fruit and boil juice until reduced to half the amount. Place fruit in juice, one layer at a time and heat gently. Lift into a crock or sterilized fruit jar and pour brandy over the hot fruit. The proportion of brandy should be ⅓ brandy to ⅔ reduced syrup. Add the syrup. Cover and store at least 24 hours in a cool place, but not in the refrigerator. Yield: about 1½ pints.

IRENE HARLAN'S APRICOT DESSERT · MANHATTAN, KANSAS

½ cup butter or margarine
1 cup confectioners' sugar
2 eggs beaten
6½ cups vanilla wafer crumbs
(1½ pounds wafers)
2 cups heavy cream, whipped
2 cans (1 pound, 13 ounces)
apricots, halved

Melt butter in top of double boiler. Add sugar and eggs; blend. Cook over boiling water, stirring constantly, until mixture thickens, about 4 minutes. Gently pack ¾ of the crumbs in 15 × 10 × 1-inch jelly roll pan. Spread cooked filling over crumbs. Spread half of whipped cream over filling. Arrange apricot halves on cream. Sprinkle nuts over apricots. Spread on remaining whipped cream. Top with remaining wafer crumbs. Chill at least 24 hours. Yield: 16 to 20 portions.

HOME-CANNED STUFFED PEACHES · GLADYS KIMBROUGH, MUNCIE, IND.

½ to ¾ cup stuffing
1 to 1½ cups syrup
2 quarts water
1 tablespoon salt
9 to 10 medium large peaches,
   clings or freestones

Get jars and canner ready. Prepare stuffing. Make syrup. Put water in pan and add salt. Wash peaches, then rinse, scald, peel and pit. Drop peaches in salted water; let remain for no longer than 20 minutes. Tightly pack stuffing into peaches. Pack peaches upright in jars. Add syrup to cover. Run knife down between jar and fruit to remove air bubbles. Adjust cap according to manufacturer's directions. Process quart jars of cling peaches 35 minutes in water-bath canner; freestone for 30 minutes. Keep water boiling steadily but not so hard as to shake jars. Yield: 1 quart peaches.

NOTE: If peaches rise to top, let jars stand until cold, then put them on their sides. Let stay in this position for a week; turn jars daily and peaches will have a better appearance.

STUFFING:
1 large slice crystallized
   pineapple
2 or 3 pieces crystallized
   orange peel
¼ cup citron

⅓ cup crystallized cherries
2 or 3 crystallized ginger slices

Finely chop all ingredients. Mix thoroughly so fruits hold together when pressed. Yield: 1 cup.

SYRUPS:
After syrups are cooked, cover pan and keep hot; do not let cook further. Yield depends upon rate of boiling. These recipes make 5 to 6 cups syrup.

Orange:
5½ cups sugar
1 cup orange juice
2 teaspoons grated orange
   rind

4 cups water
½ teaspoon salt

Mix all ingredients. Boil 5 minutes.

Brandied Syrup:
5 cups sugar
3 cups water
2 cups peach brandy

Boil sugar and water together 5 minutes. Add brandy to taste.

Filled peaches may be served in the manner of Cherry Jubilee. A sumptuous dessert is to sandwich a peach between meringue shells and pour over the sauce in which the peaches are canned. Slice the peaches and use as a garnish over ice cream, or to decorate a fruit salad or a fruit cup. The peaches, just as they come from the jar, make an interesting relish with cold meats and fowl.

Gladys says the clingstone peach looks neatest in the jar and holds together best, if properly pitted. But the freestone gives the best flavor.

She warns, don't try to pit the clingstone without a pitting spoon, a handy, inexpensive little tool costing around a dollar.

CHERRIES JUBILEE · MRS. STANLEY H. WATSON, CLEVELAND, OHIO

Take a large tin of the Bings and turn into the freezing tray of the refrigerator. Freeze until the syrup gets mushy. Then dip cherries into dessert dishes, and dollop with whipped cream, using about ¾ cup for 4 portions and adding to this 1 jigger of brandy —no more.

SPICED CRANBERRY ORANGE COMPOTE · MRS. EDWARD L. BARTHOLOMEW, WAREHAM, MASS.

3 oranges
2 cups sugar
1 cup water
2 2-inch cinnamon sticks
5 whole cloves
4 cups fresh cranberries

Peel oranges and cut in slices ½-inch thick. Boil sugar, water and spices together 5 minutes. Add orange slices, simmer 3 minutes. Add cranberries, cook 5 minutes or until skins pop open. Serve as a dessert, very cold.

Yield: 5 portions.

ORANGES JUBILEE · CALIFORNIA

1 cup fresh orange juice
1 cup water
¾ cup sugar
1½ tablespoons cornstarch
6 oranges, sectioned
½ cup toasted slivered
    almonds
½ to ⅔ cup brandy, heated
    slightly
Orange cartwheel slices
1½ cups sugar
¼ cup flour

Combine ¾ cup of the orange juice with water and sugar. Bring to a boil; simmer 5 minutes. Mix remaining ¼ cup orange juice and cornstarch to a smooth paste. Add slowly to hot mixture, stirring constantly. Cook until slightly thickened and glossy, about 10 minutes, stirring occasionally. Place orange sections in chafing dish and cover with thickened syrup. Sprinkle with almonds. (Add orange slices for eye appeal.) Heat. Add brandy, and ignite, if desired.

Yield: 4 to 6 portions.

Combine sugar and flour in 2-quart casserole. Add rhubarb pieces and stir until well coated. Add eggs,

RICE FARM RHUBARB · MRS. WILLIAM D, MC MILLAN, ITHACA, N.Y.

6 cups rhubarb, cut in ½-inch
    pieces
2 eggs, slightly beaten
1 lemon slice
2 whole cloves
1 tablespoon butter or
    margarine

stir lightly. Add lemon and cloves. Dot with butter. Bake at 300°F. about one hour or until mixture thickens. Serve as pudding. Yield: 6 portions.

STRAWBERRY WHIP · L. S. AYRES CO. DEPARTMENT STORE, INDIANAPOLIS, IND.

¾ cup frozen strawberries,
    defrosted
1 egg white
½ cup sugar
½ tablespoon lime juice

Combine ingredients and whip in an electric mixer, twenty minutes or longer until mixture is stiff. Yield: 10 portions. Serve with a thin custard sauce.

APPLE DUFFLE · PEACH RIDGE, MICHIGAN

¼ cup shortening
½ cup sugar
¼ teaspoon salt
1 egg, beaten
2 cups sifted flour
2½ teaspoons baking powder
1 cup milk
4 cups pared, diced apples

    CRUMB TOPPING:
½ cup sugar
⅓ cup flour
½ teaspoon cinnamon
¼ cup butter or margarine

Cream shortening and sugar. Beat in salt and eggs. Sift flour and baking powder and add alternately with milk to creamed mixture. Spread dough in greased 8 × 12-inch pan. Completely cover with apples. Sprinkle with topping. To make topping, mix sugar, flour and cinnamon. Cut in butter. Bake at 350°F. for 45 to 50 minutes or until topping is browned. Serve with any favorite sauce.
    Yield: 12 portions.

APPLE DUMPLINGS · MRS. THOMAS W. JENSEN, SALT LAKE CITY, UTAH

1 cup sifted flour
2 teaspoons baking powder
¼ teaspoon salt
2 eggs
⅓ cup top milk or thin cream
2 cups boiling water

3 medium-size unpared apples, sliced
¼ cup butter or margarine
½ cup sugar
1 teaspoon lemon juice

Sift flour, baking powder and salt together. Beat eggs and milk together; add flour mixture. Mix well. In a wide saucepan combine water, apples, butter, sugar and lemon juice; bring to a boil. Drop batter by tablespoonfuls into sauce. Cover pan. Cook on low heat for 15 minutes. Serve just warm with plain cream, whipped cream, or lemon sauce. Yield: 6 portions.

APPLE HONEY CRUNCH · ADELAIDE VAN WEY, NEW ORLEANS, LA.

4 apples
Juice of 1 lemon
15 whole cloves
¼ teaspoon cinnamon
½ cup honey
1 cup brown sugar, packed
3 tablespoons butter or
*   margarine*
¼ cup flour
1 cup salted peanuts

Peel and core apples, and cut into thin slices. Arrange in heat-proof glass baking dish. Sprinkle with lemon juice, cloves and cinnamon. Drizzle over 2 tablespoons of the honey. Bake at 350°F. for 30 minutes or until apples are tender. Cream brown sugar, butter and flour. Add remaining honey, mixing well. Stir in peanuts. Spread sugar mixture over cooked apples in baking dish. Place under broiler until topping melts and browns. Serve hot with ice cream or plain cream. Yield: 6 portions.

MONTAUK BERRY DUFF · JEANNETTE RATTRAY, EAST HAMPTON, N.Y.

2 cups sifted flour
1 cup sugar
2 teaspoons baking powder
2 eggs, beaten
1 cup milk

2 cups blueberries or blackberries fresh or canned,
*   well drained*

Sift flour, sugar, and baking powder. Combine eggs and milk. Add to flour and beat until smooth. Stir in berries. Turn batter into greased and floured 1½-quart mold. Steam 1½ to 2 hours. Serve with lemon sauce or thick cream. Yield: 8 portions.

CHERRY COBBLER · HAWTHORN ROOM, INDIANAPOLIS, IND.

1 quart frozen, sweetened
*   sour cherries*
3 tablespoons flour
1 cup sugar
Pinch of salt
2 tablespoons butter or
*   margarine*
½ recipe pie pastry

Combine cherries with flour, sugar, and salt. Turn into 8 × 8-inch baking dish. Dot with butter or margarine. Roll out pastry and cover cherries, making a fluted edge or cut pastry into strips and make a latticework top by placing half of the strips in one direction and weaving the other half in the other direction. Bake at 400°F. for 45 minutes or until the pastry is browned and cherries are thoroughly cooked. Yield: 6 portions.

Very Good

PEACH COBBLER · MRS. EARNST BLAZER, YUBA CITY, CALIF.

1 egg
¼ cup milk
1 tablespoon salad oil
2 tablespoons sugar
¼ teaspoon salt
½ cup pancake mix
1 tablespoon tapioca

1 can (1 pound, 13 ounces) cling peach slices

Combine egg, milk, salad oil, sugar, salt, and pancake flour. Beat with rotary beater until well blended. Cook peaches, juice and tapioca until thickened. Pour into 1½-quart casserole. Pour over the batter. Bake at 350°F. for 30 minutes. Serve with cream. Yield: 6 portions.

PLUM COBBLER · KATHLEEN LASSELLE, TIGARD, ORE.

FILLING:
1 can (1 pound, 13 ounces)
  purple plums
⅓ cup sugar
2 tablespoons flour
¼ teaspoon cinnamon
⅛ teaspoon salt
1 tablespoon butter or
  margarine

Drain plums, reserving juice. Pit plums. Place in a 1½-quart casserole. Add drained juices. Sprinkle with mixture of dry ingredients. Dot with butter. Put in 450°F. oven and bring to a boil while mixing top crust.

TOP CRUST:
1 cup sifted flour
1 teaspoon baking powder
½ teaspoon salt
⅓ cup sugar
2 tablespoons butter or
  margarine
¼ cup milk

Sift flour, baking powder, salt, and sugar. Cut in butter coarsely. Stir in milk until a ball is formed. Pat into shape of casserole and cover fruit mixture. Bake at 450°F. for 25 to 30 minutes. Serve with cream.
  Yield: 6 portions.

ORANGE DUMPLINGS · MRS. AUSTIN CARPENTER, SHERBURNE, N.Y.

1 tablespoon butter or
  margarine
¾ cup sugar
1½ cups sifted flour
1½ teaspoons baking powder
¼ teaspoon salt
½ cup milk
Orange sauce
Whipped cream

To make dumpling dough: cream together butter and sugar. Sift together flour, baking powder and salt. Add alternately with milk to creamed mixture. Drop by spoonfuls into hot orange sauce (*see next page*) in shallow baking pan. Bake at 375°F. for 20 to 25 minutes or until light brown. Serve warm, topped with whipped cream. Yield: 8 to 10 portions.

ORANGE SAUCE:
1 tablespoon butter or
    margarine
1 cup sugar
1 cup orange juice
½ teaspoon grated orange rind
2¾ cups boiling water

Place butter, sugar, orange juice and rind in saucepan. Add boiling water. Boil 10 minutes.

DORIS WESTBERG'S PEARADISE FRITTERS · YAKIMA, WASH.

1 cup sifted flour
2 tablespoons sugar
1 tablespoon baking powder
¼ teaspoon salt
¼ teaspoon mace
1 egg, beaten
1 cup milk
1 can (1 pound, 13 ounces)
    Bartlett pear halves,
    drained
Flour for dipping

Sift dry ingredients into mixing bowl. Combine egg and milk. Add to dry ingredients, beat until smooth. Roll pear halves in flour; then dip into fritter batter. Fry in deep fat (360°F.) from 3 to 4 minutes, or until fritter is nicely browned. Drain on absorbent paper. Serve hot. Yield: 8 fritters.

CORNISH FIGGIE 'OBBIN · COLORADO

2 cups sifted flour
1 teaspoon baking powder
1 teaspoon salt
2 tablespoons shortening
1 tablespoon finely chopped
    suet
½ cup milk, about
1 teaspoon grated lemon rind
¾ cup seedless raisins or
    chopped figs

Sift flour, baking powder, and salt together. Cut in shortening and suet thoroughly. Add milk and mix until a stiff dough is formed. Roll on floured surface into a rectangle ⅛-inch thick. Sprinkle lemon rind and raisins evenly on dough. Roll as for jelly roll. Place on greased baking sheet. Bake at 425°F. for about 20 minutes or until light golden brown. Serve warm with Lemon Sauce.

Yield: 6 portions.

LEMON SAUCE:
¾ cup sugar
¼ cup water
2 teaspoons butter or
    margarine
1 tablespoon lemon juice

Combine sugar and water; boil gently 5 minutes. Remove from heat. Add butter and lemon juice; stir until butter is melted. Yield: ⅔ cup sauce.

PLUM SHORTCAKE · MRS. GEORGE OTTEN, PORTLAND, ORE.

1 cup sifted flour
¼ cup sugar
1 teaspoon baking powder
½ teaspoon salt
3 tablespoons vegetable
    shortening
1 egg, beaten
1 tablespoon milk (about)
12 halves fresh purple plums,
    or 10 cooked, seeded
    dried whole prunes
1 tablespoon sugar

½ teaspoon cinnamon
2 tablespoons butter or margarine
½ cup walnuts, broken

Sift flour, sugar, baking powder, and salt together. Cut shortening into flour mixture until well blended. Stir in egg and add milk to make a soft dough. Turn mixture into greased 8-inch square baking pan. Press in plums. Dust with sugar, sprinkle with cinnamon, dot with butter, cover with walnut meats. Bake at 375°F. for 30 minutes. Serve with cream.
Yield: 6 generous portions.

OLD FASHIONED SHORTCAKE · KANSAS
   (A Quantity Recipe)

3 quarts flour
1 tablespoon salt
6 tablespoons baking powder
1½ cups shortening
6 eggs, well beaten
3 cups milk, or milk and
    water
Butter or margarine

1 gallon crushed, sweetened strawberries
Sift dry ingredients together. Cut in shortening. Add well-beaten eggs mixed with milk, mixing to as soft a dough as can be handled. Pat and roll a third of the dough at a time to ¼-inch thickness. Cut each portion into 2 8-inch squares. Put together with butter in between. Bake at 450°F. about 25 minutes. Split, spread with butter and put crushed berries between and on top. Yield: 50 portions.

SHERRY-ALMOND PUDDING · MRS. HAROLD FABIAN, JENNY LAKE, WYO.

2 tablespoons unflavored
    gelatin
½ cup cold water
1 cup hot water
⅓ cup sherry wine
½ teaspoon almond extract
¼ teaspoon salt
6 egg whites
1½ cups sugar
1 cup heavy cream, whipped
1 cup almonds, shredded
Shredded almonds
Toasted coconut

Soak gelatin in cold water; dissolve in hot water. Cool. Add wine, almond extract, and salt. When the mixture begins to thicken, beat until frothy. Beat egg whites until foamy. Gradually add the sugar and beat until stiff. Fold egg whites and whipped cream into gelatin mixture. Chill until almost firm. Pour into a 3-quart melon mold, alternating mixture with the 1 cup almonds. Chill at least 4 hours. Unmold and garnish with almonds and coconut. Serve with Sherry Sauce (*see next page*).
Yield: 10 portions.

SHERRY-CUSTARD SAUCE:

Beat 6 egg yolks thoroughly; mix in ¼ cup sugar and 2 tablespoons flour. Gradually stir in 2 cups scalded milk. Cook over low heat till thickened, stirring constantly. Cool. Add ¼ cup sherry wine. Chill. When ready to serve, whip 1 cup heavy cream and fold into custard.

APPLE PUDDING · MRS. L. K. MC CORMICK, NORTH MIAMI, FLA.

¼ cup butter or margarine
1 cup sugar
1 egg, well beaten
½ cup sifted flour
½ teaspoon cinnamon
½ teaspoon nutmeg
¼ teaspoon baking soda
1½ cups chopped apples
(about 2, peeled)

Cream butter and sugar thoroughly. Beat in egg. Sift together flour, cinnamon, nutmeg and soda. Beat into creamed mixture. Fold in chopped apples. Turn into buttered 1½-quart baking dish. Bake at 350°F. for about 35 minutes. Serve hot with hot Orange Sauce.
Yield: 4 portions.

ORANGE SAUCE:

1 cup sugar
2 tablespoons cornstarch
1 cup boiling water
½ cup orange juice
2 tablespoons butter or
margarine

Mix sugar with cornstarch. Add boiling water slowly, stirring constantly. Bring to a boil over low heat and cook until clear, stirring frequently. Remove from heat and add orange juice and butter; mix until butter is melted. Yield: 2 cups sauce.

MRS. MORTON'S APPLE CRISP PUDDING · MRS. PAUL MORTON, BRUNSWICK, GA.

4 cups peeled and sliced
apples
½ cup water
1 teaspoon cinnamon
½ cup butter or margarine
1 cup sugar
¾ cup flour
1 cup heavy cream, whipped,
or
1 pint vanilla ice cream

Turn apples into buttered casserole. Combine water and cinnamon and pour over apples. Blend butter, sugar and flour until crumbly. Sprinkle over apples. Bake at 375°F. for 35 to 45 minutes, or until top is golden and apples are done. Serve warm topped with whipped cream or ice cream.
Yield: 4 to 6 portions.

CARROT PUDDING · MRS. EZRA TAFT BENSON, SALT LAKE CITY, UTAH

1 cup sifted flour
1 teaspoon baking soda
1 teaspoon cinnamon
½ teaspoon cloves
½ teaspoon nutmeg
½ teaspoon allspice
1 cup dry bread crumbs
1 cup sugar
1 cup ground carrots
1 cup ground raw potatoes

1 cup ground suet
1 cup seedless raisins, ground
1 tablespoon dark molasses

Sift flour, baking soda and spices together. Add bread crumbs and sugar; blend. Add carrots, potatoes, and suet to dry ingredients. Mix dark molasses in thoroughly. Steam in a wide, shallow 1½-quart double boiler over boiling water for 2 hours. Serve with a sharp lemon sauce. Yield: 6 to 8 portions.

INDIAN PUDDING · MASSACHUSETTS

1 quart milk
5 tablespoons yellow corn meal
2 tablespoons butter or margarine
½ cup dark molasses
⅓ cup dark brown sugar
1 teaspoon salt
½ teaspoon ginger
½ teaspoon nutmeg
⅛ teaspoon cinnamon
2 eggs, well beaten
1 cup cold milk

Scald milk in top of double boiler over low heat. Add corn meal bit by bit, sifting it in from a little bowl in almost invisible amounts, one hand stirring all the while. Never a lump! Cook 20 minutes over hot water. Add butter, molasses, sugar, salt, spices and the eggs. Turn into a greased 2-quart casserole. Pour the cold milk over (don't stir); as the pudding cooks, the milk settles through. Bake at 350°F. about 50 to 60 minutes, or until silver knife inserted in the center comes out clean. Serve warm with plain cream or ice cream. Yield: 10 portions.

TOLL HOUSE BAKED INDIAN PUDDING · DUNCAN HINES

3 tablespoons yellow corn meal
3 cups scalded milk
⅓ cup molasses
1 egg
½ cup sugar
1 tablespoon melted butter or margarine
½ teaspoon ginger
½ teaspoon cinnamon
½ teaspoon salt

Gradually add corn meal to milk. Cook, stirring constantly, until slightly thickened. Add molasses. Beat egg. Add sugar, butter, ginger, cinnamon and salt. Add to hot corn meal mixture; mix well. Pour into greased 1½-quart baking dish. Bake at 300°F. for 2 hours. Yield: 6 portions.

BAKED INDIAN PUDDING · HERMAN SMITH, NEW YORK

5 cups milk
⅔ cup dark molasses
⅓ cup sugar
½ cup yellow corn meal
1 teaspoon salt
¾ teaspoon cinnamon
¾ teaspoon nutmeg
¼ cup butter or margarine

Scald 4 cups of the milk. Add molasses, sugar, corn meal, salt, spices and butter. Cook 20 minutes, stirring frequently, or until mixture thickens. Pour into a greased 1½-quart baking dish. Add remaining 1 cup cold milk, do not stir. Bake at 300°F. for 3 hours. Pass with thick cream flavored with nutmeg and sprinkled with maple sugar. Some prefer hard sauce, some like ice cream. Yield: 8 portions.

FLO'S INDIAN PUDDING · ELLA BOWLES, DURHAM, N.H.

½ cup corn meal
2 cups scalded milk
½ cup finely chopped suet
½ cup molasses
½ cup raisins
1 egg, well beaten
½ teaspoon salt
¼ teaspoon ginger
¼ teaspoon cinnamon

1 cup cold milk
½ cup cold water

Stir cornmeal into scalded milk and cook long enough to make a smooth batter. Add chopped suet, molasses, raisins, egg, salt and spices. Turn into a greased baking dish. Pour the cold milk and cold water over the mixture, but do not stir them in. Cover. Bake at 275°F. 3 hours. Serve each portion topped with vanilla ice cream. Yield: 6 portions.

LEMON PUDDING · MRS. THOMAS F. KNIGHT, JR., LA CANADA, CALIF.

1 cup sugar
¼ teaspoon salt
3 tablespoons lemon juice
2 teaspoons grated lemon rind
3 eggs, separated
⅓ cup sifted flour
2 tablespoons butter or
    margarine, melted
1½ cups milk

Mix together sugar, salt, lemon juice and rind. Add egg yolks and beat. Add flour, mixing well. Blend in melted butter and milk. Beat egg whites until stiff and fold into egg-yolk mixture. Pour into greased 2-quart casserole. Set in pan of hot water. Bake at 350°F. for 45 to 50 minutes.
Yield: 6 portions.

LEMON PUDDING · MRS. HOWARD S. WILLIAMS, HATTIESBURG, MISS.

3 eggs, separated
1 cup sugar
1 cup milk
2 tablespoons flour
Pinch of salt

1 lemon, rind and juice
Whipped cream

Beat egg yolks, adding sugar gradually. Gradually stir in milk. Add flour and salt a little at a time, stirring until smooth. Add lemon rind and juice. Fold in stiffly beaten egg whites. Pour into greased individual ramekins; place dishes in a pan of hot water. Bake at 350°F. for 45 minutes. Serve with whipped cream.

Yield: 6 portions.

ORANGE MARMALADE PUDDING · MRS. EWING ELMORE, BIRMINGHAM, ALA.

1⅛ cups sifted flour
1 teaspoon baking soda
1 teaspoon baking powder
½ teaspoon salt
1½ cups soft bread crumbs
1 cup suet, finely chopped
1 egg, slightly beaten
1 cup orange marmalade

1 cup milk
¼ cup sugar

Sift flour with soda, baking powder and salt. Combine with bread crumbs and suet. Add egg, marmalade, milk and sugar. Beat until thoroughly mixed. Pour into a greased 1½-quart mold. Cover. Steam for 3 hours. Yield: 6 to 8 portions.

MRS. TRUMAN'S OZARK PUDDING · SERVED TO WINSTON CHURCHILL AT FULTON, MO.

1 egg
¾ cup sugar
⅓ cup flour
1¼ teaspoon baking powder
⅛ teaspoon salt
½ cup chopped apples
½ cup chopped nuts
1 teaspoon vanilla extract
1 cup heavy cream, whipped
¼ cup rum

Beat egg well and add sugar, beating until light and creamy. Sift flour, baking powder, and salt together. Add to egg mixture; blend well. Fold in apples and nuts. Add vanilla. Pour into greased and floured 1-quart baking dish. Bake at 325°F. for 30 minutes. Serve with whipped cream, to which rum has been added.

Yield: 8 portions.

PERSIMMON PUDDING · MRS. ARTHUR B. LANGLIE, OLYMPIA, WASH.

1 cup sifted flour
¾ cup sugar
½ teaspoon baking powder
½ teaspoon salt
¼ to ½ teaspoon cinnamon
½ cup seedless raisins
½ cup chopped nuts
1 cup fresh persimmon pulp

⅓ cup milk
1 teaspoon vanilla extract

Sift dry ingredients. Stir in raisins and nuts. Combine remaining ingredients and stir into flour mixture. Turn into a greased and floured 1-quart mold, filling it about ⅔ full. Cover tightly and steam for 1 hour. Serve with vanilla-flavored hard sauce.

Yield: 8 portions.

PERSIMMON PUDDING · MRS. DONALD C. DRAKE, INDIANAPOLIS, IND.

⅓ cup butter or margarine
2 cups sugar
2 eggs, beaten
2 cups sieved persimmons
    (about 5 or 6 medium)
1 teaspoon baking soda
¼ cup hot water
2½ cups sifted flour
1½ pints milk
1 cup heavy cream, whipped

Cream butter and sugar. Add eggs and persimmon pulp, mixing well. Dissolve soda in hot water and add. Stir in flour, alternating with milk. Two methods of baking: In northern Indiana the batter is poured into a greased 16 × 10 × 2-inch pan and baked at 275°F. for 1¾ hours. In southern Indiana the preferred way is to pour batter into a greased baking bowl and place in pan of water in a 275°F. oven, baking 3 hours. Stir once every 20 minutes. Serve with whipped cream.

Yield: 12 portions.

GOVERNOR SPOTTSWOOD'S PLUM PUDDING · WILLIAMSBURG, VA.

5 eggs
1 cup sugar
¾ pound beef suet finely
    shredded
½ pound soft bread crumbs
½ nutmeg, grated
½ cup cognac
1 pound seedless raisins
1 pound currants
¼ pound citron, cut into large
    dice

Beat eggs and sugar until light. Add suet, crumbs, nutmeg and brandy; mix thoroughly. Combine fruits and add to egg mixture; mix thoroughly. Press into a well-buttered 2-quart mold. Cover. Steam for 4 hours.

Yield: 24 portions.

ELLIN NORTH'S PLUM PUDDING · FREDERICK STIEFF, BALTIMORE, MD.

1 pound seeded raisins
1 pound currants
½ pound citron, finely
    chopped
1 pound white suet
4 to 5 apples
2 cups soft bread crumbs
    (from day-old bread)
1 tablespoon salt
1½ tablespoons nutmeg
1½ tablespoons ginger
1 tablespoon flour
8 eggs, well beaten

2 cups milk
2 cups sugar
1 wine glass brandy

Combine raisins, currants and citron; dredge with flour. Chop suet and apples into small pieces. Mix bread crumbs, salt, spices and the tablespoon of flour. Combine eggs, milk and sugar. Add breadcrumb mixture, suet and apples. Add brandy. Pour into a well-greased 3-quart mold. Cover tightly. Steam for 4 hours. Yield: 1 3-quart pudding.

Sauce:

Cream ¾ cup sugar and ¼ pound butter or margarine thoroughly. Add 2 eggs, well beaten. Heat only until smooth. Add 1 cup sherry wine. Yield: about 2 cups sauce.

MOM'S POTATO PUDDING · MRS. H. C. DOPP, BOISE, IDAHO

1 cup grated carrots
1 cup grated potatoes
1 cup raisins
1 cup sugar
2 eggs, well beaten
2 cups flour (more if needed)
1 teaspoon baking soda
½ teaspoon salt
1 teaspoon cinnamon
½ teaspoon nutmeg
½ teaspoon allspice
¼ teaspoon ground cloves
3 tablespoons melted butter
*   or margarine*

Combine carrots, potatoes, raisins, and sugar. Add eggs. Combine and stir in well the flour, soda, salt, and spices. Add more flour, if needed, to make the consistency of a cake batter. Coat all sides of a 2-quart pudding mold or can with butter. Pour in the batter. Cover tightly with a lid or with aluminum foil secured with a rubber band. Place on a rack in a covered pan and steam for 3 hours. Cool. Store in refrigerator or cover mold with foil and freeze. When ready to serve, reheat in oven. Serve with this old-fashioned caramel sauce. Yield: about 12 portions.

CARAMEL SAUCE:
2 cups sugar
½ cup boiling water
½ cup heavy cream

In a heavy skillet over moderate heat, melt one cup of the sugar and cook until brown. Carefully and gradually stir in water. Cook, stirring until dissolved. Stir in remaining sugar; stir until dissolved. Blend in cream. If a thicker sauce is desired, thicken with a little cornstarch made into a paste with cream. Yield: 1½ cups sauce.

STEAMBOAT PUDDING · PITTSBURGH, PENNA.

2 cups large dry bread cubes
1 quart scalded milk
1 tablespoon butter or
*   margarine*
½ teaspoon salt
¾ cup sugar
4 eggs, lightly beaten
¾ teaspoon vanilla extract
½ cup seedless raisins

Soak bread in milk 5 minutes. (Home-style bread, cut fairly thick, makes the best cubes.) Combine with remaining ingredients. Pour into greased 1½-quart casserole. Bake at 350°F. for 1 hour. Serve warm with crushed, sweetened fruit.

Yield: 6 portions.

ALMENDRADO · MRS. ELMA VAN ZANDT, PHOENIX, ARIZ.

1 tablespoon unflavored
   gelatin
½ cup cold water
½ cup boiling water
½ cup sugar
4 eggs whites
½ teaspoon almond extract
Red and green food coloring
1 cup finely ground almonds

Soften gelatin in cold water. Add hot water and sugar and stir until dissolved. Chill until slightly thickened. Beat egg whites very stiff. Fold into gelatin mixture with almond extract. Beat until mixture resembles whipped cream. Divide into 3 bowls. Leave one uncolored, the second color red, the third green. Line an 8×8-inch pan with waxed paper. Pour in red mixture, sprinkle with ½ cup of the ground almonds. Pour in white layer and sprinkle with remaining almonds. Add green layer. Chill. Cut into 4×2-inch slices. Serve with chilled custard sauce—to stand for the Mexican eagle.

Yield: 12 portions.

ALMOND MOLD · PIRATE HOUSE, SAVANNAH, GA.

6 tablespoons sugar
3 tablespoons cornstarch
2 eggs, lightly beaten
1 quart hot milk
1 envelope unflavored gelatin
¼ cup cold water
2 teaspoons almond extract
3 tablespoons sugar
1 pint heavy cream, whipped
14 graham crackers, crumbled

Combine sugar, cornstarch and eggs in top of double boiler; stir until smooth. Gradually add milk. Cook over hot water, stirring, until custard is thick and smooth. Soften gelatin in water for 5 minutes; add to hot mixture and stir until thoroughly dissolved. Cool. Add almond extract. Add 3 tablespoons sugar to whipped cream and fold into custard, keeping out about 1 cup to use as topping. Pour into 9×12×2½-inch pan. Cover with graham cracker crumbs. Spread over the remaining cream.

Yield: 10 portions.

SWEDISH CHOCLATE PUDDING · MRS. CHARLES COOK HOWELL, JR., JACKSONVILLE, FLA.

1 egg
½ cup sugar
4 tablespoons cocoa
⅔ cup light cream
½ tablespoon unflavored
   gelatin
2 tablespoons water
1¼ cups heavy cream,
   whipped

Mix egg, sugar, cocoa and light cream in top of double boiler. Cook over hot water, stirring frequently until thick, about 10 minutes. Remove from heat. Soften gelatin in water and add to pudding mixture. Stir occasionally until cold. Fold in whipped cream. Pour into a 1-quart mold or individual molds rinsed in cold water. Chill until firm. Unmold, garnish with whipped cream, if desired.

Yield: 6 to to 8 portions.

COCONUT DESSERT · MRS. GUY ROCKWELL, EAST CLEVELAND, OHIO

1 cup milk
1 envelope unflavored gelatin
¼ cup cold water
1 cup sugar
2 cups heavy cream, whipped
Vanilla extract to taste
2 cups grated fresh coconut

Bring milk to a boil. Soften gelatin in cold water, add to the hot milk with sugar, stirring until dissolved. Let stand to cool and slightly thicken. When gelatin mixture begins to set, fold in whipped cream flavored with vanilla. Add coconut. Place in mold and chill overnight. Serve with caramel sauce.
Yield: 6 portions.

CARAMEL SAUCE:
2 cups brown sugar
1 cup light cream
1 tablespoon butter or
    margarine

½ cup chopped nuts
Combine sugar, cream, and butter in pan over low heat. Cook 5 minutes, stirring constantly, or until sauce is syrupy and smooth. Add nuts and serve warm.

FRESH CRANBERRY ICE PUDDING · MRS. EDWARD L. BARTHOLOMEW, WAREHAM, MASS.

4 cups fresh cranberries
2 cups water
⅔ cup sugar
1 cup heavy cream, whipped
1 envelope unflavored gelatin,
    softened in
¼ cup cold water
Plain cake (round single layer,
    or oblong pound cake
    shape)

Cook cranberries and water until berries are soft, about 5 minutes. Mash berries through strainer. Stir in sugar and softened gelatin until dissolved. Cool. Fold whipped cream into cranberry mixture. Pour mixture into refrigerator freezing tray. Freeze until partly frozen. Turn into a chilled bowl and beat with rotary beater until light and foamy. Return to refrigerator tray and freeze until firm. To assemble: Place cake on aluminum foil covered board. Unmold cranberry ice and place on top of cake. Cover with meringue made by beating until stiff but not dry, 3 egg whites, ⅓ cup sugar, added gradually. Bake at 450°F. 5 minutes or until meringue is lightly browned. Yield: 8–10 portions.

BRANDON PEACH RING · MRS. J. KELL BRANDON, SIMSBURY, CONN.

1 package lemon gelatin
1 cup boiling water
¼ cup sugar
1 cup canned apricot juice
1 cup heavy cream, whipped
8 peach halves, canned or
    fresh
Peach slices

Dissolve gelatin in water. Add sugar and apricot juice. Chill until it starts to set. Fold in cream. Rinse ring mold with cold water and arrange peach halves in bottom; put slices on sides if desired. Fill very carefully with gelatin mixture so as not to disturb halves. Chill until firm. Turn out; decorate with leaves. Serve with strained raspberry juice; fill center with peach slices. Yield: 8 portions.

CHARLOTTE RUSSE · MRS. RUTH MOSS CARROLL, FORT SMITH, ARK.

2 envelopes unflavored gelatin
½ cup cold water
2 cups milk
6 eggs, separated
1 cup sugar
1 teaspoon vanilla extract
1½ dozen lady fingers
2 cups heavy cream, whipped

Soften gelatin in water. Scald milk in top of double boiler. Beat egg yolks and sugar until well blended; stir into milk. Cook over boiling water, stirring constantly, until mixture coats a spoon. Remove from heat. Add gelatin; stir until dissolved. Add vanilla. Cool thoroughly. Meanwhile line sides of 10×4-inch tube pan with lady fingers. When custard is cool, beat egg whites until stiff. Fold into custard. Fold in cream. Turn into pan. Chill until set. Yield: 12 portions.

CHARLOTTE RUSSE WHEEL · MRS. JOHN MINOR WISDOM, NEW ORLEANS, LA.

2 dozen ladyfingers
2 tablespoons rum
5 tablespoons port
1 recipe Charlotte Russe,
    vanilla flavored

Sprinkle ladyfingers with rum and port. In a ring mold arrange ladyfingers on bottom to form 6 spokes. Dip Charlotte Russe (use any favorite recipe for this or preceding recipe) between spokes. Add more ladyfingers, more Charlotte Russe, until mold is filled. Chill. Unmold and serve with this butterscotch sauce.
Yield: 8 portions.

BUTTERSCOTCH SAUCE:
1 cup brown sugar
1 teaspoon cornstarch
¼ cup water
1 teaspoon vinegar
¼ cup butter or margarine

Combine ingredients. Cook to soft-ball stage (238°F.). Cool slightly and serve warm. Yield: ¾ cup sauce.

CHOCOLATE SPONGE VIENNOIS · MRS. HAMILTON POLK JONES, NEW ORLEANS, LA.

4 eggs, separated
½ cup sugar
½ cup boiling water
2 squares unsweetened
    chocolate, melted
2¼ teaspoons unflavored
    gelatin
½ cup cold water
1½ teaspoons vanilla extract

Beat the egg yolks until thick and lemon-colored. Gradually beat in sugar. Add boiling water to melted chocolate and blend well. Soften gelatin in cold water for 5 minutes. Stir into chocolate mixture until dissolved. Gradually stir into yolk mixture. Cool until slightly thickened. Fold in stiffly beaten egg whites. Add vanilla. Turn into mold and chill. If desired, garnish with whipped cream. A cold chocolate sauce poured over pudding before decorating with cream adds to the deliciousness of this dessert. Yield: 6 portions.

SCANDINAVIAN PUDDING · MRS. ARTHUR B. LANGLEY, OLYMPIA, WASH.

1 package unflavored gelatin
½ cup cold water
5 eggs, separated
¾ cup sugar
Juice of 1 lemon
1 teaspoon grated lemon
    rind (or to taste)
Pinch of salt

Soak gelatin in water 5 minutes. Dissolve over boiling water; cool to lukewarm. In a large mixing bowl beat egg yolks thoroughly. Add sugar a little at a time, beating constantly. Add lemon juice and rind, and continue beating. Add cooled gelatin mixture and beat again. Add salt to egg whites and beat until stiff. Fold into yolk mixture. Pour into a 1½-quart compote bowl. Chill until firm. Serve with whipped cream and maraschino cherries or finely ground toasted almonds as a garnish.

Yield: 8 portions.

WINE JELLY · MRS. LIONEL K. LEGG, CHARLESTON, S.C.

2 envelopes unflavored
    gelatin
½ cup cold water
1 cup boiling water
⅔ cup sugar
Pinch of Salt
¼ cup lemon juice, strained
¼ cup orange juice, strained
2 cups sherry wine

Soften gelatin in cold water. Dissolve in boiling water. Add sugar, salt, lemon and orange juice and sherry. Stir until well blended. Pour into a mold and chill until firm. Yield: 6 portions.

PEACH UPSIDE-DOWN CAKE · MRS. EARNEST BLAZER, YUBA CITY, CALIF.

½ cup butter or margarine
1 cup brown sugar
1 can (1 pound, 13 ounces)
    cling peach slices
2 tablespoons large whole
    pecans or walnuts
1 cup sifted flour
1 teaspoon baking powder
½ teaspoon salt
3 eggs, separated
1 cup sugar
5 tablespoons peach juice

Melt butter in 12×8-inch pan. Spread brown sugar evenly in pan. Arrange peach slices on sugar; fill in space with nuts. Sift flour, baking powder and salt. Beat egg yolks until light colored. Beat in sugar gradually. Blend in peach juice. Stir in sifted dry ingredients. Fold in stiffly beaten egg whites. Pour batter over peaches. Bake at 375°F. for 30 to 35 minutes. Let cool about 5 minutes. Turn upside down on cake plate. Serve with whipped cream, if desired.

Yield: 12 portions.

UPSIDE-DOWN APPLE CAKE · MRS. WILLIAM STURT, ALBANY PARK, ILL.

1 package active dry yeast
2 tablespoons warm, not
*   hot, water*
½ pound sweet butter
¾ cup sugar
3 eggs
1 cup commercial sour
*   cream*
3 cups sifted flour
Pinch of salt

FILLING:

3 tablespoons melted butter
*   or margarine*
3 tablespoons dark brown
*   sugar*
2 tablespoons currants
2 tablespoons fine graham-
*   cracker crumbs*
4 medium cooking apples

Dissolve yeast in warm water. Cream butter and sugar. Beat in eggs, one at a time. Stir in sour cream and yeast. Blend in flour and salt. Refrigerate overnight. Use only ⅛ of the dough. For filling: pour butter in the bottom of a 9×9×2-inch pan. Sprinkle with sugar, currants, and graham-cracker crumbs. Peel and core apples and cut into 8 slices. Arrange on top of butter mixture. Roll dough out on a floured surface into a 9-inch square. Place dough over apples and press against sides of pan. Let rise in a warm place for about 1½ hours. Bake at 350°F. for about 30 minutes. Invert cake on a wire rack so juice runs off and dough won't soak. Cool. Serve with cream. Yield: 6 to 8 portions.

NOTE: With the addition of enough flour to make a stiffer mixture, the remaining dough may be used for other sweet goods. For example: roll dough into a 12×8-inch rectangle. Spread with 2 tablespoons soft butter; sprinkle with 2 tablespoons brown sugar and 2 tablespoons currants. Cut the dough into 3 lengthwise strips and braid. With a sharp knife cut down the center of braid. Place on greased baking sheet. Let rise for 2 hours. Bake at 350°F. for about 30 minutes.

A CAKE FOR THE GIRLS · MRS. STUART COULTER, CALIFORNIA

1 10-inch angel-food cake
1 tablespoon unflavored
*   gelatin*
¼ cup cold water
2 tablespoons bourbon
8 egg yolks
1 cup confectioners' sugar
1 pint heavy cream, whipped
½ pound peanut or pecan
*   brittle, crushed*

Slice cake crosswise into 3 layers. Soften gelatin in cold water; dissolve over hot water. Add bourbon. Beat egg yolks until thick. Beat in sugar. Add gelatin mixture. Fold in whipped cream. Chill until mixture begins to stiffen. Spread between cake layers, sprinkling each layer with the brittle. Cover entire cake with the cream mixture and sprinkle with candy. Chill for several hours.

Yield: 1 10-inch cake.

LINDY'S CHEESECAKE · NEW YORK CITY

CHEESE FILLING:
2½ pounds cream cheese
1¾ cups sugar
3 tablespoons flour
1½ teaspoons grated orange rind
1½ teaspoons grated lemon rind
Pinch of vanilla bean (inside pulp) or ¼ teaspoon vanilla extract
5 eggs
2 egg yolks
¼ cup heavy cream

Combine cheese, sugar, flour, grated orange and lemon rind, and vanilla. Add eggs and egg yolks, one at a time, stirring lightly after each addition. Stir in cream.

COOKIE DOUGH PASTRY:
1 cup sifted flour
¼ cup sugar
1 teaspoon grated lemon rind
Pinch of vanilla bean (inside pulp)
1 egg yolk
½ cup butter or margarine

Combine flour, sugar, lemon rind and vanilla. Make a well in center and add egg yolk and butter. Work together quickly with hands until well blended. Wrap in waxed paper and chill thoroughly in refrigerator, about 1 hour. Roll out ⅛ inch thick and place over oiled bottom of 9-inch spring-form cake pan. Trim off the dough by running a rolling pin over sharp edge. Bake at 400°F. for 20 minutes, or until a light gold. Cool. Butter sides of cake form and place over base. Roll remaining dough ⅛-inch thick and cut to fit the sides of the oiled band. Fill form with cheese mixture and bake at 550°F. for 12 to 15 minutes. Reduce temperature to 200°F. and continue baking 1 hour. Let the cake cool for at least 2 hours before cutting. Yield: 12 portions.

CHERRY CHEESE PIE:
Using pastry recipe, roll pastry ⅛-inch thick and line an 11-inch oiled pan. Bake at 400°F. for 20 minutes. Add half Cheese Filling recipe. Bake at 450°F. for 10 to 12 minutes longer. Cool. Add fruit mixture, made by combining 2 cups sour cherries with ½ cup sugar, a pinch of cinnamon and ½ teaspoon lemon juice. Bring fruit to boil and add 2 teaspoons cornstarch blended with 2 tablespoons cherry syrup. Again bring to a boil and immediately remove from heat. Cool. Cover with strips of the pastry laid lattice-wise. Bake at 550°F. for 10 minutes, or until strips are brown. Yield: 10 portions.

NOTE: This recipe is both difficult and expensive to make.

LEMON ICE-BOX PUDDING · CAROL JEAN ACKLEY, CLAREMONT, CALIF.

¾ cup sugar
2 tablespoons cornstarch
Dash of salt
1 cup milk
3 eggs, separated
⅓ cup lemon juice
1 tablespoon butter or
    margarine
2 8-inch sponge cake layers
Whipped cream

Combine sugar, cornstarch, salt, and milk in top of double boiler. Cook over boiling water until thickened. Stir small amount into slightly beaten egg yolks; then gradually pour into cornstarch mixture. Continue cooking over hot water about 2 minutes, stirring constantly. Add lemon juice and butter. Cool slightly. Pour over stiffly beaten egg whites, blending thoroughly. Slice cake into 6 layers. Arrange cake and pudding in alternate layers in a round 9-inch casserole, ending with sauce. Cover and chill for 24 hours. Serve with sweetened whipped cream.

Yield: 12 portions.

CHOCOLATE ICEBOX CAKE · THE DUTCH CUPBOARD, COATESVILLE, PENNA.

1 cup sugar
2 eggs, separated
1 teaspoon vanilla extract
1½ cups sifted flour
¼ cup boiling water
1½ teaspoons baking powder
½ teaspoon salt

Beat sugar and egg yolks together until creamy. Add vanilla and 2 tablespoons of the flour, stirring in well. Add boiling water. Sift remaining flour, baking powder and salt together. Stir into sugar mixture. Beat egg whites until stiff but not dry. Fold into batter. Pour into a greased 11 × 7-inch cake pan which is waxed-paper lined, and then the paper well greased and dusted with flour. Bake at 325°F. for about 25 minutes. Watch it now, and don't get it too brown, for the cake must be soft. Place clean dish towel over cake rack, turn out cake and cool while making the filling. Remove waxed paper.

FILLING:

4 squares unsweetened
    chocolate
1½ cups confectioners' sugar
¼ cup boiling water
4 eggs, separated

Melt chocolate in top of double boiler over hot water. Beat in ¾ cup of the sugar. Add water. Beat egg yolks until smoth with remaining sugar. Add chocolate mixture, stirring well. Beat egg whites until stiff but not quite dry and fold into chocolate mixture. Cool.

Take cake, cut into thirds, then each piece into 3 layers, making 9 layers in all. Line 2 pans 8½ × 4½ × 2¾-inches, with heavy waxed paper. Lay in a layer of cake, a layer of chocolate filling and keep repeating with layers until filled. There should be 4 layers at least, and be sure to end with chocolate. Place in refrigerator for 8 hours or longer. The finished cake will keep for 2 weeks. Serve sliced with whipped cream or ice cream. If it's ice cream, you may top with butterscotch sauce.

Yield: 12 to 16 portions.

SHERRY ICEBOX CAKE · MRS. RICHARD S. WRIGHT, PIEDMONT, CALIF.

12 to 14 ladyfingers
3 egg yolks, well beaten
½ cup sugar
1 cup heavy cream
3 egg whites
1 tablespoon unflavored
    gelatin
¼ cup cold water
¼ cup hot water
1 teaspoon vanilla extract or
4 tablespoons sherry or rum
    or 2 tablespoons lemon
    juice and grated rind, or
Maple flavor to taste, or 2
    squares unsweetened
    chocolate, melted

Line a medium-sized spring-form pan with lady finger halves. Combine egg yolks and sugar. Beat cream until stiff. Beat egg whites until stiff but not dry. Soak gelatin in cold water, dissolve in hot water; combine with egg-yolk mixture. Fold in whipped cream and beaten egg whites. Add the flavoring of choice. Pour into finger-lined pan. Chill until firm.

Yield: 6 portions.

BAKED ALASKA À L'ORANGE · CALIFORNIA

8 navel oranges
¼ cup grenadine syrup
3 egg whites
½ cup sugar
1 pint very firm ice cream

Slice off tops of oranges. Cut out fruit and cut into bite-size pieces, removing membranes. Pour syrup over fruit. Chill. Refill orange "cups" with mixture. Beat egg whites until foamy. Gradually beat in sugar until mixture holds in peaks. Top oranges with ice cream. Immediately cover with meringue to edge of shell; completely seal the cream. Place filled cups on a small breadboard or a shallow pan lined with several thicknesses of aluminum foil. Bake at 400°F. for 3 to 5 minutes. Serve immediately.

Yield: 8 portions.

CRANBERRY FRAPPÉ · MRS. EDWARD L. BARTHOLOMEW, WAREHAM, MASS.

4 cups fresh cranberries
2 cups sugar
1¾ cups water
Juice of 1 lemon
Juice of 1 orange
1 egg white, stiffly beaten

Cook cranberries, sugar and water together for 5 minutes, or until cranberry skins pop open. Put through fine sieve. Add fruit juices. Cool. Pour in refrigerator freezing tray and freeze until mushy. Turn into a chilled bowl. Fold in stiffly beaten egg white, then beat for 2 to 3 minutes. Return to freezer tray and freeze until firm.   Yield: 6 to 8 portions.

LEMON ICE CREAM · MRS. THOMAS E. DEWEY, PAWLING, N.Y.

3 tablespoons lemon juice
2 teaspoons grated lemon
    rind
1 cup sugar
1 pint light cream
2 drops yellow vegetable
    coloring

Add lemon juice and rind to sugar, blending well. Slowly stir in cream and add vegetable coloring, mixing thoroughly. Place in ice-cube tray of refrigerator and set to fast freezing for 3 hours. Do not stir and it freezes smooth. Yield: 6 portions.

LEMON ICE CREAM · MRS. THOMAS E. DEWEY, PAWLING, N.Y.

4 cups light cream
Rind of 2 lemons, finely
    grated
Juice of 1 lemon
¾ cup sugar
Few grains salt

Heat 1 cup of the cream. Add grated lemon rind, lemon juice, remainder of cream, sugar and salt. Pour into freezer and freeze, using 8 parts ice to 1 part salt. When firm remove dasher, pack freezer in 3 parts ice to 1 part salt. Let ripen 2 hours. Yield: 1 quart ice cream.

PEACH ICE CREAM · MRS. DAVID HUGHES, SOUTH CAROLINA

1 quart crushed fresh
    peaches
1½ cups sugar
½ pint light cream
½ pint heavy cream
1 quart milk
1 tablespoon vanilla extract
1 tablespoon almond extract

Combine peaches and sugar, mixing well; let stand for 10 minutes. Add light and heavy cream, milk and flavorings. Pour into freezer can of electric freezer or hand-crank type to about ⅔ full. Assemble parts in usual way and lock. Turn freezer shaft with fingers to be certain gears will mesh. Pack freezer with 1 cup rock salt to each 6 cups crushed ice in alternate layers. Place container under spout to catch salt water during freezing. Turn speed control gradually to 4 and freeze 10 to 15 minutes in electric freezer or until it is very difficult to turn the crank freezer. Remove freezer whip from can, pack down cream, cover and close opening. Repack with ice and salt to keep and to "ripen."

Yield: 1 gallon ice cream.

MILDORA'S PEACH ICE CREAM · TAYLOR FAMILY, BROWNSVILLE, TENN.

18 medium, very ripe
   peaches
4 cups sugar
½ cup water
2 egg whites
3½ cups milk (about)
1 pint heavy cream

Wash peaches and place in strainer; dip into boiling water and then into cold; peel and remove pits. Mash peaches or put through a food mill. Blend with 2 cups of the sugar and chill thoroughly. Combine remaining sugar and water, and boil until syrup spins a thread (230 to 234°F.) when dropped from a spoon. Meanwhile, beat egg whites until very stiff, but not dry. Add hot syrup slowly, in a long stream, beating constantly until mixture is stiff. Blend in ½ cup milk; chill. Add egg-white mixture with heavy cream to peaches, blending well. Pour mixture into chilled gallon freezer container; add enough milk to fill container to within 2 inches from top, about 3 cups.

Cover and adjust dasher so handle turns smoothly. Have ready 8 parts finely cracked ice to 1 part rock salt (crush ice in canvas bag, or grind in machine). Fill tub with 2-inch layer of cracked ice; add a layer of salt and continue with alternate layers of each until ice comes three-fourths of the way up the sides of the container. Turn handle slowly and steadily until resistance is felt, then turn rapidly until mixture is as thick as corn-meal mush, about 15 minutes. Follow directions of manufacturers for electric ice cream freezers. Drain off excess brine. Wipe off and remove cover, take out dasher, scrape cream from sides of can and pack with spoon. Replace cover and close lid opening with cork. Using 3 or 4 parts crushed ice to 1 part rock salt, repack cream in ice and salt, covering container completely. Cover freezer with heavy canvas, carpet or newspaper and ripen 3½ to 4 hours.

Yield: 1 gallon.

GREENGAGE PLUM ICE CREAM · WILLIAMSBURG, VA.

2½ cups stewed or canned
    greengage plums
2 cups sugar
⅓ cup lemon juice
1 quart heavy cream
1½ quarts milk

Peel plums, remove pits and put through fine sieve. Add remaining ingredients; mix until sugar is dissolved. For best results use a churn freezer, though the cream may be frozen in the freezing compartment of refrigerator, if stirred once or twice during freezing period, 2 to 4 hours.

Yield: 3 to 3½ quarts.

STRAWBERRY ICE CREAM · KANSAS

3 cups crushed strawberries
4 cups sugar
3 quarts light cream
12 eggs
Dash of salt
3 tablespoons vanilla extract

Mix berries with ⅓ of the sugar and let stand in a warm place 1 to 2 hours or until juices are drawn out. Or, if fruit is firm, heat gently until the juices run freely. Then chill. Scald cream. Beat eggs thoroughly; add salt and remaining sugar. Add cream slowly, mixing well. Cook over simmering water 10 minutes or until mixture coats a spoon. Cool and then chill. Strain. Add juice drained from berries. Turn into freezer and freeze in a mixture of 1 part salt to 8 parts ice. When partially frozen, add fruit and continue to freeze until firm. Yield: 1 gallon ice cream.

Some like their strawberry ice cream unadorned. Others want more crushed berries ladled over all, to run like rivulets to the saucer to form a crimson lake. For this, slightly crush the fruit as for shortcake, adding as much sugar as the palate dictates, then set to ripen in a warmish place.

IOWA ICE CREAM · MRS. JOHN MC DERMOTT, OTTUMWA, IOWA

1¼ cups sugar
1 pint heavy cream
6 eggs, separated
2 quarts milk
1½ tablespoons vanilla extract
⅛ teaspoon salt
Milk

Mix sugar with cream, stirring to dissolve thoroughly and turn into 1-gallon can of freezer. Beat egg yolks until thick and mix with milk; add vanilla and salt. Combine the two mixtures. Whip egg whites until stiff but not dry. Blend into mixture, then add enough milk to fill within 1 inch of the top. Freeze, using 8 parts ice to 1 part salt. Yield: 1 gallon.

PHILADELPHIA ICE CREAM · BASSETT'S, PHILADELPHIA, PENNA.

1 quart light cream
¾ cup sugar
⅛ teaspoon salt
1 vanilla bean or
2 teaspoons vanilla extract

Combine one pint of the cream, sugar and salt, and split vanilla bean in top of double boiler over boiling water. Stir constantly for 10 minutes until cream is scalded. Remove from heat, scrape seed and pulpy part from vanilla bean, discarding pod. Mix seed with cream and cool. (If extract is used, add after cream is removed from the heat.) Add remaining cream and chill. Turn into freezer can and freeze, using a mixture of 3 parts ice to 1 part salt. Yield: 6 portions.

With strawberries: add to chilled mixture 2 cups mashed strawberries which have been mixed with ¾ cup sugar and allowed to stand 2 hours. Freeze as above.

CRÈME BRÛLÉE · MRS. ORREN SAFFORD, MINNEAPOLIS, MINN.

1 quart light cream
8 egg yolks
5 tablespoons granulated
    sugar
2 teaspoons vanilla extract
2 tablespoons brown sugar

Scald cream. Beat egg yolks and sugar together. Pour cream very slowly into egg mixture, stirring constantly. Add vanilla. Pour mixture in baking dish and place in pan of hot water. Bake at 350°F. about 1 hour or until silver knife inserted in center comes out clean. When done sprinkle with brown sugar. Place under broiler until sugar melts and forms a glaze. Serve cool as an ice cube.

Yield: 8 portions.

SPANISH CUSTARD · COLUMBIA RESTAURANT, YBOR CITY, FLA.

3 cups sugar
½ cup boiling water
6 eggs
1 tablespoon anisette
1 teaspoon vanilla extract
Dash of nutmeg
Dash of salt
2 cups boiled milk

Melt 1 cup of the sugar over low heat, stirring constantly. When light brown, remove from heat and add boiling water slowly. Heat and stir until caramel is dissolved. Pour into custard cups. Beat eggs until frothy. Add remaining sugar, anisette, vanilla, nutmeg and salt; beat well. Add milk gradually. Pour mixture into caramel cups. Place cups in a pan of hot water. Bake at 350°F. for 30 to 40 minutes or until custard is set. Cool, then chill in refrigerator. When ready to serve, loosen edges of custard with a spatula and turn mold upside down. The caramel tops the custard.

Yield: 8 portions.

SWEDISH RICE PORRIDGE · MRS. WESLEY C. HEISE, PORTLAND, ORE.

*1½ cups long-grained rice,
    washed*
1¼ cups boiling water
1 teaspoon salt
5 cups milk
½ cup sugar
1 teaspoon cinnamon
1 almond

Place rice in top of double boiler. Add boiling salted water. Cook over boiling water, adding milk as the rice absorbs the moisture. After an hour's slow cooking, stir in sugar and cinnamon. Cook, covered, 2 hours. Serve not warm, not cold. The consistency should be about that of blanc mange. Nan serves the pudding in wooden bowls, adding a spoonful of lingonberries, or again plain, a jug of thick cream for the sauce. Don't forget the almond—it's good luck.
Yield: 6 servings.

SWISS FASTNACHT KUECHEN · MRS. ELSIE GERBER, MONROE, WIS.

1 egg
3 tablespoons heavy cream
½ teaspoon salt
¾ cup sifted flour (about)
Sugar
Fat for frying

Beat egg slightly with fork; beat in cream and salt. Add just enough flour to make a dough that can be rolled out, not stiff, yet not too sticky. Divide into 4 portions. Roll on lightly floured surface into circles, about 8 inches in diameter and gossamer-thin. (If making more, cover 4 pieces with a towel, then add a second layer over this.) Lift pieces, one at a time, with 2 spoons or spatulas and drop into hot fat (350 to 370°F.); give each a twiddle-twirl with spoons so the pieces curl. When golden brown, in about 2 minutes, remove from fat and place on absorbent paper to drain. Sprinkle with sugar while warm. Serve as a dessert with whipped cream or plain with wine, coffee or tea. Yield: 4 portions.

FRENCH PANCAKES À LA GELÉE · ANTOINE'S, NEW ORLEANS, LA.

½ cup sifted flour
1 egg
1 egg yolk
⅛ teaspoon salt
5 tablespoons milk (about)
*3 tablespoons currant or red
    raspberry jelly*
Confectioners' sugar

Combine flour, egg, egg yolk, salt and milk. Beat with rotary beater until smooth. If necessary, add more milk to make batter the consistency of light cream. Cover, chill ½ hour in refrigerator. Heat heavy iron skillet; wipe out with waxed paper which has been dipped in butter. Pour in enough batter barely to cover bottom of skillet, tipping while adding batter. Brown pancakes on both sides. Remove from skillet;

spread with jelly. Roll up jelly-roll fashion. Sprinkle with a little sugar. Place under broiler to glaze. Serve immediately. Yield: 12 to 15 5-inch pancakes.

CRÊPES CITRON · LOUISE SAVIN, CALIFORNIA

12 crêpes (very thin French
  pancakes)
⅛ pound sweet butter
½ cup sugar
1½ tablespoons lemon juice

Spread pancakes with butter; sprinkle with sugar. (You may use recipe above or your own favorite.) Moisten each with lemon juice and roll like little flat cigarettes. Sprinkle with sugar and put into a hot oven (400°F.) until thoroughly heated.
  Yield: 6 portions.

PURPLE-PLUM SOUFFLÉ · MRS. S. ELTON LASSELLE, TIGARD, ORE.

1 can (1 pound, 13 ounces)
  purple plums
¼ cup cold water
1 envelope unflavored gelatin
¾ cup plum juice
2 tablespoons lemon juice
Grated rind of 1 lemon
½ cup sugar
¼ teaspoon salt
¼ teaspoon cinnamon
½ cup heavy cream, whipped
1 egg white, stiffly beaten
½ cup chopped nuts

Drain plums, reserving juice. Pit plums; mash to a pulp. Pour cold water into bowl and sprinkle gelatin on top; stir to soften. Heat plum pulp with the plum juice, lemon juice and rind, sugar, salt and cinnamon. Add to gelatin mixture. Chill. Fold in cream, egg white and nuts. Chill in sherbet glasses. Top with whipped cream if desired. Yield: 6 portions.

WALNUT SOUFFLÉ · MRS. J. KELL BRANDON, SIMSBURY, CONN.

4 eggs, separated
10 tablespoons confectioners'
  sugar
½ teaspoon vanilla
¾ cup ground walnuts
⅛ teaspoon salt
Brandy sauce

Beat egg yolks until light; gradually add sugar and beat until creamy. Mix in vanilla and walnuts. Beat egg whites and salt together until stiff. Fold into yolk mixture. Pour into a greased 2-quart baking dish. Place in pan of hot water. Bake at 325°F. for 45 to 55 minutes or until firm. Serve hot with brandy sauce.
  Yield: 6 portions.

DEVONSHIRE CREAM · MINERAL POINT, WIS.

Combine 2 quarts milk and 1 quart cream and refrigerate overnight. The following day place over the lowest heat possible. If heat cannot be reduced sufficiently, immerse mixture in a pan of hot water, and let stand 3 to 5 hours, or until a wrinkled, leathery look appears on the surface, this containing little pockets filled with a liquid resembling melted butter. The mixture should be in a room where there are no strong scents such as onion, fish or any food from which it may absorb an off flavor. Do not disturb the cream on the surface by stirring or shaking. Don't let the mixture boil. When it becomes very wrinkled and drawn-looking, cool and again refrigerate overnight. The following day skim off the thick top cream. Serve with preserved fruit or fresh strawberries. Yield: about 1 pint.

Dessert Sauces

BUTTERSCOTCH SAUCE · DARTMOUTH COLLEGE, HANOVER, N.H.

2 cups white sugar
2 cups brown sugar
2 cups light corn syrup
2 cups water
⅔ cup sweetened condensed
    milk
¼ cup butter or margarine
1 14½-ounce can evaporated
    milk
1 teaspoon vanilla extract

Combine sugars, syrup and water in saucepan and place over low heat. Bring to a rolling boil and boil 10 minutes. Add sweetened condensed milk. Add butter if sauce is to be used immediately. (If being stored for now-and-then use, omit butter or the mixture will become granular.) Cool. Add evaporated milk and vanilla. Yield: about 2 quarts.

CHOCOLATE SAUCE · DARTMOUTH COLLEGE, HANOVER, N.H.

¾ pound unsweetened
    chocolate
4 cups sugar
1 cup cocoa
2 cups hot water
2 cups light corn syrup
⅔ cup sweetened condensed
    milk
¼ cup butter
1 14½-ounce can evaporated
    milk
1 teaspoon vanilla extract

Melt chocolate over hot water. Mix sugar and cocoa and add to chocolate. Add hot water and corn syrup. Stir until dissolved. Bring to a rolling boil and boil 10 minutes. Add sweetened condensed milk. Add butter if sauce is to be used immediately. (If being stored for now-and-then use, omit butter or the mixture will become granular.) Cool. Add evaporated milk and stir in well. Add vanilla. Yield: about 2 quarts. Serve it on ice cream, pudding or cake.

CHOCOLATE FUDGE SAUCE · CAMELBACK INN, PHOENIX, ARIZ.

1½ squares unsweetened
   chocolate
½ cup boiling water
1 tablespoon butter or
   margarine
2 tablespoons corn syrup
1 tablespoon marshmallow
   sauce
1 cup sugar
⅛ teaspoon salt
½ teaspoon vanilla extract

Melt chocolate in top of double boiler over hot water. Add water, butter, corn syrup, marshmallow sauce, sugar and salt, stirring constantly until ingredients are dissolved. Place saucepan over direct heat and boil for 3 minutes. Stir in vanilla. Serve hot or cold.

Yield: 1½ cups sauce.

RASPBERRY SAUCE · MRS. J. KELL BRANDON, SIMSBURY, CONN.

Defrost package frozen raspberries, then heat. Press through sieve to remove seeds; add 1 teaspoon unflavored gelatin, 2 tablespoons sugar, 2 tablespoons port wine and chill in the refrigerator until serving time. Serve over a ball of ice cream with a brandied peach.

RUM SAUCE · MISS SUE TOKES, WINCHESTER, VA.

1 cup brown sugar
½ cup butter or margarine
2 egg yolks, beaten
½ cup dark rum

Combine sugar, butter and egg yolks and simmer until blended, stirring constantly. Add rum and continue cooking about 2 minutes, stirring well. Serve hot with apple dumplings. Yield: 2 cups sauce.

Pies

SCHNITZ DRIED-APPLE PIE · MRS. WILLIAM FREE, HUNGERFORD, PENNA.

1 pound dried, sour schnitz
1 quart cold water
1 tablespoon cinnamon
1 to 1½ cups sugar
4 teaspoons grated orange
  rind
½ cup orange juice
Pastry for 9-inch double-
  crust pie

Put the schnitz and water into a covered saucepan and gently cook to a soft pulp, about 30 to 45 minutes. Add cinnamon, sugar, grated orange rind and orange juice, and mix well together. Line a pie pan with pastry, fill with the schnitz makings and cover top with pastry; make slits in top crust. Bake in a 450°F. over for 10 minutes. Reduce the heat to 350°F. and continue baking 30 minutes.

A schnitz pie filling is packed commercially by a Pennsylvania firm, in jars of one pound, one ounce net content, one jar holding the exact amount for an eight-inch pie. Write to the Hungerford Packing Co., Inc., Hungerford, York County, Pennsylvania.

VIRGINIA APPLE PIE · MISS SUE TOKES, WINCHESTER, VA.

6 medium cooking apples
Pastry for 2-crust 9-inch pie
⅓ cup white sugar
⅓ cup brown sugar
3 tablespoons butter or
    margarine

Pare apples. Core and cut in eighths. Cook for about 5 minutes in a small amount of water. Put wedges close together in chilled unbaked 9-inch pie shell. Sprinkle with mixture of sugars. Dot with butter. Cover with top crust. Bake at 450°F. for 30 to 35 minutes.

FRIED APPLE PIES · MOUNTAIN BROOK CLUB, BIRMINGHAM, ALA.

2 cups sifted flour
3 teaspoons baking powder
1 teaspoon salt
¼ cup shortening
⅔ cup milk (approximately)
1½ cups thick, sieved
    applesauce
1 cup sugar
3 teaspoons cinnamon

Mix and sift flour, baking powder and salt. Then cut in shortening until well blended. Add milk gradually to make a soft dough. Turn out on lightly floured surface and knead with a light touch. Roll out dough very thin. Lay on saucer and cut around edge with sharp-pointed knife; make 8 to 10 circles. Place on one side of each circle 3 tablespoons applesauce; fold in half, moisten and seal edges with fork. Fry in 1½ inches hot fat (350°F.) in heavy-bottomed frying pan. When brown on one side, turn and brown the other. Have ready a flat pan, the bottom covered with mixture of sugar and cinnamon. Lift pie from fat, drain, then into the sugar, turn, giving both sides a good sugar coating. Quickly serve while hot with plain cream or vanilla ice cream.

Yield: 8 to 10 pies.

COTTAGE CHEESE APPLE PIE · MRS. FRANK SCHIESSER, NEW CLARUS, WIS.

1 9-inch unbaked pie shell
2 eggs
½ cup cottage cheese
¾ cup sugar
½ cup heavy cream
⅛ teaspoon salt
1 teaspoon grated lemon rind
1½ cups finely chopped
    apples
½ teaspoon cinnamon
½ teaspoon nutmeg

Prepare pie shell and set aside. Beat eggs slightly, add cheese, ½ cup of the sugar, cream, salt, and lemon rind; mix well. Cover bottom of pie shell with chopped apples. Blend remaining ¼ cup sugar with cinnamon and nutmeg and sprinkle over apples. Pour cheese mixture on top. Bake at 425°F. for 10 minutes; reduce heat to 350°F. and bake 30 minutes longer.

Yield: 1 9-inch pie.

CONGRESSIONAL APPLE PIE · WASHINGTON, D.C.

Pastry for 2-crust 9-inch pie
8 large tart apples
½ cup sugar
¼ cup brown sugar or honey
½ teaspoon cinnamon
¼ teaspoon salt
1 tablespoon lemon juice
1 tablespoon butter or
    margarine

Line a 9-inch pie pan with pastry. Combine sugars, cinnamon, salt and lemon juice. Add to apples and toss lightly to mix. Arrange in pastry-lined pie pan. Dot with butter. Moisten edges of under crust and cover with top crust which has been gashed to allow escape of steam. Fold upper crust under lower crust and seal edges with fork. Bake at 450°F. for 10 minutes; reduce heat to 350°F. and bake 40 to 50 minutes longer, or until apples are tender. Yield: 1 9-inch pie.

LOTWARRICK MERINGUE BOI (APPLE BUTTER MERINGUE PIE)
LANCASTER COUNTY, PENNA.

Pastry for 2-crust 9-inch pie
2 cups thick applesauce
½ teaspoon grated lemon rind
½ teaspoon cinnamon
½ teaspoon cloves
¼ teaspoon allspice
½ teaspoon ginger
¼ teaspoon mace
1 cup sugar
½ cup butter, melted
3 egg yolks, well beaten
3 egg whites*
¼ teaspoon cream of tartar
6 tablespoons sugar
¼ teaspoon ginger

Line 9-inch pie pan with half the pastry. Combine apple sauce, grated lemon rind, and first 5 spices. Mix the 1 cup sugar, butter and egg yolks; add to applesauce mixture; pour mixture into pastry-lined pie pan. Cover with remaining pastry. Trim, turn under, and flute edge. Bake at 350°F. for 1 hour. Let stand until cold. Beat egg whites until foamy; add cream of tartar and beat until whites stand in soft peaks. Beat in remaining sugar, 1 tablespoon at a time; continue beating until meringue is stiff and glossy. Spread meringue over top crust of pie. Bake at 300°F. for 15 to 20 minutes, or until lightly browned. Sprinkle with ¼ teaspoon ginger. Cool away from draft. Yield: 1 9-inch pie.

*Meringue may be omitted and pie topped with whipped cream that has been sweetened with ½ teaspoon cinnamon or ginger.

APPLESAUCE CUSTARD PIE · NORTHERN NEW ENGLAND

1½ cups applesauce
½ cup sugar
1 teaspoon cinnamon
3 eggs beaten
¼ teaspoon salt
½ cup milk
1 unbaked 9-inch pie shell

Mix ingredients in order as given. Pour custard mix into unbaked pie shell. Bake at 450°F. for 10 minutes. Then reduce heat to 350°F. and bake for 35 minutes or until a silver knife comes out clean.

Yield: one 9-inch pie.

SARAH WHEELER'S BUTTERSCOTCH PIE · CONNERSVILLE, IND.

2½ cups milk
2 eggs, separated
¼ cup flour
1 cup dark brown sugar,
    firmly packed
½ cup water
⅛ teaspoon salt
1½ tablespoons butter or
    margarine
1 teaspoon vanilla extract
1 8-inch baked pastry shell
¼ teaspoon cream of tartar
¼ cup sugar

Thoroughly combine ½ cup of the milk, egg yolks, and flour. Set aside. Scald remaining 2 cups of milk over hot water. Combine brown sugar, water, and salt in skillet. Place over low heat and bring to a gentle boil. Cook until mixture thickens and a few bubbles break sending up not whiffs, but puffs, of smoke. Add caramelized sugar very slowly, stirring constantly, to scalded milk. When smooth, gradually stir in egg-yolk mixture and cook, stirring constantly, over hot water until thick. Remove and add butter and vanilla; stir well. Cool. Pour filling into cooled pie shell. Make a meringue using egg whites, cream of tartar and sugar. Spread over pie. Bake at 400°F. for 8 to 10 minutes or until delicately browned. Yield: 1 8-inch pie.

BUTTERSCOTCH PIE · TAYLOR FAMILY, BROWNSVILLE, TENN.

4 tablespoons cornstarch
2 cups brown sugar
5 eggs, separated
2 cups milk
3 tablespoons butter or
    margarine
1 8-inch baked pastry shell
1 teaspoon baking powder

Mix cornstarch with brown sugar. Beat the egg yolks until thick and lemon-colored; add the brown sugar mixture. Add milk and beat well. Place butter in frying pan and brown lightly. Pour the custard into the pan with the butter and stir until thick; start over slow heat and gradually increase to moderately hot. This will take about 20 minutes. Cool mixture and pour into baked pastry shell. Beat egg whites until frothy; gradually add the baking powder. Continue beating until whites are stiff and stand in peaks. Top custard with meringue, spreading to edges of pie. Bake at 350°F. until lightly browned. Yield: 1 8-inch pie.

CHESS PIE · THE NUT TREE, VACAVILLE, CALIF.

1 cup sugar
⅓ cup brown sugar
2 tablespoons flour
1 cup chopped walnuts
⅔ cup seedless raisins
3 eggs
⅔ cup milk

2 tablespoons butter or margarine
Unbaked 9-inch pastry shell

Combine dry ingredients, nuts and raisins. Combine eggs, milk, and butter. Blend with nut mixture. Pour into pastry-lined pan. Bake at 275°F. for about 1 hour and 45 minutes, or until firm. Yield: 1 9-inch chess pie.

CHESS PIE · TAYLOR FAMILY, BROWNSVILLE, TENN.

1 8-inch unbaked pie shell or
    6 to 8 tart shells
½ cup butter or margarine
1 cup sugar
3 eggs
1 teaspoon vanilla extract

Make pie or tart shells and chill 30 minutes. Cream butter and sugar thoroughly. Add unbeaten eggs, 1 at a time, and stir well. Add vanilla. Pour into chilled pie shell or individual tarts. Bake at 450°F. 10 minutes for pie and 5 minutes for tarts. Reduce heat to 300°F. and bake 20 to 25 minutes longer for pie and 10 to 15 minutes longer for tarts.

Yield: 6 to 8 portions (1 8-inch pie shell or 6 to 8 tarts).

CHERRY PIE · LUCY CORBETT, GROSSE ILE, MICH.

1 quart fresh or quick-frozen
    sour cherries
2 tablespoons quick-cooking
    tapioca
1½ cups sugar
⅛ teaspoon salt
2 drops almond extract

Remove pits from cherries. Combine cherries, tapioca, sugar, salt and extract. Turn into pie shell. Cover with twisted pastry strips to make lattice design. Bake at 450°F. for 10 minutes. Reduce heat to 350°F. and bake 20 to 30 minutes or until the pie is golden brown.

Yield: 6 portions.

MARRINER PIE CRUST:

1 cup sifted flour
¼ pound cream cheese
¼ pound butter or
    margarine

Place ingredients in bowl. Work together with fingers until it's a putty-like mass. Pat mass into ball. Wrap in waxed paper and place in refrigerator to chill and blend overnight. Remove and let stand at room temperature for at least 2 hours. Otherwise, Lucy says, you must roll it with a sledge hammer. That pastry is solid until baked, then a tender, flaky delight. Roll on floured surface to ⅛-inch thickness. Line a lightly greased 8-inch pie pan. Re-roll remaining pastry and cut into 8 strips 1 inch wide; twist strips and lay across filled pie shell.

CITRUS CHIFFON PIE · MRS. JOHN POWELL, CALIFORNIA

1 envelope unflavored gelatin
⅓ cup orange juice
4 eggs, separated
½ cup sugar
½ cup lemon juice

⅛ teaspoon salt
¼ teaspoon cinnamon
¼ teaspoon cloves
1 9-inch baked pastry shell
1 cup cranberry sauce, chilled

Soften gelatin in orange juice. Beat egg yolks and sugar until well blended. Add lemon juice, salt, and spices. Cook in top of double boiler over hot water until mixture thickens and coats a metal spoon. Add softened gelatin and stir until dissolved. Remove from heat. Chill until almost set. Beat egg whites until soft peaks form. Fold white into the chilled mixture. Spread the bottom and sides of the pastry shell with chilled cranberry sauce. Turn the filling into shell. Chill in refrigerator 1 hour. Cut pie into small wedges and garnish each with a teaspoon of cranberry sauce and an orange section. Pie may also be topped with whipped cream. Yield: 1 9-inch pie.

COCONUT MERINGUE PIE · MRS. MARIO MARTINEZ, HIALEAH, FLA.

1 cup fresh grated coconut
2 cups milk
1 cup plus 2 tablespoons
    sugar
1 tablespoon butter or
    margarine
3 tablespoons cornstarch
3 tablespoons cold water
3 eggs, separated
⅛ teaspoon salt
1 teaspoon vanilla extract
1 baked 9-inch pie shell

Heat coconut and milk in top of double boiler. Add ¾ cup sugar and butter. Dissolve cornstarch in cold water; stir into coconut mixture. Cook over boiling water, stirring constantly, until mixture thickens. Add well-beaten egg yolks, salt, vanilla. Cook 1 minute longer, stirring constantly. Pour into baked pie shell; cool 5 minutes. Beat egg whites until foamy; gradually add 6 tablespoons sugar, beating until whites are stiff but not dry. Bake at 425°F. until meringue is golden brown.
    Yield: 1 9-inch pie.

CRACKER PIE · MRS. GORDON S. CLINTON, SEATTLE, WASH.

3 eggs whites
1 cup sugar
14 soda crackers, coarsely
    crumbled
¾ cup slivered walnuts
1 teaspoon baking powder
1 teaspoon vanilla extract
1 cup heavy cream, whipped

Beat egg whites until foamy. Gradually add sugar, beating until stiff. Combine crackers, walnuts and baking powder. Fold into egg mixture along with vanilla. Spread in a buttered 9-inch pie pan. Bake at 350°F. for about 45 minutes, or until dry. Cool and spread with sweetened whipped cream. Refrigerate at least 2 hours. Yield: 6 to 8 portions.

MOTHER BOWLES' CUSTARD PIE · ELLA BOWLES, DURHAM, N.H.

½ recipe plain pastry
3 cups milk, scalded
3 eggs, beaten
5 tablespoons sugar
¼ teaspoon salt
1 teaspoon vanilla extract
Grated nutmeg

Line a 9-inch pie pan with pastry and make a fluted, standing rim. Stir scalded milk into beaten eggs. (The eggs should not be foamy.) Add sugar, salt and vanilla. Cool slightly. Pour into the unbaked pie shell; sprinkle with nutmeg. Bake at 325°F. about 1 hour, or until custard is set and crust is brown. Yield: one 9-inch pie. Note: To make Raspberry Custard Pie, add 1 cup raspberries to the Custard Pie recipe and increase sugar to ½ cup.

EGGNOG PIE · MRS. LAWRENCE ADAMS, JACKSONVILLE, FLA.

1 envelope unflavored gelatin
¼ cup cold water
4 eggs, separated
1 cup sugar
½ teaspoon salt
½ cup hot water
¼ cup rum
1 teaspoon grated nutmeg
1 8-inch baked pie shell
Whipped cream for garnish

Soften gelatin in ¼ cup cold water and let stand for 5 minutes. Meanwhile beat egg yolks with ½ cup of the sugar and salt. Gradually stir in hot water. Cook in double boiler over rapidly boiling water until of custard consistency; stir constantly. Add softened gelatin and stir until thoroughly dissolved. Cool. Add rum and ½ teaspoon nutmeg. Beat egg whites until foamy; gradually add remaining ½ cup sugar and beat until stiff but not dry. Fold into custard when it begins to thicken. Turn into baked pie shell. Chill. Garnish with whipped cream and sprinkle with remaining ½ teaspoon nutmeg. Yield: 1 8-inch pie.

HOLIDAY EGGNOG PIE · CAMELBACK INN, PHOENIX, ARIZ.

1 envelope unflavored gelatin
¼ cup cold water
½ cup sugar
½ teaspoon salt
¾ cup milk
½ cup light cream
3 eggs, separated
1 teaspoon vanilla extract
⅛ teaspoon nutmeg
¼ teaspoon cream of tartar
½ cup sugar
Rum flavoring
1 9-inch baked pie shell
Whipped cream

Soften gelatin in cold water. Combine ½ cup sugar, salt, milk, cream and beaten egg yolks in a double boiler. Cook over hot water until mixture thickens. Add gelatin and stir until dissolved. Add vanilla and nutmeg. Pour into a bowl and place in a pan of ice cubes. Beat egg whites and cream of tartar until foamy; gradually beat in ½ cup sugar until stiff. Fold into cooled mixture. Add rum flavoring to taste. Pour into cooled pie shell. Chill and top with whipped cream. Sprinkle with more nutmeg if desired.

Yield: 1 9-inch pie.

FUDGE PIE · MARY CALL COLLINS, TALLAHASSEE, FLA.

¼ pound butter or margarine
1 cup sugar
2 eggs
2 squares unsweetened
    chocolate, melted
¼ cup flour
¼ teaspoon salt
1 teaspoon vanilla extract
½ cup chopped pecans
1 pint ice cream

Cream butter and sugar. Add eggs, singly, beating thoroughly after each addition. Blend in melted chocolate. Add flour, salt and vanilla and beat slightly. Stir in pecans. Spread in a hot greased 8-inch pie pan. Bake at 350°F. for 20 to 25 minutes, or until edge is dry. Let cool in pan. Serve warm topped with ice cream. Yield: 6 portions.

GUAVA TARTS · MRS. ROBERT EUGENE OTTO, KEY WEST, FLA.

1 pastry for 2-crust pie
1 15-ounce bar prepared
    guava paste
2 teaspoons cinnamon
2 teaspoons nutmeg
8 teaspoons butter or
    margarine

Roll pastry ⅛ inch thick on a lightly floured surface. Cut into circles, 5½ to 6 inches in diameter. Butter 8 muffin cups and fit the pastry into cups. Fill with pieces of guava paste (cut 15-ounce bar into eighths), sprinkle each tart with ¼ teaspoon cinnamon, ¼ teaspoon nutmeg and place 1 teaspoon butter on top. Lightly moisten edges of pastry and seal tightly by pinching moistened edges together. Be sure there are no open seams or guava paste will leak out. Bake at 400°F. about 30 minutes.
    Yield: 8 tarts.

JEFF DAVIS PIE · MRS. ROY ANTHONY, FULTON, MO.

4 eggs, separated
1 cup light cream
2 cups brown sugar (1 cup
    firmly packed)
2 tablespoons flour
½ cup melted butter or
    margarine
1 baked 9-inch pastry shell
⅓ cup sugar

Beat egg yolks and blend in cream. Combine brown sugar with flour and add to egg mixture, creaming well. Gradually stir in butter. Turn into pastry shell. Bake at 250°F. for 20 minutes. Cover with meringue made by gradually beating ⅓ cup sugar into 4 stiffly beaten egg whites. Bake at 350°F. for 15 minutes, or until delicately browned. Yield: 1 9-inch pie.

ZAIDEE'S JELLY PIE · TAYLOR FAMILY, BROWNSVILLE, TENN.

½ cup butter or margarine
1 cup tart jelly (plum or
    currant)
3 eggs, beaten

½ cup sugar
2 tablespoons cracker meal
1 8-inch unbaked pie shell

Cream butter and gradually add jelly, blending well. Beat eggs, sugar and cracker meal thoroughly. Blend with the butter and jelly. Pour mixture into pie shell that has chilled 30 minutes. Bake at 450°F. for 10 minutes. Then reduce heat to 350°F. and bake 25 to 30 minutes longer. Cool. Yield: 6 portions.

LITTLE FELLOW LEMON PIES · ROBIN WOODS, LITTLE ROCK, ARK.

½ cup butter or margarine
2 cups sugar
4 eggs
1 tablespoon flour
⅓ cup lemon juice
Pastry

Cream butter and sugar. Add eggs, singly, beating only until blended after each addition. Add flour; mix well. Stir in lemon juice. Fill pastry-lined muffin pans ⅔ full. Bake at 350°F. for 30 minutes or until golden brown. Yield: 4 dozen small pies.

FROZEN LEMON PIE · MRS. RUTH MOSS CARROLL, FORT SMITH, ARK.

½ cup lemon juice
1 can (14 ounces) sweetened condensed milk
5 egg whites
2 tablespoons sugar
1 tablespoon grated lemon rind
1 9-inch pie shell (graham cracker or baked plain pastry)

Add lemon juice to milk, stirring until a thick, smooth mixture is formed. Beat egg whites until foamy. Add sugar, a tablespoon at a time, and beat until stiff peaks are formed. Fold in lemon-milk mixture. Sprinkle lemon rind on bottom of pie shell. Turn filling into shell. Chill until set.
Yield: 1 9-inch pie.
NOTE: Pie may be frozen.

LEMON MIST PIE · MRS. THOMAS F. KNIGHT, JR., LA CANADA, CALIF.

3 eggs, separated
⅔ cup sugar
¼ teaspoon salt
2¼ teaspoons grated lemon rind
3 tablespoons lemon juice
6 tablespoons boiling water
3 tablespoons lemon-flavored gelatin
¼ teaspoon cream of tartar
8-inch baked pastry shell

Beat egg yolks slightly. Stir in ⅓ cup of the sugar, salt, lemon rind, and juice. Cook over hot water, stirring constantly, until mixture thickens. Stir boiling water into gelatin. Beat in hot custard. Cool until mixture begins to set. Beat slightly and let stand while making meringue. Beat egg whites with cream of tartar until stiff; gradually beat in remaining ⅓ cup sugar. Continue beating until mixture stiffens and is glossy. Carefully fold into the cooled custard. Pile into cool, baked pie shell. Chill.
Yield: 1 8-inch pie.

LIME CHIFFON PIE · MRS. THOMAS SWANN, WINTER HAVEN, FLA.

4 egg yolks
1 can (15 ounces) sweetened
    condensed milk
⅓ cup lime juice
¼ teaspoon salt
6 egg whites
½ cup sugar
1 9-inch baked pastry shell

Beat egg yolks until thick and lemon-colored. Stir in milk, lime juice and salt, blending well. Beat egg whites until foamy; gradually add sugar, continue beating until meringue stands in peaks. Fold ¼ cup of meringue into egg-yolk mixture. Pour into baked pie shell. Cover top with remaining meringue. Bake at 400°F. for 8 to 10 minutes, or until lightly browned. Yield: 6 portions.

MAPLE SYRUP PIE · MRS. JAMES EGERTON, VERMONT

1½ tablespoons butter or
    or margarine
2 tablespoons flour
2 eggs, separated
1 cup maple syrup
½ cup water
½ cup finely chopped walnuts
1 8-inch baked pie shell
¼ cup sugar
¼ teaspoon vanilla extract

Blend butter and flour in top of double boiler. Blend in egg yolks, maple syrup and water. Cook over boiling water, stirring constantly, until thick, about 10 minutes. Mix in nuts. Cool. Pour into cooled pie shell. Beat egg whites until stiff. Add sugar, 1 tablespoon at a time, beating well after each addition. Continue beating until stiff peaks form. Blend in vanilla. Spread meringue over filling. Bake at 325°F. for 25 to 30 minutes or until firm and lightly browned. Yield: one 8-inch pie.

DEERFIELD MARLBOROUGH PIE · MRS. HELEN JUDD, LEXINGTON, MASS.

2 cups tart applesauce, sieved
3 tablespoons butter or
    margarine, melted
1 cup sugar
½ teaspoon salt
3 tablespoons lemon juice
1 teaspoon grated lemon rind
4 eggs, slightly beaten
1 9-inch unbaked pie shell
    (deep)

Combine applesauce, butter, sugar and salt. Add lemon juice and rind to eggs and stir into sauce. Stir until well blended. Pour into pastry shell. Bake at 450°F. for 15 minutes; reduce heat to 275°F. and bake 1 hour or longer. The pie should be a golden brown and cut like a custard pie.

Yield: 1 9-inch pie.

BOSTON MARLBOROUGH PIE · MISS. SUSAN L. BALL, LEXINGTON, MASS.

1 cup tart applesauce, sieved
3 tablespoons lemon juice
1 cup sugar (to taste)
4 eggs, slightly beaten

2 tablespoons butter or margarine, melted
½ teaspoon nutmeg (if desired)
½ teaspoon salt
1 9-inch unbaked pastry shell (deep)

Combine applesauce with lemon juice, sugar, eggs, butter, nutmeg and salt. Blend thoroughly. Pour into pastry shell. Bake at 450°F. for 15 minutes; reduce heat to 275°F. and bake 1 hour or longer. The pie should be a rich yellow and cut like firm jelly. Yield: 1 9-inch pie.

MINCEMEAT · MRS. STUART COULTER, CALIFORNIA

1 pound seeded raisins
1 pound seedless raisins
1 pound currants
½ pound citron, chopped
½ teaspoon salt
1 tablespoon nutmeg
1½ teaspoon cinnamon
1½ teaspoons mace
1 teaspoon cloves
1 pound beef suet, ground twice
¼ pound mixed candied peels
2 pounds apples, chopped

1 pound brown sugar
1 pint sherry wine
1 pint brandy
Juice and rind of 1 lemon
Juice and rind of 1 orange

Mix ingredients well (do *not* cook). Pack into sterilized quart jars; seal well. Store in refrigerator. Should keep perfectly six to eight weeks. Yield: 5 quarts mincemeat.

DEAN'S GUILD MINCEMEAT · SPOKANE, WASH.

4½ pounds lean beef, cooked and ground
6 cups cider
3 cups cider vinegar
11 cups (5½ pounds) sugar
8½ pints chopped tart apples (nicer peeled but not necessary)
2 cups ground suet
4 cups seeded raisins
2 cups seedless raisins
2 cups currants
1 cup finely chopped orange rind
1 cup finely chopped lemon rind

1 cup chopped citron (more is even better)
2 tablespoons cinnamon
1 tablespoon cloves
1 tablespoon nutmeg
1 tablespoon salt
1 tablespoon black pepper

Mix together all ingredients and store in stone crocks. Cover tightly. Dip out as ready to use, or spoon into jars to present as gifts. Stored in a cold place, the mincemeat keeps splendidly for a period of months. This recipe requires no cooking. Yield: 2¼ gallons.

INDIANA MINCEMEAT · MRS. DONALD C. DRAKE, INDIANAPOLIS, IND.

2 pounds suet
4 pounds beef-neck meat
8 pounds apples (Winesap
    preferred)
3 pounds quinces
1 pound citron
1 pound seedless raisins
1 pound currants
2 pounds sugar
1 quart molasses
2 tablespoons salt
4 tablespoons cinnamon
2 tablespoons cloves
2 tablespoons allspice
1 tablespoon nutmeg
1 tablespoon pepper
3 cups boiled cider

Cover suet and meat with cold water and bring to a boil. Reduce heat and let simmer until tender, about 3 hours. Meanwhile prepare fruit. Peel and dice apples and quinces. Dice citron; add other fruits, sugar, molasses, and seasonings. When meat is tender, cool in stock, then grind. Combine meat and fruit. Place in roasting pan; add meat stock and cider. Simmer 1 hour for final blending and the mincemeat is ready to can. Yield: 6 quarts mincemeat.

NOTE: Those who like a "stick" in their Christmas pie, add a cup of brandy.

MOCK CHERRY PIE · MRS. EDWARD L. BARTHOLOMEW, WAREHAM, MASS.

3 cups fresh cranberries
½ cup raisins
1¼ cups sugar
1½ tablespoons flour
½ cup hot water
Grated rind of ¼ lemon
Pastry for two-crust 8-inch pie

Combine cranberries and raisins. Mix sugar and flour, blend with cranberry mixture. Stir in water and lemon rind. Turn into pastry lined 8-inch pie pan. Cover with top crust, seal edges, cut vents, and brush with milk. Bake at 400°F. for about 45 minutes. Yield: one 8-inch pie.

MOLASSES PIE · TAYLOR FAMILY, BROWNSVILLE, TENN.

2 cups molasses
¼ cup lemon juice
2 tablespoons flour
3 tablespoons water
½ teaspoon cinnamon
½ teaspoon nutmeg
2 tablespoons melted butter
3 eggs, separated
½ cup sugar
1 unbaked 8-inch pastry shell

Combine molasses and lemon juice. Moisten flour with water and add cinnamon, nutmeg and melted butter; mix well. Beat egg yolks with sugar until light. Add to molasses mixture, mixing well. Fold in stiffly beaten egg white. Bake pie shell at 425°F. for 5 minutes. Then add filling. Bake at 350°F. 30 to 40 minutes or until filling is set. Yield: 1 8-inch pie.

MY MOTHER'S DEEP-DISH PEACH PIE · MRS. DAVID HUGHES, SOUTH CAROLINA

PASTRY:
2 cups whole-wheat flour
½ teaspoon salt
¾ cup shortening
5 tablespoons cold water

FILLING:
1 tablespoon flour
1 cup sugar
8 large fresh peaches, peeled
    and sliced
1 teaspoon cinnamon
1 teaspoon nutmeg
¼ cup butter or margarine
5 tablespoons warm water
1 cup heavy cream, whipped
Sugar to taste
1 teaspoon almond extract

Pastry: Place flour and salt in bowl. Cut in shortening until mixture crumbles. Stir in cold water with fork. Chill for at least 1 hour. Roll out ⅛ inch thick on lightly floured surface. Cut into 1-inch strips.

Pie: Lay ⅓ of strips crisscross fashion on bottom of 8×8-inch baking dish. Sprinkle with 1 tablespoon flour and 1 tablespoon sugar. Lay in half the peaches; sprinkle with cinnamon, nutmeg and ½ cup sugar. Cover with another third of pastry strips; add remaining peach slices and sprinkle over remaining sugar. Dot with butter; add warm water. Cover with remainder of pastry. Bake at 450°F. for 20 minutes. Reduce heat to 350°F. and bake 20 minutes longer. Whip cream until slightly thickened; add sugar gradually and beat until stiff; flavor with almond extract. Serve over warm pie. Yield: 6 portions.

PEACH GLAZE PIE · MRS. GORDON S. CLINTON, SEATTLE, WASH.

1 quart sliced fresh peaches
¾ cup water
1 cup sugar
3 tablespoons cornstarch
1 tablespoon lemon juice
1 tablespoon butter or
    margarine
Pinch of salt
Baked 9-inch pie shell
Whipped cream

Cut up 1 cup of the peaches. Add water and cook 4 minutes. Mix sugar and cornstarch and add to fruit mixture. Cook until thick and clear. Add lemon juice, butter, and salt; cool. Arrange remaining fruit in cooled pie shell. Pour cooled glaze over. Chill. Top with whipped cream and a few peach slices.
Yield: 6 to 8 portions.

MRS. GEORGE ESCHBACK'S PEARADISE PIE · YAKIMA, WASH.

1 can (1 pound, 13 ounces)
    Bartlett pear halves
¾ cup sugar
1 tablespoon cornstarch
½ cup light cream
1 tablespoon orange juice

Remove pears from syrup and drain thoroughly. Combine sugar and cornstarch, then stir in cream. Add orange juice and lemon juice and mix well. Line pie pan with pastry. Slice 8 pear halves into pan. Pour cream mixture over pears and dot with butter. Sprinkle with spices. Roll out top crust and cut into ½-inch

1 tablespoon lemon juice
Pastry for 8-inch double-crust
    pie
1 tablespoon butter or
    margarine
⅛ teaspoon cinnamon
⅛ teaspoon nutmeg

strips. Arrange pastry strips in lattice pattern on top of pear slices. Seal. Bake at 425°F. for 35 minutes, or until done. Serve warm. Top with ice cream, if desired.

Yield: 6 portions.

CALLIE'S PECAN PIE · RICH'S DEPARTMENT STORE, ATLANTA, GA.

3 eggs
2 tablespoons melted butter
    or margarine
2 tablespoons flour
¼ teaspoon vanilla extract
⅛ teaspoon salt
½ cup sugar
1½ cups dark corn syrup
1½ cups broken pecan halves
1 unbaked 8-inch pie shell

Beat eggs. Blend in melted butter, flour, vanilla extract, salt, sugar and syrup. Sprinkle nuts over bottom of unbaked pastry shell. Now gently pour over syrup mixture. Bake at 425°F. for 10 minutes. Reduce heat to 325°F. and bake about 40 minutes. Yield: 1 8-inch pie to serve six.

SOUTHERN PECAN PIE · WILLIAMSBURG, VA.

1 9-inch unbaked pastry shell
1 cup pecans
3 eggs
1 cup dark corn syrup
⅓ cup sugar
⅛ teaspoon salt
¼ cup melted butter or
    margarine

Line pastry shell with pecans. Beat eggs well. Add corn syrup, sugar, salt and butter; mix well. Pour over nuts in crust. Bake at 425°F. for 10 minutes. Reduce heat to 350°F. and bake 40 minutes longer. Cool before serving. Yield: 1 9-inch pie.

LOWELL INN PECAN PIE · STILLWATER, MINN.

3 eggs
¾ cup sugar
¼ pound butter or margarine,
    melted
1 cup dark corn syrup
1 cup pecan halves
1 unbaked 9-inch pie shell

Beat eggs until light. Add sugar, butter and syrup, gradually beating each ingredient in until blended. Pour into pie shell. Bake at 425°F. for 10 minutes. Reduce heat to 350°F. and bake for 30 minutes longer. Remove pie and cover with pecan halves and return to oven to bake 10 to 15 minutes longer or until firm. Serve just warm with whipped cream. Yield: 1 9-inch pie.

PURPLE-PLUM PIE · KATHLEEN LASSELLE, TIGARD, ORE.

PASTRY:
1½ cups sifted flour
½ teaspoon salt
½ cup shortening
¼ cup cold water

Combine flour and salt. Cut in half of shortening finely; cut in remainder coarsely. Add water and stir until particles hold together. Divide dough. Roll into bottom and top crusts for an 8-inch pie.

FILLING:
1 can (1 pound, 13 ounces)
   purple plums
¾ cup plum juice
½ cup sugar
2 tablespoons flour
¼ teaspoon salt
¼ teaspoon cinnamon
1 tablespoon butter or
   margarine

Drain plums, reserving juice. Pit and lay plums on bottom crust of pie. Add plum juice; sprinkle with mixture of sugar, flour, salt, and cinnamon. Dot with butter. Add top crust, seal, make vent openings, brush with cream. Bake at 425°F. for 30 to 40 minutes. Yield one 8-inch pie.

HOOSIER "PUNKIN" PIE · HAWTHORN ROOM, INDIANAPOLIS, IND.

½ recipe pie pastry
1½ cups cooked, strained
   pumpkin
1 cup milk
⅞ cup sugar
¼ teaspoon salt
¼ teaspoon nutmeg
¼ teaspoon cinnamon
2 eggs, slightly beaten
1 tablespoon melted butter or
   margarine

Line an 8-inch pie pan with pastry and make a fluted, standing rim. Place pumpkin in bowl; add milk gradually, stirring constantly. Add remaining ingredients in the order given and beat well with a rotary beater or electric mixer. Pour into pastry-lined pie pan. Bake at 400°F. for 35 to 45 minutes or until a silver knife inserted into the custard draws out clean. Yield: 1 8-inch pie.

ONE-HALF RECIPE FOR PASTRY:
¾ cup sifted flour
½ teaspoon salt
⅓ cup vegetable shortening
2 to 3 tablespoons water

Sift flour and salt into bowl. Cut in ¾ of the shortening until mixture is crumbly, then cut in other ¼ until mixture is slightly coarser. Mix in water until mixture holds together and forms a ball, not too stiff yet not sticky. Knead once or twice on lightly floured surface, pat out slightly, and roll into a square shape for crust or rectangular shape for lattice top.

FLUFFY PUMPKIN PIE · NEW HAMPSHIRE

½ cup sugar
1 teaspoon cinnamon
½ teaspoon nutmeg
¼ teaspoon cloves
¼ teaspoon ginger
¼ teaspoon salt
1 cup cooked or canned
    pumpkin
1 cup milk
2 eggs and 1 egg yolk, well
    beaten

1 egg white, stiffly beaten
1 9-inch unbaked pastry shell
Whipped cream

Mix sugar, spices and salt. Combine with pumpkin. Add milk and mix well. Stir in well-beaten eggs and egg yolk. Fold in stiffly beaten egg white. Pour into pastry shell. Bake at 425°F. for 45 minutes. Cool. Top with swirls of whipped cream and serve at once. Yield: 1 9-inch pie.

MRS. LAWRENCE'S BROWN SUGAR PUMPKIN PIE · EAST HAMPTON, N.Y.

½ recipe plain pastry
¾ cup brown sugar, firmly
    packed
½ teaspoon salt
1 teaspoon grated lemon
    rind
½ teaspoon ginger
¼ teaspoon mace
¼ teaspoon nutmeg
⅛ teaspoon vanilla extract
2 cups cooked pumpkin

3 eggs, beaten slightly
1¾ cup rich milk, scalded

Line a 9-inch pie pan with pastry and make fluted, standing rim. Mix the brown sugar, salt, lemon rind, spices and vanilla thoroughly with the pumpkin. Then stir in eggs and add milk gradually. Pour mixture into pastry-lined pan. Bake at 450°F. for 10 minutes; then reduce heat to 350°F. and bake 30 to 40 minutes longer, or until knife comes out clean when inserted in custard. Yield: one 9-inch pie.

SOUR CREAM RAISIN PIE · HAWTHORN ROOM, INDIANAPOLIS, IND.

1 cup brown sugar, firmly
    packed
2 tablespoons flour
½ teaspoon nutmeg
½ teaspoon cinnamon
¼ teaspoon salt
1 cup commercial sour cream
3 eggs, separated
1 cup raisins
1 8-inch baked pastry shell
⅓ cup sugar

Combine brown sugar, flour, spices, salt, and sour cream in top of double boiler, mixing well. Place over boiling water and cook, stirring occasionally until slightly thickened. Beat egg yolks; add a little of the hot mixture and then add the yolk mixture to the hot mixture, stirring constantly. Cook for about 5 minutes longer and add raisins. Cool. Pour into baked pie shell. Cover with meringue made by beating the 3 egg whites until frothy, gradually adding ⅓ cup of sugar, beating until stiff but not dry. Bake at 400°F. for 8 to 10 minutes or until meringue is delicately brown. Yield: 1 8-inch pie.

FRESH RHUBARB MERINGUE PIE · CAMELBACK INN, PHOENIX, ARIZ.

2 tablespoons butter or
    margarine
1½ cups sugar
½ cup flour
¼ teaspoon salt
3 eggs, separated
4 cups diced rhubarb
1 baked 9-inch pie shell
6 tablespoons sugar

Blend butter, the 1½ cups sugar, flour, and salt thoroughly. Add beaten egg yolks; mix well. Stir in rhubarb. Turn into pie shell. Bake at 350°F. for 30 to 40 minutes, or until rhubarb is tender. Make a meringue from egg whites and the 6 tablespoons sugar. Spread on warm pie. Bake at 400°F. for 8 to 10 minutes or until brown. Cool before serving. Yield: 1 9-inch pie.

RHUBARB CUSTARD PIE · MRS. LILY W. HANSEN, IDAHO

2½ cups unpeeled rhubarb,
    cut in 1-inch lengths
1½ cups sugar
2 tablespoons flour
2 eggs, slightly beaten
1½ teaspoons lemon juice
Pinch of salt
Pastry for two-crust 9-inch pie
2 tablespoons butter or
    margarine
2 teaspoons sugar

Mix together fruit, sugar, flour, eggs, lemon juice, and salt. Turn into the pastry-lined pie pan. Dot with butter. Lay on top pastry, fold bottom pastry edge over top crust and flute edges to seal in juice. Sprinkle with the 2 teaspoons sugar. Bake at 450°F. for 10 minutes. Reduce heat to 350°F. and bake 30 minutes longer. Yield: 1 9-inch pie.

U.S. SENATE RUM PIE · WASHINGTON, D.C.

2 cups milk
¾ cup sugar
Pinch of salt
4 tablespoons flour
2 tablespoons cornstarch
5 egg yolks, slightly beaten
¼ pound butter or margarine,
    softened
2 tablespoons dark rum
Whipped cream
Chopped pecans
Unsweetened chocolate

Combine 1½ cups of the milk, sugar and salt. Bring almost to the boiling point. Combine flour and cornstarch. Stir in remaining milk and egg yolks; mix until smooth. Stir into the heated milk mixture. Cook until thick and smooth. Let cool to room temperature. Beat in butter. Blend in rum. Pour into Graham Cracker Crust. Chill thoroughly. When ready to serve top with whipped cream and sprinkle with nuts and chocolate. Serve cold. Yield: 1 9-inch pie.

GRAHAM CRACKER CRUST:

*1½ cups Graham Cracker
    crumbs
½ cup confectioners' sugar
½ teaspoon nutmeg
½ cup butter or margarine,
    melted*

Mix crumbs, sugar and spice together. Add melted butter and mix thoroughly. Line a 9-inch pie pan with mixture and press firmly into place. Chill ½ hour before filling.

SHOO-FLY PIE (DRY) · EDNA EBY HELLER, BUENA VISTA, PENNA.

PASTRY FOR THREE 8-INCH PIE SHELLS

CRUMB MIXTURE:

*4 cups sifted flour
¾ cup lard
1 cup brown sugar*

LIQUID:

*1 cup molasses
1 teaspoon baking soda
1 cup boiling water*

Line 3, 8-inch pie pans with pastry. Combine ingredients for crumb mixture, using hands to blend well. Combine ingredients for liquid; pour into pie pans. Top with crumbs. Bake at 350°F. for about 25 minutes. Yield: 3 8-inch pies.

SHOO-FLY PIE (WET) · EDNA EBY HELLER, BUENA VISTA, PENNA.

PASTRY FOR ONE 9-INCH PIE SHELL

CRUMB MIXTURE:

*¾ cup sifted flour
½ teaspoon salt
½ teaspoon cinnamon
½ teaspoon ginger
⅛ teaspoon nutmeg
⅛ teaspoon ground cloves
½ cup brown sugar
2 tablespoons shortening*

LIQUID:

*½ cup dark molasses
¾ cup boiling water
1 egg yolk, well beaten
½ teaspoon baking soda*

Line a 9-inch pie pan with pastry. Combine ingredients for crumb mixture using hands to blend. Combine ingredients for liquid; pour into pie pan. Top with crumbs. Bake at 400°F. until it starts to brown, about 10 minutes. Reduce heat to 325°F.; bake until firm, about 30 minutes.
    Yield: 1 9-inch pie.

SHOO-FLY PIE (CAKE-TYPE) · EDNA EBY HELLER, BUENA VISTA, PENNA.

PASTRY FOR ONE 8- OR 9-INCH PASTRY SHELL

CRUMB MIXTURE:
1½ cups sifted flour
½ cup sugar (brown and
    white mixed)
1 teaspoon baking powder
2 tablespoons shortening

Line an 8- or 9-inch pan with pastry. Combine ingredients for crumb mixture, using hands to blend. Combine ingredients for liquid, pour ⅓ into pie pan. Add ⅓ of crumbs; continue alternating, ending with crumbs. Bake at 350°F. for about 30 minutes. Yield: 1 8- or 9-inch pie.

LIQUID:
½ cup dark molasses
¾ teaspoon baking soda
½ cup boiling water

FRESH STRAWBERRY PIE · LOWELL INN, STILLWATER, MINN.

PASTRY:
2 cups sifted flour
1 cup shortening
1 teaspoon salt
2 tablespoons cold water

Sift flour and cut in shortening. Combine salt and cold water, and add to flour mixture, stirring quickly until a soft dough is formed. Roll on floured surface to ¼-inch thickness. Fit into 10-inch pie pan. Bake at 425°F. for 15 minutes or until golden brown.

FILLING:
1 cup crushed fresh straw-
    berries
1 cup sugar
1 tablespoon cornstarch
Fresh strawberries—enough
    to fill pie shell

Mix crushed strawberries with sugar and cornstarch. Boil until transparent. Fill pie shell with fresh whole strawberries, washed and hulled. Pour over hot berry syrup. Chill. Serve with whipped cream.
Yield: 1 10-inch pie.

SYRUP-CUSTARD PIE · MRS. HENRIETTA DULL, ATLANTA, GA.

4 eggs
¾ cup sugar
1½ cups cane syrup
2 tablespoons butter or
    margarine
1 tablespoon flour
¼ teaspoon salt

1 teaspoon vanilla extract
1 9-inch unbaked pie shell

Beat eggs lightly. Add sugar, then remaining ingredients, mixing well. Pour into pie shell. Bake at 450°F. for 10 minutes. Reduce heat to 350°F. and bake for 25 minutes, or until firm. Serve cold. Yield: 6 portions.

ENGLISH TOFFEE PIE · MINERAL POINT, WISCONSIN

3 cups heavy sour cream
2¼ cups sugar
1 teaspoon cloves
3 eggs
2 egg yolks
3 cups seedless raisins
¾ cup chopped walnuts
¾ cup quartered blanched
    almonds
1 teaspoon vanilla extract
¼ cup sherry
2 unbaked 9-inch pastry shells

Combine sour cream, sugar, and cloves. Add whole eggs and egg yolks (beaten together). Stir in raisins, nuts, vanilla extract and sherry wine. Pour mixture into pie shells and bake in a hot oven (400°F.) 15 minutes. Reduce to moderate heat (350°F.) and bake 35 to 40 minutes or until a silver knife inserted in center comes out clean. Serve with vanilla ice cream, if you like.

Yield: 2 9-inch toffee pies.

WALNUT TARTS · MRS. J. KELL BRANDON, SIMSBURY, CONN.

1 cup walnuts, coarsely
    chopped
⅓ cup hot milk
6 tablespoons sugar
2 teaspoons rum
4 unbaked 3-inch tarts

Mix filling ingredients well. Pour into tarts. Bake at 425°F. for 15 to 20 minutes.

Yield: 4 tarts

PERFECT PIE CRUST TOPPING · MADELEINE BURRAGE, WISCASSET, MAINE

1 cup sifted flour
¼ teaspoon salt
½ cup butter or margarine
2 tablespoons water

Combine flour and salt. Cut in butter until size of large peas. Sprinkle water, a tablespoon at a time, over mixture. Mix quickly until a dough is formed. Shape lightly into a round. Wrap in waxed paper. Refrigerate for 2 hours or more. Roll dough on well-floured surface to desired size.

Yield: pastry for top of a 9-inch pie.

Cakes

BASIC CAKE · MRS. ROBERT ADAMS, JACKSONVILLE, FLA.

1½ cups sifted cake flour
2 teaspoons baking powder
½ teaspoon salt
½ cup butter or margarine
1 cup sugar
1 teaspoon vanilla extract
2 eggs, separated
½ cup milk

Sift together flour, baking powder and salt. Cream butter and sugar until very fluffy. Beat in vanilla and well-beaten egg yolks. Add flour mixture alternately with milk, beating well after each addition. Fold in egg whites, beaten stiff but not dry. Turn into 2 greased and paper-lined 8-inch layer-cake pans. Bake at 350°F. for 30 minutes. Cover layers with chocolate frosting. Yield: 1 8-inch layer cake. For a loaf cake, pour batter of basic cake into a greased and floured 10×5×3-inch loaf pan. Bake at 350°F. for 50 to 60 minutes. Serve sliced with ice cream. Yield: 8 portions.

For tea muffins, pour basic cake batter into small-sized muffin pans which have been greased and floured. Onto each muffin cup of batter drop 4 or 5 seeded raisins and a half pecan. Bake at 400°F. about 15 minutes. Serve warm. Yield: 1½ to 2 dozen small muffins.

For cake to serve with a sauce, pour batter into a greased and floured 9-inch square pan. Bake at 350°F.

about 45 minutes. While still warm cut and serve immediately, dolloping each square with this fresh strawberry hard sauce. Yield: 8 portions.

STRAWBERRY HARD SAUCE:

⅔ cup butter or margarine
2½ cups confectioners' sugar
1 cup mashed fresh strawberries

Cream butter until soft. Gradually beat in sugar until smooth and well blended. Gradually add mashed fresh strawberries and beat until light. Serve over warm cake. Yield: 2 cups sauce.

ANGEL FOOD CAKE · MRS. DOUGLAS MC KAY, SALEM, ORE.

1½ cups fresh egg whites
 (about 13 large)
Pinch of salt
1¼ teaspoons cream of tartar
1½ cups sugar
1 cup and 1 tablespoon
 sifted cake flour
1 teaspoon vanilla extract

Turn egg whites onto large platter, dust with 2 shakes of salt. Beat with a wire whip until whites are frothy. Add cream of tartar and continue beating until the mixture makes little mountains, but not too stiff. Sift sugar 6 times, adding this to the egg whites 1 tablespoon at a time, folding it in gently, so gently. Next the flour is added, this too sifted 6 times and added 1 tablespoon at a time. At the very last, the vanilla. The batter is poured into a 10-inch flour-dusted aluminum tube pan which Mrs. McKay uses for angel food only. The cake is started in a cold oven, set at 150°F. for 10 minutes, then to 200° for another 10 minutes. Next, increase the temperature 25° every 10 minutes until the oven is at 300°. Now give the cake another full 10 minutes, and at this point increase the temperature to 350° and leave it in 10 minutes longer to take on that delicate macaroon color. In all, 1 hour and 10 minutes and out comes the cake to turn upside-down on a rack and let cool for 2 hours. Remove from the pan, frost or leave plain. Yield: 12 portions.

ANGEL CAKE · MRS. HELEN BENDER, SUMMIT, N.J.

11 egg whites (1⅜ cups)
½ teaspoon salt
1 teaspoon cream of tartar
1 cup sifted flour
1½ cups sugar
1 teaspoon vanilla extract

Beat egg whites until foamy. Add salt and cream of tartar and continue beating until whites are just stiff enough to form soft peaks. Sift flour and sugar twice together. Gently fold into egg white mixture, sifting in 2 tablespoonfuls at a time. Fold in vanilla. Turn into ungreased 9-inch tube pan. Bake at 375°F. for 40 minutes. Invert pan on cake rack until cake is cold. Yield: 1 9-inch tube cake.

MRS. ROY ANTHONY'S ANGEL FOOD CAKE · BAKED FOR WINSTON CHURCHILL AT FULTON, MO.

12 egg whites
⅛ teaspoon salt
1 teaspoon cream of tartar
1½ cups sugar
1 cup sifted cake flour
1 teaspoon vanilla extract
1 teaspoon lemon extract

Combine egg whites and salt and beat until foamy. Add cream of tartar and continue beating until whites cling to the bowl. Gradually fold in the sugar, adding a little at a time. Fold in flour in the same way. Add flavorings and continue folding for a few minutes longer. Turn into an ungreased 10-inch tube pan. Place in a cold oven and bring to 325°F. Bake for 1 hour. Remove cake from oven and invert on a wire rack until cold. Frost with Seven Minute Icing (see any basic cook book). Yield: 1 10-inch cake.

CUSTARD ANGEL FOOD CAKE · MRS. ROSA B. CONNELL, OREGON

1¼ cups sugar
½ cup water
8 eggs, separated
1 teaspoon orange juice
1 cup sifted cake flour
¼ teaspoon salt
1 teaspoon cream of tartar
1 cup filberts, finely chopped

Boil sugar and water until mixture reaches the thread state (230°F.). Meanwhile, beat egg yolks until thick and lemon-colored. Add orange juice. Pour hot syrup over yolks a little at a time and continue to beat until thick. Let cool. Sift flour with salt 7 or 8 times. Fold into egg-yolk mixture. Beat egg whites until frothy, add cream of tartar and beat until stiff. Fold into cooled batter. Fold in filberts. Pour into ungreased 10-inch tube pan. Bake at 300°F. for 1¼ to 1½ hours. Yield: 1 10-inch tube cake.

FILBERT APPLESAUCE CAKE · MRS. ROSA B. CONNELL, OREGON

½ cup shortening
1 cup sugar
1 egg, beaten
1 teaspoon vanilla extract
1 cup cooked prunes, finely chopped
1½ cups applesauce
1 cup raisins
1 cup filberts, finely chopped
½ teaspoon cinnamon
½ teaspoon cloves
2 cups sifted flour
2 teaspoons baking soda

Cream shortening and sugar thoroughly. Beat in egg. Add vanilla. Stir in prunes, applesauce, raisins, nuts and spices. Sift flour with soda and add to mixture, stirring in well. Turn into a well-greased and floured 10½ × 5½ × 3-inch loaf pan. Bake at 350°F. for 1 hour. Yield: 1 loaf cake.

APPLESAUCE CAKE · MRS. THOMAS E. DEWEY, PAWLING, N.Y.

1 cup butter or other
    shortening
2 cups sugar
2 eggs
3 cups sifted flour
1 tablespoon baking soda
½ teaspoon salt
1 tablespoon cinnamon
1½ teaspoons nutmeg
1 teaspoon cloves

2½ cups applesauce
2 tablespoons corn syrup
1 cup raisins
1 cup chopped nuts

Cream butter and sugar thoroughly. Beat in eggs one at a time. Sift together flour, soda, salt and spices. Add alternately with combined applesauce and syrup. Fold in raisins and nuts. Pour batter into two greased 8 by 8-inch pans. Bake at 300°F. for about 1 hour. Yield: 2 8-inch squares.

BLACK WALNUT CAKE · MRS. JOHN ISE, LAWRENCE, KAN.

½ cup butter or margarine
1½ cups sugar
2 cups sifted flour
4 teaspoons baking powder
½ teaspoon salt
1 cup milk
1 cup finely ground black
    walnuts
1 teaspoon vanilla extract
4 egg whites
¼ teaspoon cream of tartar

Cream butter and sugar thoroughly. Sift flour with baking powder and salt. Add to creamed mixture alternately with milk, mixing well after each addition. Add ground nuts and flavoring. Fold in egg whites which have been beaten with cream of tartar until stiff but not dry. Cover the bottom of a 9-inch tube pan with waxed paper; oil sides. Pour in batter. Bake at 325°F. for 15 minutes; then increase heat to 350°F. and bake about 30 to 40 minutes longer, or until top springs back when lightly pressed with finger. Yield: 1 9-inch cake.

CAPP'S BLACKBERRY-JAM CAKE · TAYLOR FAMILY, BROWNSVILLE, TENN.

1 cup seeded raisins
1 cup Burgundy wine or
    grape juice
1 cup finely chopped citron
1 cup finely chopped pecans
3½ cups sifted flour
2 teaspoons baking powder
1 teaspoon baking soda
1 teaspoon salt
1 cup butter or margarine
1 cup sugar
5 eggs
1 cup seedless blackberry
    jam (or strained)

¾ cup buttermilk
1 tablespoon confectioners' sugar

Soak raisins overnight in wine or grape juice. The following morning strain raisins, reserving juice. Dredge raisins, citron, and pecans in ½ cup of the flour. Sift together remaining flour, baking powder, soda and salt. Cream butter and sugar, beating until fluffy. Beat in 1 egg at a time. Add jam and beat until smooth. Add flour mixture alternately with buttermilk, beating until smooth after each addition. Blend in reserved wine or grape juice. Add dredged fruit to mixture and mix thoroughly. Pour into greased 9-inch tube pan. Bake at 350°F. for 1¼ hours, or until done. Cool. Dust confectioners' sugar over top of cake. Yield: 12 to 16 portions.

BURNT SUGAR CAKE · MRS. W. H. CALDWELL, DALLAS, TEX.

2 cups sugar
½ cup boiling water
¾ cup butter or margarine
2 teaspoons vanilla extract
2 eggs, separated
3 cups sifted cake flour
1 teaspoon baking soda
½ teaspoon baking powder
¼ teaspoon salt
1 cup water

Caramelize ½ cup of the sugar by melting over low heat, stirring until liquid becomes very dark. Remove from heat. Very gradually stir in boiling water, then simmer until caramel is dissolved and syrupy; cool. Cream butter, vanilla and remaining sugar. Add beaten egg yolks. Stir in cooled syrup. Sift dry ingredients together 3 times. Add to creamed mixture alternately with water, adding flour first and last. Fold in stiffly beaten egg whites. Pour into two greased and floured 9-inch layer pans. Bake at 375°F. for 25 to 30 minutes. Cool and frost. Yield: 1 9-inch layer cake.

FROSTING:
4 cups sugar
1 cup milk
2 tablespoons butter or
    margarine
1 teaspoon vanilla extract
4 tablespoons light cream

Put 3 cups of the sugar and milk into saucepan. Put remaining sugar and 1 tablespoon of the butter in heavy frying pan. Place both on low heat at same time. Caramelize sugar in frying pan to a dark brown color. Add very gradually to boiling sugar and milk mixture. Cook until mixture forms a soft ball when tested in (235°F.) cold water. Remove from heat; allow to cool. Add remaining butter and vanilla. Beat until creamy. Add cream and beat until mixture forms proper spreading consistency.

CHERRY CAKE · MRS. AUSTIN CARPENTER, SHERBURNE, N.Y.

½ cup butter or margarine
1 cup sugar
2 eggs
3 tablespoons sour cream or
    milk
2 cups sifted flour
1 teaspoon baking soda
½ teaspoon salt
2 teaspoons cinnamon
1 cup canned, sour, red,
    pitted cherries and juice

Cream together butter and sugar. Add eggs one at a time, beating after each addition. Stir in cream. Sift together flour, baking soda, salt and cinnamon. Add to creamed mixture. Add cherries and juice; stir until mixed. Pour into 3 greased 8-inch layer pans. Bake at 350°F. for 25 to 30 minutes. Cool 5 minutes; turn out on cake racks. Cool. Put together with seven-minute frosting (see any basic cook book), substituting cherry juice for part of the water.

Yield: one 3-layer cake.

SOUR-MILK CHOCOLATE CAKE · MRS. DOUGLAS MC KAY, SALEM, ORE.

½ cup butter or margarine
1½ cups sugar
2 eggs, well beaten
2 squares unsweetened
    chocolate, melted
2 cups sifted cake flour
1 teaspoon baking soda
1 teaspoon salt
1 cup sour milk or buttermilk

1 tablespoon sour cream
1 teaspoon vanilla extract

Cream butter and sugar thoroughly. Beat in eggs, then the melted chocolate. Sift flour, soda, and salt together. Add alternately to creamed mixture with the sour milk and sour cream. Add vanilla. Pour into 2 greased 9-inch layer cake pans. Bake at 350°F. for 30 minutes. Yield: 1 9-inch layer cake.

DEVIL'S FOOD CAKE · WHITE SPRINGS, FLORIDA

4 ounces unsweetened
    chocolate
1 egg, separated
1½ cups sugar
1½ cups milk
¼ pound butter or margarine
2 eggs or 1 egg and 2 egg
    yolks (reserve whites for
    icing)
1 teaspoon baking soda
2 cups sifted flour
½ teaspoon salt
2 teaspoons vanilla extract

Melt chocolate in top of double boiler. Mix 1 egg yolk with ½ cup of the sugar; gradually stir in ½ cup of the milk. Add egg mixture to melted chocolate and cook over hot water until thick, stirring occasionally. Set aside to cool before using.

Cream remaining 1 cup sugar with butter. Beat in eggs. Dissolve soda in remaining 1 cup milk and add alternately with flour to creamed mixture. Blend in chocolate mixture, salt and vanilla. Pour into 2 greased and floured 9-inch pans. Bake at 350°F. for 25 to 30 minutes. Cool layers and frost with this icing:

Thoroughly mix 3 cups sugar and 9 tablespoons cold water in top of double boiler. Set pan over rapidly boiling water and add 3 egg whites. Beat with rotary beater for 7 minutes or until stiff enough to spread. Add pinch of salt, 2 teaspoons vanilla extract and 2 teaspoons fresh lemon juice. Beat until cool.

OX-BLOOD CAKE · MRS. GORDON S. CLINTON, SEATTLE, WASH.

⅔ cup shortening
2 cups sugar
2 eggs
2½ cups sifted flour
1 cup sour milk or buttermilk
¾ cup cocoa
2 teaspoons baking soda

1 teaspoon salt
¾ cup boiling water

Cream shortening and sugar. Beat in eggs singly. Add flour and milk alternately. Combine cocoa, soda, salt, and water. Fold into batter. Pour into a greased 13×9×2-inch pan. Bake at 350°F. for 1 hour. Cool and frost with Fudge Icing (see next page).

FUDGE ICING:

1½ cups confectioners' sugar
3 tablespoons cocoa
¼ cup melted butter or
    margarine
3 tablespoons hot coffee
1 teaspoon vanilla extract

Combine sugar and cocoa; blend in butter. Gradually add hot coffee and vanilla; beat well.

GRANDMOTHER GILETTE'S ELECTION CAKE · MABEL MANGANO, CONNECTICUT

2 packages or cakes yeast,
    active dry or compressed
¼ cup warm, not hot, water
    (lukewarm for
    compressed)
¾ cup lukewarm milk
1 teaspoon salt
2½ cups sifted flour
½ cup lard
1 cup sugar
2 eggs
¾ teaspoon nutmeg
½ cup chopped citron
⅓ cup seedless raisins, cut in
    half

Dissolve yeast in water. Stir in milk and salt. Add 1½ cups of the flour; beat thoroughly. Let rise until light, 45 minutes to 1 hour. Cream shortening and sugar. Add eggs, singly, beating well after each addition. Stir in yeast mixture. Combine remaining 1 cup flour and nutmeg. Add to yeast batter; beat until smooth. Stir in citron and raisins. Turn into greased and floured 9-inch tube pan. Let rise in warm place until doubled in bulk, about 1 hour. Bake at 375°F. for 35 to 40 minutes. Frost with creamy vanilla frosting. Decorate with strips of citron, if desired. Yield: one 9-inch tube cake.

APPLESAUCE FRUIT CAKE · MRS. KENNETH BIXLER, WASHINGTON

2 cups raisins
1½ cups shortening
2 cups sugar
5 eggs
2 cups applesauce
3½ cups sifted flour
2 teaspoons baking soda
1 teaspoon salt
1 teaspoon cinnamon
1 teaspoon cloves
2 teaspoons nutmeg
1 pound diced fruit mix

1 cup diced candied pineapple
1 cup candied cherries, halved
1 cup chopped dates
½ cup cut-up candied lemon peel
½ cup cut-up candied orange peel
2 cups chopped nuts

Soak raisins in warm water; drain and dry. Cream shortening and sugar. Beat in eggs, one at a time. Stir in applesauce. Sift dry ingredients 3 times and add to creamed mixture, mixing well. Blend in raisins, fruits and nuts. Pour into three 9×5×3-inch loaf pans which

have been lined with 2 thicknesses of greased brown paper. Bake at 300°F. for 2 to 2½ hours.
Yield: 6 pounds fruit cake.

FRUIT CAKE · MRS. CLEO WRIGHT, UTAH

1 cup salad oil
1½ cups brown sugar
4 eggs
3 cups sifted flour
1 teaspoon baking powder
2 teaspoons salt
2 teaspoons cinnamon
2 teaspoons allspice
1 teaspoon cloves
1 cup fruit juice (apple,
   pineapple or orange)
1 cup shaved citron
1 cup chopped candied
   pineapple
1½ cups whole candied
   cherries
1 cup seedless raisins

1 cup chopped figs or dates
3 cups chopped nuts

Combine oil, sugar and eggs, and beat for 2 minutes. Sift together 2 cups of the flour with baking powder, salt and spices. Stir into oil mixture with fruit juice. Mix remaining cup of flour with fruits and nuts. Combine with batter and mix thoroughly. Pour batter into two 9×5×3-inch loaf pans lined with waxed or greased brown paper. Bake at 275°F. for 2½ to 3 hours. Remove cakes, leaving paper on. When cool, glaze and decorate.

Cake glaze: Combine 2 tablespoons brown sugar, 1 tablespoon corn syrup, and 2 tablespoons water. Boil for 2 minutes. Pour over cake tops. Decorate with glacéed fruits and nuts.

GOLD CAKE · MRS. HELEN BENDER, SUMMIT, N.J.

½ cup butter or margarine
1¼ cups sugar
11 egg yolks (⅞ cup)
½ cup milk
1¼ cups sifted cake flour
½ teaspoon salt
⅓ teaspoon each, orange,
   lemon, almond extract
2 teaspoons baking powder

  ICING:
¼ cup butter or margarine
1 pound confectioners' sugar
Orange juice

Cream butter and sugar thoroughly. Add yolks, beating until creamy. Add milk alternately with cake flour sifted with salt, beating well after each addition. Add extracts, and at the very last the baking powder, stirring well. Turn mixture into an ungreased 9-inch tube pan. Bake at 350°F. about 45 minutes, or until done. Invert on rack to cool. Remove by running spatula along sides. Cover with icing made by blending butter with confectioners' sugar and adding orange juice, just enough to give icing a nice spreading consistency. Yield: 1 9-in. tube cake.

HICKORY-NUT LAYER CAKE · MRS. REBA CAREY, INDIANA

3 cups sifted flour
4 teaspoons baking powder
1 teaspoon salt
1 cup butter or margarine
1¾ cups sugar
1 teaspoon vanilla extract
½ to 1 teaspoon maple
    flavoring
4 eggs
2 cups chopped hickory nuts
1 cup milk

Sift flour, baking powder, and salt together. Cream butter and sugar until very light and lemon-colored. Add vanilla and maple flavoring. Beat in eggs one at a time. Stir in 1½ cups of the hickory nuts. Blend in sifted dry ingredients alternately with milk, beginning and ending with the addition of dry ingredients. Turn batter into well-greased 12 × 9 × 3-inch pan or 2 9-inch layer pans. Bake at 375°F. for 35 to 40 minutes. When cool, frost with your favorite icing and sprinkle with the remaining nuts. Yield: 1 rectangular, or 1 9-inch layer cake. NOTE: For real maple flavor, substitute ¼ cup maple syrup for the maple flavoring and reduce milk by 1 tablespoon.

LADY BALTIMORE CAKE · ADELAIDE R. READ, CHARLESTON, S.C.

3½ cups sifted cake flour
3½ teaspoons baking powder
1 cup butter or margarine
3 cups sugar
4 eggs
1 cup milk
½ cup water
2 teaspoons vanilla extract
2 teaspoons almond extract

Sift together flour and baking powder. Cream butter until soft. Gradually beat in 2 cups of the sugar until mixture is light and fluffy. Add eggs, one at a time, and beat thoroughly. Add flour mixture, alternately with milk, blending until smooth after each addition. Pour into two greased and floured 9-inch layer pans. Bake at 350°F. for 30 to 35 minutes. Then combine remaining 1 cup sugar and water and cook until a thick syrup is formed. Stir in extracts. Remove cakes from pans and spread tops with syrups. Cool. Frost and fill with Lady Baltimore Frosting.

Yield: 1 9-inch layer cake.

LADY BALTIMORE FROSTING:

2 cups sugar
⅔ cup water
2 teaspoons corn syrup
2 egg whites
2 cups seeded raisins, cut in
    small pieces
12 figs, cut in small pieces
2 cups pecans, chopped
Almond and vanilla extracts

Combine sugar, water and corn syrup. Stir over low heat until sugar is dissolved. Boil gently until a small amount of syrup forms a firm ball in cold water (244°F.) Beat egg whites until stiff. Pour syrup in a fine stream over egg whites, beating constantly. Continue to beat until frosting is cool, and a proper spreading consistency. Blend in raisins, figs and pecans. Add extracts to taste. NOTE: Raisins and figs may be soaked overnight in a small amount of sherry or brandy if desired.

GRANDMA PADDLEFORD'S MARBLE LAYER CAKE · STOCKDALE, KANSAS

2 cups sifted cake flour
2½ teaspoons baking powder
¼ teaspoon salt
½ cup shortening
1 cup sugar
1 teaspoon vanilla extract
2 eggs, separated
¾ cup milk
1 square unsweetened
    chocolate, melted

Sift flour, baking powder, and salt together. Cream shortening and sugar thoroughly. Add vanilla. Beat in well-beaten egg yolks. Add flour alternately with milk, beating until smooth after each addition. Fold in the stiffly-beaten egg whites. Divide batter into 2 parts. To one half, add chocolate. Put by spoonfuls into 2 greased and floured 9-inch layer pans, alternating light and dark batters. Bake at 375°F. about 25 minutes. Put layers together and cover with chocolate butter frosting.

Yield: 2 9-inch layers.

COCONUT MARSHMALLOW CAKE · MISS ETTA PATTERSON, KEY WEST, FLA.
BAKED FOR PRESIDENT TRUMAN

¾ cup butter or margarine
1 cup sugar
4 eggs, reserving 2 whites for
    frosting
2 cups sifted cake flour
1½ teaspoons baking powder
¼ teaspoon salt
½ cup milk
1 teaspoon vanilla extract

Cream butter and sugar until light and fluffy. Beat in eggs 1 at a time (reserving 2 egg whites for frosting). Sift together flour, baking powder and salt. Add to creamed mixture alternately with milk, starting and ending with flour. Blend in vanilla. Turn into 2 well-greased 9-inch or 3 8-inch layer-cake pans. Bake at 350°F. about 25 minutes. Frost with Marshmallow Frosting.

Yield: 1 layer cake.

MARSHMALLOW FROSTING:

1 cup sugar
½ cup boiling water
¼ teaspoon vinegar
2 egg whites, stiffly beaten
10 marshmallows, cut in
    small pieces
1 coconut, grated, or 1 cup
    moist-pack

Combine sugar, boiling water and vinegar in a saucepan and stir over heat until sugar is dissolved. Cover for 2 minutes to prevent crystals forming and cook without stirring. Remove cover and cook until candy thermometer registers 238°F., or until a small amount dropped into a cup of cold water forms a soft ball. Pour in a thin stream over stiffly beaten egg whites, beating constantly. Add marshmallow pieces and continue beating until cool and thick enough to spread. Spread on cake and sprinkle generously with coconut.

MAZUREK KROLEWSKI · MRS. MICHAEL LASKOWSKI, MILWAUKEE, WIS.

1 pound sweet butter
2 cups sugar
6 egg yolks
1 cup almonds, chopped
4 cups sifted flour
Melted chocolate
Almonds, orange peel and
*   citron for garnish*

Cream butter and sugar. Add egg yolks, one by one, mixing well after each addition. Add almonds. Sift in half of the flour, blending thoroughly. Add remainder of flour and stir batter until mixed. Divide into two parts and turn onto two well-greased baking sheets covered with oiled brown paper. Take a spatula, press each of the two lumps of dough into rectangles of ½-inch thickness. Bake at 325°F. for 30 to 35 minutes or to a golden brown. Cool. Frost with chocolate. Lay on almonds with orange-peel flowers, using citron for stems. The decoration is a matter of each woman's skill.

Yield: 2 rectangular cakes.

PECAN CAKE · MRS. THOMAS HART BENTON, KANSAS CITY, MO.

½ cup butter or margarine
1 cup sugar
3 eggs
1 cup sifted flour
½ teaspoon baking powder
½ teaspoon cinnamon
½ teaspoon nutmeg
Dash of salt
1 jigger (2 ounces) brandy,
*   rum or whiskey*
2 cups raisins
2 cups pecans

Cream butter and sugar thoroughly. Add eggs, stirring well. Sift flour with dry ingredients; add a little at a time to the egg mixture, stirring in each addition thoroughly. Add brandy. Flour the raisins and stir in with pecans. Turn into a well greased 9-inch tube pan. Bake at 350°F. about 1 hour and 10 minutes. Yield: 1 9-inch cake.

NOTE: This cake will keep many weeks in a tight-lidded tin, and stay moist if brandy is poured over from time to time.

QUICK-TO-MAKE PLUM CAKE · KATHLEEN LASSELLE, TIGARD, ORE.

1 can (1 pound, 13 ounces)
*   purple plums*
½ cup butter or margarine
2 teaspoons baking soda
2 cups sifted flour
1 cup sugar
½ teaspoon salt
½ teaspoon cinnamon
½ teaspoon cloves

½ cup raisins or chopped citron
½ cup chopped nuts

Drain plums; pit and mash to a pulp. Combine with butter. Heat. Add soda; let cool. When cool, add flour and remaining ingredients; mix well. Pour into a greased 9 × 5 × 2½-inch loaf pan. Bake at 350°F. for 60 to 70 minutes. Yield: 1 loaf cake.

DELICIOUS POTATO CAKE · MRS. HOLLIS BECKER, OAKLAND VALLEY, IDAHO

⅔ cup butter or margarine
2 cups sugar
4 eggs, separated
2 cups sifted flour
2 teaspoons baking powder
1 teaspoon cinnamon
½ teaspoon cloves
½ teaspoon nutmeg
½ cup milk
½ cup hot mashed potatoes
2 tablespoons cocoa
1 cup chopped nuts

Cream butter and sugar thoroughly. Beat in well-beaten egg yolks. Sift flour, baking powder, and spices together. Add to creamed mixture alternately with milk. Blend together and add mashed potatoes, cocoa, and nuts. Mix until blended. Fold in stiffly beaten egg whites. Pour into 2 greased 9-inch layer cake pans. Bake at 375°F. for about 25 minutes, or until cake springs back when lightly touched with finger. Cool 10 minutes; remove from pans and cool. Frost with a caramel icing.

Yield: 1 9-inch layer cake.

SAUTTER'S OLD-FASHIONED POUND CAKE · JACOB YACKLE, PHILADELPHIA, PENNA.

1 pound butter
1 pound sugar
1 pound eggs, separated
1 tablespoon vanilla extract
2 teaspoons orange extract
1 pound flour, sifted

Cream butter and beat in sugar gradually. Cream together well. Add the egg yolks bit by bit and continue beating until thoroughly blended. Add extracts. Gently fold in flour. Beat egg whites just barely stiff. Fold into flour mixture, and oh so gently. Pour into 2 buttered 8×4×3-inch loaf pans lined with heavy waxed paper. Bake at 325°F. for 1½ hours. Yield: 2 loaves.

NOTE: This recipe is both difficult and expensive to make.

BEULAH MICHAEL'S POUND CAKE · MRS. A. B. MICHAEL, INDIAN RIVER, FLA.

1 pound butter or margarine
3⅓ cups sugar
1 pound, or 2 cups, eggs
    (9 large)
4 cups sifted flour

Cream butter and sugar until very light and fluffy. (Sugar must be thoroughly absorbed.) Add eggs, one at a time, and beat well. (The entire beating process takes about 1 hour.) Fold in the sifted flour, a cupful at a time, and be careful that no white streaks remain. Pour batter into buttered 10-inch angel food pan. Place cake in a cold oven; set the thermostat at 250°F. and bake for 1½ hours. Increase temperature to 300°F. and bake for 1 hour or until done. Cool cake; then chill thoroughly in refrigerator. Remove from pan. Serve plain or toasted. Yield: 1 10-inch cake.

POUND CAKE · MRS. HELEN DUPREY BULLOCK, WASHINGTON, D.C.

Mrs. Bullock suggests a ready-mix for the Monticello pound-cake base, this one of the historic "name" series. Here is her version of how to use the mix for a truly down-South dessert:

Use three packages commercial pound cake mix. Stir in 1 teaspoon mace or nutmeg. Prepare according to box directions substituting ½ cup brandy and 1 cup milk for the 1½ cups milk called for. (For a richer cake, use 4 eggs instead of 3.) Pour into a greased and floured 10-inch tube pan or, preferably, an iron or earthen Turk's Head mold, as the early cake pans were called. Bake at 325° for 1½ hours. Serve with the brandied fruit. Yield: 1 10-inch tube cake.

PRUNE CAKE · MRS. WILLIAM BRACY, SALT LAKE CITY, UTAH

2¼ cups sifted flour
1 teaspoon baking soda
1 teaspoon allspice
1 teaspoon cinnamon
½ teaspoon cloves
¼ teaspoon salt
½ cup butter or margarine
1½ cups sugar
2 eggs, well beaten
1 cup cooked pitted prunes,
    puréed
1 cup sour milk or buttermilk

Sift flour, baking powder, spices, and salt together. Cream butter and sugar, beating until creamy. Blend in eggs, then prunes. Mix well. Add flour alternately with milk, adding a small amount at a time and beating until smooth after each addition. Pour into a greased 10-inch square pan. Bake at 350°F. for 40 to 45 minutes. Cool and frost with Creamy Frosting.

Yield: 9 to 12 portions.

CREAMY FROSTING:
¼ cup butter or margarine
2 cups sifted confectioners'
    sugar
3 tablespoons evaporated
    milk (about)
1 teaspoon vanilla extract

Cream butter until soft. Blend in half of the sugar and add milk. Cream well. Add remaining sugar and vanilla and beat until of spreading consistency. More sugar or milk may be added for desired thickness.

PRUNE CAKE DELUXE · LILLIAN JOHNSON, HOLLISTER, CALIF.

2 cups sifted flour
1 teaspoon baking soda
½ teaspoon salt
2 teaspoons cinnamon
1 teaspoon nutmeg
½ cup powdered chocolate or
    cocoa

Sift together flour, soda, salt, spices and chocolate. Cream shortening and sugar thoroughly. Add egg and beat until well blended. Add flour mixture and prunes and juice alternately, beating thoroughly after each addition. Stir in raisins, currants and nuts. Pour into well-greased 10×7×2-inch baking pan. Bake at

½ cup butter or other
    shortening
1½ cups sugar
1 egg
2 cups cooked pitted prunes,
    and juice (at least ½ cup
    juice)
1 cup seedless raisins
1 cup currants
1 cup coarsely chopped nuts

350°F. about 1¼ hours, or until done. Cool and frost with Mocha Butter Frosting. Yield: 8 portions.

MOCHA BUTTER FROSTING:

Sift 2 cups sifted confectioners' sugar with 3 teaspoons cocoa. Cream 3 tablespoons softened butter or margarine. Gradually add ½ cup of the sugar. Add remaining sugar alternately with 3 tablespoons (about) hot coffee, to bring to easy spreading consistency.

SPICE CAKE · MRS. HELEN BENDER, SUMMIT, N.J.

½ cup shortening
1 tablespoon molasses
1½ cups sugar
½ teaspoon salt
¼ teaspoon cloves
¼ teaspoon nutmeg
⅛ teaspoon allspice
1 teaspoon vanilla extract
2 eggs
1 cup milk
2½ cups sifted cake flour
1 tablespoon baking powder

Cream shortening, molasses and sugar thoroughly. Add salt, spices and vanilla and blend thoroughly. Beat in eggs. Add milk alternately with cake flour, beating in well after each addition. Blend in baking powder. Pour batter into 2 deep greased 9-inch cake pans lined with greased waxed paper. Bake at 375°F. for 25 minutes. Cool layers. Frost with 7-minute icing (see any basic cook book), flavoring with cinnamon or nutmeg instead of vanilla. Yield: 1 9-inch layer cake.

BANANA SPICE CAKE · TERRANCE HANOLD, MINNEAPOLIS, MINN.

2 cups sifted cake flour
2½ teaspoons baking powder
1 teaspoon salt
1 teaspoon cinnamon
1 teaspoon allspice
½ teaspoon cloves
⅛ teaspoon nutmeg
¾ cup granulated sugar
½ cup firmly packed brown
    sugar
½ cup soft shortening
¾ cup milk
2 eggs
1 teaspoon vanilla extract

Sift first 8 ingredients together into a bowl. Add brown sugar, shortening and ½ cup of the milk; beat 2 minutes. Add remaining ¼ cup milk, eggs, and vanilla. Beat 2 minutes. Pour into 2 greased and floured 8-inch layer pans. Bake at 350°F. for 25 to 30 minutes. Cool layers. Frost with banana frosting. Yield: 1 8-inch layer cake.

BANANA FROSTING:

Mix ½ cup mashed ripe banana and ½ teaspoon lemon juice. Cream 4 tablespoons butter or margarine. Add about 3 cups confectioners' sugar alternately with the banana mixture to the creamed butter.

FOUR-EGG SPONGE CAKE · MRS. L. K. MC CORMICK, NORTH MIAMI, FLA.

4 eggs, separated
½ teaspoon salt
2 tablespoons cold water
½ cup hot water
1½ cups sugar
1 teaspoon vanilla extract
1½ cups sifted flour
½ teaspoon cream of tartar

Beat egg yolks and ¼ teaspoon of the salt in a 3½-quart mixing bowl until very thick, and light-colored. Add cold water and beat for 1 minute. Add hot water and beat about 5 minutes or until mixture fills bowl ¾ full. Gradually beat in sugar; stir in vanilla. Beat until very fluffy. Blend in flour. Beat egg whites until frothy; add cream of tartar and remaining salt and continue beating until stiff but not dry. Fold whites into egg-yolk mixture. Pour into an ungreased 10-inch tube pan. Bake at 325°F. for 1 hour. Invert pan on cake rack and let cool for 20 minutes. Cut cake away from pan with sharp knife and turn out on rack to cool. Frost with orange icing.

Yield: 1 10-inch tube cake.

ORANGE ICING:
4 tablespoons butter or
    margarine
2 cups sifted confectioners'
    sugar
1 tablespoon grated orange
    rind
4 to 6 tablespoons orange
    juice
1 cup flaked coconut

Combine butter with sugar, creaming well. Add grated orange rind and enough orange juice to bring the icing to an easy spreading consistency. Beat until fluffy. Cover top and sides of cake with icing and sprinkle iced surface with grated coconut.

HOT-MILK SPONGE CAKE · MRS. MILDRED M. RUTHERFORD, SOUTH WOODSTOCK, VT.

2 eggs
1 cup sugar
1 cup sifted cake flour
1½ teaspoons baking powder
½ cup hot milk
1 tablespoon vegetable
    shortening, melted
¼ teaspoon salt
½ teaspoon vanilla extract
½ teaspoon lemon extract

Beat eggs, add sugar beating in thoroughly. Sift flour with baking powder and stir into egg mixture. Add milk, shortening, salt and extracts. Mix quickly and turn into an 8-inch-square greased pan. Bake at 350°F. for about 30 minutes. Remove from oven and invert pan for 1 hour or until cake is cold. Yield: 8 portions. Serve plain or with a lemon or cocoa sauce:

COCOA SAUCE:

1 cup heavy cream
3 tablespoons sugar
3 tablespoons cocoa

Combine ingredients and place in refrigerator for a full 3 hours. Whip until stiff just before serving to give the desired consistency. Yield: 1½ cups.

MRS. DULL'S PERFECTION SPONGE CAKE · MRS. HENRIETTA DULL, ATLANTA, GA.

6 eggs, separated
⅛ teaspoon salt
½ teaspoon cream of tartar
1¼ cups sifted sugar
1½ tablespoons lemon juice
1¼ cups sifted cake flour

Beat white of eggs with salt until foamy. Add cream of tartar and continue beating until whites are stiff. Add sugar gradually, beating for three minutes until mixture holds shape. Beat egg yolks until light and creamy; add lemon juice. Now fold in the whites and blend well together. Fold in flour a little at a time. Pour into ungreased 10×5×3-inch loaf pan. Bake at 300°F. about one hour and 10 minutes. Invert cake on rack and let cool before removing from pan. Yield: 1 loaf cake.

SANPETE COUNTY STARCH CAKE · MRS. THOMAS W. JENSEN, SALT LAKE CITY, UTAH

6 eggs, separated
1 cup sugar
1 cup sifted potato starch
2 teaspoons baking powder
¼ teaspoon salt
3 tablespoons water
1 teaspoon lemon extract

Beat egg yolks until they are a pale yellow color. Then very slowly add sugar, a little at a time, and beat well. Sift in starch, baking powder, and salt; add water. Beat thoroughly. Beat egg whites until stiff but not dry and fold into the mixture, with flavoring. Pour batter into a 9-inch tube pan. Bake at 300°F. for 1 hour. Yield: 1 9-inch tube cake. Serve plain, frosted, or with a tart lemon sauce.

EDITH WALLACE'S CRACKER TORTE · TULSA, OKLA.

¾ cup fine soda cracker
    crumbs
1 teaspoon baking powder
3 egg whites
1 teaspoon vanilla extract
⅛ teaspoon salt
1 cup sugar
¾ cup chopped nuts
½ cup heavy cream
1 tablespoon confectioners'
    sugar

Combine cracker crumbs and baking powder. Combine egg whites, vanilla and salt; beat until stiff. Add the 1 cup sugar gradually, beating thoroughly after each addition. Fold crumb mixture and nuts into beaten egg whites. Spread in buttered 9-inch pie pan. Bake at 350°F. for 25 minutes or until light golden brown. Cool. Whip cream and confectioners' sugar until stiff. Spread over top of torte. Cover with foil; chill for 8 hours or overnight. Yield: 6 portions.

MADER'S CHEESE TORTE · MADER'S RESTAURANT, MILWAUKEE, WIS.

CRUST:

3 cups graham-cracker
    crumbs
1 cup sugar
½ cup melted butter or other
    shortening
1 teaspoon cinnamon

Mix graham-cracker crumbs, sugar, butter and cinnamon together. Line a 19×11×2½-inch pan with crumb mixture, reserving about ½ cup for topping.

FILLING:

5 eggs, separated
2½ cups sugar
1½ teaspoons salt
2 cups milk
5 envelopes unflavored
    gelatin
¾ cup cold water
3 tablespoons lemon juice
2½ pounds bakers' cheese (fine
    dry cottage cheese)
1 quart heavy cream,
    whipped

Beat egg yolks slightly. Add sugar, salt and milk, and mix well. Cook in top of double boiler over boiling water until thickened, stirring frequently. Soften gelatin in water and lemon juice. Remove custard mixture from heat and add softened gelatin. Stir until dissolved. Cool about 20 minutes. Add bakers' cheese, which has been sieved, and stir until light and fluffy. Fold in whipped cream and egg whites, beaten stiff but not dry. Pour into crumb-lined pan. Top with remaining crumbs. Chill in refrigerator for several hours. Yield: 20 portions.

SASHA FLAMBÉ · TY LONG, NORWALK, CONN.
(A Quantity Recipe)

TORTE:

10 eggs, separated
2½ cups sifted confectioners'
    sugar
⅓ cup sifted flour
½ teaspoon baking powder
1 teaspoon vanilla extract
2 tablespoons rum
¾ pound walnuts, finely
    ground
½ pound pecans, finely ground
Apricot brandy

Beat egg yolks until very thick and lemon-colored. Gradually beat in sugar. Add flour, baking powder, vanilla and rum; mix well. Fold in stiffly beaten egg whites and ground nuts. Spread evenly in 2 greased and floured 15½×10½×1-inch pans. Bake at 300°F. for 30 to 35 minutes. Turn out of pans and cool. Cut each layer in half crosswise. Brush well with apricot brandy.

MOUSSE:

¾ cup lemon juice
2 teaspoons grated lemon
    rind
2 cups sugar
Dash of salt
½ cup water
6 eggs, separated
1 quart heavy cream,
    whipped
¾ cup cognac

Combine lemon juice, rind, 1¼ cups of the sugar, salt and ¼ cup of the water. Stir over heat until sugar dissolves; bring to boil and simmer for 20 minutes. Beat egg yolks until thick and lemon-colored. Add remaining water and lemon mixture gradually. Cook over hot water until thickened, stirring constantly. Cool. Mix whipped cream and lemon sauce thoroughly. Turn into 15½ × 10½ × 1-inch pan and freeze. When very firm, unmold and cut cross-wise into 3 sections. Alternate layers of torte and mousse (4 of torte and 3 of mousse). Refreeze for ½ hour. Cover sides and top with meringue made by beating egg whites until stiff but not dry, and gradually beat in remaining ¾ cup sugar. Bake at 500°F. for 3 to 5 minutes, until lightly browned. Pour heated cognac over Sasha and light. Yield: 30 portions.

NUT TORTE · MRS. ALVORD BAKER, FREEVILLE, N.Y.

3 eggs, separated
1 cup sugar
1 tablespoon flour
½ teaspoon baking powder
1 cup nut meats (black
    walnuts or hickory nuts)
1 cup heavy cream, whipped

Beat egg yolks thoroughly. Beat in sugar. Sift flour and baking powder. Fold into egg mixture. Stir in nuts. Fold in stiffly beaten egg whites. Pour into greased 9-inch pie pan. Bake at 325°F. for 40 minutes. Serve with whipped cream. Yield: 8 portions.

MOLLY WOODWARD'S PECAN TORTE · MRS. CARL WOODWARD, NEW ORLEANS, LA.

6 tablespoons butter or
    margarine
1½ cups brown sugar
4 eggs, separated
3½ cups ground pecans
1 teaspoon vanilla extract
2 cups whipped cream
½ cup ground pecans

Cream butter and sugar. Mix in well-beaten yolks of eggs. Stir in the 3½ cups ground pecans and vanilla. Fold in stiffly beaten whites. Turn into two 9-inch layer pans lightly oiled. Bake at 350°F. for about 25 minutes. Cool. Just before serving, layer with whipped cream, cover top with whipped cream and sprinkle with remaining pecans. Yield: 8 portions.

POLSKI TORTE · MRS. MICHAEL LASKOWSKI, MILWAUKEE, WIS.

6 eggs, separated
1 cup granulated sugar
1 cup chopped or ground
   walnuts or pecans
2 tablespoons graham-cracker
   crumbs
1 teaspoon vanilla extract
1 cup sweet butter
1 cup confectioners' sugar
4 squares unsweetened
   chocolate
Marmalade or strawberry jam
2 teaspoons sherry wine

Beat egg yolks. Gradually add the granulated sugar; beat until thick and lemon-colored. Add nuts and cracker crumbs, then vanilla. Fold into stiffly beaten egg whites. Turn into two greased and floured 9-inch layer pans. Bake at 350°F. about 30 minutes. Cool. Cream butter. Add confectioners' sugar and whip until fluffy. Melt chocolate in top of double boiler. Add to butter mixture, blending well. Spread one layer of the torte with marmalade or strawberry jam to a thickness of ¼ inch. Sprinkle with sherry. Place on top layer and cover top and sides of cake with butter icing. Decorate as you will with Easter flowers and salutations. Place in refrigerator and it will keep at least 2 weeks, or without refrigeration for 2 to 3 days.

SACHER TORTE · ANNA MARIA SCHWARZENBERG, BETHEL, VT.

1 6-ounce package semi-sweet
   chocolate pieces
¾ cup butter or margarine
¾ cup sugar
¼ teaspoon salt
6 eggs, separated
1½ cups sifted cake flour
Raspberry or apricot jam
¾ cup semi-sweet chocolate
   pieces
½ cup butter or margarine

Melt package of chocolate over hot water. Cream the ¾ cup butter. Gradually add sugar and continue creaming until fluffy. Add salt and melted chocolate, blending well. Add egg yolks one at a time, beating well after each addition. Beat egg whites until stiff but not dry and fold into chocolate-yolk mixture. Fold in flour. Turn into a greased and floured 9×3½-inch spring-form pan. Bake at 305°F. for 40 to 50 minutes. Cool; remove from pan. Spread raspberry jam over top and sides. Melt remaining chocolate over hot water. Add remaining butter and stir until blended. Cool until of spreading consistency. Spread over cake. Serve with whipped cream if desired.
   Yield: 8 portions.

SCHAUM TORTE · MRS. F. W. GLANTZ, FOX POINT, WIS.

8 egg whites, at room
   temperature
½ teaspoon cream of tartar
2 cups sugar
1 teaspoon vanilla extract
1 teaspoon vinegar

Beat egg whites until frothy. Add cream of tartar and beat until almost dry. Slowly add 1 cup of the sugar, vanilla and vinegar, beating in well. Slowly add remaining 1 cup of sugar, beating until well blended and the mixture is stiff. Turn into a well-greased 8-inch spring-form pan. Bake at 250°F. for 1¼ hours. The cake has a marshmallow texture but is tender and doesn't stick to the fork. Warning: never bake the Schaum Torte if the day is humid. As Mrs. Glantz says, "It will be a mess if you do." Serve topped with berries and heaped with whipped cream.

Yield: 1 8-inch torte.

MAPLE FROSTING · MRS. JAMES EGERTON, VERMONT

1¾ cups maple syrup
1 egg white, stiffly beaten
½ cup chopped walnuts

Cook maple syrup until a small amount of syrup forms a firm ball in cold water (248°)F. Pour in thin stream over beaten egg white and beat until thickened. Place over hot water and continue beating until mixture stands in peaks. Add nuts and spread immediately.

COCONUT DULCE · MRS. MARIO MARTINEZ, HIALEAH, FLA.

3 cups sugar
4 cups water
1 fresh coconut, grated

Boil sugar and water until of a thin-syrup consistency, about 10 minutes. Add coconut, grated, or if desired, run through food chopper using fine blade. Cook until coconut becomes transparent, about 25 minutes. Chill. Serve with cream cheese or use as a cake filling. Yield: 1 quart.

APRICOT PULP · LILLIAN JOHNSON, HOLLISTER, CALIF.

Make in quantity and keep on hand as a ready filling for cookies. Fold it into stiffly beaten egg white for a delicate fruited dessert, allowing ½ cup pulp to each egg white used. Delicious as a chocolate-cake filler, this made by folding pulp from 1 pound apricots into 1 cup whipped cream. Split 2 layers of chocolate cake to make 4 layers and sandwich together with the puréed fruit.

PULP: Take a pound of apricots, soak 2 hours with water to cover, then cook in the same water until mushy and thick. Press through a strainer, measure, and add half as much sugar as purée.

Cookies

BUTTERSCOTCH COOKIES · Salt Lake City, Utah

½ cup butter or margarine
1½ cups brown sugar, firmly
    packed
2 eggs
1 teaspoon vanilla extract
2½ cups sifted flour
1 teaspoon baking soda
½ teaspoon baking powder
½ teaspoon salt
1 cup sour cream
⅔ cup finely chopped nuts

BROWN-BUTTER ICING:
¼ cup butter (no substitute)
2 cups sifted confectioners'
    sugar
2 to 3 tablespoons boiling
    water
½ teaspoon vanilla extract

Cream butter and sugar thoroughly. Add eggs and beat until light and fluffy. Blend in vanilla. Add sifted dry ingredients alternately with sour cream. Stir in nuts. Drop by teaspoonfuls onto greased baking sheet. Bake at 350°F. for 10 minutes or until very lightly browned. Frost with Brown-Butter Icing. Yield: about 5 dozen cookies.

NOTE: To make sour cream, best results are had by using soured evaporated milk. To make this, measure 1 tablespoon vinegar into a 1-cup measure, then fill to 1 cup mark with undiluted evaporated milk.

Melt butter in small saucepan. Continue to cook until butter stops bubbling and is nut-brown in color. Pour over confectioners' sugar in mixing bowl and beat, adding enough boiling water to make of right consistency to spread. Stir in vanilla. Add a little more hot water if frosting becomes too stiff.

BUTTERSCOTCH COOKIES · MRS. FLORENCE RICHARDS, HARTFORD, IOWA

10 tablespoons butter or
    margarine (1 stick plus 2
    tablespoons)
1 cup brown sugar, firmly
    packed
¼ cup sorghum
2½ cups sifted flour
1 egg, well beaten
1 teaspoon baking soda
Dash of mace

Melt butter over low heat in heavy saucepan. Add sugar and sorghum. Stir until sugar has melted. Bring to a rolling boil, remove from heat. Cool. Add ½ of the flour, the beaten egg, and then the remaining flour sifted with soda and mace. Mix well to a soft dough. Drop from a spoon onto a greased baking sheet about 1 inch apart. Bake at 375°F. about 10 minutes or until light brown. When cool the cookies are crisp; if stored in a tight container with a cut apple they will absorb moisture to fairly melt in the mouth. Yield: 3 dozen cookies.

MRS. ENGLE'S CHRISTMAS COOKIES · MRS. ROBERT GEMMILL, ABILENE, KAN.

¾ cup butter or margarine
1 cup sugar
1 egg, separated
1 can (3 ounces) candied
    cherries, chopped
1 red candied pineapple ring,
    diced
1 green candied pineapple
    ring, diced
1 cup walnuts, chopped
1 cup sifted flour
⅛ teaspoon salt

Cream butter and sugar thoroughly. Add egg yolk and milk thoroughly. Blend in chopped fruits and nuts. Add flour and salt gradually and work in well. Beat egg white until stiff but not dry and fold into cooky mixture. Drop from teaspoon, 2 inches apart, on aluminum-foil-lined baking sheet. Bake at 350°F. for 15 minutes. Cool before removing from foil. Yield: 5 to 6 dozen cookies.

NOTE: If you cannot get the colored pineapple rings, soak uncolored candied pineapple in ½ cup hot water in which 4 to 5 drops of food coloring have been dissolved. After pineapple has soaked for 2 or 3 hours, drain on wire rack and let dry for 2 hours.

SOUR-CREAM COOKIES · MRS. WILLIAM D. MC MILLAN, ITHACA, N.Y.

1 cup shortening
2 cups sugar
2 large eggs
1 cup sour cream
½ teaspoon vanilla extract
4½ cups sifted flour
4 teaspoons baking powder
½ teaspoon baking soda
¼ teaspoon salt
½ cup coarsely chopped
    hickory nuts

Cream shortening and sugar thoroughly. Add eggs, one at a time, beating until well blended. Stir in sour cream and vanilla. Sift together flour, baking powder, baking soda and salt. Stir into creamed mixture. Drop batter by tablespoonfuls onto greased cooky sheet. Sprinkle with hickory nuts. Bake at 350°F. for 20 minutes. The cookies should be large, soft and fairly thick. Yield: 3½ dozen.

GREAT-GRANDMA JOAN HUNTTING'S SOFT MOLASSES COOKIES

JEANNETTE RATTRAY, EAST HAMPTON, N.Y.

1 cup molasses
½ cup shortening (originally lard)
½ cup sugar
½ cup undiluted evaporated milk, soured with 1 teaspoon vinegar
2 eggs
2 teaspoons ginger
1¾ teaspoon baking soda
Pinch of salt

3 cups sifted flour, about
3 tablespoons sugar

Mix the first eight ingredients together in order given. Stir in flour until the mixture is stiff enough to hold a spoon upright. Drop from teaspoon to greased, floured cooky sheet placing cookies 1½ inches apart. Flatten with wet cloth wrapped over bottom of tumbler. Sprinkle with sugar. Bake at 400°F. for 10 to 15 minutes. Yield: 4 dozen medium-sized cookies.

SPONGE COOKIES · MRS. MILDRED M. RUTHERFORD, SOUTH WOODSTOCK, VT.

3 eggs
¾ cup sugar
1½ cups sifted cake flour
2 teaspoons baking powder
¾ teaspoon lemon extract

Beat eggs until frothy. Add sugar, beating well. Sift flour with baking powder and slowly stir into mixture. Add extract. Drop batter, ½ teaspoon at a time, on a greased cooky sheet placing cookies about 3 inches apart. Bake at 400°F. about 5 minutes. Yield: approximately 5 dozen. Watch closely; these cookies scorch easily. A cooky quickly made and delicious with ice cream or to pass with a fruit compote.

ANISPLÄTZCHEN (SELF-FROSTING ANISE DROPS) · MRS. NORVIN H. VAUGHAN, CHICAGO, ILL.

3 eggs, room temperature
1 cup, plus 2 tablespoons, sugar
1¾ cups sifted flour
½ teaspoon baking powder
½ teaspoon salt
3 teaspoons anise seed or 1 teaspoon anise extract

Beat eggs in electric mixer at medium speed until fluffy. Then add sugar gradually, beating constantly. Continue to beat for 20 minutes more. Reduce speed of mixer and add flour which has been sifted with baking powder and salt. Beat another 3 minutes. Add anise. Drop by heaping teaspoonfuls onto a well-greased and floured baking sheet, swirling the dough to form a perfectly round cookie. Let stand for at least 8 hours to dry, preferably overnight. Bake at 325°F. for about 10 minutes or until cookies are a creamy golden color, not brown, on the bottom. Store in airtight tins. Yield: about 90 1½-inch cookies. NOTE: Don't try to make when humidity tops 50 per cent.

HOLIDAY "BILLY GOATS" · MRS. ROBERT GEMMILL, ABILENE, KAN.

1 cup butter or margarine
1½ cups sugar
3 egg yolks
1 teaspoon vanilla extract
2½ cups sifted flour
1 teaspoon baking soda
⅛ teaspoon salt
1 teaspoon cinnamon
¼ teaspoon cloves
2 tablespoons sour milk or
    buttermilk
1 pound walnuts, chopped
1 pound dates, chopped

Cream butter and sugar thoroughly. Add egg yolks and vanilla and beat until light and fluffy. Sift together flour, soda, salt, and spices. Add dry ingredients to egg mixture with sour milk. Bleed well by hand. Add walnuts and dates and blend thoroughly. Drop by teaspoonfuls 1 inch apart on greased baking sheet. Bake at 325°F. for 20 minutes. Yield: 7 to 8 dozen cookies

SCHOKOLADEPLÄTZCHEN (LITTLE CHOCOLATE DROPS)

MRS. NORVIN H. VAUGHAN, CHICAGO, ILL.

3 egg whites
⅛ teaspoon salt
½ cup sugar
¾ cup unblanched almonds,
    grated (not ground)
1 bar (4 ounces) German
    sweet chocolate, grated
    (not ground)

Beat egg whites with salt to firm moist peaks. Add sugar slowly, beating constantly. After adding last of sugar, beat another 2 minutes. Fold in grated almonds and chocolate. Drop by teaspoonfuls onto a well-greased baking sheet. Bake at 275°F. for 35 to 40 minutes, or until dry, so they can be easily removed from sheet. Yield: about 50 cookies.

DROP GINGERSNAPS · MRS. JACOB ROHWER, SPOKANE COUNTY, WASH.

1¼ cups sugar
½ cup shortening
2 eggs
1 teaspoon vanilla extract
1¼ teaspoons baking soda
½ teaspoon salt
2 teaspoons ginger
1 teaspoon cinnamon
¾ cup sorghum
3 cups sifted flour

Cream sugar and shortening thoroughly. Add egg, mixing well. Add vanilla. Combine soda, salt, spices, and sorghum. Blend into creamed mixture. Add flour, stirring well. Drop by teaspoonfuls onto ungreased baking sheet. Bake at 400°F. for 10 to 15 minutes.

Yield: 100 gingersnaps, about 2½ inches in diameter.

SESAME SEED WAFERS · CHARLESTON, S.C.

1 cup sifted flour
½ teaspoon baking powder
¼ teaspoon salt
¾ cup butter or margarine
2 cups brown sugar, firmly
    packed
2 eggs, beaten
1 teaspoon vanilla extract
¾ cup sesame seeds, toasted

Sift together flour, baking powder and salt. Cream butter and sugar until light and fluffy. Beat in eggs. Stir in flour mixture until well blended. Add vanilla and sesame seeds. Drop by teaspoonfuls onto a well-greased baking sheet, allowing 2 inches between each cooky (bake only a few at a time). Bake at 325°F. for 8 to 10 minutes, or until lightly browned. Allow to cool a minute before removing from baking sheet, then remove quickly and gently with a spatula. If cookies get too crisp for easy removal, return them to the oven for a minute or so to soften. Yield: 8 to 10 dozen wafers.

NOTE: To toast sesame seeds, place in a heavy iron skillet over medium heat. Stir seeds constantly until lightly toasted.

PUCHITAS (SHORTBREAD WAFERS) · ANA BEGUE DE PACKMAN, CALIFORNIA

½ cup water
Juice of 1 lime or ½ lemon
1 teaspoon anise seed
1 tablespoon sugar
3 cups sifted flour
1 cup sugar
1 teaspoon salt
1 teaspoon baking powder
¾ cup shortening
1 egg, well beaten

Boil water, juice and anise seed. Add the 1 table-spoon sugar; cool. Sift flour, sugar, salt and baking powder into bowl. Cut in shortening finely. Stir in egg and cooled liquid; mix well. Chill, if desired. Form a dough into marble-size balls or drop by tablespoon-fuls onto a greased baking sheet; flatten with fork or mold. Bake at 375°F. for 10 to 12 minutes.

Yield: about 4 dozen cookies.

MRS. RAFERTY'S OATMEAL MACAROONS · MRS. JAMES RAFERTY, MIAMI, FLA.

1¼ cups sugar
⅓ cup shortening
1 egg
1½ teaspoons vanilla
⅔ cup flour
5 tablespoons cocoa
2 teaspoons baking powder
½ teaspoon salt
⅓ cup milk
2½ cups quick-cooking oats

Cream sugar and shortening; add egg and cream again. Blend in vanilla. Sift dry ingredients and add to shortening mixture alternately with milk; mix well. Stir in oats. Drop by tablespoonfuls onto a greased baking sheet. Bake at 350°F. for 12 to 15 minutes. Yield: 3½ dozen cookies.

BROWN CHRISTMAS COOKIES · MRS. NORVIN H. VAUGHAN, CHICAGO, ILL.

1 cup butter or margarine
1 cup dark brown sugar
1 cup sorghum or mild-
    flavored molasses
4½ cups sifted flour
1 tablespoon ginger
2 teaspoons baking soda
½ teaspoon salt
Colored sugar

Cream shortening and sugar thoroughly. Stir in sorghum. Add sifted dry ingredients and mix well. Roll out on floured surface to about ⅛-inch thickness. Cut with fancy cookie cutters. Decorate with colored sugar. Place on ungreased baking sheet. Bake at 350°F. for 6 to 8 minutes. Yield: about 12 dozen 2½-inch cookies.

NOTE: These are a cross between the Swedish pepparkakor and our American gingersnap, and keep for a fairly long time in tin cans.

MRS. STEVENSON'S FILLED DATE COOKIES · MRS. ROY STEVENSON, SUMMIT, N.J.

FILLING:

1 large or 2 small packages
    pitted dates, cut fine
1 cup sugar
1 cup water
1 teaspoon grated orange rind
¾ cup finely chopped walnuts
    or pecans

Combine dates, sugar, and water. Boil for 2 minutes, stirring constantly. Beat until smooth. Add orange rind and nuts. Cool.

DOUGH:

1 cup butter or margarine
1½ cups dark brown sugar,
    firmly packed
2 eggs
1½ cups quick oats
3¾ cups sifted flour
1 teaspoon baking soda
1 teaspoon cream of tartar
½ teaspoon salt
1 teaspoon vanilla extract

Cream butter and sugar thoroughly. Add eggs, one at a time, and beat until light and fluffy. Add oats. Beat in sifted dry ingredients and vanilla. Chill dough several hours. Roll out a quarter of dough at a time on well-floured surface, to ⅛-inch thickness. Cut with a 2½-inch round or fluted cutter. Spread 1 teaspoon of the date filling on half of each cookie and fold over. (If filling is too thick to spread, add a little water.) Sealing of the edges is not necessary. Place on ungreased baking sheet. Bake at 375°F. for 8 to 10 minutes or until delicate tan.

Yield: 7 dozen cookies.

CARD GINGERBREAD · MRS. MARY MC BAY, PROVIDENCE, R.I.

⅓ cup butter or margarine
⅓ cup brown sugar
1 egg, slightly beaten
½ cup dark molasses
2½ cups sifted flour
½ teaspoon baking soda
½ tablespoon ginger (scant)
¼ teaspoon cinnamon
¼ teaspoon salt

Cream butter and sugar. Mix in beaten egg; stir in molasses. Sift flour with dry ingredients and add to batter. Roll out on floured surface to ¼-inch thickness. Cut in oblongs—playing card shape and size, 3 by 4 inches. Score cards with knife in ½-inch parallel lines. Place on greased baking sheet. Bake at 325°F. for 10 minutes. Yield: 2 dozen.

18TH CENTURY GINGER COOKIES · WILLIAMSBURG, VA.

1 cup butter or margarine
4 tablespoons ginger
1 tablespoon nutmeg
1 tablespoon cinnamon
Dash of salt
1 cup sugar
2 cups dark molasses
½ pint light cream or
    evaporated milk
8 to 9 cups sifted flour

Blend butter, spices and salt. Add sugar and cream thoroughly. Warm together molasses and cream; add gradually to butter mixture, mixing well. Stir in flour until a moderately stiff dough is formed. Roll out on floured surface to ⅛-inch thickness. Cut with cookie cutter. Place on baking sheet. Bake at 375°F. for 10 to 12 minutes.

Yield: about 8 dozen 3-inch cookies.

NOTE: This recipe makes a very hard cookie.

HAZELNUT RINGS · MRS. HORACE F. TANGEMAN, CINCINNATI, OHIO

½ pound butter or margarine
1½ cups sugar
½ pound hazelnuts, ground
2 cups sifted flour
½ teaspoon salt
2 egg whites, stiffly beaten

Cream butter with 1 cup of the sugar and hazelnuts. Sift flour and salt. Add slowly, mixing well. Pat out a small piece of dough on lightly floured surface; cover with waxed paper and roll out to ½-inch thickness. Cut with a doughnut cutter. Place rings and centers on greased and floured baking sheet. Using a pastry tube or a teaspoon, place a ribbon of meringue around the cookie ring, just wide enough so that an edge of the cookie shows on each side of the ribbon. To make meringue, fold remaining half cup of sugar into the stiffly beaten egg whites. Bake at 300°F. for 12 to 15 minutes. Yield: 5 dozen rings, plus 5 dozen centers.

JOE FROGGERS · STURBRIDGE VILLAGE, MASS.

Sift 7 cups sifted flour with 1 tablespoon salt, 1 tablespoon ginger, 1 teaspoon cloves, 1 teaspoon nutmeg, ½ teaspoon allspice. Combine ¾ cup water with ¼ cup rum. Combine 2 teaspoons baking soda with 2 cups dark molasses. Cream 1 cup shortening and 2 cups sugar. Add sifted dry ingredients, water mixture and molasses mixture in 2 sections to creamed mixture, blending well after each addition. Chill dough, preferably overnight. Roll to ¼-inch thickness on floured board. Cut with 4-inch cutter. Place on greased baking sheet. Bake at 375°F. for 10 to 12 minutes. Let stand on sheet a few minutes before removing to prevent breaking. Store in a covered cookie jar.

Yield: 2 dozen 5-inch cookies.

JUMBLES · AVERY ISLAND, LA.

½ pound butter or margarine
2 cups sugar
4 eggs, well-beaten
2 teaspoons rose water
1 teaspoon lemon or vanilla
    extract
5 cups sifted flour
1 teaspoon nutmeg
Sugar for sprinkling

Cream butter and sugar until fluffy. Add eggs; mix well. Add rose water and lemon extract. Mix in flour and nutmeg. Wrap in waxed paper and store in refrigerator for several hours. Take out just enough at a time to roll easily. (The secret of very thin jumbles lies in the dough being kept well chilled.) Roll to ⅛-inch thickness on lightly floured surface. Cut with a 2½-inch cooky cutter. Place on greased baking sheet. Bake at 375°F. for 5 to 8 minutes. After baking, sprinkle with granulated sugar.

Yield: about 12 dozen cookies.

GRANDMOTHER TANGEMAN'S MERINGUE COOKIES · MRS. HORACE F. TANGEMAN, CINCINNATI, OHIO

1 cup butter or margarine
2 cups sugar
6 eggs, separated
2 cups sifted flour
1 teaspoon baking powder
2 cups blanched almonds,
    thinly sliced
¼ cup currant jelly

Cream butter with ½ cup of the sugar. Beat in egg yolks. Sift flour with baking powder and add, stirring in a little at a time. Cover bowl of dough and place in refrigerator for 1 hour or until firm enough to roll out (very important). Beat egg whites until stiff but not dry, fold in remaining 1½ cups sugar. Take a small piece of dough from the refrigerator—one piece at a time as this dough is hard to handle when soft. Turn onto floured pastry cloth, and we mean a pastry cloth, using a rolling pin covered with stockinette. Roll to the thinness of pie crust. Cut in 2-inch diamonds. To each diamond add 2 teaspoons meringue. Sprinkle with almonds. Make a slight indentation in the center. Bake at 425°F. for 5 to 7 minutes. Reduce heat to 300°F. and bake 5 to 10 minutes to set meringue. Cool. Place a dab of jelly in indented center of each cookie. Yield: about 5 dozen cookies.

"MODEL TEAS" · MRS. HENRY FORD, DEARBORN, MICH.

½ cup sifted cake flour
¼ cup sifted all-purpose flour
2 teaspoons baking powder
½ teaspoon salt
¾ cup wheat germ
2 tablespoons very firm butter
   or margarine
¼ cup ice water

Sift flours, baking powder and salt into bowl. Mix in ½ cup of the wheat germ. Cut in butter finely. Add water, blending well, without too much handling. Turn onto a floured surface and shape into a ball. Roll lightly to about ½ inch thickness. Sprinkle with remaining ¼ cup wheat germ and continue to roll until wafer thin, keeping wheat germ spread evenly over top. Cut with a 2-inch cutter. Place wafers on ungreased baking sheet. Bake at 325°F. for 12 to 15 minutes or until softness has disappeared. Yield: about 30 dollar-sized wafers.

SUGAR COOKIES · MRS. EARNEST BLAZER, YUBA CITY, CALIF.

1 cup shortening
1¼ cups sugar
3 eggs
1 tablespoon vanilla extract
3 cups sifted flour
3 teaspoons baking powder
1¼ teaspoons salt
Sugar

Cream shortening and sugar. Beat in eggs and vanilla. Mix in sifted dry ingredients. Roll dough on floured surface to ⅛-inch thickness. Cut in fancy shapes to appeal to the children. Place on ungreased baking sheet. Sprinkle with sugar. Bake at 375°F. for 8 to 10 minutes.
Yield: about 5 dozen 2½-inch cookies.

LEAF SUGAR COOKIES · MRS. MARY MC BAY, PROVIDENCE, R.I.

1 cup sugar
1 cup butter or margarine
1 egg
3 cups sifted flour
1 teaspoon baking soda
¼ teaspoon nutmeg

Cream sugar and butter. Beat in egg. Sift flour, soda and nutmeg and add to creamed mixture. Mix well. Roll out on floured surface to ⅛-inch thickness. Lay over an oak leaf pattern, cut from cardboard, and with a sharp pointed knife, outline edges. Sprinkle with sugar. With spatula, carefully lift cookies from board to greased baking sheet. Bake at 425°F. for 8 minutes.
Yield: 3 dozen.

MONDCHENS (LITTLE CRESCENT MOONS) · MRS. NORVIN H. VAUGHN, CHICAGO, ILL.

1 cup butter or margarine
  (or half and half)
1¼ cups sugar
2 teaspoons grated lemon rind
¼ teaspoon salt
1⅓ cups sifted flour
1½ cups unblanched almonds,
  grated (not ground)
1 teaspoon vanilla extract

Cream butter and sugar thoroughly. Add remaining ingredients, mixing thoroughly. Chill dough about 1 hour. Roll out on well-floured surface to about ⅛-inch thickness. Cut with crescent cutter. Place on ungreased baking sheets. Bake at 375°F. for 8 to 10 minutes, or until light tan colored. Ice as soon as removed from oven.

Yield: about 7 dozen medium crescents.

ICING:
1½ cups confectioners' sugar
2 tablespoons boiling water
1 teaspoon vanilla extract

Combine sugar, water, and vanilla. Spread thinly on cookie, thinning out if necessary with more boiling water.

FRENCH NUT STICKS · MRS. ROY BRADEN, DALLAS, TEX.

¾ cup butter or margarine
2 cups sugar
2 eggs
3 cups sifted cake flour
1 teaspoon vanilla extract
Apricot jam
2 egg whites
Pinch of salt
1 tablespoon flour
1 cup chopped pecans

Cream together butter and 1 cup of the sugar until light and fluffy. Beat in eggs until blended. Gradually add cake flour, beating until smooth. Stir in vanilla. Roll out ¼-inch thick on greased baking sheet. Spread with a thin layer of apricot jam. Bake at 350°F. for 6 minutes. Beat egg whites with salt until frothy. Gradually beat in remaining sugar combined with 1 tablespoon flour. Fold in pecans. Spread over the cooky dough. Chill. Cut into sticks, 2 by ½ inches. Place on baking sheet. Bake at 375°F. for about 15 minutes. Yield: 3 dozen cookies.

COFFEE FINGERS · MRS. GRAVANDER, MILL VALLEY, CALIF.

1 cup butter or margarine
⅓ cup sugar
½ teaspoon almond extract
2½ cups sifted flour
1 egg, beaten
15 blanched almonds,
  chopped
2 tablespoons sugar

Cream butter and ⅓ cup sugar until fluffy. Add extract and flour. Mix thoroughly. Chill. Roll dough to ½-inch thickness. Cut into 2 × ½-inch strips. Brush with egg; sprinkle with mixture of almonds and sugar. Place on ungreased baking sheet. Bake at 350°F. for 8 to 10 minutes or until golden yellow.

Yield: 55 cookies.

RASPBERRY TEAS · MRS. NORVIN H. VAUGHAN, CHICAGO, ILL.

1 cup butter or margarine
½ cup granulated sugar
½ cup confectioners' sugar
⅛ teaspoon salt
1 egg yolk
1 teaspoon vanilla extract
2¼ cups sifted flour
½ cup nuts, pecans or walnuts, finely chopped
½ cup raspberry jam

Cream butter, sugars and salt thoroughly. Add egg yolk and vanilla and mix well. Blend in flour. Chill ⅔ of the dough. Form the remainder into 48 balls. Roll in nuts. Roll out chilled dough on floured surface to ⅛-inch thickness. Cut with a heart, round or fluted cutter into 48 cookies. Place on an ungreased baking sheet. Place ¼ teaspoon of raspberry jam in the center of each cooky. Place ball on top of the jam; press down lightly. Indent the center of each ball and place another ¼ teaspoon jam in each depression. Bake at 350°F. for 12 to 15 minutes, or until pale cream-colored. Yield: 48 2½-inch cookies.

ZIMTSTERNE (CINNAMON STARS) · MRS. NORVIN H. VAUGHAN, CHICAGO, ILL.

1 cup sugar
1 teaspoon cinnamon
1 teaspoon grated lemon rind
3 egg whites
¼ teaspoon salt
1½ cups unblanched almonds, grated (not ground)

Combine sugar, cinnamon and lemon rind. Beat egg whites and salt to stiff, moist peaks. Add sugar mixture gradually, beating constantly. Continue to beat until thick and glossy and holds shape. Set aside ½ cup for the frosting. Stir in grated almonds. Chill well. Roll out in small amounts (rather difficult to roll) to ⅛-inch thickness, using a generous amount of a mixture of equal parts of sugar and flour, or confectioners' sugar on board or cloth. Cut out with a star cutter. Spread small amounts of reserved frosting mixture in center of each cookie. Place on well greased baking sheet. Bake at 300°F. for 20 to 25 minutes or until dry. Yield: about 80 1¾-inch cookies.

ZIMTSTERNE (CINNAMON STARS) · MRS. HORACE F. TANGEMAN, CINCINNATI, OHIO

3 egg whites
1 cup confectioners' sugar
½ pound unblanched almonds, ground*
1 tablespoon cinnamon
¼ teaspoon salt
¼ cup flour
¼ cup granulated sugar
2 egg yolks, beaten
2 teaspoons water

Beat egg whites until stiff. Add the confectioners' sugar gradually, beating thoroughly after each addition. Combine almonds, cinnamon and salt; fold into egg whites. Mix flour and granulated sugar together and sprinkle on board or waxed paper. Place 1 tablespoon of dough at a time on sugared surface. With spatula, pat to ¼-inch thickness. Cut with floured, star-shaped cutter. Place on lightly buttered and floured baking sheet. Brush with combined egg yolk and water. Bake at 350°F. for 15 minutes. Remove from baking sheet immediately. Yield: about 2½ dozen 3-inch cinnamon stars.

NOTE: Instead of egg yolk glaze, cookies may be brushed with cinnamon syrup. To make syrup, boil ½ cup water, ¼ cup sugar, and 1 tablespoon cinnamon until slightly thickened. Brush on cookies after 10 minutes of baking; then bake 5 minutes longer.

*The almonds should be ground one day in advance to allow time to dry.

BUTTER BALLS · MRS. J. V. GUERIN, ARIZONA

½ cup butter or margarine
¼ cup sugar
1 egg yolk
½ teaspoon vanilla extract
1 tablespoon lemon juice
1 cup sifted flour
1 egg white, slightly beaten
½ cup ground or finely
    chopped filberts
Candied cherries

Cream butter and sugar thoroughly. Add egg yolk, vanilla and lemon juice and blend well. Stir flour into creamed mixture. Cover bowl and store in refrigerator 3 to 4 days. When ready to bake, roll into tiny balls using ¼ teaspoon dough for each. Dip into egg white and roll in filberts. Place 2 inches apart on ungreased baking sheet. Press ¼ cherry into each cookie. Bake at 325°F. for 10 to 12 minutes. Place in a tightly covered jar as soon as cooled. Yield: 16 dozen cookies.

MRS. THORNTON SCOTT'S COCOONS · ABILENE, KANSAS

½ cup butter or margarine
⅔ cup confectioners' sugar
1 teaspoon vanilla extract
1 cup sifted flour
1 cup finely chopped
    walnuts

Cream butter and ⅓ cup of the sugar until light and fluffy. Add vanilla. Blend flour in gradually. Add chopped nuts. Pinch off small quantities and shape into 1½-inch cocoons with palms of hands. Place 1 inch apart on greased baking sheet. Bake at 350°F. for 12 minutes, or just long enough for the cocoons to "dry out." While still warm, roll in remaining ⅓ cup confectioners' sugar. Yield: 3 dozen 1½-inch cocoons.

FRENCH-SWISS COOKIES · MELANIE DE BEN, PASS CHRISTIAN, MISS.

½ pound butter or margarine
1 cup sugar
1 egg, separated
2 cups sifted flour
2½ teaspoons cinnamon
Colored candies or ground
    nuts

Cream butter and sugar thoroughly. Beat in egg yolk. Add flour and cinnamon and blend well. Roll pieces of the dough between buttered palms into 1-inch balls. Place balls on ungreased baking sheet about 2 inches apart. Press out paper thin with a floured spatula. Paint with egg white and sprinkle with colored candies or ground nuts. Bake at 350°F. for 10 to 12 minutes. Yield: 6 dozen 2½-inch cookies.

SWEDISH CHRISTMAS COOKIES · MRS. HARRY LEONARD, JR., ABILENE, KAN.

½ cup butter or margarine
¼ cup sugar
1 egg, separated
2 teaspoons vanilla extract
1 tablespoon grated orange
    rind
1 tablespoon lemon juice
⅛ teaspoon salt
1 cup sifted cake flour
1 cup finely chopped walnuts
25 candied cherries, halved
    (both red and green)

Cream butter and sugar until light and fluffy. Add egg yolk and beat well. Add vanilla, orange rind, lemon juice, and salt; blend thoroughly. Add cake flour gradually, mixing in well. Chill dough for about 2 hours. Shape into small balls, dip into slightly beaten egg white and roll in chopped nuts. Place a half a cherry on top of each cookie (use both red and green cherries for holiday effect) and arrange 1 inch apart on greased baking sheet. Bake at 325°F. about 20 minutes.

Yield: 50 small cookies.

SWEDISH OATMEAL COOKIES · MRS. CHARLES C. HOWELL, JR., JACKSONVILLE, FLA.

⅔ cup butter or margarine
3 cups rolled oatmeal
½ cup sugar
1 egg, beaten
1 teaspoon almond extract

Reserve 1 tablespoon of the butter to grease the cooky sheet. Using fingers, knead together in a solid mass remaining butter, oatmeal and sugar. Add egg and almond extract. Form into tiny balls the size of marbles, and place on buttered cooky sheet. Press down each cooky with tines of fork. Bake at 325°F. for 10 to 15 minutes or until golden brown. Yield: 2½ dozen cookies.

NOTE: Our kitchen changed this recipe, adding the egg and the extract. Mrs. Howell used only butter, oatmeal and sugar, in slightly different proportions. The cookies were delicious but too crumbly to store.

CAROL'S SAND TARTS · CAROL JEAN ACKLEY, CLAREMONT, CALIF.

1 cup plus 1 tablespoon
    butter or margarine
¼ cup confectioners' sugar
1½ to 2 cups sifted flour
⅛ teaspoon salt
1 tablespoon plus 1 teaspoon
    cold water
½ teaspoon vanilla extract
Walnut halves

Cream butter and sugar. Combine ½ cup of the flour and salt and blend into creamed mixture. Add water and vanilla and work in remaining flour. Chill dough. Pinch off small amounts of dough and roll into 1½-inch balls. Top each with walnut. Place on ungreased baking sheet. Bake at 375°F. for 10 minutes. Reduce heat to 325°F. and continue baking for 15 to 20 minutes. Cool before frosting. Run a confectioners'-sugar icing through a pastry tube making a thread-like line around and around the top of the cookie. Sprinkle with confetti-colored sugar or other candy decorations. Yield: about 30 cookies.

Icing: Combine ¾ cup confectioners' sugar, 2 tablespoons hot milk, and ¼ teaspoon vanilla extract. Mix until smooth.

SAND TARTS · MRS. J. V. GUERIN, ARIZONA

1 cup butter or margarine
3 tablespoons confectioners'
   sugar
1 cup ground almonds
2½ cups sifted cake flour
1 teaspoon vanilla extract

Mix ingredients together well, using a wooden spoon. Pinch off small pieces of dough and roll to thickness of a pencil and form into crescents. Place on ungreased baking sheet. Bake at 325°F. for 15 to 18 minutes or until cookies are a very delicate brown. Roll in confectioners' sugar while still warm.

Yield: about 40 cookies.

ZUCCARINI · MRS. J. V. GUERIN, ARIZONA

¼ pound butter or margarine
⅓ cup peanut oil
¼ cup sugar
6 eggs, beaten
1 teaspoon lemon or almond
   extract
1 teaspoon anise extract
5 cups sifted cake flour
4 tablespoons baking powder
Pinch of salt
Anise seed (optional)

Blend butter and oil together. Add sugar and cream thoroughly. Beat in eggs and extracts. Sift flour, baking powder and salt. Mix into batter. Pinch off small pieces of dough using 1 tablespoon of dough for each sweet. Roll on a floured board to thickness of pencil, then form into small knots. Place on ungreased baking sheet. Sprinkle with anise seeds if desired. Bake at 400°F. for 12 to 15 minutes. Coat with frosting. Yield: 5 dozen cookies.

FROSTING:
1½ cups sugar
½ cup water
1 teaspoon anise extract

Combine ingredients in saucepan and boil until mixture forms a soft ball in cold water (234°F.). Drop baked cookies into this syrup and stir well until coated. The frosting will dry on the sweets to look like a sugar frosting.

NOTE: Mrs. Guerin places cookies in a large container, a turkey roaster or any big pan, pours the frosting over and shakes sweets around. Do not overstir or they'll break.

RUSSIAN TEA COOKIES · MRS. J. V. GUERIN, ARIZONA

1 cup butter or margarine
½ cup confectioners' sugar
1 teaspoon vanilla extract
2¼ cups sifted flour
¼ teaspoon salt
¾ cup finely chopped nuts

Cream butter and sugar thoroughly. Add vanilla extract, flour, salt, and nuts; mix well. Form into dime-size balls, or flatten if preferred. Place on ungreased baking sheet. Bake at 400°F. for 12 to 15 minutes. While still warm, roll in confectioners' sugar. After cooling roll again in confectioners' sugar.
Yield: 9 dozen cookies.

VANILLA KIPFEL · MRS. HORACE F. TANGEMAN, CINCINNATI, OHIO

1 cup butter or margarine
½ cup sugar
½ teaspoon salt
2 cups sifted flour
2 cups ground almonds
    (no need to blanch)
1 cup confectioners' sugar
⅛ teaspoon vanilla bean pulp

Cream butter, sugar, and salt thoroughly. Add flour, a little at a time, stirring in thoroughly. Add almonds. Take 1 teaspoonful of mixture at a time, roll in palm of hand to form crescent. Lay in rows on a greased baking sheet. Bake at 400°F. for 2 minutes. Reduce temperature to 300°F. and bake about 10 minutes longer, or until cookies are a pale yellow color. Cool slightly. Roll in sugar mixed with vanilla bean pulp.
Yield: 6 dozen crescents.

LADYFINGERS · JACOB YACKLE, PHILADELPHIA, PENNA.

7 eggs, separated
Pinch of salt
1½ cups confectioners' sugar
½ teaspoon vanilla extract
2¼ cups sifted cake flour
Sifted confectioners' sugar

Beat egg whites with salt until frothy. Gradually beat in ½ cup of the sugar. Beat egg yolks until thick and lemon-colored. Gradually whip in remaining cup of sugar and add vanilla. Gently fold sweetened yolks into meringue. Gradually fold in flour. Press mixture through pastry bag (using plain tube) to cooky sheet lined with brown paper. Make fingers to measure 4×¾-inches. Dust with confectioners' sugar. Lift paper by 2 corners on one side and shake off the surplus sugar. Bake at 350°F. for 10 to 12 minutes, or until fingers are pale gold. Immediately remove paper with ladyfingers from sheet to prevent drying. When cool, turn upside down on table; wet back of paper. Remove fingers, sandwiching together in pairs. Arrange in rows and lightly dust with sifted confectioners' sugar. Yield: 52 ladyfingers.

GINGER COOKIES · MRS. GRAVANDER, MILL VALLEY, CALIF.

1¼ cups butter or margarine
1 cup sugar
1 cup dark corn syrup
1 tablespoon ginger
2 teaspoons cinnamon
2 teaspoons cloves
1 teaspoon crushed carda-
    mom seed
1 cup blanched almonds,
    coarsely chopped
2 tablespoons cognac or
    brandy
5 to 6 cups sifted flour

Cream butter and sugar until fluffy. Blend in syrup and spices. Combine nuts and cognac. Mix with flour on a rolling surface. Add creamed mixture, blend well. Divide dough into 2 or 4 rolls, about 2 inches in diameter. Wrap rolls in waxed paper. Place in refrigerator overnight. Slice very thin. Place on greased baking sheet. Bake at 350°F. for 6 to 8 minutes. Use the dough as needed; it keeps for weeks in the refrigerator. Yield: about 14 dozen cookies.

PETTICOAT TAILS · WILLIAMSBURG, VA.

1 pound butter or margarine
1 cup confectioners' sugar
1 teaspoon vanilla extract
5 cups sifted flour

Cream butter until very soft. Add sugar and beat well. Blend in vanilla. Add flour gradually, beating until smooth after each addition. Form dough into four rolls, 1 inch in diameter. Wrap in wax paper. Chill until firm. Cut into ⅛-inch slices. Place on ungreased baking sheets. Bake at 350°F. for 7 minutes, or until light brown. Cool before removing from pan. Yield: about 23 dozen cookies.

NOTE: This is a primitive recipe for icebox cookies. And we had always thought this was an idea that came in with modern refrigeration!

ALMOND TARTS · MRS. GRAVANDER, MILL VALLEY, CALIF.

⅔ cup butter or margarine
⅓ cup sugar
1 egg yolk
¼ teaspoon almond extract
½ cup blanched almonds,
    grated
1½ cups sifted flour

Cream butter and sugar until fluffy. Add egg yolk, extract, almonds and flour; mix thoroughly. Chill. Butter small (about 2-inch) fluted tins. Using about 1 tablespoon of dough, press in pan with floured thumbs. Bake at 325°F. about 10 minutes or until light brown. Cool in tins, then unmold. Serve plain or filled with jam and whipped cream. Yield: about 30 cookies.

TORCETTI (ITALIAN PASTRY) · MRS. J. V. GUERIN, ARIZONA

1 pound butter or margarine
1 pound vegetable shortening
10 cups sifted flour
1 cup warm milk
1 tablespoon sugar
1 tablespoon vanilla extract
2 packages active dry yeast
4 eggs, beaten
2 pounds confectioners' sugar

Cut butter and shortening into flour until mixture is as fine as corn-meal. Combine milk, sugar and vanilla extract; stir in yeast until dissolved. Add yeast liquid to flour mixture. Beat in eggs. Add more flour if necessary. Knead slightly. Let rise until double in bulk, about 1 hour. Cover breadboard with confectioners' sugar. Break off small pieces of dough, roll in sugar and shape in figure eights or crescents. Place on greased baking sheet. Bake at 375°F. for 12 to 15 minutes.

Yield: about 12 dozen cookies.

MERINGUES · FLORIDA

3 egg whites
¼ teaspoon cream of tartar
⅛ teaspoon salt
¾ cup sugar

Beat egg whites until foamy; add cream of tartar and salt; beat until stiff but not dry. Add sugar gradually, beating until very stiff. Cover baking sheet with heavy brown paper. Pile meringue into 6 mounds, about 3 inches in diameter. Make a 2-inch depression in center of each. Bake at 275°F. for 1 hour. Cool shells, fill with Lime Filling. (For a soft meringue shell chill 6 to 24 hours.)

Yield: 6 portions.

LIME FILLING:
3 egg yolks
¼ cup sugar
4 tablespoons lime juice
1½ teaspoons grated lime rind
1 cup heavy cream, whipped
Green food coloring

Beat egg yolks; add sugar and lime juice. Cook over boiling water, stirring constantly, until thick. Add lime rind. Remove from heat; chill. Fold into whipped cream. Tint filling with a small amount of green food coloring.

HOLIDAY MERINGUES · MRS. GRAVANDER, MILL VALLEY, CALIF.

3 cups sugar
12 egg whites
Dash of salt
1½ cups finely chopped
    walnuts

Mix in heatproof bowl the sugar, egg whites and salt. Place over kettle of boiling water and beat with rotary beater until mixture holds its shape. Fold in nuts. Butter baking sheet and dust lightly with flour. Drop mixture onto sheet using 2 teaspoons, one to dip, one to push the dip. Bake at 250°F. for 1 hour, or until meringues are thoroughly dry.

Yield: about 6 dozen 2-inch meringues.

AUNT IDA'S PRALINE KISSES · MRS. PAUL KUECHLE, MILWAUKEE, WIS.

3 egg whites from medium
   eggs
Pinch of salt
½ cup granulated sugar
½ cup light brown sugar,
   firmly packed
1 cup chopped filberts
   (hazelnuts)

Beat egg whites with salt to soft moist peaks. Add sugars slowly, beating constantly. Beat until thick and glossy and mixture holds shape. Fold in nuts. Drop by heaping teaspoonfuls onto lightly greased baking sheets. Bake at 275°F. for 35 to 40 minutes or until dry. Remove from sheets at once; store in airtight tins. Yield: 50 to 60 kisses.

NOTE: Don't try to make when humidity tops 50 per cent.

WHEAT RANCH BROWNIES · MRS. JACOB ROHWER, SPOKANE COUNTY, WASH.

4 squares unsweetened
   chocolate
¾ cup butter or margarine,
   melted
6 eggs
3 cups sugar
2 cups sifted flour
½ teaspoon salt
⅓ cup nuts, chopped
2 teaspoons vanilla extract

Melt chocolate in butter. Beat eggs; add sugar. Sift flour with salt; add to egg mixture. Add melted butter-chocolate mixture, nuts, and vanilla. Turn into 2 oiled 14 × 10-inch pans. Bake at 450°F. for 12 to 15 minutes. Just before the brownies are done, run under broiler to give a rich brown. Cut into squares while warm. Yield: 48 brownies.

Pickles, Relishes and Jams

NINE-DAY PICKLES · MRS. ADA NELLIS, PALATINE BRIDGE, N.Y.

3 quarts water
1 cup non-iodized salt
7 pounds cucumbers
1 cup cider vinegar
2 quarts water
5 grape leaves
¼ teaspoon alum
6 cups vinegar
3 pounds sugar
⅓ cup allspice
¼ cup cassia buds

Combine the 3 quarts water and salt. Pour over washed cucumbers and let stand 3 days. Drain; cover with water for 3 days, changing water daily. Wipe cucumbers dry and cut into large-size pieces. Combine the 1 cup vinegar with the 2 quarts water in a large kettle. Add cucumbers, grape leaves and alum (or soak 2 hours in lime water made by dissolving 1 tablespoon calcium oxide in 2 quarts cold water) and simmer 1 hour; drain. Combine 6 cups vinegar, sugar, allspice and cassia buds. Boil 5 minutes. Pour this over drained cucumbers; let stand about 3 hours. Drain off syrup; reboil 1 minute and pour over cucumbers. Let stand for 3 days. Pack into sterilized jars and seal. Yield: 3 quarts.

GINGER GAPICKELTI ROATA REEVA (GINGER PICKLED BEETS)

LANCASTER COUNTY, PENNA.

Cooked beets (10-15 depend-
    ing on size)
3 cups vinegar
1 cup water
1 teaspoon ground mace
1 teaspoon ground ginger
½ teaspoon ground cloves

2 tablespoons prepared horseradish
2 tablespoons sugar

If beets are small, leave whole. If they are large, slice them. Heat vinegar with other ingredients. Place beets in hot, sterilized quart jar. When vinegar is boiling, pour over beets. Let stand 24 hours before using. Yield: 1 quart.

DILL PICKLES · MRS. ADA NELLIS, PALATINE BRIDGE, N.Y.

Small uniform-sized
    cucumbers
6 grape leaves
6 slices peeled horseradish
    root
6 sprays of dill
3 pints vinegar
3 pints water
½ cup non-iodized salt

Wash cucumbers well. Into bottom of 3 sterilized quart jars place 1 grape leaf, 1 slice horseradish root and 1 spray of dill. Pack cucumbers into jars as tightly as possible; add another spray of dill, slice of horseradish root and 1 grape leaf to each jar. Combine vinegar, water and salt. Pour into jars to cover cucumbers. Cover jars with lids only half closed. Store in a warm place 2 to 3 weeks. Add new brine (vinegar, water and salt mixture) when necessary, to keep cucumbers covered. Remove scum as soon as it forms. When gas formation ceases (after 2 to 3 weeks), cover with paraffin and seal tightly. Yield: 3 quarts.

KOSHER DILL PICKLES · MRS. MARSHALL KENNADY, EAGLE MOUNTAIN LAKE, TEX.

4 to 5 cucumbers, 3 to 5
    inches
1 bunch fresh dill
2 garlic cloves
2 bay leaves
2 grape leaves
2 medium red hot peppers
2 medium green hot peppers
1½ tablespoons mixed pickling
    spice
1 quart water
¼ cup vinegar
¼ cup salt

Wash cucumbers well. Sterilize half-gallon jar. Pack 1 inch of fresh dill into jar. Over this arrange on end 3 big cucumbers with 1 or 2 smaller ones; place in garlic cloves, bay leaves, grape leaves, peppers and spice. Pack each jar tightly at top with dill. Bring water, vinegar and salt to a rolling boil. Fill jar with the brine. Seal. Ice pickles before serving. Cut into slices to use as a relish with meat or in thick chunks when served as an appetizer with drinks and pretzels. Yield: 4 to 5 pickles.

MOTHER PATRICK'S ICE WATER PICKLES · MRS. LEONARD W. SCOTT, MINNEAPOLIS, MINN.

6 pounds medium cucumbers
36 medium pickling onions
6 pieces celery
2 tablespoons mustard seed
3 quarts white vinegar
1 cup salt
3 cups sugar

Cut cucumbers into 4 to 8 pieces and soak in ice water to cover for 3 hours. Drain, pack into sterilized jars. Add 6 onions, 1 piece celery, and 1 teaspoon mustard seed to each jar. Bring to boil vinegar, salt, sugar, and pour over cucumbers. Seal jars. Yield: 6 quarts.

PICKLED DRIED APRICOTS · LILLIAN JOHNSON, HOLLISTER, CALIF.

1 cup large dried apricots
Water
1 cup sugar
3 tablespoons vinegar
12 whole cloves
¼ teaspoon mustard seed
Stick of cinnamon

Wash apricots. Cover with water. Simmer gently for 10 minutes. Add sugar, vinegar, and spices. Cook until apricots are tender but still hold shape. Fill small sterilized jars with the apricots, cover with syrup and seal.

NOTE: Prepare prunes the same way.

MUSTARD BOONA (MUSTARD BEANS) · PENNSYLVANIA DUTCH

2 pounds string beans, cut
    into 1-inch pieces
½ cup flour
3 tablespoons dry mustard
2 teaspoons turmeric
3 cups vinegar
1 cup water
1 cup sugar
1½ teaspoons celery seed
½ teaspoon mustard seed

Cook beans in boiling salted water until just barely tender. Drain. Combine flour, mustard and turmeric. Bring vinegar, water, sugar and seeds to a boil. Simmer 5 minutes. Combine both mixtures and stir until smooth. It will be slightly thick. Add beans. Cook 5 minutes and pour into sterilized jars. Seal.

Yield: 2 quarts.

MUSTARD PICKLES · TAYLOR FAMILY, BROWNSVILLE, TENN.

1 quart shredded cabbage
1 quart chopped onions
1 quart diced green tomatoes
6 hot green peppers, chopped
1 cup salt
3 quarts hot water

1 quart sliced, unpeeled cucumbers
4 large green peppers, cored and chopped
2 sweet red peppers, chopped

Combine all ingredients and let stand for 8 hours; stir occasionally; drain off liquid and rinse under cold water.

Into another pan, place:

½ cup prepared mustard
½ cup flour
1 cup sugar
2 teaspoons celery seed
1 quart cider vinegar

Blend all ingredients well and cook until thick; add the chopped, drained ingredients and bring to a boil. Remove from heat and pack immediately into sterilized jars; seal. Yield: 7 pints.

PICKLED OYSTERS · MRS. ARCHIBALD MC CREA, CARTER'S GROVE, VA.

1 quart large oysters
1 quart oyster liquor
1 tablespoon whole black
*   pepper*
1 tablespoon whole allspice
1 lemon, cut in thin slices
Salt, vinegar, Cayenne
*   pepper to taste*

Put oysters and liquor in top of double boiler over hot water. Heat just enough to curl edges of oysters. Drain; reserve liquor. Wipe off oysters with a clean cloth. Boil liquor with spices until a strong infusion is made, about 30 minutes. Pour over oysters and sliced lemon. Add salt, vinegar and cayenne. Let stand in refrigerator for at least 24 hours. Yield: 1 quart oysters. NOTE: oysters will keep in refrigerator for about 3 weeks.

PEACH PICKLE · MRS. DAVID HUGHES, SOUTH CAROLINA

4 quarts peaches
*   (about 24 large peaches)*
3 pounds sugar
3 cups cider vinegar
4 3-inch pieces cinnamon
4 teaspoons whole cloves

Put the peaches in large strainer and dip into kettle of boiling water for about ½ minute; rinse with cold water and remove skins. Boil the sugar, vinegar and cinnamon together for 20 minutes. Place about 5 peaches in syrup at a time and cook for 5 minutes or until tender. Pack into hot, sterilized jars, placing teaspoon of cloves in each jar. Fill jars to overflowing with hot syrup. Adjust covers; seal at once.
    Yield: 4 quarts.

SPICED PEACHES · MRS. FREDERICK P. STIEFF, SR., BALTIMORE, MD.

5 pounds medium peaches
1 tablespoon (scant) whole
*   allspice*
1 tablespoon (scant) whole
*   cloves*
1 tablespoon (scant) broken
*   cinnamon stick*
3 pounds sugar
1 cup cider vinegar

Peel peaches. Tie spices in a bag and crush. Combine sugar, vinegar and spice bag in a large pot and bring to a boil. Place peaches several at a time, into the syrup and cook slowly until tender but not soft. Remove and let stand. When all peaches are cooked, continue cooking syrup and spices until syrup is rather thick. Return peaches to syrup and set aside to cool. Fill sterilized jars with peaches and syrup. Seal. Yield: 3 to 4 pints.

PICKLED PEACHES · MRS. MARTIN A. MOORE, PENNSYLVANIA

3 pounds sugar
1 quart cider vinegar
¼ cup water
6 pounds small fresh peaches

Boil sugar, vinegar and water until sugar is dissolved. Wash peaches. Then add to the syrup and boil gently until fruit is fork-tender. Pack peaches in hot sterilized jars and fill with pickling liquid. Serve as relish with meats. Yield: 3 quarts.

NOTE: This pickling liquid may be used also for cantaloupe cut in 2-inch pieces with thin outer part of rind removed. It's a Dutch thrifty idea to use melons of little flavor. After pickles are eaten, remaining juice may be reused by adding an equal portion of pickling syrup newly made. Or add the leftover to mincemeat for an added smack in flavor.

PEAR PICKLES · MRS. LEONARD W. SCOTT, MINNEAPOLIS, MINN.

3 pints vinegar
5 pounds sugar
1 ounce whole cloves
2 sticks cinnamon
7 pounds pears (Bartletts)

Combine vinegar and sugar and cook 10 minutes. Add spices tied in bag. Peel pears and leave whole with stem, or cut in half and core. Drop fruit into boiling syrup, one or two pieces at a time. Cook until pears can be pierced with a toothpick. Let stand in syrup in a covered kettle overnight. Then pack into clean jars to within one-half inch of top. Cover with the syrup. Adjust covers and process in a water bath 20 minutes. For variation, add green food coloring to syrup and a few drops of mint flavoring, this instead of spice bag. Yield: 3 quarts.

GAPICKELTI BEERA (SLICED PEARS) · LANCASTER COUNTY, PENNA.

1 can (1 pound, 3 ounces)
    pear halves
1 1-inch stick cinnamon
5 whole cloves
4 whole allspice
Green food coloring

Drain pears. Add spices to syrup and simmer gently for 10 minutes. Add a few drops of green coloring. Pour the hot liquid over the pears and chill in refrigerator. Drain before serving. Yield: 8 to 10 pear halves.

APPLE RELISH · EDITH DAVISON, DES MOINES WOMEN'S CLUB, DES MOINES, IOWA

1 pound large red apples
2 dill pickles
1 medium onion
½ cup sugar
¼ cup vinegar

Core apples but do not peel; grind together with pickles and onion. Add sugar and vinegar. Serve well chilled with pork or turkey. Yield: 1 pint relish.

HYDEN RELISH SALAD · MRS. ARCHIBALD MC CREA, CARTER'S GROVE, VA.

1 gallon finely chopped
  cabbage
½ gallon green tomatoes,
  chopped fine
1½ cups brown sugar
3 tablespoons white mustard
  seed
2 tablespoons celery seed
2 tablespoons salt

1½ tablespoons cinnamon
1½ teaspoons cloves
½ gallon vinegar

Combine all ingredients. Cook until vegetables are tender, about 25 minutes. Serve cold. Yield: about 1 gallon relish.

MRS. GRADY STRAIN'S RELISH · DALLAS, TEX.

1 cup salt
1 gallon ground green
  tomatoes
1 gallon ground cabbage
1 dozen medium onions,
  ground
1 dozen sweet peppers,
  ground
12 to 16 hot peppers,
  chopped (according to
  taste)
6 cups sugar (or more)
2 teaspoons dry mustard
1 teaspoon cloves

1 teaspoon cinnamon
1 teaspoon turmeric
½ gallon vinegar (or more)
1 teaspoon celery seed

Add salt to ground tomatoes and let stand. Drain the remaining vegetables in a cloth bag. Mix drained vegetables with tomato mixture. Add sugar, mustard, cloves, cinnamon, turmeric and vinegar. Boil 5 minutes. Add celery seed. Pour, while hot, into sterilized jars and seal.
Yield: 20 pints relish.

GARDEN-FRESH RELISH · CAROL JEAN ACKLEY, CLAREMONT, CALIF.

1 cup sliced celery
½ cup finely chopped green
  pepper
1 cup finely chopped
  cabbage
½ cup finely chopped onion
1 cup sugar
1 tablespoon salt
1 hot pepper (optional)
1 tablespoon mustard seed
  (optional)

½ teaspoon celery seed
1 cup lemon juice
2 tablespoons grated lemon peel

Combine all ingredients; stir well. Chill in refrigerator overnight.
Yield: about 3 cups.
NOTE: Serve over hamburgers or other barbecued meats. It's a crisp, fresh-tasting relish to serve with baked beans or with a tuna casserole.

SALSA · MRS. DOROTHEA DALTON, CALIFORNIA

1 quart drained, canned
   tomatoes
1 clove garlic, minced
1 teaspoon sugar
Salt to taste
1 tablespoon olive oil
1 tablespoon vinegar

2 medium onions, chopped very fine
1 can (1 ounce) green medium-hot chilis, chopped

Mash tomatoes. Add remaining ingredients, mixing well. Store in refrigerator. Serve over beans or tortillas. Yield: 1 quart relish.

SPICED WATERMELON RIND · MRS. ELLA MC GIBBON, RED HOOK, N.Y.

3 pounds white portion of
   watermelon, cubed
5 cups sugar
2 cups cider vinegar
1 cup cold water
1 tablespoon whole cloves
1 tablespoon whole allspice
1 tablespoon broken-up
   cinnamon stick
1 lemon, sliced

Let watermelon stand in salted water to cover overnight (½ cup salt to 1 quart water). Drain, cover with fresh cold water. Cook until tender. Drain. Combine sugar, vinegar, and water. Tie cloves, allspice, cinnamon and lemon in a bag; add to syrup. Boil 5 minutes. Add watermelon and cook until transparent, about 45 minutes. Pack in hot, sterilized jars.
Yield: 3 pints.

MRS. NELLIS' CHILI SAUCE · MRS. ADA NELLIS, PALATINE BRIDGE, N.Y.

8 pounds skinned ripe
   tomatoes, finely chopped
1½ cups sugar
2 tablespoons salt
1 quart vinegar
¼ cup whole cloves
¼ cup allspice
4 sticks cinnamon

6 medium-sized onions, finely chopped
6 seeded green peppers, finely chopped

Combine chopped tomatoes, onions and green peppers in large kettle. Add sugar, salt and vinegar. Tie spices securely in a cheesecloth bag and place in kettle. Cook mixture slowly until thick, about 2½ hours, stirring occasionally. Yield: 3 pints.

TAYLOR-FAMILY CHILI SAUCE · BROWNSVILLE, TENN.

8 quarts finely chopped
   tomatoes
2 cups sugar
¼ cup salt
4 cups cider vinegar
1 teaspoon cinnamon
½ teaspoon cloves
½ teaspoon curry powder
½ teaspoon pepper

12 large onions, finely chopped
12 green peppers, finely chopped, plus seeds of
   2 peppers

Combine ingredients in large pot and cook slowly until thick, about 3 hours. Pour boiling mixture into hot sterilized jars, filling to overflowing, and seal at once.
Yield: 3 quarts.

INDIANA PEACH CHUTNEY · GLADYS KIMBROUGH, MUNCIE, IND.

3½ pounds peaches
4 ounces green ginger root,
    diced*
3½ cups sugar
1½ cups vinegar
4 tablespoons Worcestershire
    sauce
2 large cloves garlic, minced
1 cup chopped onion
¾ cup lime juice
¾ teaspoon ground ginger
1 pod chili, crushed
½ cup white raisins
½ cup seedless raisins
Red, yellow and green food
    coloring

Peel and slice peaches ¼-inch thick. Cover with brine made with 2 tablespoons salt to 1 quart water and let stand 24 to 36 hours. Drain. Cook ginger in water to cover until almost tender. Drain; reserve water. Mix 4 tablespoons of reserved ginger water, sugar, vinegar, Worcestershire sauce and garlic. Bring to a boil. Add peaches. Cook slowly until peaches are clear. Remove peaches from syrup. Add cooked ginger and remaining ingredients. Cook until onions are soft, and mixture is thickness desired. Return peaches to syrup. Add food coloring to get a rich brown tone. Return to heat and bring to a boil. Pour into hot sterilized jars; seal. Yield: 2½ pints.

* NOTE: The best chutney is made with green ginger root and this is available in Chinese and Spanish markets in large cities. Though less potent, crystallized ginger may be substituted. Soak in water to cover until sugar crystals dissolve; dice. Use soaking water as a substitute for that in which the green ginger is cooked.

PINEAPPLE CHUTNEY · MRS. HAROLD HOLCOMB, SCOTTSDALE, ARIZ.

1 large pineapple, or 2 cans
    (1 pound, 13 ounces
    each) pineapple
4 cups brown sugar
3 cups cider vinegar
2 cloves garlic
1 pound seeded raisins
1 pound currants
1 pound blanched almonds or
    walnuts, broken up
2 tablespoons green ginger
    root, peeled and chopped
1½ teaspoons salt
⅛ teaspoon pepper
½ teaspoon whole cloves
½ teaspoon ground cinnamon
½ teaspoon allspice

Cut pineapple into small pieces. Combine all ingredients in a 4-quart saucepan and boil until thick, about 20 minutes. Remove garlic and cloves. Pour mixture into hot sterilized jars and seal with paraffin immediately. Yield: 4 8-ounce jars chutney.

IDAHO PURPLE PLUM CHUTNEY · MRS. ROBERT E. SMYLIE, BOISE, IDAHO

1 cup light brown sugar,
    firmly packed
1 cup granulated sugar
¾ cup cider vinegar
1½ teaspoons crushed red
    peppers
2 teaspoons salt
2 teaspoons mustard seed
2 fat cloves garlic, thinly
    sliced
1 small onion, thinly sliced
½ cup preserved ginger, cut in
    thin slices
1 cup seedless white raisins
3½ cups fresh purple plums,
    halved and pitted (about
    20)

Mix together sugars and vinegar and bring to the boiling point. Add remaining ingredients except plums, and mix well. Then stir in plum halves. Simmer until thickened, about 50 minutes, stirring frequently and gently. Fill hot sterilized jars. Seal. Store in dark place.

Yield: 3 half-pint jars.

DICK'S CANDIED APPLES · DICK TAYLOR, BROWNSVILLE, TENN.

10 cooking apples, peeled and
    cored
8 cups sugar
½ cup hot water

Place apples in large baking pan. Cover with sugar and water. Cook on top of range, uncovered, over lowest possible heat, stirring sugar and water together as sugar settles to bottom of pan. Cook 1 to 1½ hours, or until apples become transparent, basting apples occasionally. Bake at 350°F. for 30 minutes. Allow apples to cool about 10 minutes before serving. Serve with or without syrup and as an accompaniment to baked ham, chicken or roast pork. Yield: 10 portions.

PEAR JAM · MRS. GEORGE VOLZ, PLACERVILLE, CALIF.

4 cups (2 pounds) very ripe
    crushed pears
½ cup Maraschino cherries,
    minced
7⅓ cups sugar
1 bottle (6 ounces)
    commercial pectin

Place pears, cherries, and sugar in 5- to 6-quart saucepan; mix well. Bring to a full rolling boil over high heat and boil 1 minute, stirring constantly. Remove from heat and immediately stir in pectin. Then stir and skim alternately for 5 minutes. Pour into sterilized glasses, leaving ½ inch space at top. Seal with ⅛-inch hot paraffin. Yield: 11 to 12 six-ounce glasses.

MRS. KENNADY'S MARMALADE · MRS. MARSHALL KENNADY,
EAGLE MOUNTAIN LAKE, TEX.

1 dozen grapefruit
1 dozen lemons
1 dozen oranges
Water
Sugar
3 pounds whole candied
cherries
2 pounds candied pineapple,
cut up
1 pound preserved ginger,
cut up

Cut off ends of the three fruits; cut fruit into ⅛-inch slices; cut slices crosswise into ½-inch strips. Measure the fruit into quarts and add to it as many quarts of water as there are of fruit and juice. Let stand overnight. The following day, cook until the rind is tender and again let stand overnight. On the third day, measure and add sugar measure for measure with fruit. Cook about 2 hours, stirring frequently. Add cherries, pineapple and ginger with their juices. Continue cooking until syrup sheets from spoon (217°F.). Then pour into hot sterilized jars, filling them to within ¼ inch from top. Cover immediately with a layer of melted paraffin; when cool add a second layer.

Yield: 16 quarts marmalade.

TANGERINE MARMALADE · MRS. LAWRENCE ADAMS, JACKSONVILLE, FLA.

6 large, firm tangerines
6 large lemons
Water
Sugar
1 bottle (8 ounces) pectin
(optional)

Put whole fruits through coarse blade of food grinder. Measure. Add 3 cups water to each cup of ground fruit. Let stand for 24 hours. Add 1 cup sugar to each cup of fruit and bring to a boil. Let stand another 24 hours. Cook to jelly stage (220°F.) or until syrup "sheets" from spoon. If firmer marmalade is desired, add pectin. Pour into hot sterilized glasses and immediately cover with ⅛-inch melted paraffin. When cool, add another ⅛-inch layer of paraffin.

Yield: 10 8-ounce glasses.

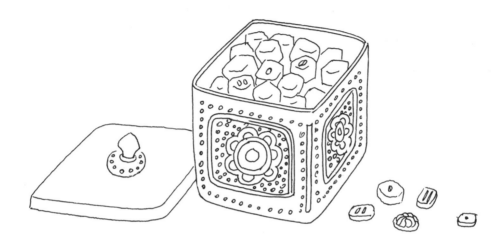

Confectionery

APRICOT CONFECTION · LILLIAN JOHNSON, HOLLISTER, CALIF.

Steam dried fruit in sieve over hot water 5 minutes until warm but not overly moist. While still hot, roll in granulated sugar. Dry on waxed paper and serve as a confection —not quite a candy but very, very good.

MRS. COULTER'S BRANDY BALLS · MRS. STUART COULTER, CALIFORNIA

2 packages (4¾ ounces each)
    vanilla wafers, crushed
¼ cup brandy
¼ cup rum
½ cup strained honey
Confectioners' sugar

Mix ingredients, except sugar, thoroughly. Using a level tablespoon for each, form into balls. Roll in sugar. Store in stone jar; cover tightly.

Yield: about 4½ dozen.

NOTE: Brandy balls keep moist and fragrant for as long as six weeks.

HICKORY-NUT BRITTLE · C. R. SALLY, PACIFIC, MO.

2 cups sugar
¾ cup light corn syrup
¾ cup water
1 tablespoon butter or
   margarine
1¼ cups chopped hickory nuts
2 teaspoons baking soda
1 tablespoon vanilla

Combine sugar, corn syrup, water, butter, and nuts in saucepan. Cook over high heat, stirring until sugar is dissolved. Continue boiling over moderate heat, stirring after mixture is amber colored, to hard-crack stage (290°F.). Remove from heat. Add soda and vanilla, stirring slightly. Pour onto buttered baking sheets and spread very thin. Break into pieces.
Yield: 1½ pounds candy.

BUTTERSCOTCH · C. R. SALLY, PACIFIC, MO.

4 cups sugar
1⅓ cups dark corn syrup
1 tablespoon salt
1 tablespoon butter or
   margarine

Combine ingredients and cook over high heat, stirring constantly, until sugar dissolves. Boil quickly, stirring frequently, to hard-crack stage (290°F.). Pour into buttered 15½×10½×1-inch pan. Score into squares with knife. Yield: 2½ pounds candy.
NOTE: This is the recipe Mr. Sally uses for his lollypops.

VANILLA CARAMELS · MRS. ALVORD BAKER, FREEVILLE, N.Y.

1 cup sugar
1 cup heavy cream
1 cup light corn syrup
¼ cup sweetened condensed
   milk
¼ cup butter or margarine
1 teaspoon vanilla extract

Cook together sugar, cream and syrup to thread-spinning stage (230°F.). Add condensed milk and cook until a small amount of syrup forms a firm ball in cold water (240°F.). Add butter and vanilla; remove from heat, stirring just enough to mix. Pour into greased pan to cool. Cut when cold and wrap the pieces in waxed paper. Yield: about 36 small pieces.

VANILLA CARAMELS · C. R. SALLY, PACIFIC, MO.

2 cans (14½ ounces each)
   evaporated milk
4 cups sugar
2 cups dark corn syrup
1 tablespoon butter or
   margarine
1 tablespoon vanilla extract
1 cup finely chopped black
   walnuts

Mix one can of the milk with sugar, corn syrup, and butter. Bring to brisk boil, stirring constantly. Add second can of milk, pouring very slowly so that mixture never gets below boiling point. Never cease stirring or the mixture will scorch. (A long-handled wooden spoon is best for this.) Cook to soft ball stage (234°F.). Remove from heat and stir in vanilla and black walnuts. Pour into 2 buttered 8-inch layer pans. When cool, cut into squares. Yield: 3½ pounds candy.

CARAMEL HICKORY-NUT FUDGE · MRS. ALVORD BAKER, FREEVILLE, N.Y.

3 cups sugar
2 tablespoons hot water
1 cup light cream
½ cup chopped hickory nuts
1 teaspoon vanilla extract

Melt 1½ cups of the sugar in heavy skillet; stirring constantly. Add hot water when entirely melted. Cook until smooth, stirring constantly. Place remaining 1½ cups sugar in saucepan. Add caramel syrup and cream. Cook to soft-ball stage (238°F.). Cool thoroughly. Beat until stiff. Add nuts and vanilla, stirring in well. Pour into greased pan. Cool before cutting.
Yield: 30 pieces, 1-inch square

MRS. ROLAND'S FUDGE · MRS. O. M. ROLAND, DALLAS, TEX.

4 cups sugar
4 squares unsweetened
*   chocolate*
¼ cup white corn syrup
1⅓ cups milk
5 tablespoons butter or
*   margarine*
1 tablespoon vanilla extract
1 cup pecans, broken

Combine sugar, chocolate, syrup and milk in saucepan over low heat. Stir while increasing heat to medium and stir constantly until well blended. Increase heat and cook without stirring until thermometer reaches 236°F. or mixture forms a soft ball in cold water. Remove from heat and add butter; don't stir. Let cool to 110°F. (lukewarm), then beat mixture until it becomes dull looking. (Mrs. Roland uses electric beater until smooth and finishes with a spoon. Don't pour too soon. When the mixture loses sheen it's almost ready.) Add vanilla and pecans. Pour into waxed-paper-lined pan. After it's poured Mrs. Roland takes a spoon and gives the fudge a few swirls for a rippled homemade appearance.
Yield: 2 pounds fudge.

BLACK WALNUT FUDGE · C. R. SALLY, PACIFIC, MO.

4 cups sugar
2¼ cups heavy cream
1 tablespoon light corn syrup
4 squares unsweetened
*   chocolate*
¼ teaspoon salt
1 tablespoon vanilla extract
1 cup chopped black walnuts

Combine sugar, cream, corn syrup, chocolate, and salt in saucepan. Cook, stirring constantly, until sugar dissolves. Continue boiling gently, stirring occasionally, to soft ball stage (236°F.). Pour onto buttered marble slab, counter or table top (not wood). When lukewarm, work candy with spatula, putty knife or back of wooden spoon. Work in vanilla and nuts. When firm enough, knead with buttered hands until cool. Spread on waxed paper to thickness desired and cut into squares, or roll and slice. Yield: 2½ pounds candy.

SOUR-CREAM FUDGE · MRS. ALVORD BAKER, FREEVILLE, N.Y.

3 cups sugar
1 cup sour cream
2 squares unsweetened
    chocolate, or
    6 tablespoons cocoa

Cook ingredients to 232°F. or just a little under the soft-ball stage; that is, when it just holds together when a bit is poured in cold water. Cool. Beat until stiff. Pour into greased pan. Cut into 1-inch squares. Yield: 36 pieces.

HOREHOUND CANDY · C. R. SALLY, PACIFIC, MO.

3 pints boiling water
1 quart loosely packed hore-
    hound leaves and stems
4 cups sugar
1¼ cups dark corn syrup
1 tablespoon butter or
    margarine

Pour boiling water over horehound. Steep 5 minutes. Tea should be bitter-tasting and dark, but not black. Strain. Measure 2 cups of this tea and combine with sugar, corn syrup, and butter. Bring to boil and cook, stirring occasionally, to hard-crack stage (300°F.). If residue forms around sides of pan during the cooking period, skim off. Pour into buttered 15¼ × 10½ × 1-inch pan. Score with knife. Break into squares. Yield: 2½ pounds candy.

PECAN BALLS · EDITH CRUMB, DEARBORN, MICH.

¼ pound butter or margarine
1 teaspoon vanilla extract
2 tablespoons granulated
    sugar
1 cup sifted flour
1 cup pecans, chopped
    medium fine
½ cup confectioners' sugar

Cream butter and vanilla until smooth. Blend in the combined sugar, flour, and nuts. Roll between palms into small balls. Place on an ungreased baking sheet. Bake at 350°F. for 15 minutes. Remove from oven while still hot. Roll in confectioners' sugar divided into 2 piles; roll first in one, then the other. Yield: 24 balls.

CREOLE PECAN PRALINES · NEW ORLEANS, LA.

1 pound light brown sugar
½ cup warm water
1 tablespoon butter or
    margarine
½ pound pecans

Combine sugar, water and butter. Boil over medium heat, stirring, to thread stage (228°F.). Add pecans. Continue to boil gently, with stirring, until a small amount of mixture forms a very soft ball in cold water (236°F.). Remove from heat. Cool to lukewarm (110°F.) without stirring. Beat until candy begins to thicken. Drop by tablespoonfuls onto waxed paper. Yield: 12 large pralines.

SUGARED WALNUTS · MRS. J. V. GUERIN, ARIZONA

1 cup sugar
⅓ cup concentrated orange
　juice
1 teaspoon lemon extract
2 tablespoons butter or
　margarine
2½ cups walnut halves

Combine sugar and orange juice and cook until mixture forms a soft ball in cold water (234°F.). Add extract and butter. Beat well until mixture has a very creamy look and begins to thicken. Add walnut halves and stir until nuts are well coated. Pour out on waxed paper and pull apart to form small clusters. Cool.

Yield: 1 pound walnuts.

CANDIED GRAPEFRUIT PEEL · MRS. ROBERT ADAMS, JACKSONVILLE, FLA.

Peel of 1 medium grapefruit
3½ cups water
1 teaspoon salt
1¼ cups sugar
1 cup water

Wash peel; cut into strips (about 3×½ inches). Combine the 3½ cups water with salt and pour over grapefruit in bowl; let stand 8 to 10 hours. Boil peel in same water 10 minutes; drain. Dissolve 1 cup of the sugar in the 1 cup water; boil until syrup spins a thread (232° to 234°F.). Add peel and cook slowly 15 minutes. Remove from syrup; lay on waxed paper to dry for 1 hour. Roll in remaining sugar if desired.

Yield: about 1½ dozen pieces candied peel.

LEMON SOURS · MRS. THOMAS F. KNIGHT, JR., LA CANADA, CALIF.

¾ cup sifted flour
⅓ cup butter or margarine
2 eggs
1 cup brown sugar
¾ cup shredded coconut
½ cup chopped nuts
⅛ teaspoon baking powder
½ teaspoon vanilla extract
1 teaspoon grated lemon rind
1½ tablespoons lemon juice
⅔ cup confectioners' sugar
　(about)

Mix together flour and butter to a fine crumb. Sprinkle evenly in 11×7-inch pan. Bake at 350°F. for 10 minutes. Meanwhile beat eggs; mix in brown sugar, coconut, chopped nuts, baking powder and vanilla. Spread on first mixture as you take it from the oven; return to oven and bake 20 minutes longer. Mix lemon rind and juice and add confectioners' sugar to make a creamy mixture. Spread this over the top as soon as pan is taken from oven. Cool and cut into squares.

Yield: 24 pieces.

Beverages

CAFÉ-AU-LAIT · NEW ORLEANS, LA.

Pour milk, or ½ milk and ½ cream, into a saucepan and heat to the boiling point while your coffee is dripping in a French drip pot. The dripping must be slow, "as slow as New Orleans molasses in January," for according to a Creole saying that still serves: "Honey, if you can hear it drippin', it's drippin' too fast."

When the last drop has dripped, fill the cup halfway with the boiling hot milk and add the jet-black coffee until it's the coffee-and-cream shade you like.

CAFÉ BRÛLOT DIABOLIQUE · ANTOINE'S, NEW ORLEANS, LA.

1 1-inch stick cinnamon
8 whole cloves
Peel of 1 lemon, cut thin
3 lumps sugar
3 jiggers brandy
3 cups strong coffee

Place in a silver brûlot bowl (or chafing dish) cinnamon, cloves, lemon peel and sugar. Place brandy in large ladle; ignite brandy and pour over ingredients in bowl. Keep ladling brandy over ingredients until sugar is dissolved. Gradually add coffee, ladling the mixture until the flames fade. Serve immediately.

Yield: 8 small cups or 4 portions.

FRENCH CHOCOLATE · EDITH DAVISON, DES MOINES WOMEN'S CLUB, DES MOINES, IOWA

2½ squares unsweetened chocolate
½ cup water
¾ cup sugar
Pinch of salt
½ cup heavy cream, whipped
6 cups hot milk

Melt chocolate over hot water. Add ½ cup water; stir constantly for 4 minutes. Add sugar and salt, and cook 4 minutes longer, stirring all the while. Cool. Fold in whipped cream. When ready to serve, place a heaping tablespoonful of this chocolate mixture into each serving cup and pour over the hot milk almost to fill cup. Stir lightly to blend.

Yield: 8 portions.

CRANBERRY SHRUB · WILLIAMSBURG, VA.

Mix 1 quart cranberry juice cocktail, 1 quart grapefruit juice, 1 quart apricot nectar and 1 quart pineapple juice. Chill. Pour over ice in a punch bowl. Garnish with orange slices or spoonfuls of orange sherbert.

Yield: 4 quarts.

FRUIT SHRUB · MRS. MARTIN A. MOORE, PENNSYLVANIA

Currants, black or red rasp-
berries, blueberries,
grapes, elderberries in
any amount to make
1 pint fruit juice
1 pound sugar

Wash any one of the above fruits. Simmer in water to cover until soft. Empty into colander and drain off juice. Strain juice through one layer of cheesecloth. Measure juice. Add sugar and boil for about 15 minutes. Skim and pour into sterilized bottles (Mrs. Moore saves empty vinegar bottles for this purpose). Cork tightly and when cool dip into melted paraffin water or ginger ale.

Yield: about 2 cups fruit base.

RASPBERRY SHRUB SYRUP · SENATOR MARGARET CHASE SMITH, MAINE

4 quarts raspberries
1 quart cider vinegar
Sugar

Clean and pick over berries. Cover with vinegar and let stand 4 days. Strain. To each cup of juice add 1 cup sugar. Boil 15 minutes. Bottle when cold.

Yield: 5 cups syrup. Serve diluted with three parts cold water to one part syrup. Fill a tall glass with crushed ice and pour in the perfume. Tinkle it, whiff it, sip it and smile.

SYLLABUB · MRS. JACK WILKINSON, CHATTANOOGA, TENN.

No namby-pamby fare. Ingredients: 1 pint whipping cream, 1 pint milk, ½ cup sugar and bourbon to taste, ½-cup a guest. That gives service for 8. It takes a syllabub churn to whip the stuff to a fluff and these churns are rare things. Mrs. Wilkinson has her grandma's churn, meaning Grandma Hatcher Hughes Riley of Amelia Courthouse, Virginia. But the churn was an heirloom even in Grandma's day, brought over from England. Now if you are syllabub making use your egg beater.

Mix all ingredients in a deep bowl, place beater in center and get busy. When the top of the bowl is well covered with froth, skim with a spoon and dip into tall glasses. Continue beating and skimming until the mixture is used. Syllabub can be beaten over and over again as long as it lasts. To serve, sprinkle with grated rind of lemon and a dust of nutmeg.

Sherry may be used instead of bourbon, then serve over fruit.

SYLLABUB · MRS. STUART DAWSON, CHARLESTON, S.C.

Peel of 2 lemons
1 cup sweet wine
1 cup Madeira wine
1 quart heavy cream
6 tablespoons lemon juice
Sugar to taste
Nutmeg

Soak lemon peel in the sweet wine and Madeira until the flavor is extracted. Discard lemon peel. Whip cream until it just begins to hold its shape. Gradually whisk in the wines, lemon juice, sugar to taste and nutmeg. Heap in glasses and serve. Yield: 3 quarts or 12 portions.

HOLIDAY GLUGG · MRS. WESLEY C. HEISE, PORTLAND, ORE.

1½ pounds seedless raisins
3 cups water (about)
1½ cups sugar
1 tablespoon broken
    cinnamon stick
1 tablespoon whole cloves
2 dozen cardamom seeds
1 gallon red Burgundy wine
⅖ quart brandy or bourban

Cover raisins with water. Add sugar, cinnamon, and cloves. Crack cardamom seeds, drop in with shells. Simmer, covered, for 2 hours or until raisins swell. If necessary add more water from time to time. Remove from heat. Add wine, bring almost to simmer, not quite, and keep hot at about 160°F. for 2 hours. Cool; leave spices in the brew overnight. Drain. Squeeze raisins to get out every last drop of wine. Pour into bottles until ready to use. Reheat when ready to serve, adding brandy or bourbon.

Yield: 4 quarts glugg.

ARTILLERY PUNCH · MRS. HANSON HILLYER, SAVANNAH, GA.

Here are the amounts for serving two hundred: the yield, ten gallons. But you divide into units to suit the crowd and its capacity. Combine two gallons Santa Cruz rum, one gallon Hennessey's Three Star Brandy, one gallon of gin, one gallon of rye whiskey, two gallons of green tea (made with one pound tea and two gallons of cold water, soaked overnight). Add pineapple cubes and cherries and sweeten to taste. Let this rest for two weeks. When ready to serve place ice block in the punch bowl and pour mixture to half full, then serve in champagne glasses very well chilled.

JIFFY PUNCH · L. S. AYRES CO. DEPARTMENT STORE, INDIANAPOLIS, IND.

Place orange ice, three-fourths of a gallon, in large chunks in a well-chilled punch bowl, then pour over five quarts of chilled ginger ale, garnish with mint leaves and maraschino cherries and serve it at once. Yield: 55 cups.

ORANGE-BLOSSOM PUNCH · MARY CALL COLLINS, TALLAHASSEE, FLA.

2½ cups sugar
2½ cups water
1½ cups lime juice
1½ quarts ginger ale, chilled
1½ quarts fresh, frozen or
    canned grapefruit juice,
    chilled

1½ quarts fresh, frozen or canned orange juice,
    chilled

Combine sugar and water in a saucepan; place over heat and stir until sugar is dissolved. Boil 5 minutes without stirring. Cool. Add fruit juices. Just before serving, add ginger ale. Pour over orange-blossom ice ring. Yield: 44 ½-cup servings.

ORANGE-BLOSSOM ICE RING:

Use a deep saucepan, about 7 inches in diameter. Put 2 layers of ice cubes in the bottom and then place an empty No. 2 can (20 ounces) in the center. Pile cubes around can. Weight the can down with something heavy inside so that it will not float to top. Fill pan almost to top with water. Float fresh orange blossoms, halved orange and lime slices in the water. Put saucepan in freezing compartment to freeze solid. Arrange additional citrus and orange blossoms around top of ring. Carefully add water to depth of ¼-inch; freeze until solid, about 1½ hours. To remove solid ice from pan, run hot water over inverted pan, turn over, put small amount of water in empty can, then lift out ring. Fill center with mint sprigs.

CHOWNING'S HOT SPICED PUNCH · WILLIAMSBURG, VA.
  (Used at Yule Log Ceremony)

Pour 1 quart apple cider into a pan with 3 cinnamon sticks and the juice of 1 lemon. Allow to simmer gently for ½ hour. Make a cheesecloth bag and fill with 1 teaspoon nutmeg and 1 teaspoon cloves. Drop into apple cider and steep until punch is spicy enough to suit your taste. Yield: 8 portions.

Index

304   INDEX